THE

PUBLICATIONS

OF THE

Lincoln Record Society

FOUNDED IN THE YEAR

1910

VOLUME 99

ISSN 0267–2634

THE CORRESPONDENCE OF THE SPALDING GENTLEMEN'S SOCIETY

1710–1761

EDITED BY

DIANA HONEYBONE and MICHAEL HONEYBONE

The Lincoln Record Society

The Boydell Press

First published 2010

A Lincoln Record Society Publication
published by The Boydell Press
an imprint of Boydell & Brewer Ltd
PO Box 9, Woodbridge, Suffolk IP12 3DF, UK
and of Boydell & Brewer Inc.
668 Mt Hope Avenue, Rochester, NY 14620, USA
website: www.boydellandbrewer.com

ISBN 978–0–901503–87–9

A CIP catalogue record for this book is available
from the British Library

Details of other Lincoln Record Society volumes are available
from Boydell & Brewer Ltd

The publisher has no responsibility for the continued existence or accuracy of URLs for
external or third-party internet websites referred to in this book, and does not guarantee
that any content on such websites is, or will remain, accurate or appropriate.

This publication is printed on acid-free paper

Printed in Great Britain by
CPI Antony Rowe, Chippenham and Eastbourne

CONTENTS

ILLUSTRATIONS

On pp. 205–216:

1. Coat of arms of the Spalding Gentlemen's Society, designed by Maurice Johnson and engraved by George Vertue in 1746
2. John Grundy's map of Spalding, 1732
3. Spalding Market Place, showing the Town Hall where the Society met on occasions during its early years. Engraving by Hilkiah Burgess, 1822
4. Sketch of the Society's meeting-rooms from 1727 to 1743, from the margin of John Grundy's map of Spalding, 1732
5. Gayton (Holyrood) House, Spalding, meeting-place of the Society from 1743 to 1755. Painting by Thomas Albin, 1872
6. Mr Cox's Rooms, the meeting-place of the Society from 1755 to the 1880s. Engraving by Hilkiah Burgess, 1827
7. The Society's meeting-room in Mr Cox's Rooms, from *The Gentlemen's Society at Spalding*, printed by William Pickering, London, 1851
8. The Society's new rooms and museum, opened in 1911
9. Letter from Maurice Johnson in London to his stepbrother Richard Falkner, dated 6 July 1734 (no.227 in this calendar)
10. Letter from Maurice Johnson (son) in London to his father Maurice Johnson in Spalding, with his sketches of the new music room at Ranelagh, dated from Charing Cross, 19 March 1741/2 (no.390 in this calendar)

Illustrations 1–10 are in the possession of the Spalding Gentlemen's Society, and are reproduced by kind permission of the President and Council of the Society.

Front cover: Miniature of Maurice Johnson by George Vertue, 1731. National Portrait Gallery, no.4684

ACKNOWLEDGEMENTS

Thanks are due to the President and Council of the Spalding Gentlemen's Society, to the previous President, Mr Bill Belsham, and to their Curators past and present, especially the late Mr Tom Royce, for providing access to the correspondence and other papers in their archives, and to Mrs Marion Brassington for help with finding the eighteenth-century books in the Society's library.

Help has also been received from the staff of the British Library, the Bodleian Library and the library of Christ Church, Oxford, Lincolnshire Archives, the University of East Anglia Library and the Dean and Chapter's Library at Norwich Cathedral.

The Open University has kindly given access to an extensive range of electronic reference sites, in particular the website of the *Oxford Dictionary of National Biography* and *Eighteenth-Century Collections On-line*. The *Clergy of the Church of England Database* and the *COPAC* on-line catalogue of university libraries have provided valuable data. The Google index has allowed us to consult a wide range of eighteenth- and nineteenth-century books.

ABBREVIATIONS

Some of these abbreviations are found in the transcribed letters, e.g. 'L^r' for 'Letter'.

BD	Bachelor of Divinity
Bodl.	Bodleian Library, Oxford
c.	circa
CP	*Complete Peerage*
d.	died
DCL	Doctor of Civil Law
DD	Doctor of Divinity
D^o	ditto
ed.	edited, editor
fl.	flourished
fol.	folio
FRCP	Fellow of the Royal College of Physicians
FRS	Fellow of the Royal Society
FSA	Fellow of the Society of Antiquaries
LAO	Lincolnshire Archives
LL.B	Bachelor of Laws
LL.D	Doctor of Laws
Longden	H. I. Longden, *Northamptonshire and Rutland Clergy from 1500*, 15 vols (Northampton, 1938–43)
L^r	letter
LRCP	Licentiate of the Royal College of Physicians
LRS	Lincoln Record Society
MB	Minute Book of the Spalding Gentlemen's Society (e.g. MB1) Bachelor of Medicine
MD	Doctor of Medicine
MS(S)	manuscript(s)
No	number
ODNB	*Oxford Dictionary of National Biography*
OED	*Oxford English Dictionary*
PGS	Peterborough Gentlemen's Society
Rev., Revd	Reverend
RS	Royal Society
SA	Society of Antiquaries
SGS	Spalding Gentlemen's Society
S^r	Sir
Stukeley	W. C. Lukis (ed.), *The Family Memoirs of the Rev. William Stukeley*, 3 vols (Surtees Society 73, 76, 80, 1882–87)
vol.	volume
Xst	Christ
y^r	your

INTRODUCTION

'This Society was instituted for Supporting mutual Benevolence, raising and preserving, & rendring of general Use a Publick Lending Library pursuant to the Statute of the 7th of Queen Ann Chapt. 14th And the Improvement of the Members in All Arts and Sciences, Upon Proposals tryed from & approved of and subscribed to, 3d November 1712.' This statement by Maurice Johnson, the founder of the Spalding Gentlemen's Society, in the Society's first Minute Book (folio 217A) sums up his vision for the society which he created and maintained with ceaseless energy and effort for over forty years, and which has survived in various forms to the present day. This volume is a calendar of the wide-ranging correspondence received by Johnson and by his society, dating from 1710, just around the time of its foundation, to 1761, six years after his death. It gives a fascinating insight into this remarkable institution and the enthusiasts, some of them local Lincolnshire men, who founded and maintained it in its astonishing early years as a learned society flourishing in what was then a remote corner of the Lincolnshire fens. As its founder frequently referred to it by the initials SGS, we have followed his example in this volume.

It is not intended to provide in this introduction a comprehensive general history of the Spalding Gentlemen's Society, as this has already been covered in some detail. Its foundation, activities and governing principles have been clearly outlined in the introduction to Dorothy Owen's volume on the early minute-books of the Society.[1] Besides earlier histories of the Society such as those by Richard Gough and William Moore,[2] there are modern theses by R. J. Evans and by Michael Honeybone.[3] Honeybone also investigated the Society's scientific activities in depth.[4] In addition, the Spalding Gentlemen's Society is planning a history of the Society from its foundation to its current activities, to commemorate its tercentenary in 2010.

The better-known members of the SGS have biographical entries in the *Oxford Dictionary of National Biography* (*ODNB*) (2004); these include Maurice Johnson himself, William Stukeley and Roger Gale among many others. Appendix 2 of this volume lists those SGS members who are represented as correspondents in

---

[1] D. M. Owen (ed.), *The Minute-Books of The Spalding Gentlemen's Society 1712–1755* (LRS 73, 1981).

[2] Richard Gough, 'An account of the Gentlemen's Society at Spalding', in John Nichols (ed.), *Bibliotheca Topographica Britannica* III (1784); W. Moore, *The Gentlemen's Society at Spalding: its Origin and Progress* (London, 1851).

[3] R. J. Evans, 'The Diffusion of Science: the geographical transmission of natural philosophy into the English provinces, 1660–1760' (unpublished Ph.D. thesis, University of Cambridge, 1982); Michael Honeybone, 'The Spalding Gentlemen's Society: the communication of science in the East Midlands of England 1710–60' (unpublished Ph.D. thesis, Open University, 2001).

[4] Michael Honeybone, 'Sociability, utility and curiosity in the Spalding Gentlemen's Society, 1710–60', in David M. Knight and Matthew D. Eddy (eds), *Science and Beliefs: from Natural Philosophy to Natural Science, 1700–1900* (Aldershot, 2005).

this calendar, and their brief biographies in this appendix indicate those who have entries in the *ODNB*. The newest initiative of the editors of the *ODNB* is the current production of a set of group biographies; Michael Honeybone has contributed a group biography of the Spalding Gentlemen's Society in the eighteenth century.

This calendar concentrates on the voluminous correspondence which the SGS received in its early years, much of which has survived in its archive at Spalding today. Maurice Johnson was convinced that a central function of his society should be correspondence with other learned societies and with individuals who, like the Society's members, were 'curious', as the eighteenth century expressed it, interested in the study of the world around them and keen to share their findings with fellow-enthusiasts. Johnson frequently referred to the advice he had received in an interview with the ageing Sir Isaac Newton in 1724, when he persuaded Newton to become a member of the SGS, that it was through correspondence that such a society as the SGS could develop and prosper. The SGS's correspondence over almost half a century effectively demonstrates the nature of the national and international 'Republic of Letters' for which the eighteenth century was distinguished.

Origins and development of the SGS

At this point, it would be useful to offer a brief outline of the development of the SGS with particular reference to the importance of its correspondence in its activities. Maurice Johnson (1688–1755)[5] was born in Spalding and received his first education at the local Grammar School before transferring to Eton for a few years and then studying law at the Inner Temple in preparation for a career as a barrister. He then returned to Spalding, which remained his base for the rest of his life, although he frequently spent the three short legal terms of each year in London on business and travelled regularly to attend the Assize Court on the Midland Circuit. His acquaintance with the social and intellectual life of the capital, at a time when Englishmen were becoming notably 'clubable' to use Dr Samuel Johnson's term, created a wish for a similar group in his home town of Spalding which would reflect something of the sociability and intelligent discussion he had known in London in the first years of the eighteenth century.

---

[5]   The Johnson family of Spalding gave the name 'Maurice' to six generations of its members, which can be rather confusing. The founder of the SGS was the son of the first Maurice Johnson (1661–1747), a Lincolnshire lawyer trained at Clement's Inn in London, who acquired Ayscoughfee Hall through marriage (see family genealogy, Appendix 5). For much of his life, until his father's death in 1747, the SGS's founder signed himself 'Maurice Johnson junior' or 'MJ jun.' to distinguish himself from his father, who was one of the founder members of his son's society. The confusion is deepened by the fact that he also named his eldest son Maurice, and this third Maurice also became a member of the SGS and a frequent correspondent. In this volume, they will be distinguished by using 'Maurice Johnson senior' for the eldest of the three, 'Maurice Johnson' to refer exclusively to the SGS's founder and 'Maurice Johnson (son)' to refer to the youngest of the three. Although later holders of the name were associated with the SGS's history, they fortunately do not enter into the historical period covered by this volume. If the surname 'Johnson' occurs in this volume it will refer to the founder of the SGS; any references to the better-known eighteenth-century figure Dr Samuel Johnson (no relation) will use his full name to avoid confusion.

The society that he created at Spalding was, in many respects, unique. Many provincial towns in the early eighteenth century had a gentlemen's club, often, though not always, a mainly social gathering. There are traces of such groups across the Midlands, such as the Northampton Philosophical Society of 1743 founded by Philip Doddridge and the Deepings and Grantham societies. Some were, or became, simply dining or drinking clubs; others concentrated on a specialised function, becoming book clubs or musical societies. Few kept minutes, and those of others have mostly been lost. What distinguished the society at Spalding from these was the range and breadth of its activities, the detail and precision of its minutes from 1712 to 1758, still preserved in six folio volumes in the SGS's archive, and the voluminous correspondence that it maintained. These contributed to its longevity; it prospered under Maurice Johnson and continued under his sons Walter and John and the Revd John Rowning who took over as secretary in the 1760s. A letter of 1764 from Walter Johnson to William Stukeley and a letter of 1769 to the Spalding Gentlemen's Society from one of its members, Joseph Mills, minister of neighbouring Cowbit, show that the organisation was still very active up to that time.[6] The survival of the Society's archives encouraged later revivals after periods of relative inactivity; it remains today as England's longest-surviving active provincial learned society.

It is the more remarkable that such a society began and flourished in the Lincolnshire Fens, regarded at that time as a remote and inaccessible part of the country, as comments by some of the correspondents show. William Bogdani, Clerk to the Ordnance at the Tower of London, referred to 'Spalding (a Town separated from the rest of Mankind)'.[7] The antiquarian Roger Gale wrote from London in 1735 that the Spalding gentlemen were 'a sett of Virtuosi allmost out of the world and who would never have been known but by the emanations of theyr own light'.[8] The Society's survival and success at this stage of its history were mainly the result of the enthusiasm and efforts of Maurice Johnson, who was determined to give it the same range of interests as the great urban learned societies. The SGS modelled itself consciously on the London learned societies, the Royal Society and the Society of Antiquaries, with which it maintained contact.[9]

It is interesting to trace, from its records, the SGS's changing form and functions. Johnson began it when a remarkably young man of 22, fresh from his legal studies at the Inns of Court. There, his friendship with the poet and dramatist John Gay (then secretary to the Duchess of Buccleuch for whose Lincolnshire lands Johnson's father was steward) brought him into the stimulating world of London coffee-house clubs. Here he met Addison and Steele the essayists, Alexander Pope, Laurence Eusden (soon to be Poet Laureate) and other significant figures of the London literary scene, and he determined to re-create that atmosphere of

---

6   Joseph Mills was minister of the chapel of Cowbit from 1760 until his death in 1804 (LAO, Episcopal Register 38, 580). His letter was printed in Joseph Mills, *A Collection of Letters and Verses on Several Occasions* (Spalding, 1771). For a transcription of these two letters, see Appendix 4.
7   Letter No 93 (29 October 1728).
8   Letter No 259 (4 September 1735).
9   In 1717 Johnson was one of the re-founders of the Society of Antiquaries, or 'Antiquarian Society' as he often wrote of it. See Joan Evans, *A History of the Society of Antiquaries* (Oxford, 1956), 49–54.

enquiry and debate on his return to Spalding.[10] He documents fully in Minute Book 1 of the SGS minutes the conversation with Steele which confirmed his resolve:

> ... the Hint was taken and pursued from Conversations with Secretary Addyson, Sr Richard Steele, Laur. Euden now the Poet Laurat, Mr Alexander Pope the Poet, Col. Brett, Mr Jn. Gay & other Gentlemen at their Clubb at Buttons Coffee house in Cavent Garden London by me M. Johnson.[11]

Beginning with a small group of local gentry and professional men, Maurice Johnson established weekly meetings in Spalding which lasted in a virtually unbroken sequence until the 1770s as 'an Universal Literary meeting for the sake of Improvement in Friendship and Knowledge'.[12] The first topics for discussion arose from the reading, by 'the men of Sense & Letters' as Johnson described them, of the London papers and periodicals in a local coffee-house.[13] This was coupled with work in progress to catalogue and preserve the local parish library in the church of St Mary and St Nicholas in Spalding, following the Parish Libraries Act of 1708, which led in turn to the creation of a lending library for the SGS.

As it became established, the Society expanded its activities to include the antiquarian topics dear to Maurice Johnson's heart and, partly under William Stukeley's influence, natural philosophy. Eventually no topic was barred except disputes over religion and politics; Johnson was anxious to avoid the contentions and divisions that could arise through taking sides over such thorny contemporary problem areas. In turn this contributed to the stability and prosperity of his society, unlike its daughter the Peterborough Gentlemen's Society, which foundered over disputes between clerics and physicians.[14]

The importance of the SGS's correspondence

It was, however, correspondence that extended the SGS's scope beyond local knowledge and preoccupations. Maurice Johnson became aware at an early stage that his own considerable efforts, which kept the Society afloat through its first years, and the contributions from the small group of local members were not enough to achieve his aims of extending active research and communication of knowledge in his neighbourhood. He set about building up as wide a body of correspondents as possible. In addition, he sent regular reports to his society during his absences in London, including information on newly-published books, new inventions, events and exhibitions in the city and meetings of the Royal and Antiquarian societies that he had attended. Correspondence proved very valuable in providing an impetus for meetings to continue in his absence; when he was present it formed a major part of the material for discussion at their weekly

---

[10] Eusden (1688–1730), not one of the most distinguished holders of the Laureateship, later took holy orders and in 1730 was appointed Rector of Coningsby where he died five months later (H. B. Williams, 'Lincolnshire's parson Poet Laureate', *Lincolnshire History and Archaeology* 30 (1995), 63–65).
[11] SGS, Minute Book 1, fol.16 (marginal note). There are entries for all those mentioned in *ODNB*.
[12] SGS, Minute Book 1, fol.73 (2 January 1724).
[13] SGS, Minute Book 1, fol.15.
[14] The statutes and 'Oeconomical Rule' which ordered the activities of the Society and governed its weekly meetings are transcribed in Owen, *Minute-Books of the Spalding Gentlemen's Society*, p. x.

Thursday meetings. The contents of letters received by the Society were then recorded meticulously in the six folio volumes of Minute Books by Maurice Johnson as SGS Secretary and by Dr John Green, his son-in-law, the second secretary.

The aims of this correspondence with fellow enthusiasts for knowledge were threefold: to keep the Spalding society, in its remote location, in touch with the latest discoveries in the world beyond the Fens; to pass on this knowledge to other interested members of the 'Republic of Letters' and to communicate to others the discoveries made by local Spalding members. By the mid-1720s the correspondence preserved in the SGS archive shows that the Society's interests had expanded to encompass all branches of knowledge which interested the 'virtuosi' or the 'curious', as learned people described themselves at the time. The topics receiving the greatest attention were natural history, antiquities, numismatics and literature, though the letters calendared below indicate widespread interest in art, medicine, astronomy, travel and a range of other topics.

The creation of contacts by letter was made possible by the recent improvements in the postal system. Some letters were still given to friends to bring, as the writers indicate, but most were delivered by post. These were still the days of the folded letter rather than the use of a separate envelope, and the outside of many of the letters carry instructions for their journey such as the frequent 'Turn at Stilton' for letters from London and 'By Caxton Bag' on letters from Cambridge and the east of England. The journey of these letters was remarkably quick; the Minute Book's account of the meetings at which they were read is often dated three or even two days after the date shown on the letter.

One significant factor in this improvement was the system of 'cross posts' and 'bye-posts' developed by Ralph Allen, Deputy Postmaster of Bath, by 1720.[15] This established cross-country routes which meant that letters did not have to be sent via London, so shortening the time required for their delivery. The cost of postage was still paid by the recipient. The SGS was helped in this by members or friends, notably MPs, who had the right to 'frank' their letters, thus escaping postal charges because of the important office they held, usually in Government. Such a person could frank a letter for a friend, and some of the letters received at Spalding bear handwritten franks. A valuable member of the SGS was George Shelvocke, Secretary to the Post Office; he agreed to send the SGS's foreign correspondence free of charge, as he also did for the Royal Society.[16] Nonetheless, the cost of postage could still be considerable for a small group like the SGS's 'regular' members and it was likely that Maurice Johnson himself bore the brunt of it. Perhaps this explains why the Society's vast correspondence seems to have diminished very soon after his death.

The creation of a network of correspondents

Although Newton was by 1724 too old to be a correspondent, his advice spurred Maurice Johnson to action. The Society had already admitted non-Spalding members whose contributions came mainly through correspondence because of

---

[15]   This is referred to in James Rowland's letter (No 122, 18 June 1730).
[16]   Letter No 453 (5 November 1745).

problems of travelling even short distances from Fenland villages for evening meetings, particularly in winter. The first of these to be recorded, in 1714, was Francis Curtis, schoolmaster of nearby Moulton and an enthusiast for the Society's aims.

A fruitful source of correspondents was Johnson's own large family. The extended family was of great importance in the eighteenth century and his sociable and hospitable nature led him to enjoy keeping contacts even with distant relations. A number of regular correspondents were addressed, or addressed him, as 'cousin'; indeed, the recipient of one letter from him addressed simply to 'My Couzen' cannot be more precisely identified for this reason. His family history gave him connections with the Lynns of Southwick, including the meteorologist George Lynn senior and his medical brother Walter, and the numismatist Beaupré Bell among others; they became active correspondents. Of the twenty-seven children born to Johnson and his wife Elizabeth, seventeen survived into adulthood, many of whom became correspondents. His eldest son, Maurice, contributed over twenty letters to the SGS from his travels. Local members also brought in their friends; for example, Benjamin Ray, the incumbent of Cowbit and a regular attender at SGS meetings, encouraged his friend, the scholarly Samuel Pegge, to correspond from Kent.

Johnson could also draw on his legal contacts in London and on the Midland Circuit to find corresponding members. During his regular visits to London for the legal terms, he was able to recruit correspondents when he attended the Society of Antiquaries as a member or went to the Royal Society's meetings as a guest of friends such as William Stukeley and William Bogdani, Clerk of the Ordnance at the Tower of London. As the SGS became well-known, membership was requested by interested members of the 'Republic of Letters' who heard of the SGS from friends and colleagues. Many SGS members were also members of the Royal Society or Society of Antiquaries, and some belonged to both. Those who were also active correspondents of the SGS are documented in Appendix 2.[17] Other academic connections were made through the attendance of family members at the universities; Maurice Johnson's son John made useful contacts while at St John's College, Cambridge, as did other young Spalding men at Oxford.

The network of correspondents also spread overseas as the SGS established international links. Some were via family members such as 'cousins' Henry Johnson, a merchant who reported on his travels in Spain and Central America, and William Johnson, serving with the East India Company. As a young man, Dr John Green, later to become Johnson's son-in-law and the SGS's second secretary, wrote about his medical studies at Leiden University under the great Boerhaave. As mentioned above, Maurice Johnson's eldest son, Captain (later Colonel) Maurice Johnson, sent descriptions of his travels in Europe with his regiment, the '1st of Foot' (Grenadier Guards), during the War of the Austrian Succession (1740–1748), with accounts of antiquities and works of art that he had seen there. The Minute Books indicate that letters were also received from two of Johnson's younger sons overseas, Martin, a midshipman in the Navy serving in the Caribbean, and Henry Eustace, an East India Company man travelling to India; unfortunately these have not survived. Accounts of travels in the British Isles were sent

---

[17] Further details are available in Michael Honeybone's article on the SGS in *ODNB*.

to the SGS by members such as William Stukeley and Roger Gale reporting on their antiquarian tours and Calamy Ives describing his visit to Ireland.

Other correspondents arose through links with the Spalding area; for example, Johnson acted as steward for the Lincolnshire lands around Crowland belonging to Major-General Sir Robert Hunter, Governor-General in Jamaica. A valuable source of correspondence was the network of merchants who traded goods to and from the port of Spalding, then much closer to the sea and on the tidal reaches of the River Welland, and from Boston and King's Lynn. One such was Richard Norcliffe, based in south Norway for the Scandinavian timber trade; he in turn introduced Andreas Bing, a Norwegian astronomer and former missionary to Greenland. Correspondence with men of learning who did not speak English was facilitated by Maurice Johnson's ability to write fluently in Latin. This came almost as naturally to him as writing English; he exchanged letters in Latin on occasions with friends such as Francis Curtis, Samuel Whiting and Roger Gale.

Links with other learned societies

One regular source of letters was the SGS's contact with other learned societies. From the 1720s onwards there was a steady flow of official correspondence with the Royal Society and with the Society of Antiquaries who referred to the SGS as 'our Cell at Spalding'. The SGS regularly received the Royal Society's *Philosophical Transactions* until the 1770s and subscribed to the Antiquaries' sets of prints of coins and historic buildings; this kept the provincial society in touch with the latest intellectual developments in the capital. In return, the SGS sent transcripts and summaries of their minutes; some of these are recorded in the *Philosophical Transactions*, including their description of a metal thermometer in the Spalding Society's museum and observations of a waterspout in Deeping Fen.

One of the mainstays of the SGS's correspondence was its interchange of letters with its daughter society, the Peterborough Gentlemen's Society (hereafter referred to by the abbreviation PGS, frequently used by Maurice Johnson). The PGS was founded in 1730 by Timothy Neve, who had recently moved from Spalding to be a minor canon of Peterborough Cathedral. He had previously been Master of Spalding Grammar School and was an early and enthusiastic member of the SGS, acting as its Treasurer for some years. The PGS aimed at an equally wide membership, electing corresponding members from across Britain and overseas. Frequent reports of its meetings, activities and news received were sent to Spalding in letters from Neve to Johnson. In his earlier years, Maurice Johnson had shared with his friend William Stukeley the hope of creating a network of learned societies across the towns of the Fens and the East Midlands, all enquiring into 'the Arts and Sciences' and disseminating their knowledge to their fellow societies by correspondence, a form of early postal internet. As Johnson stated in his annual review of the Society's activities in 1724, he had kept his minutes in detail partly in the hope of

> Assisting other Gentlemen my Acquaintance and friends in Lincoln City, Peterborough, Stamford, Boston, Oundle, Wisbeach and elsewhere to Institute & promote the like Designe, and hold Correspondence with us …[18]

---

[18]   SGS, Minute Book 1, fol.73 (2 January 1724).

Several of these societies came into existence, but they tended to depend on the leadership of a strong enthusiast as President or Secretary and declined when that person moved on. In addition to Neve's PGS, which flourished between 1730 and 1752 before diminishing into a book club, there was a short-lived society at Wisbech which declined when its moving spirit, Johnson's friend Dr Richard Middleton Massey, moved to London. Stukeley, after his move to Stamford in 1729 to become Rector of All Saints' Church, attempted to revive the earlier short-lived Brazen-nose Society, but on the death of his wife his enthusiasm was dampened and the Stamford society declined again. The letters in this calendar show an attempt by Stukeley, Maurice Johnson and others to set up similar societies at Ancaster and Market Deeping. The factors ensuring the survival of Johnson's society at Spalding included his own determined efforts and those of his extended family, his connections with other national and professional groups, his dominant position in Spalding as one of the leading men of the town and district and his own hospitable disposition which helped in the avoidance of destructive quarrels between members.

Once the letters had been received, the SGS heard them read at a Thursday meeting. Their contents were then summarised in that week's minutes and a reply was drafted. Some of these drafts survive in the Spalding archive. Maurice Johnson was officially appointed Secretary in 1713 in the very early days of the Society. He retained this position until 1748 when he took over as President on the death of Stephen Lyon, minister of Spalding, who had held the office since 1713.[19] As the extent of the correspondence and of the topics it covered increased, a second or assistant secretary, Dr John Green, was appointed to deal with letters on scientific, medical and mathematical topics while Johnson concentrated on those relating to the arts, antiquities, history and literature.

The role of 'corresponding' members of the SGS

Of the voluminous correspondence received by the SGS during its first active period in the early eighteenth century, a large amount survives from 1712 to 1753. After that, even though the Minute Books continue for a few years and letters from members conserved in other archives such as the Bodleian Library and the British Library indicate that the SGS was active as a learned society until the early 1770s, no further letters from this period have been preserved at Spalding. The minutes become much briefer after Johnson's death and cease in 1758, with a final entry on 29 June, not to resume until 1828 when they were re-started by J. H. Marsden, later Professor of Archæology at Cambridge. Even after this there are further gaps; between 1828 and 1889 only thirty-six meetings were held. There was a significant gap when no meetings were held between 1875 and 1889. The SGS was 'revivified' when Dr Marten Perry became President at

---

[19] Stephen Lyon was born in Rouen and came to England as a Huguenot refugee, 'under the guardianship of his mother'. He was ordained priest by the Bishop of London in 1696 and was licensed to serve the cure of Spalding in 1709. He married Grace, daughter of George Lynn of Southwick (Northants), a kinswoman of Maurice Johnson. He died in 1748. See John, Lord Monson (ed.), *Lincolnshire Church Notes made by William John Monson 1828–1840* (LRS 31, 1936), 332; R. E. G. Cole (ed.), *Speculum Diœceseos Lincolniensis sub episcopis Gul: Wake et Edm: Gibson 1705–1723* (LRS 4, 1913), 112.

the end of the nineteenth century.[20] As Perry wrote, 'The few remaining members met on July 15th 1889 and decided that an earnest effort should be made to revivify the Society.'[21] It is thus not possible to check on the systematic receipt of letters from the SGS's early years after 1753.

The archive of letters at Spalding, though comprehensive, does not contain every letter received by the Society during this period. The Minute Books record some letters which have not survived, including Midshipman Martin Johnson's reports from the West Indies. One particularly sad loss is the series of letters from the well-known engraver George Vertue who was one of the SGS's official artists and engraved the portrait of Maurice Johnson now in the National Portrait Gallery. Some letters from regular correspondents like Stukeley, Neve and William Bogdani, recorded in the minutes, are not present in the modern collection. This helps to explain apparent gaps in the regular correspondence, caused by missing letters rather than interruption to the friendships. Nonetheless, the present Spalding archive contains 580 letters, calendared in this volume.

Some writers of letters in the Spalding archive were not members of the SGS. These are usually represented there by one letter, though a few contributed more than one. Some are from people who shared Johnson's antiquarian interests and wrote to offer information he would find helpful or to request his help in solving an antiquarian problem. Notable among these were Francis Peck, the historian of Stamford, who offered an exchange of historical documents with Johnson, Edward Saul, chaplain to the Duke of Rutland and author of a book on the barometer, who asked about the mediæval ownership of land in Lincolnshire, and Dr Patrick Kennedy, the numismatist, enquiring about a coin of the Emperor Carausius. Other letters are originals or copies of letters on matters which would interest the SGS, passed on from their original recipients to Johnson. This was evidently one of the ways in which the latest discoveries were notified around the early eighteenth-century 'Republic of Letters'. A few, such as an order for candles and a letter to John Johnson, Maurice's brother, from a client in Lincoln Prison, have probably got into the collection from among the Johnson family papers.

One group of letters included in this calendar is not strictly related to the affairs of the SGS, though it deals with a topic of great concern to many of its members. The legal specialism of Maurice Johnson and his younger brother John was law relating to drainage, and this was one of the great ages of drainage schemes for the South Holland Fens. Several letters in the collection passed between the Johnsons in their work for the Court of Sewers in South Holland and the Lincolnshire MPs, Sigismund Trafford and Robert Vyner. They are concerned with the Duke of Bedford's schemes for drainage and its probable impact on the Spalding area, in particular the perennial problem of where the water would go when removed from the Bedford Level. Other letters reflect this interest in drainage; the well-known drainage engineers the John Grundys, father and son, were SGS members and some of their correspondence relates to the drainage of the Spalding area.

---

[20] Chris Renn, 'The revivification of the Spalding Gentlemen's Society' (unpublished MA thesis, University of Lincoln, 2008).
[21] Marten Perry, 'The origin, progress and present state of the Spalding Gentlemen's Society', *Journal of the British Archaeological Association* new series 5 (1899), 39.

Letters from SGS members

However, the vast majority of these letters were contributed by members of the SGS. These letters confirm the evidence from the Minute Books that the SGS developed three categories of members. The first were the 'regular' members, the small group of local clergy, professional men and merchants who met weekly on Thursday evenings throughout the year, to the surprise of the Society of Antiquaries and Royal Society where meetings were often suspended during the summer. They came together to hear dissertations and letters, to bring their own 'curious' items such as verses, coins, plants or medical specimens and to communicate their meteorological and astronomical observations; members were expected to 'communicate to the Society something new or Curious' at meetings.[22] Since they were present at meetings, these members provide few of the letters in the collection, though there are reports of travels by some of them.

The second group were the 'honorary' members, elected because their position in society or the academic world gave dignity to the SGS. Letters survive from Johnson inviting them to become members, and there are replies from some of them, often offering a book for the Society's library, which was a condition of membership. A notable example was the Duke of Buccleuch, Lord of the Manor of Spalding and a former schoolfellow of Maurice Johnson's at Eton. He agreed to be the SGS's patron and was named among the Society's benefactors for his donations of expensive books such as Pine's beautifully produced and bound edition of the poems of Horace, still in the SGS's collection. Such members did not usually correspond on a regular basis. Other correspondents who are represented by a single letter in this calendar have written on similar lines, either thanking the SGS for the honour of their election to membership or promising a book for the Society's library.

Significant correspondents

A smaller group of writers made a much greater contribution to the body of correspondence. Maurice Johnson distinguished some members as 'corresponding' members, whose membership had been encouraged because they had an interest shared by the Society and had indicated their willingness to enter into a dialogue by letter about it. In some cases, only a few of their letters are represented in the current archive at Spalding. Some wrote regularly for the limited period of time in which they were connected with the SGS; for example, Alexander Gordon, the Secretary of the Society of Antiquaries, was a regular correspondent on antiquarian topics in 1738–9 but his letters appear to have ceased when he left London for a post in the relatively new colony of Carolina. Dr Musgrave Heighington, the SGS's composer, was a regular correspondent during his time in Great Yarmouth as organist at St Nicholas' Church in the late 1730s and early 1740s. He travelled to Spalding each summer for the SGS's yearly Anniversary Concerts, often performing his own settings of verses written or chosen by the Society's members. His letters cease on his move to Spalding and then Leicester.

Some members continued to correspond over many years, and it is the letters from this small group of people that make up a major section of the current

---

[22] SGS, Minute Book 1, fol.26.

archive, as Appendix 1 indicates. Johnson distinguished these in the Minute Books as 'beneficient members' alongside those who had made particularly generous donations, regarding their donation of information as equally valuable. Perhaps unsurprisingly, Maurice Johnson himself made the largest contribution; 75 letters from him remain at Spalding. A few of these are drafts of letters, particularly from his early years when he was anxious to perfect his style for addressing important people. Most, however, are the regular reports that this assiduous and indefatigable correspondent sent to the SGS whenever he was absent from Spalding, in his determination that there should be adequate material to sustain the weekly meetings. As his friend and relative Benjamin Ray said of him, 'you so kindly & so generously feast us, to our great satisfaction, with one fine entertainement or other, during your absence from us' by letter.[23]

Johnson's letters are chiefly reports from his yearly short visits to London for the three legal terms. Although some are addressed to his wife or later to one of his sons, only the sections intended for the SGS have been preserved; since they were intended to convey intellectual information for the Society's meetings, very little of the personal parts of the letters have remained in this archive. These sections may have been kept among the family's personal papers and so dispersed. Occasionally items of information which he assumed would interest the recipient have survived, such as accounts of his journeys to London or Lincoln in letters written to his wife. The main body of these letters contains information about meetings of the Royal and Antiquarian societies, about exhibitions of natural history or other 'curiosities', about the latest plays and publications. The sheer energy required to maintain this level of communication, in addition to the personal letters to individuals which survive in other archives and the replies to letters received by the SGS, together with his assiduous minute-keeping, his legal career, his hospitality to visitors, his care for his own antiquarian and numismatic collections and extensive garden and, certainly not least, his affectionate concern for his large family, leave one feeling exhausted by simply reading about it! One is driven to a sentence more typical of Maurice Johnson's length, just to record his activities.

Some of his friends and fellow-SGS members made their own considerable contributions to the flow of correspondence. Biographical details of these people are given in Appendix 2, and a number of them also have entries in the *Oxford Dictionary of National Biography*. William Stukeley is the classic example. A lifelong friend of Johnson's since their boyhood in the Fens, he sent more than the thirty-three letters which remain in the Spalding archive and are calendared in this volume; others, now missing, are reported in the Minute Books. Stukeley and Johnson shared a passion for antiquities and coins and were concerned to conserve the Abbey ruins at Crowland.[24]

The letters from Timothy Neve have already been referred to; a total of thirty remain in the SGS's archive. He and Maurice Johnson became friends when the

---

[23] Letter No 420 (26 November 1743).
[24] Although these letters form an important aspect of this correspondence, it was decided not to select any for complete transcription here (although they are, of course, calendared), since we are in the process of preparing a further volume for the LRS which will contain a full transcription of Stukeley's correspondence with Johnson together with Johnson's replies, which are housed in the Bodleian Library, Oxford.

young Neve came to Spalding in 1716 as Master of the Grammar School;[25] he soon joined the SGS and became its Treasurer. His earliest letters are reports from Spalding to Johnson in London about the SGS meetings which have taken place in Johnson's absence and about his plans to provide a permanent meeting-room for the Society. He had moved to Peterborough by 1729 and continued to correspond over the years about the activities of his own PGS and his own discoveries and observations relating to Roman antiquities and natural phenomena such as the Aurora Borealis.

Several other major correspondents supported the SGS by their regular letters. The best-known of these was the antiquarian Roger Gale, a friend of Johnson's from the Society of Antiquaries, who contributed at least the 30 letters recorded here, sending the first of them from his work in London. His letters were of particular interest in giving the latest news of discoveries such as the Chichester inscription and the Corbridge silver plate. On his enforced retirement to his Yorkshire estate, he continued to correspond, describing his visit to Scotland with the Scottish scholar Sir John Clerk, whom he introduced to the SGS as a member. While Roger's antiquarian brother Samuel was also an SGS member, no letters from him have survived.

Beaupré Bell, one of Maurice Johnson's extended family of 'cousins', and famous for his passion for numismatics which exceeded even Johnson's, regularly contributed his very extensive knowledge of coins, particularly those from the Roman Empire, in 37 letters extending over much of his adult life. Bell was also a frequent visitor to the SGS's Thursday meetings, travelling to Spalding from his home at Beaupré Hall in Outwell, just beyond the Norfolk border. After Bell's death the SGS was anxious to have his tables of Roman coins published, and some of the correspondence with Bell's old college, Trinity College Cambridge, deals with this; unfortunately, this did not result in publication by Trinity and the SGS lacked the funds to publish them themselves.

A surprisingly little-known SGS member and very regular correspondent was William Bogdani, Clerk to the Ordnance at the Tower of London and a member of the London intellectual scene as a member of both the Royal Society and Society of Antiquaries. There appears to have been some family connection between him and the Johnsons, but it has so far eluded detection; his father was an émigré Hungarian Protestant artist and his wife, Penelope Bowell, has no traceable connection with families to whom the Johnsons were related. A letter from Charles Green of Spalding to the *Gentleman's Magazine* in 1797 speaks of Bogdani as 'a near relation and intimate friend' of Maurice Johnson. Maurice Johnson and he were godfathers to each other's sons, so the relationship may perhaps have been of that nature. He contributed at least the 39 letters to the SGS which survive and others we know of from references in the Society's minutes. They are full of reports from the learned societies of London, national and international news, political comment and also the latest London scandals. His correspondence is of national interest, coming from the Tower of London, the headquarters of Britain's military and naval gunnery.

Other frequent correspondents were among the younger members that Maurice Johnson was determined to attract, to ensure the continued survival of his society.

---

[25] See Letter No 23.

One of his last letters to Stukeley, now in the Bodleian Library, expresses his pleasure at the list of young men of promise that he has been able to secure as SGS members. Two, in particular, sent over 20 letters each. The contribution of Maurice Johnson's eldest son, another Maurice, has already been mentioned; letters during his military training and service with the 1st Regiment of Foot are dated from as far afield as London, Ghent and the Rhine valley. His father's careful training of his children of both sexes as artists is shown in the sketches which accompany his letters as well as in his sister Anne Alethea's illustrations for the Minute Books.

Another Johnson connection, Richard Falkner, contributed 22 letters from Oxford in the period 1733 to 1736. Falkner was, in fact, the stepbrother of Maurice Johnson the SGS Secretary, though they belonged to different generations, as Falkner was of the same age as Johnson's son, the younger Maurice, with whom he was firm friends. 'Mr Secretary Johnson's' father, also confusingly called Maurice, had married three times.[26] His first marriage produced his only surviving children, Maurice of the SGS and his younger brother John, for many years the SGS Treasurer following Neve's move to Peterborough. The third marriage, in 1726, was to a Boston widow who was herself embarking on a third marriage. Ann Falkner, née Wood, was the widow first of William Gonville of Alford and then of Thomas Falkner, a Boston merchant referred to in a letter from Stukeley.[27] Most of her children were grown up; the letter from her to Richard in the Spalding archive refers to a married daughter, and an adult son was the incumbent of Saleby in Lincolnshire.[28] Her youngest child, Richard, accompanied her to Spalding on her marriage to Maurice Johnson senior.

A promising young man, he decided on a career in medicine and went to Lincoln College, Oxford, in 1733, probably on one of the scholarships at the college open to young men from Lincolnshire. He reported back diligently to the SGS on happenings at the University, enclosing drawings of antiquities in its museums and copies of Latin verses written by his fellow-undergraduates. An amusing verse by him 'An Oxonian to his Owl', survives in Johnson's MS collection of poems, now in the Osborn Collection in the Library of Yale University. Whether this level of correspondence would have been maintained cannot be known; like that of Francis Curtis early in the SGS's history, it was cut short by his early death in 1737.

Other young men at university also corresponded during their time there, though with less intensity. Timothy Neve's son, Timothy Neve junior, contributed a set of letters from Oxford when he was a student in the late 1740s. His friend George Johnson, son of Maurice Johnson's cousin Walter, wrote accounts of his Oxford student life in the early 1750s and sent matters of interest to the SGS, including a list of the portraits in the hall at Christ Church. Young men making a career in London, particularly John Hill and Emanuel Mendes da Costa, also corresponded with the SGS as a means of becoming known and looking for patronage, all-important in the eighteenth century.

---

[26] See family genealogy, Appendix 5.
[27] Letter No 20 (6 June 1716).
[28] Letter No 193 (26 September 1733). Thomas Falkner was Vicar of Saleby from 1728 until his death in 1764 (LAO, Episcopal Register 38, p. 191; Episcopal Register 39, p. 37).

The number of letters received by the Society shows considerable variation from year to year. The development of the correspondence and the increase in corresponding members can be seen in Table 1 below. Its figures represent the numbers of letters surviving in the Society's archive; the Minute Books record others, received and read, which do not remain there, but these were not in such numbers as to make a major difference to the overall pattern of numbers received.

Table 1: Letters in the SGS archive by year of receipt

1710: **1**	1720: **2**	1730: **23**	1740: **20**	1750: **24**	1760: **1**
1711: **0**	1721: **3**	1731: **19**	1741: **18**	1751: **17**	1761: **3**
1712: **3**	1722: **4**	1732: **26**	1742: **23**	1752: **5**	1762: **0**
1713: **5**	1723: **7**	1733: **25**	1743: **17**	1753: **5**	
1714: **3**	1724: **10**	1734: **35**	1744: **18**	1754: **0**	
1715: **4**	1725: **10**	1735: **28**	1745: **11**	1755: **0**	
1716: **7**	1726: **12**	1736: **22**	1746: **21**	1756: **1**	
1717: **3**	1727: **4**	1737: **15**	1747: **23**	1757: **0**	
1718: **7**	1728: **6**	1738: **14**	1748: **8**	1758: **0**	
1719: **2**	1729: **16**	1739: **30**	1749: **9**	1759: **0**	
		Also: 1782:1		Undated: 10	

In the first decade of the Society's existence, 1710–19, the idea of having corresponding members had not been fully considered; each year shows only a handful of letters, mainly from the same people who were usually Johnson's friends such as Stukeley and Francis Curtis. As the 1720s progressed, more corresponding members were elected, and the range of correspondents widened, so that 74 letters are archived from the 1720s, compared with the 35 from the 1710s.

The 1730s were the great decade in the SGS's correspondence, with a large number of individual letters and of correspondents, some contributing only one letter and others writing at least once a year or sending several in a short period of time. A remarkable total of 237 letters from that decade remain in the SGS's archive. The largest number of letters is recorded for 1734, when 35 letters were received, the same amount as during the whole of the 1710s. Other years, such as 1735 and 1739, fall little short of this total with 28 and 30 respectively. A similar pattern, though on a rather reduced scale, prevailed in the 1740s, with new correspondents being introduced as earlier ones died or ceased to communicate. The 1740s produced 168 surviving letters, with the best years being 1742 and 1747, each with 23 letters. It is possible that the Jacobite rising of 1745 may have affected some correspondents in mid-century; Sir John Clerk, for one, moved from Edinburgh to Durham to avoid the invasion and Maurice Johnson's eldest son was involved in military campaigns against Prince Charles's forces.

By the end of the 1740s, a significant decline can be seen: 1748 has only 8 letters in the archive and there are only 9 for 1749. This may reflect Maurice Johnson's increasing age and ill-health; he gave up the Secretaryship in 1748 to become President, and he was to a large extent the moving force of the Society's correspondence. Some regular correspondents such as Roger Gale died during the 1740s. The 1750s get off to a good start, however, with some new younger correspondents and SGS members; the first two years return to the earlier amounts of letters, with 24 archived from 1750 and 17 from 1751. After that, there is a dramatic decline in letters received; the archive contains five letters each year in the next two years. The minutes become much shorter at this point and do not record letters read at meetings which have not survived, so it is not possible to work out whether it was the archiving rather than the efforts of the correspondents that was declining. However, Maurice Johnson himself was failing at this time; he died at the beginning of 1755, at the point where the regular correspondence appears to cease.

A few letters survive from the later years up to 1763, indicating that the Society itself did not cease to function. There are regular entries in the Minutes up to 1758, and the Treasurer's Accounts show regular meetings well beyond this date. The two letters in Appendix 4, though they are in the British Library, not the SGS's archive, are included to give evidence of the continuing activity and varied interests of the SGS into the 1760s. Both the SGS Minutes and the Treasurer's Accounts detail the change of activity to that of a book club and library in the late 1700s and early 1800s; the Society experienced revivals in the nineteenth century, a temporary one in the 1830s and a more lasting one in the 1890s and 1900s, though these did not produce the same system of corresponding members and the same range and volume of letters. Such correspondence as survives from the later periods is mainly concerned with business and membership matters.

Style

The styles of the correspondents in this archive are as varied as the correspondents and their subject-matter; this is apparent from the selection of letters transcribed in this calendar. Between Maurice Johnson and his old friends such as Stukeley or Roger Gale, and in Johnson's letters addressed to his family, a familiar tone often appears, with use of contracted forms such as 'I'll', 'it's' or ''tis' and 'you've'; sentences are shorter and vocabulary simpler. Correspondence intended for a more public reception or sent to persons of importance or rank has a more dignified style, with a more Latinate vocabulary and complex sentence-structure. At times, Johnson's sentences have an intricacy of subordinate clauses probably derived from the legal documents with which he was familiar; this public style is also found in other correspondents.

Style and deportment were key aspects of a gentleman's public life in the early eighteenth century; they were apparent in his style of speech and writing as much as in his dress and physical self-presentation through his way of walking, dancing and bowing, and were taught from an early age. Some of the letters in the Spalding archive show evidence of a desire to create a good impression on the reader by the adoption of a formal style of address in the salutation, conclusion and expression of contents and the use of dignified, lengthy sentences. It is as though the writers were proving their right to membership of the 'Republic of Letters' and to a reputation for civilised conduct and learning not only by what knowledge they are communicating but by their expression of it.

In this regard it is interesting to note the number of drafts that survive among the letters written by Maurice Johnson, as he attempts to ensure an appropriate expression for the occasion. This was partly because it was usually expected that letters such as those sent for the use of the SGS would reach a public audience, either by being read aloud at meetings or by being passed on to other 'virtuosi' of the world of learning, and perhaps eventually even being published in the transactions of a learned society. It could cause concern to a gentleman if a letter he had regarded as informally personal was given public exposure. Two of the letters in the Spalding collection express such concerns.[29] They are from good friends and relatives of Maurice Johnson's, William Bogdani and Beaupré Bell; both object to having a previous letter read out at an SGS meeting because they had written in what they had regarded as too informal and casual a style for a public audience, although it may not strike a modern reader as such.

Conservation of the letters

Most of the letters calendared in this volume have been in the possession of the SGS ever since they came into the hands of its secretaries and have travelled with the Society's papers in their various removals. The earliest ones were stored in the Society's first official meeting-place after its removal from the coffee-house, a room attached to the parsonage in Churchgate. Later accretions of correspondence swelled the collection as the Society moved, after a brief attempt to use the new Town Hall, to a room off the Abbey Yard, leased from Joseph Sparke of Peterborough, where the SGS remained until 1743, building up their collection of books, antiquities and specimens of natural history.

Their next move was to Gayton or Holyrood House, which had come to Maurice Johnson through his wife Elizabeth and was next to Maurice Johnson's home at Ayscoughfee Hall beside the River Welland. Their final move at this stage of the SGS's life was in 1755, on the death of Maurice Johnson, to rooms belonging to Mr Cox, the SGS's Operator, at the junction of Bridge Street and Double Street. The collections stayed there for over 100 years until road-widening demolished the premises in the 1880s. The Society's books, papers and remnants of their collections were removed for a brief time to the boardroom of the newly-built Johnson Hospital in Spalding, founded with funds from two surviving Johnsons, the Misses Elizabeth and Mary Johnson. The revival of the SGS towards the end of the nineteenth century under Dr Marten Perry (a president of Johnsonian enthusiasm and drive) and his colleagues brought about the establishment of a purpose-built home for the Society and its collections at its present base in Broad Street, opened in 1911. This has been the home of the correspondence from then onwards.

Other letters addressed to Maurice Johnson have come into the SGS's possession through the purchase of items of his personal papers, particularly during the two sales of the Johnson books and papers organised by Sotheby's. The first of these was in 1898 after the death of the sixth and last Maurice Johnson, who had retired to Suffolk, and a second and larger one took place in 1970. It was decided to include these letters in this calendar, since they are in the SGS's archive and relate to the activities of the SGS or of an individual member of it, or throw light on Maurice Johnson himself as an antiquary or as a practising lawyer. This is particularly the case in the letters relating to the drainage of the South Lincolnshire Fens and the business of the Court of Sewers, of which Maurice Johnson and his brother John were officers.

---

[29] Letter No 80 (22 October 1726) and Letter No 141 (18 March 1731).

In the SGS's early years, before 1755, an original system of cataloguing and storage for this correspondence was developed by Maurice Johnson and John Green as secretaries. The early eighteenth century was a time when experiments in categorising and cataloguing were becoming widespread. There was a growing awareness of the need to systematise the rapidly-expanding knowledge in the arts, natural philosophy and medicine and the increasingly extensive private and public libraries such as that of the SGS, and as yet no standard systems of organisation existed. Maurice Johnson was very interested in various systems of library cataloguing, as his entries in the Minute Books show. He repeatedly reorganised and updated the SGS's library catalogues and in the late 1740s John Green was creating a 'useful catalogue of the Water Fowles'.[30] The SGS developed its own original system of cataloguing and storing its growing correspondence.

Johnson originally dealt with all the correspondence, but as it grew in volume and became more specialised in content, John Green was appointed to assist him, as was mentioned above. The letters were usually read and discussed at a meeting of the SGS, their contents summarised in the Minute Book and a reply written by the appropriate secretary. They were then filed in one of eight, or perhaps nine large, strong brown folders; details of only eight survive, along with a further sheet labelled 'X'. As far as can be ascertained, each letter was assigned to one of eight groups, depending on three factors. The first two are relatively easy to identify: its content and the size of paper on which it was written. The third was whether it was a 'letter' or a 'dissertation'; the dividing line between these two types of document was, however, less clearly drawn than in modern documents, so some of Johnson's 'dissertations', which were in letter form, are included in this calendar. Others, clearly papers, are not included.

Letters and dissertations categorised as 'Theological, Ethical, Juridical & Historical Topics' were Johnson's province. He divided them further into folio or quarto size, and filed them in one of four folders dependent on this. John Green did the same with correspondence categorised as 'Physical, Philosophical & Mathematical Subjects', sorting them among the four folders of which he had charge. Each letter was entered, in order of receipt, in a numbered list written on the inside of the appropriate folder, and this number was written at the head of the relevant letter, usually in the form 'SGS No 23' (for example) but sometimes simply as 'No 23'. This numbering has been reproduced in the individual entries in this calendar. There was no further annotation to distinguish between 'No 23' in arts or sciences, in quarto or folio, as the secretaries assumed that this would be obvious since the letters would remain in their folders in future. These original catalogues of the letters, as written in the brown folders, are transcribed as Appendix 3 in this volume.

Johnson gave up the secretaryship when he became President in 1748 on the death of the long-serving Stephen Lyon. After Johnson's death in 1755, his meticulous system of storage and recording seems to have broken down. There are only three letters in this collection received after 1753. It may be that other letters received by the SGS were stored elsewhere, for example with the personal papers of John Green or of John Rowning who became Secretary in the 1760s, and were lost with them, or were mislaid during the move to Mr Cox's rooms

---

[30] See Letter No 481 below.

in 1755. As the Society moved to becoming mainly a book club towards the end of the century, the volume of correspondence would inevitably decrease; Johnson's energy and enthusiasm and his wide circle of acquaintances were the main driving forces behind the extensive network of correspondence.

Later systems of storage

As long as this system of filing in the brown files was retained, there was no confusion, since the contents and the paper size of a letter made it clear which 'No 23' was being referred to. At some stage at the end of the nineteenth or early twentieth century, however, perhaps during the use of the Johnson Hospital Board Room or at the time of the SGS's move in 1910 to its Broad Street premises, it was decided that this system was no longer appropriate. As far as we know there is no record of this decision, presumably made by the Curators of the period. The letters were removed from these folders and re-arranged alphabetically by surname of author. They were then stored in green paper wrappings, sometimes using one such package for a single correspondent and sometimes grouping several together, with the name or names of the writers on the outside of each package. The handwriting on the packages is almost certainly that of Dr Marten Perry, the outstanding President who revived the Society in the 1890s and organised the building of the Broad Street premises, so perhaps he was responsible for this reorganisation of the letters. While this new system was in many respects more efficient, it broke up the numerical sequence of 'SGS numbers' and rendered it incomprehensible.

At a later stage in the twentieth century, while the letters remained in these green packages in the SGS's strong room, the alphabetical sequence seems to have been disturbed. A Curator at this time gave to each package a pencilled number, from 1 to 100, but these did not correspond to the alphabetical order of the writers of the letters. For example, the letters from Cornelius Little were in the package numbered 1 and package 100 contained the letters of Benjamin Ray, while the 'W's came somewhere in between. When the staff of the Lincolnshire Archive Office visited the SGS in the late 1950s and early 1960s, it was this rather confusing numerical order that they recorded in their printed list of the SGS's papers. It was in this form that we first encountered these letters. Very recently, however, it was agreed that this system was no longer adequate for the preservation of these fragile documents, in the light of modern conservation techniques. The letters have now been transferred into acid-free individual envelopes and the alphabetical order by writer's surname has been restored.

System adopted for this calendar

In calendaring the letters for this volume, however, a strict chronological order has been established, integrating the letters from different correspondents into the sequence in which they were written and the SGS received and recorded them. This is of particular value since some of them are answers to questions posed in previous letters. Others form part of an extended dialogue on topics of interest to the learned world of the time. The breadth of the interests of the SGS and their associates becomes apparent from these discussions. Groups of letters cluster around discoveries such as the applications of the recently-systematised 'fluxions' or calculus, especially to water-flow with its implications for Fen drainage. Natural phenomena such as the Aurora Borealis and earthquakes are discussed and observations exchanged on eclipses. Antiquarian discoveries such as the Chichester inscription, the Corbridge plate and the coinage of Roman emperors produce fascinating sequences of letters. The chronological sequence also makes it possible to follow the growth of the SGS, its relations with other societies and the changes in its interests.

It would perhaps have been ideal to produce a transcription of all of these letters, but there were several strong reasons why this was not practicable. The size of the correspondence, approaching 600 letters, some of them extending to eight folio pages, made for a very extensive task. Maurice Johnson's prodigious output took a lifetime to produce; it would perhaps take another to make it all available in printed form. Secondly, the specialised nature of some of the letters meant that they would be of interest to numismatists or mathematicians rather than the wider reading public, and it therefore seemed preferable to offer a summary of their contents so that those with a particular interest could follow up these letters in the SGS's archive. Also, many of the letters contain drawings and diagrams of everything from heraldry to medical specimens. These add to the interest of the letters and indicate how information was communicated in the early eighteenth century, but would be very difficult and expensive to reproduce. Facsimile reproductions of some of them as copied into the Minute Books can be seen in Dorothy Owen's volume of the Minutes for 1733.[31]

It was decided, nonetheless, to transcribe a portion of this correspondence, approximately one-tenth of the total. This gives a flavour of the style, content and range of this remarkable collection. The criteria for selecting letters to transcribe were:

1. They give valuable information about the SGS, its organisation, activities and relationships with other similar societies and with learned individuals.
2. They give information about Maurice Johnson in his roles as SGS Secretary, noted antiquary, lawyer, friend or family member.
3. They contain information about specific members of the SGS who are themselves of significance, or about other public figures and events of the period, especially those with Lincolnshire connections.
4. They contain descriptions or comments about Lincolnshire, its life, people and countryside at that period, or its history and antiquities.

There is one notable exception to the above criteria; as mentioned above, it has been decided not to transcribe for this volume any of the letters from William Stukeley to Maurice Johnson. This is because this correspondence merits fuller attention. We are currently preparing a further volume, for future publication by the LRS, which will contain a full transcription of Stukeley's letters to Johnson, kept at Spalding, and also the letters which form Johnson's side of the correspondence, most of which are in the collection of Stukeley papers in the Bodleian Library, Oxford. This will give a more extensive and balanced view of the correspondence and relationship between these two important Lincolnshire antiquaries and avoid duplication of material.

---

[31] Owen (ed.), *Minute-Books of the Spalding Gentlemen's Society*.

The organisation of this calendar

As stated above, in this calendar the letters in the SGS archive from 1710 to 1761 are arranged chronologically in order of date of writing, though they may have been received much later because of delays in delivery, for example those from Norway or Central America. Each letter's contents are summarised, except where a full transcription is given. The letters are numbered in chronological order for ease of reference. Where Maurice Johnson or John Green had allocated an SGS number to a particular letter this is also given, e.g. 'SGS No 17' or 'No 17'.

The place and date of writing are given at the head of each summary, either as specified by the writer or as deduced from the contents of the letter or from the relevant entry in the SGS Minute Books, in which case square brackets are used. Most of the letters included in this calendar are mentioned in the Minute Books' accounts of the SGS's weekly meetings. Where this is the case, a reference is then given to the volume of the Minute Books, the folio on which the reference occurs and the date of the meeting at which the letter was read to members, e.g. 'MB3 fol.52B, 27 March 1740'. Transcribed letters which had been read at an SGS meeting are also given their Minute Book reference in the same format. Any points in individual entries requiring further explanation are clarified in footnotes at the end of the summary or transcription.

As most of the writers of these letters were members of the SGS, a brief biography of each of the members who contributed letters calendared in this volume is given, in alphabetical order, in Appendix 2 with the date of their election to membership. If they have a biographical entry in the *Oxford Dictionary of National Biography* (*ODNB*), as many of them do, reference is made to this so that fuller information can be obtained from it. The much smaller number of correspondents who were not SGS members are identified in a footnote at the end of the entry summarising their letter. The appendices are:

1: List of all correspondents with the numbers and dates of their letters in this calendar;
2: Brief biographies of those correspondents who were members of the SGS;
3: Transcription of the original lists of letters as made by Maurice Johnson and John Green in the brown storage files;
4: Letter from Walter Johnson to William Stukeley in April 1764, and letter from Joseph Mills to the Spalding Gentlemen's Society in December 1769, both indicating the continuing activity at the SGS;
5: A simplified genealogy of the Johnson family of Spalding.

Problems encountered

In preparing this calendar of the SGS's correspondence in the Spalding archives, we encountered problems common in working with documents of this period. First, and most significant for establishing the chronological sequence of the letters, was the matter of dating. There were three aspects to this difficulty:

1. Establishing the date of a letter if the date was not specified or only partially given, for example the day and month but not the year. The full date could often be found by using internal evidence such as political events or natural phenomena specified in other texts, or references to the publication of a book.

In some cases the letter was obviously a reply to a previous, clearly dated letter. The greatest help in dating was gained from the entries in the SGS's Minute Books where the contents of letters read at meetings were summarised and dated. The Index Book to the Minute Books, created by Maurice Johnson and kept in the SGS archive, was also of value, though he had his own idiosyncratic method of referring to entries in it. In a few cases, no date could be found; these letters are listed at the end of the calendar, together with one of a much later date which had found its way into this collection of letters.

2. Establishing the correct year if a letter was dated between 1 January and 25 March of a given year. This was because the change of year took place on 25 March, the feast of the Annunciation or Lady Day, which was the first day of the year, officially and legally, until 1752. There appears to have been no consistency among the correspondents as to their dating practices. Some used the date of the previous year until 25 March. Others used the new year's date from 1 January. Some preferred the 'double indication' writing both dates. So three letters from different correspondents received on the same day in February could be dated '3 February 1741' or '3 February 1742' or '3 February 1741/2'. Some correspondents were even inconsistent in their own usage, sometimes using one method and sometimes another, so that internal or external evidence has had to be drawn on to date the letter accurately. If a letter is dated by its writer to the early spring of one year, but its contents or the reference to it in the SGS Minute Books show it to be from the following year, we have given it the date provided by the writer but added a note indicating the correct date according to modern usage.

3. Confirming which calendar was being used. The countries of Continental Western Europe were using the reformed Gregorian calendar. In Britain, however, the Julian calendar was still used, and continued to be used until the calendar reform of 1752 when the more accurate Gregorian calendar was introduced. This is well-known because of the method of its introduction; to bring Britain into line with the date in Western Europe, eleven days were removed, for one year only, from September 1752, so days of that month jumped from 2 to 14 September. In dating the letters in this collection there was no difficulty over letters sent within Britain, but some came from correspondents travelling in Europe, such as Maurice Johnson's son Captain Johnson, Emanuel Mendes da Costa and the young John Green when he was studying in Leiden. They were aware of the difference in calendars between Britain and the country they were writing from; the usual practice was to adopt the local dating system but indicate it by writing 'New Style' or simply 'N.S.' after the date. On occasions a letter from Europe is dated by the Julian system in use in England, in which case the writer adds 'Old Style' or 'O.S.' after the date. If the letter was delivered quickly there could be interesting anomalies such as its being recorded as read at a Spalding meeting at a date preceding that on the letter.

The fragmentary nature of some letters also presented problems in reading them. Some are preserved as parts of a letter; in particular, Maurice Johnson often saved the expense of more than one letter home when in London by including material intended for an SGS meeting in a more personal letter to a member of his family. In this case, only the postscript or the section of the letter which contained information for the Society was archived by the SGS's secretaries at the time of its receipt. Some letters have clearly been cut by the recipient; the more personal section was presumably kept by Mrs Johnson or another family member and the section intended for the SGS handed over to one of the Society's officers.

The paper on which they were written varies in quality; some is excellent, so that the letter is still in very good condition, but others have become more fragile. On one occasion, Timothy Neve apologised for 'Sad paper but the best I have here'.[32] In some cases this has resulted in damage where a small segment, usually at the edge of a page or on the fold of a letter, has become detached and is missing. A further cause of damage resulted at some time in the past when the wax seals with which the letter were sealed were cut out, leaving a hole in the paper so that certain words are lost. This was presumably the action of a collector; the seals, usually made by the seal-ring of the sender, have imprints such as coats of arms or copies of Roman coins. We have indicated in the relevant entries in the calendar where these gaps occur in a document.

It has been fascinating to piece together from this patchwork of letters, a picture of a remarkable and perhaps unique group. The flowering of this 'sett of virtuosi allmost out of the world' (in Roger Gale's phrase) is a considerable one. We are fortunate that the assiduity of the SGS's officers from 1710 to 1753 and the care exercised by subsequent Curators of the Society have preserved so much documentary evidence for later readers to enjoy and to appreciate these achievements in 'Friendship and Knowledge'.

---

[32] Letter No 151 (23 December 1731).

THE CORRESPONDENCE OF
THE SPALDING GENTLEMEN'S SOCIETY

1710–1761

Correspondents who are members of the Spalding Gentlemen's Society are given a brief biographical statement in Appendix 2, and therefore they are not identified in a footnote at the end of their letter. Those correspondents who are not members of the Society are identified in a footnote at the end of their letter, or of their first letter if there is more than one by them included in this collection. The location of the sender is stated in the heading of each entry wherever it is possible to do so. The recipient of the letter is in Spalding unless another location is specified.

A significant number of the letters kept by Maurice Johnson as Secretary were given an SGS number as listed in Appendix 3 and discussed in the Introduction, p. xxv. This is included in the entry for the letter. If a letter was read to a meeting of the Society, it was recorded in the Minutes for that meeting. These references are listed in the entry for the relevant letter, noting the volume of the Minutes, the folio on which the letter is referred to and the date of the meeting at which the letter was read, e.g. 'MB2 fol.3B, 6 March 1729'; see the explanation in the Introduction, p. xxv.

1710

1. SGS No 50: From J. Mason to Revd Mr Henley at Melton Mowbray.
St John's [College Cambridge], 30 May 1710.
MB6 fol.23B, 12 August 1756.[1]
Gives an account of Mr Henley's son John Henley's excellent behaviour while 'here amongst us' [as a student].

[1]   The letter was presumably passed on to the SGS by Revd John Hardy, a later incumbent of Melton Mowbray (Leics) and a member of the SGS. It was read at an SGS meeting on 12 August 1756, and contrasted at that meeting with Henley's more flamboyant later character as 'Orator Henley' criticised by Pope and others. For a full biography of Henley, see his entry in *ODNB*.

1712

2. SGS No 4: Draft of letter from Maurice Johnson to Dr Edward Green[1] in London.
[Spalding], 17 November 1712.
MB1 fol.30A, 5 January 1713.
Also transcribed into MB1 fol.31B.

To Mr Edward Green the Chirurgion at his house in Newgate Street   London
Sr

The Candor of your Temper & my own Interest (Two very strong motives) induced me to write to you in favour of a Laudable Designe which Wee in the Inhospitable Fenns have formed for our Improvement in Literature & the passing our Lives with more Comfort I mean a Clubb or Society of Gentlemen of all the Learned Professions who meet every Monday[2] And would esteem It a singular favour from You Sr, who are a Part of the living learned World not the lest distinguishd if You would be pleased to spare a Quarter of an houre twice or thrice in a Yeare for the communicating to Us any of the many thousand occurrences in any part of Learning which You (who are every day conversant in all Parts of It) shall think fit. I beleive if you are pleased to oblige Us in our

Request, that I may modestly affirme Your Letters will more promote Science[3] amongst us Fenn Men, who are thought to labour under a very stupid Air,[4] than the Missionarys from Rome have Relligion (truly so calld) amongst the Chinese.[5] Ill detain you no longer than to add that I am – S[r] –

Your most obliged &

Spalding   most obedient humble Servant

17 Nov[r] 1712   Maur. Johnson jun[r]

[1]   Dr Green, a significant London surgeon and principal surgeon at St Bartholomew's Hospital, was related to the family of Maurice Johnson and was the uncle of Dr John Green who later became the SGS's Second Secretary.

[2]   The SGS originally met on Mondays. The meetings changed to Thursday evenings in 1719 and continue so today.

[3]   At this period, 'science' had the broader meaning of 'knowledge' and was not confined to 'natural philosophy' although it included this.

[4]   This reflects the eighteenth-century belief that health depended on good or bad air, and that the air of the Fens was popularly thought to be bad for health.

[5]   The Jesuit mission to China had begun in the seventeenth century.

Also a copy of reply from Edward Green, London, 12 December 1712. See next letter (No 3) for the original of this reply.

3. SGS No 5: From Edward Green to Maurice Johnson.
London, 12 December 1712.
There is also a transcribed copy of this letter in MB1 fol.31B.

S[r]   [SGS] No A5   London Decbr 12 1712
I thank you for your kind Complement & am very sorry that I have neither leisure or Capacity to answer your Intentions but if I take you right there are helps enough come out every day that may supply my defects such as the Journal des Scavans[1] Mercure Gallant[2] the belles lettres,[3] monthly mercury,[4] Fabritius his Bibliotheca Græca & Latina,[5] Hookes[6] posthumus works & Hawksbyes[7] book of experiments in natural Philosophy. all the great Bacons[8] works are never enough to be commended, Ruysch[9] in Anatomical dissections & preparations has gone the farthest of any witness his thesauri anatomici, I am just reading Blackmor's Creation[10] & believe shall hardly be able to get through him the 6th book so much celebrated for the Anatomical part, I am so dull as not to admire in short my opinion is if he had read more he would have writ less & notwithstanding this best of his peices because the shortest. I am not a bit the less in love with the charming Lucretius[11] one of the best poems in my poor opinion that ere was writ, don't think in the mean time I forget Homer Virgil & Horace –
wishing all happiness & satisfaction in their enquiryes to your learn'd society   the like to your self & Lady
I am   S[r]

Very much your humble servant
E Green

Mr Maur Johnson jun
at Spalding Lincolnshire
My thanks for your hares

[1]   The *Journal des Savants*, first published in Paris in 1665 by Denis de Sallo de la Coudraye; it was the first scientific journal to be published.

[2]   First published 1672 by Jean Donneau de Visé, later called *Mercure de France,* a literary magazine.

[3]   A literary magazine which it has not been possible to trace.

[4]   An English magazine dealing with historical and political topics, begun in 1690.

[5]   J.A.Fabricius (1638–1736) a major European bibliographer; published *Bibliotheca Latina in* 1697.

[6]   Robert Hooke (1635–1703): secretary of the Royal Society, a significant experimental philosopher contemporary with Newton.

[7]   Francis Hauksbee (d.1713): published *Physico-Mechanical Experiments* in 1709.

[8]   Sir Francis Bacon (1561–1626).

[9]   Frederik Ruysch (1638–1731): Dutch botanist and anatomist, best known for his *Thesaurus Anatomicus* (1702).

[10]   Sir Richard Blackmore (c.1655–1729), *Creation, A Philosophical Poem. Demonstrating the existence of God. In seven books.* The second edition was published in 1712.

[11]   Lucretius, Roman author of *De Rerum Natura,* frequently reprinted in the seventeenth and eighteenth centuries.

4. From Revd Francis Curtis to Maurice Johnson.

Moulton, Xr 12 [12 December 1712].

MB1 fol.29B, Monday 29 December 1712.[1]

He is sending the second volume of *Remarks on Freethinking;*[2] invites Johnson to visit, or will visit him; provides a note in Latin about a Greek epigram, which he quotes, and a translation of it into Latin and English verse; sends Christmas greetings.

[1]   The Minute Book entry records a 'Familiar Epistle' to Johnson from Revd Mr Curtis, 'written after a Free and Ingenious manner.' Curtis was Master of Moulton Grammar School; see his entry in Appendix 2.

[2]   It has not proved possible to trace this book as this may not be the full title. A possibility is *Remarks upon a late Discourse of Free Thinking* (1713), Dr Richard Bentley's response to Anthony Collins' *A Discourse of Free Thinking* (1713), though the dating of this presents a problem.

1713

5. SGS No 1: From Maurice Johnson to Revd Francis Curtis in Moulton.

Spalding, 111 Nona[rum] Jan MDCCXIII [3 January 1713].

Transcribed in MB1 fol.33B.

Letter in Latin. Sends Latin verses on the subject of discord and its resolution, and good wishes from the SGS.

6. From Revd Francis Curtis to Maurice Johnson.

[Moulton] 5 Id. Jan [9 January 1713].

MB1 f.30B Monday 19 January 1713.[1]

Letter in Latin; replies to Johnson's verses, approving of their contents; gives news of how he spent the Christmas period, including the composition of two Latin verses.[2]

The letter is annotated by Johnson: 'Mr Curtis his Answer.'

[1]   The Minute Book entry states: 'Communicated by Mr Curtis a Copy of Versis of on the Nativity of our Lord in Latin & another Upon a Snow Ball in Latin & Translated'.

[2]   The verses are not filed with the letter in the SGS archives.

7. From Revd Francis Curtis to Maurice Johnson.
[Moulton] April 1713 [no day given].

Tuesday.

Dear S^r

I have herewith sent you the Memoirs of Lit:[1] as to the two Poems, our friend Mr Cock borrows them of you. if you have the Month of March come yet, the sight of it will be aggreeable. Mr Rustat has been so entirely taken up in studying his new Lady, that he has foregott all the Commissions that he had from time to time to buy books for mine & your use. For I was in hopes of sending you something or other new & delightful. however I beg of you that you would not forgett what

the reading of

I mention'd lately of putting our selves into a way of having ^   all the valuable things that come out, at a Cheap rate.[2] Multorum manibus grande levatur onus tho' it is too much for any one man. I believe I can secure my neighbours Rustat & Tipping for pretty handsome contributions, & I dare say, Mr Moreton would come in if apply'd to. Spalding I leave to you. I am fond of the thought, & propose great delight from it. For my part I think ther is little in this world worth living for besides good books & good friends, at least I know of nothing that can be put in competition with them. The Memoirs of Literature I think extremely useful. it was the saying of a very great man, viz.that it was no small part of Learning to know well the History of Learning & where to read on all subjects. I intend to reserve a place in my Common place book for titles of books that I think valuable, & which I may purchase at one time or other. I have abundance of thoughts upon this Subject which I will propose when I see you, et si quid novisti rectius imperti candidus & among other things I would humbly propose that at the Dividend of the books, our friend Mr Lyon may claim no extraordinary priviledge above his Copartners, nor be suffer'd to follow the ungodly example of his namesake in the 1st book of Phædrus[3] (fab.5) sic totam prædam sola improbitas auferet. I w'd have due regard had to the Ladys[4] that are lovers of Learning Ten pound per Annum will buy abundance of Pamphletts, & some more substantial books into the bargain, & I concieve it will be no hard matter to gett ten people to subscribe a Crown per quarter, but if 10s I shall like it better, & then 20l. per Annum will furnish us with I believe almost all that comes out. Pardon these hasty thoughts which I communicate with the freedom of a friend & such you will always find

Y^r Humble Servant

Tuesday   Fr. Curtis

Pray present my wive's & my humble service to your good father & mother & Spouse (cui Lucina sit, precor, dextra)[5]

& Br John.

Annotated by Johnson: 'L^r from the Rev^d & Learnd Fr. Curtis MA SGS No 2'. On reverse, in another hand, probably Maurice Johnson's: 'April 1713. Read 5 May being Tuesday'.

---

[1] MS 'of of'. *The Memoirs of Literature* (1713) is still in the SGS library.

[2] His proposal, discussed more fully below, was for forming a subscription group to buy and share the latest books and pamphlets published in London, since these were too expensive for a single individual to buy on a regular basis. This suggestion encouraged the formation of the SGS library, whose contents were loaned to members, though at this stage it appears that the books were to be

shared out among subscribers after all members had had the opportunity to read them. The following Latin phrase is the equivalent of 'Many hands make light work'.

3   Curtis refers to the fables of Phædrus, the first-century AD Roman poet, known for his verse fables, similar to those of Æsop, in which human failings are satirised through stories about animals. In this case the quotation 'Thus wickedness alone carries off the whole prey' refers to a fable about a greedy lion who took all four portions of a dead deer which he should have shared with other animals. This is a pun on the name of Revd Stephen Lyon, incumbent of Spalding and President of the SGS.

4   Maurice Johnson was equally interested in including women participants, even in the SGS, but this does not appear to have been implemented.

5   'To whom I pray that Lucina [Roman goddess of childbirth] will be favourable.' Johnson's second surviving child and second daughter, Elizabeth, was born in 1713 and baptised on 14 May 1713. Curtis's frequent use of Latin and reference to Classical authors indicates both his work as Master of Moulton Grammar School and the classical education which he and Maurice Johnson had shared at Eton. Curtis was also a graduate of King's College, Cambridge.

8. From John Johnson[1] to Maurice Johnson.
London, 2 May 1713.

Dear Brother

As you expressed a Desire of hearing from me when wee parted, I can't in gratitude any longer forbear writeing tho' I am conscious to my self that it's impossible for any thing which comes from my Dull Pen to give you the pleasure or Satisfaction you might justly expect in reading the Various Occurences which daily happen in this Place had I (as oh I wish I had) it in my Power to give you an Agreeable Account thereof But since you know the Small Stock of Sence I am Master off and how little even that has been improved which joined with an Innate Bashfullnes renders me wholly unfitt for the Company of those bright Men that frequent Tom's[2] and the great Coffeehouses about Towne from whence alone one gathers Variety of News

You are not to expect much from me expecially haveing been & being to stay soe little a tyme in Towne however as a Man (tho never so obscure) can't be in this Place without hearing something more than you doe in the Country I must acquaint you that the Tragedy of Cato[3] is published, continues still to be acted, and is universally admired, and recommended by all the Prints from the most Ingenious Guardian to the most Ignominious Postboy & Flying Post[4] Each Party as you thereby see espousing the Play & I fear by the Examiner[4]of yesterday will goe so farre as ₐto apply the Characters to men of the Present Age how unjustly soever which may possibly be a Prejudice to the Author and prevent his Prosecuting the Good design he seems to have in his head of reforming the Stage & makeing

> Such plays alone to please a Brittish Ear
> As Cato's self had not disdained to hear[5]

There being nothing in this Play which can possibly cause a Vitious thought save only the 2 vile Characters which in their end don't faile to meet with their deserved Punishment. The word Liberty which must of necessity be frequently used never failes of a Whigg Clap but more especially in one Place where Cato laments the Loss of Rome & Liberty more than that of his son who lyes dead before him. But what part of the Play gives occasion for a Tory clap I have not yet heard however it is plain they[6] are much pleased with it or else the Ministry would not have honoured with with their Presence as they all did this day sevenight except the Treasurer and After the Play the Lord Bolingbrooke gave

Mr Booth (who acted the Part of Cato) 50 Gwynneas which he had collected & told him It was given∧him for acting soe well the part of that great Man who chose rather to dye than see his Country enslaved by a Perpetuall Dictator. The Duke of Ormond likewise 10 Gwynneas – I am told at the Dutchess[7] Mr Gay's every day at the Playhouse morning & afternoone seeing his Play rehearsed. they don't seem displeased at it but kindly concerned for the Succes of it. he is well & presents his Service to you. Now I am writeing of Plays I cannot help sending the meloncholly news of Poor Ashtons untimely end who after he left Huntington went to Ely & passing from thence to Lynn was together with his wife & child drowned: Judge Powell[8] is extreamly ill of the Gout & tis thought cant live long but if he recovers will have his Quietas granted him & a Pension of £2000 a year allowd & will be succeeded by Hooper or Cheshyre. You will this Post receive News of the Ratifications of the Peace[9] being exchanged by the Queen & her adherents Portugall & Savoy with France & Spain The Duke of Montague has leave from the Queen to travaile & Is going to Germany to Visitt his Grace of Marlbrou. The Commons have voted a Suspension of the tax of 325 a Tunn on French wines for 3 Months. And have ordered that Dr Sacheverell[10] be desired to preach before them on the 29th of this Month. Which I suppose he wont refuse to graitfye them (and himself) in.

Pray make my Duty love & Service acceptable to all my Friends but in particular your wife Sister Jenny & the 3 little ones[11] especially Jenny & beleive me to be what I really am

2 May 1713   Yr sincere freind   J Johnson

	I desire you will returne the money I am to pay for you & let me know what I can do more for you by the
Huntington Coach	next Post for I have [taken a p][12]lace in the Coach for Wednesday the 13 if not for [Th]ursday the 14 of this Month I have sent the Childs Blankett & with some things for my Ant Ambler & Coz Tyrrell in a Box directed to my Father to the Carryers to night

To Maurice Johnson junr Esq
Att Spalding
in Lincolnshire   These

Annotated by Maurice Johnson: My Brother May 2d 1713
                                   Cato, the Success of that Tragedy &c.

[1]   Maurice Johnson's younger brother. See his entry in Appendix 2 and also the genealogy of the Johnsons of Spalding in Appendix 5.
[2]   Tom's Coffee House, run by Thomas Twining the tea-merchant in Devereux Court, close to the Inner Temple. It was a meeting-place for an informal club of London wits.
[3]   The tragedy *Cato*, set in ancient Rome but seen as reflecting on the political situation at the beginning of the eighteenth century, was written by Addison in 1713 and proved a great success. As suggested in this letter by John Johnson, both the leading political parties of the day, Whigs and Tories, saw the play as supporting their own views. Maurice Johnson would be interested in Addison's success, since he had met him at the club in Button's coffee house in London; it was there that Steele, Addison's fellow-essayist, had suggested to Johnson that he should form a society at Spalding. John Gay the poet, another member of the Button's group, who is referred to later in John Johnson's letter and who became a member of the SGS, praised the success of *Cato* in a letter to Maurice Johnson on 23 April 1713, published in C. F. Burgess (ed.), *The Letters of John Gay* (Oxford, 1966), 2.
[4]   London newspapers of the period.

[5] This is a quotation of the closing lines of Pope's prefatory speech to Addison's tragedy *Cato*. Pope was a member of the literary club to which Maurice Johnson was attached in London; he became a member of the SGS in 1728.

[6] This gives an indication of the Johnson's family's political viewpoint; they were Whigs, although Maurice Johnson insisted that political discussion was forbidden at the SGS, along with arguments about religion, to avoid quarrels and divisions among members. The 'Ministry', the government of the time, was Tory. The Lord Treasurer was Robert Harley, first Earl of Oxford; Lord Bolingbroke was Secretary of State and Lord Ormond was Lord Lieutenant of Ireland and Commander in Chief of the army.

[7] The Duchess of Buccleuch; Maurice Johnson's father was the steward of her lands in Spalding. At the time, John Gay the dramatist and poet was her secretary, and also a friend of Maurice Johnson's through membership of Addison's coffee-house club. The play written by Gay which was currently in rehearsal was *The Wife of Bath*; it followed *Cato* at Drury Lane, but was unsuccessful.

[8] Lord Chief Justice Sir John Powell (1645–1713) died in June 1713. He was known for his judgement in the case of Jane Wenham in 1712 which ended trials for witchcraft in England.

[9] The Treaty of Utrecht, negotiated by Bolingbroke, which ended the War of the Spanish Succession.

[10] A very High Church clergyman (1674–1724), suspected of Jacobite tendencies; in 1710 he was tried for publishing a sermon against the Whig government, but as a result of the associated riots the government fell and he was given only a nominal fine.

[11] MS 'little one'.

[12] There is a gap in the text here, caused by the removal of a seal.

9. From Revd Francis Curtis to Maurice Johnson.
[Moulton] Undated. [1713?]
Expresses concern that Johnson has been ill; recommends 'Dr Diet, Dr Quiet & Dr Merryman' despite Sir Thomas Browne's distrust of proverbial advice; comments on a strong wind which has blown down trees and thatch at Curtis's house in Moulton.

1714

10. Draft of letter[1] from Maurice Johnson to William Stukeley.
[Spalding], 6 April 1714.
Gives news of the birth of Johnson's son;[2] offers advice on Stukeley's plans for historical study, providing a reading list and sending a poem written by himself about Stukeley's studies and the course of English history from the pre-Roman Britons to Edward VI.

[1] The letter as sent is in Stukeley's letter-book, Bodl., MS Eng. Misc. c.113, fol.296. Letters from Stukeley to Johnson or from Johnson to Stukeley are not among those selected for transcription in this volume, since a further volume in the LRS series, containing the full text of the correspondence between William Stukeley and Maurice Johnson, is in preparation.

[2] Johnson's eldest son Maurice was born on 14 March 1714 and baptised on 5 April 1714. His letters are calendared below; see his entry in Appendix 2 and the genealogy of the Johnsons of Spalding in Appendix 5.

11. SGS No 2: From William Stukeley[1] to Maurice Johnson.
Boston, 19 May 1714.
Comments on his increasing practice as a doctor in Boston; explains in detail his plans to put together his genealogical tables of British princes and rulers, commenting on Brutus or Brito and discussing whether he was of Trojan descent; discusses his aims and methods in studying history and his great love of antiquity; comments on some British antiquities found near Lincoln.

¹   The well-known antiquarian and writer, born at Holbeach. See Stukeley's entry in Appendix 2 and note 1 to No 10 above.

12. SGS No 73: Draft of letter¹ from Maurice Johnson to William Stukeley. [Spalding], 7 November 1714.
Discusses a golden Roman-British ring and offers references to Classical authors about the wearing of gold rings in ancient Greek and Roman periods; expresses pleasure at the SGS's prosperity.

¹   The letter as sent is in Stukeley's letter-book, MS Eng.Misc. c.113 fols 297A and B. It offers useful evidence of the early activities of the SGS since it is dated at a period when weekly minutes were not kept or have not survived. The original minutes were kept in loose-leaf form by Johnson and when several years' minutes had been completed they were then bound into folio volumes by Johnson's bookbinder in London.

1715

13. From Charles Green¹ to Maurice Johnson.
London, 4 January 1715 [perhaps 1716].²
Passes on the latest gossip about London society and current political arguments about the country's prosperity; gives information about the Prince and Princess of Wales and the present Parliament.

¹   Johnson notes in his list of donors of books to the SGS library: 'Carolus Green in Offic. Magno Cancellar. Scribarum unus 1717' i.e. a legal clerk to the Chancery office. It is possible that he was a friend of Maurice Johnson's from his London legal studies.
²   As this letter is not recorded in the SGS minutes, its year cannot be precisely determined; see the Introduction for discussion of dating methods used by Johnson's correspondents.

14. SGS No 56: From William Stukeley to Maurice Johnson.
[Boston], 23 July 1715.
MB1 fol.99A, 28 July 1726.
Discusses the value of the study of antiquities; expresses his conviction of the superiority of the Ancients over the Moderns and his conviction that modern men are inferior to their Classical counterparts, especially in their writings; discusses the evidence that their works provide of the immortality of the soul; refers to doubts about the antiquity of Dr Woodward's shield,¹ relating it to the practical joke played by Dr Bobart, Keeper of the Oxford Physic Garden,² who claimed that a stuffed rat was a flying dragon caught in the garden.

¹   Dr John Woodward the antiquarian (1665/68–1728; see his entry in *ODNB*) possessed a metal circle, embossed with Classical figures, which he claimed was a Roman shield; other authorities challenged this, stating that it was of much more recent date and was perhaps not even a shield. A more detailed discussion of this is in Joseph M. Levine, *Dr Woodward's Shield: History, Science and Satire in Augustan England* (Cornell, 1991).
²   Jacob Bobart (1641–1719); see his entry in *ODNB*.

15. SGS No 16: Draft of letter from Maurice Johnson to Richard Middleton Massey.¹ [Spalding], August 1715 (day not specified).
Discusses a pamphlet about the Cheshire Prophecy² and quotes Horace to disprove its validity; discusses the latest books, particularly Pope's translation of Homer which he says is better than 'our finicall Frenchified versions'; expresses concern over the Harleian Library and its possible dispersal; provides drawing of

a Roman helmet,[3] speculating that it may be connected with Carausius; asks for details about the Hereford College of Canons, asking if there is a relevant book in Wisbech library, which Middleton Massey had catalogued.

The letter is annotated by Johnson: To Dr Richard Middleton Massey at his house in Wisbech

These Augst 1715.

[1]   See his entry in Appendix 2.

[2]   This was a popular set of rhyming prophecies, reprinted in 1714 and 1715. They were attributed to Robert Nixon who was claimed to have lived in Cheshire either in the late fifteenth century or in the reign of James I. The prophecies relate in particular to Vale Royal Abbey in Cheshire and the family who lived there after the Dissolution of the Monasteries, but like those of Nostradamus, they were extended and interpreted to suit later political circumstances, in particular the Jacobite rebellions of the eighteenth century.

[3]   Johnson's sketch is very similar to John Kemp's iron helmet, claimed as Roman, now in the British Museum, and may be a drawing of it. Kemp's helmet is illustrated in Levine, *Dr Woodward's Shield*, 180–181, 214 (see No 14 n.1 above). The note which accompanies the sketch of the helmet states that Johnson had seen it 'in Museo Kempeano', the museum or collection of John Kemp (1665–1717) the antiquary and collector; see his entry in *ODNB*.

16. As above, with annotations in another hand (Massey's?); perhaps the letter as sent, later returned to Maurice Johnson?

1716

17. SGS No 68: From Revd Samuel Addenbrooke to Maurice Johnson senior.[1]
Chesterton, 9 February 1715 [actually 1716; see next letter by Maurice Johnson, No 18 below].

Addenbrooke has been ill but has not forgotten his promise to send Roman coins for 'Mr Johnson your son' and has promise of two 'Saxon pieces'; asks for attention to the enclosed document [not present – a legal document].

The letter is annotated by Maurice Johnson: 'Letter from and to the Revd. Mr Samuel Addenbrooke of Chesterton concerning Roman Coins many found there.'

[1]   Samuel Addenbrooke was the incumbent of Haddon near Peterborough (LAO, SPE 1, p.280), but he resided with his father at neighbouring Chesterton where Roman remains, including coins,were being found at this period. He is writing to the father of Maurice Johnson, a lawyer and land steward of the same name practising in the Spalding area; see the Johnson family tree in Appendix 5.

18. Draft reply by Maurice Johnson to Revd Mr Samuel Addenbrooke.
Spalding, 18 February 1715/6.

Addenbrooke's letter about his legal business has been forwarded to Johnson's father in London; Johnson reminds Addenbrooke that he had met him at Holbeach; he explains in detail the three sizes of Roman coins as designated by coin collectors; discusses their current value depending on their scarcity and metal, and explains that those of earlier emperors are more valuable than those of the later ones; also discusses Saxon and Norman coins and English and Scottish coins from the Conquest to Queen Elizabeth and James VI.[1]

[1]   This reply to the preceding letter is a valuable letter for understanding Maurice Johnson's methods as a coin collector.

19. Draft of letter from Maurice Johnson to Mr W. Jarvis.
[Spalding], 3 May 1716.
Discusses an engraving by Vertue[1] from an original picture of Ben Jonson[2] by Honthorst, which he has heard was in the late Lord Sommers' collection; if it is for sale, and worth the price, he requests Jarvis to obtain it for him.

[1]   George Vertue (1684–1756) became a member of the SGS and was one of their official artists and engravers. In 1731 he painted a miniature of Maurice Johnson, now in the National Portrait Gallery. See his entry in *ODNB*.
[2]   The Johnson family to which Maurice Johnson belonged claimed that the Jacobean poet and dramatist Ben Jonson was an ancestor, though this has not been proved.

20. SGS No 17: From William Stukeley to Maurice Johnson.
[Boston], 6 June 1716.
MB2 fol.82A, 8 February 1733, where it is misdated by Maurice Johnson to 1715.
Discusses an improved telescope owned by his relative Mr Hill and his own astronomical observations made at King's Lynn, including the ring of Saturn, which he sketches in the margin; refers to a lunar model made by Sir Christopher Wren; explains about a model of Stonehenge which he has just made; comments on Roman pottery found at Boston by Mr Falkner's workmen.[1]

[1]   Mr Falkner's widow Ann later married Maurice Johnson senior (Maurice Johnson's father) in 1726 as his third wife and moved to Ayscoughfee Hall, Spalding, with her son Richard Falkner. Richard became a member of the SGS and his letters to the Society from Oxford and Boston, from 1733 to 1736, are calendared below.

21. SGS No 84: From Revd John Taylor[1] to Revd John Hardy.
Kirkstead, Lincolnshire, 13 July 1716.

Christead [Kirkstead] Abbey, 13 July 1716
Mr Hardy   SGS No 84
You were pleased to order me to give you an Account of the meteor which made it's dreadful appearance in these parts. I wish the Country had at the Time been bless'd with a more accurate Observer. However having compared notes with several Honest Country People, who were, with many Hundreds besides, Eye witnesses of what they relate, I'll venture to join the little which I saw to their Reports, & try whether or no I can advance any Thing that shall be satisfactory. On Monday June the 20th 1715, about 2 or 3 in the afternoon, I took a walk into the Fields; but had ∧not been there long before I perceiv'd an alteration in the Air, which before was very ˣ hot & sultry.
The skie began to lower, & threaten Rain. The wind began to stir, & blew still stronger & stronger. Being in Discourse with a Friend I was detain'd till I observ'd (near to the North West point) a notable cone jutting out of a Black Cloud with its vertex hanging perpendicular to the Earth. It was of the same Colour with the Cloud, thick at the Base & as yet but short. I took not much notice of it then,

[Written as marginal note:] ˣ very hot Gleams were frequent, in so much that they grew almost intolerable to the Labourers who were in the Fields. An honest Goodwife of my parish tells me that the Monday was her washing Day; & that at the time she was not very well provided of Fewel to boil her water with: but coming to the pit, she to her great satisfaction found the water so warm that she ventures for once to break an old rule & wash with it just as it came from the pit.

imagining that the wind had only accidentally thrown it into that Figure. But observing that it still dropt down nearer to the Earth, & so came nearer to an infinite Cone; I cou'd not but be surprised at it. Now it begins to be very stormy; the Wind is very high, the Thunder very Loud; the Day very black, & the Lightning (to me) very terrible, & the air very cold. Insomuch that how strong soever my Curiosity was, yet (being then sorely greiv'd with a lingring Hectick Fever for fear of the Lightning, & of catching Cold), I cou'd not prevail with my self to stay any longer out of Doors. I therefore made to a House with all speed. Before I cou'd get into a House it's lower end was fallen below our Horizon, & to the best of my Judgement the Whole of it much resembled the Figure A in the inclosed paper.[2] I observ'd the Storm grew greater as the Meteor[3] improv'd it self: and indeed very terrible it was when I was in the House. I stept out once I think to see it, but it was soon after I got in; there ^I ₌found it almost in the same posture that I left it, only I observed that it grew still smaller ^{at}₌^{the lower} end & bended more: & seemed to be something white towards the Top about the places CCC.[4] All that quarter of the Skie was horribly black, & dismal and seemed to be all one Continued Cloud. I tarry'd I believe 3 Hours or more at the House before I cou'd think it safe venturing Home: and then I found the Air pretty well settled, & all Things almost at Ease. Within a Day or two after the Meteor was become the Countrie's Talk, & many Things which I thought very Extraordinary were reported of it. Being therefore willing to know the certainty, I purpos'd to go in quest of some better Information: which Purpose I cou'd not well accomplish, till [erasure] Monday July the 11th. Then did I set forth towards Southray, a Village about 4 Miles distant from Christead; bearing N.W. & N. I suppose. When I came there, I found that it had fixed a Seriousness in the Looks of every one that I spake with; & I spake with a many before I cou'd meet with one that cou'd give me a satisfactory particular account. At last I met with one Mr Fox, an honest Gentleman I really beleive. He first told me the common story, that it was the most dreadful Thing that ever he saw in all his Life, & did not think he shou'd ever see the Like in this world: & that in the apprehensions of the Generality, it was a Prelude to the great Day, the Day of Judgement. Then he proceeded to Particulars, as follows. Upon the Day & about the time above mention'd his Family being most of them within Doors, his Son alarmed them with a Discovery of a very strange Thing in the air hanging over the Cliff, towards Nocton; Mr Fox did not take any Notice of what he said, till they brought him word that it grew smaller & smaller, & approach'd nearer to the Ground; & made as if it wou'd advance to Southray: That the small End was thrown into several postures (one of which may be seen in the enclosed paper Fig.b.) That abundance of smoke issu'd out of the small End, which almost obscur'd the whole Body of it. These Reports prevail'd with Mr Fox to take a view of it: but was almost hindered by the smoke which proceeded from it. It continu'd to smoke for some considerable Time & then they cou'd see it stretch directly towards the Ground, & discharge (as all the Spectators apprehended) a vast quantity of Fire. The Fire seemed to him & all with him to stream down violently from the Skie to the Ground as if it had run thro'some very large straight Tube. The smoke increased with the Fire; but did ₌^{not} totally obscure it at that Distance. It burst in Sir William Ellis's Fen, about a mile from Southray. And now it proceeded more slowly than before, making a great Roar, as it went along. (N.B. The Fen was then very deep in water.) But when it came to the River, which lay about ½ a mile from the spectators, it then multiply'd it's Roar to the great Terror of those who saw & heard it. Mr Fox cou'd compare the Noise to nothing more aptly than that which he imagin'd a vast mass of red hot Iron wou'd make, were it thrown into the River. It staid about a quarter of an Hour upon the River (tho' it is but about 30 yards broad) & the Spectators apprehended [page 2] It cry'd quits with the River, which prehended that it would ha' spent it self there. But they found themselves mistaken I am informed by another Hand [erasure] was found afterward to be very muddy. And now it advances up the Common Field Directly towards Southray Town about as fast as a man [erasure] can walk. The first Thing the Gentleman took notice of, after it was past the River, was a Crow which flew about 10 yards[5] before it, in the middle, if we may say it flew, for it was rather driven or if it flew, it flew side-wayes, aiming, as we may guess, to leave it's troublesome Companion by slipping out at a side. But it was all in vain, for it was unaccountably lost & thrown about, & squeal'd prodigiously, as long as the Gentleman saw the meteor. All the Cattle that were grazing in the Field, run from it as if distracted. You know, Sir, it is a Rule with$_\wedge$out an Exception among sheep that if one do but venture in any perilous cases to take such a[6] Course, the whole Flock will follow, tho' through fire & water. So it happen'd in this case. The sheep made the best of their way as well as other their comrades. But they all took one way: So that 4 of them were taken tardy for their perversely adhering to old Customs. Two were catch'd about the middle of the meteor, & therefore one was found dead immediately after, & the other died within a quarter of an Hour. Both of them were prodigiously swollen. The other two were catch'd about the skirts of it, & therefore were [erasure] both alive, yea, when I [erasure] received this Account from Mr Fox, & he hopes they wou'd live, tho' all the Leather pilled of them. It came over some Lands where Mr Fox had laid some manure in little Heaps. The Manuer it swept away so clean that no man cou'd say there had ever any come upon the Ground, and Mr Fox declared that for a quarter of a mile of it's course he cou'd not see that any of it was scattered. Nor cou'd he hear of any man that cou'd tell him what was become of his manure. There was a Plough lying under a Bank two yards high. It whipt the plough up; but moving an unwieldy tool, the Head struck into the Top of the Bank, & so secured it self. It scorch'd the Leaves and the Trees that it touch'd: But only Laid the Grass & corn flatt upon the Ground; the Corn tho' in the Ears, came up again in a Day or two's time & the owner hoped he shou'd never have the worse crop for't. There happen'd to be a Staff-Hedge which lay parallel to it's Course; this it swept away every stick of't. As it past over any hedge it scorcht [erasure] those parts of them that were green. And took up the staff Hedging, & any Tree that was a little eminent in the Hedge, if it lay so as to fall into the middle of it. It broke some laly Trees (we call 'em) a little before it's entrance into a wood, & left them Hanging among Trees of the wood. As it enter'd the wood & came out of it, it broke some principle Boughs of Trees, but did no Manner of Harm that was observable as it went thro' the Body of the wood. It [erasure] broke two $_\wedge$oak trees (near to one another) at Tupham Hall, the Stump of one was torn up by the Roots. The Trees were as thick as an ordinary man, or thicker. At Bucknal, about two miles from Southray, a Tree that lay in it's Course was after found with the Head standing where the Root shou'd ha' been. This Mr Fox had from one that he thought he cou'd safely credit in other matters. As it drew nearer to the spectators it seem'd still more formidable & was so environ'd with smoke that they cou'd see nothing of the middle part: It

was of a considerable Bredth. Mr Fox told me that he measured two Trees opposite to each other, between which it[7] had passed, & both which he knew it had toucht, because he found the Trees ruffled, some little Boughs broke, & the Leaves a little scorch, & he found the Distance to be 240 yards. He was very peremptory & positive in deposing this. It made a most hideous Roar. Thunder Mr Fox said was nothing to it. It was rather a complication of our ordinary Thunder-Roars. It came directly upon the Town when it had left the River; but before it reach'd the Town providence so ordered it that the wind turn'd more westerly & so brought the meteor about by the end of the Town without touching any House: Tho' it came within twenty or 30 yards of the Relators' Houses. At Southray, a great shower follow'd it. At <u>Bardnay</u> about half a mile N.West from Southray it hail'd large Hail Stones, as it passed by Southray. There was one who told me he himself saw the Hailstones, & he observ'd one to be as broad & Thick as a half Crown piece, & I suppose they were all of the same Figure & perhaps not much short in Largeness I ask'd Mr Fox if he did not feel some unusual smell or other when he was so near it: He told me others apprehended a smell of Brimstone, but he for his part wou'd not say that he felt any such smell, Tho' if I be not mistaken for fault with his smelling, else I myself conceited it was but ordinary. Thus Sir, I have given you as large & true account of the Meteor as I can: Excuse the writing: I had purpos'd to have transcribed, but circumstances to far alter'd their expected posture that I am straightened for Time. I am
your Very humble Servant

John Taylor

Christead Abby July 13th 1716

My humble Service to Mr Thorsby. Mr Hardy, if you can in your Travels pick up any Book which you think will be [erasure] useful to me, I desire you to lay Hands on it, & I will stand to the charge. I do not desire you take up any Books of the Booksellers (except of a very little value) because I cannot be satisfy'd that you should lay down much money for me, & empty your own pocket. But I speak of Books which you perhaps may meet with amongst some of my rever'd learned Brethren, which are grown out of Date with them & which you can take upon Trust. I wou'd gladly finger <u>Burnet's Expos of 39 Artic</u>.[8]

1 See the biography of John Taylor in *ODNB*; he was not an SGS member. He was a Dissenting minister and teacher; his first appointment was as minister and schoolmaster to a congregation which met in the extra-parochial chapel at Kirkstead, in the Witham valley, the remaining building of the ruined Kirkstead Abbey, which Taylor refers to as 'Christead', presumably his name for it as more appropriate to his religious viewpoint. This letter is significant for its precise and detailed description of the meteorological phenomenon which appears to have been a tornado. The letter was sent to Revd John Hardy, who at the time was a fellow Dissenting minister, but moved to the Church of England and became vicar of Kinoulton (Notts), then of Melton Mowbray (Leics). He was a member of the SGS from 1724; he presumably passed on the letter to the SGS.

2 A diagram was presumably attached to the letter originally but it has not been preserved with the letter.

3 At this period 'meteor' was not confined to its modern meaning, but was used to describe any phenomenon occurring within the earth's atmosphere; this included unusual features of the weather, such as a tornado, hence the modern term 'meteorology'. This description, though more detailed, is similar to the 'Water-Spout, rais'd off the Land, in Deeping-Fen, Lincolnshire' reported by the Benjamin Ray to the SGS on 7 May 1752. Ray's account was later sent to the RS and was published in their *Philosophical Transactions* 47 (1751), 524–6.

4 This appears to be another reference to the missing diagram.

5 MS 'years'.

⁶ MS 'such a such a'.
⁷ MS 'hit'.
⁸ *An Exposition of the Thirty-Nine Articles of the Church of England*, published by Gilbert Burnet, Bishop of Salisbury, in 1699. Burnet's biography in *ODNB* states that Burnet saw the book as 'a proper addition to the History of the Reformation, to explain and prove the doctrine that was then established ... the avowed aim of the Exposition was to help heal the breaches, both within the Church of England, and between Anglicans and other protestants'. As a Dissenter, Taylor would be very interested in this possibility.

22. Early draft of a letter from Maurice Johnson to William Stukeley in Boston. [Spalding] Undated, dateable to 6 October 1716.¹
Describes a British coin of Boadicea; he will write more fully when he returns from the Midland Circuit.
Annotated by Johnson: 'Not sent but the enclosure was.'

¹ This letter can be dated from the following more complete draft, No 23.

23. SGS No 8: Later draft of letter¹ from Maurice Johnson to William Stukeley in Boston.
[Spalding], 6 October 1716.
Replies to Stukeley's letter; comments favourably on the arrival of Revd Timothy Neve in Spalding as schoolmaster; discusses a coin of Agrippa; gives a very full description of Thorpe Hall, near Peterborough, and its statues; describes Maurice Johnson's coin of Boadicea; passes on comments about Stonehenge which his stepmother² was told by her first husband.

¹ The completed letter, which was sent to Stukeley, is in Bodl. MS Eng. Misc. c.113, fol.296, misfiled as 6 October 1726; in 1726 Stukeley was no longer in Boston but had moved to Grantham.
² This refers to the second wife of Maurice Johnson senior. Maurice Johnson the Secretary of the SGS was the son of the first wife.

1717

24. SGS No 67: From Revd Joseph Sparke¹ to Maurice Johnson.
[Peterborough], 28 January 1716–17.
Offers to send [unspecified] books by Caius and Wood and Van Beughen's book on early printed books; discusses his methods in transcribing details from early printed books and the tedium of doing so; requests details of Spalding Church Library.

¹ See his entry in Appendix 2.

25. From Revd Timothy Neve¹ to Maurice Johnson in London.
Spalding, 11 February 1717.

Sʳ   Spalding, Feb: 11 1716/7
    I received your kind letter with the enclosed papers² which I suppose will be as welcome to the Gent. of the Society, as the particular direction of them, was extreamly obliging to me. I need not communicate my judgment of any of them to you; But however I must say that Mr Pope wou'd have more admirers, if he had more modesty, and I think he sinks even below his own natural deformity, by so often indulging one obscene thought and making his wit acceptable to none but bawds and Libertines. I wish he does not make a modest Heathen speak what I

dare say he was ashamed to think. The specimen which you've given us of the ability of the Censor[3] will, (I doubt not) make the continuance of them acceptable to the Society. Mr Præses and my Chum's[4] don't seem very fond of inviting Chaucer to revisit Spalding, and they think it somewhat Preposterous, to found modern politeness upon an antiquated Author, and except he comes dress'd in the modish language of this fantastic age, they're not for entertaining him in the native unintelligible simplicity of his own. But I'm more inclined to subscribe to such an Author, than to such judgments, which think Antiquity mysterious, because they'll not give themselves the trouble to understand it. The Memoirs of Literature are desir'd to be provided, and what other things you please to oblige and divert us with. Prior's Eccles.[5] I suppose will be subscrib'd for, as being more modern than Chaucer and perhaps for that reason, the three hours after Marriage[6] might go down here. We are all here in statu quo, as indolent in Politick as ever. I've not read the other Censor which you sent us, but design after five this afternoon to regale myself over a dish of Coffee in order to examine it with greater perspicacity. Be pleased S^r to excuse this hasty Epistle from
Sr Your most obedient & most humble Servant
My humble Service to Mr Johnson & your Bro. and Mr Lynn   Tim: Neve

To
Maurice Johnson Esq
at the Widdows Coffee
house in Devoreux Court[7]
near the Temple.   London.

[1]   Master of Spalding Grammar School. See his entry in Appendix 2.
[2]   These are no longer preserved with the letter; they were evidently items sent by Johnson as of interest for the SGS at its Thursday meeting. Several correspondents, including Neve, thank Johnson for his constant efforts in sending material for the Society's meetings when he is not able to be present. In this case, the 'papers' appear to be recent publications of poems, including one by Pope, or copies of them made by Johnson. The SGS was particularly interested in Pope as a London acquaintance of Johnson's; Pope became an honorary member of the SGS in 1728 but played little, if any part in the Society's activities. Neve's letter contains a useful account of a typical SGS meeting at a time from which no minutes survive; it also indicates what other items Johnson had sent for discussion at their meeting.
[3]   A journal published in London. Johnson has sent a specimen copy to see whether the SGS is interested in subscribing to it.
[4]   The SGS President, Revd Stephen Lyon, and the other members of the Society.
[5]   Matthew Prior's collected poems were published by subscription in 1717.
[6]   The satirical comedy written jointly by Arbuthnot, Gay and Pope, which was successfully staged for a week in January 1717.
[7]   Maurice Johnson spent the legal terms in London for many years, as explained in the Introduction. He followed the custom of visitors to London of using a coffee-house as a postal address; Devereux Court is close to the Inner Temple of which Johnson was a member.

26. SGS No 39: From William Stukeley to Maurice Johnson.
[Ormond Street, London], 13 June 1717.
Sets out the advantages of his move from Boston to London, explaining that he will still be able to see his Lincolnshire friends and that his medical practice will pay better; describes the pleasant situation of his lodgings in Ormond Street; gives account of his visit to French anatomical waxworks which show nerves and

arteries; gives news of family acquaintances and London gossip, including the impeachment of Robert Harley, first Earl of Oxford.

1718

27. From Revd Timothy Neve to Maurice Johnson in London.
Spalding, 15 February 1718.

S^r   SGS No 64
    In compliance with yours and the order of the rest of the Gent. here, I am to acquaint you of the state of our affairs at Spalding, which are just the same as when you left us. Our Society does still subsist as well as can be expected in the absence of one who is the Life & Cement of it; we meet, we drink, we smoak, & except you send us a little quickening, ₍very speedily₎ I'm afraid the next time we meet we must have a greater quantity of Coffee than usual to prevent the closing of our Eyes too soon.[1] There's one frequent Transgressor of Rule & Order,[2] who takes advantage of your absence to excuse his own, & unless there be some proper expedient found out, or some wholsom severity inflicted upon such   to prevent such abuses for the future offenders the authority of our Establishment may by degrees grow into contempt. I've been viewing the room at Mr Lyons[3] old house, which with no great expence may be fitted up handsomly to receive us, Mr Lyon is not willing to be at the expence of it him self, I will alwaies pay the rent of it, if he or the rest of the Gent. wou'd contribute to put it in Tenentable repair.

The remainder of the letter sends complex information about some Spalding tenants and social life in Spalding.
Annotated by Maurice Johnson: 'Rev^d Mr Neve ab^t fitting up the Vicarage Outhouse for SGS over which he has a Chamber which was afterwards done & they met there'.[4]

1   This emphasises Maurice Johnson's concern to have an active society, involved in scholarship and research; he and some of his colleagues such as Neve, were aware that such societies could easily degenerate into purely social meetings or drinking clubs. Several later letters, including some from Neve about his own Peterborough society, refer to this problem.
2   It has not proved possible to identify this member.
3   Revd Stephen Lyon, incumbent of Spalding and President of the SGS.
4   Maurice Johnson frequently added annotations to letters on re-reading them some years after they had been received; sometimes this was in connection with his summaries of the history of the SGS, which he entered in the Minute Books. The first part of this annotation was probably written soon after the letter was received, and the second part, from 'which was afterwards …' was added at a later date.

28. From Revd Timothy Neve to Maurice Johnson in London.
[Spalding], 1 March 1717/8.
Comments more fully on fitting up the Vicarage outhouse for the SGS and on the improvement in recent meetings; discusses the Bangorian controversy.[1]

1   A theological controversy within the Church of England between the Tory non-jurors who had refused to take the oath of allegiance to William III and their Whig opponents. The Bishop of Bangor, the Latitudinarian Benjamin Hoadly, reignited it by preaching a sermon before George I on 31 March 1717, claiming that the Church should not interfere in matters of political government; this was

attacked in publications by William Law and Thomas Sherlock, Dean of Chichester. The point at issue was whether the King ruled by Divine right or by the people's assent, with Parliament retaining overall mastery.

29. From Maurice Johnson to William Stukeley.
Woburn, Monday 10 March 1717/8.
Regrets he missed seeing Stukeley in London; gives an account of the SA's activities at their meetings and of his travels, explaining the need for a young barrister to become known on the legal Circuit; discusses antiquities seen in Dunstable, particularly the church and its contents.

30. SGS No 54: From William Stukeley to Maurice Johnson.
[London], 10 April 1718.
Discusses the progress of the recently re-founded SA and its new members; explains that the SA want him to publish his map of Holland, Lincolnshire and asks for Johnson's help in preparing it; comments on a Saxon inscription on a key, discussed at the SA meeting, and offers a proposed translation of it.
Attached; drawing of the key, copy of the inscription, sketch of a seal-ring.

31. SGS No 62: From William Stukeley to Maurice Johnson.
Ormond Street, London, 19 June 1718.
Sends thanks from the SA to Johnson for information about Ely; gives an account of SA activities and discoveries; explains their plans to take a room in the Temple for meetings; comments on European political affairs, especially in Italy and Hungary, and on the election of a Chamberlain for the City of London.

32. From Dr Edward Green to Mrs Johnson.[1]
London, 10 July 1718.
He is sorry to hear she is ill; he plans to get one of 'poor Widdow Wareing's'[2] children into Christ's Hospital on a scholarship related to Spalding, though there are currently disputes among those who have the rights of presentation to these.

[1]   He addresses her as 'Dear Sister'; presumably she is Maurice Johnson senior's second wife, and 'Sister' is a courtesy title since she would be of an appropriate age-group, rather than the young wife of Maurice Johnson the Secretary. This letter would have been of interest to Maurice Johnson as offering possibilities for the education of his own sons; among Johnson's papers at the SGS is a note by Johnson listing his sons, their ages and possible schools at which they might gain closed scholarships of this kind.
[2]   Revd John Waring, an early member of the SGS and Master of Spalding Grammar School, died in 1714. Maurice Johnson dedicated his Latin account of a visit to Bath in 1710, *Iter Bathonense*, to Waring who had taught him at Spalding. After his death, the SGS bought his books from his widow and incorporated them in their own library.

33. From Revd Timothy Neve to Maurice Johnson in London.
[Spalding], 3 December 1718.
Discusses SGS matters; gives an account of Neve's pupils' dramatic activities at the Grammar School; comments on Dr Wotton, 'Defender of the Modern'[1] and his work on an edition of the 'Laws of Hywel Dda'; discusses recent publications including Dr Woodward's latest book.[2]

[1]   He describes Dr Wotton or Wootton (1666–1727; see his entry in *ODNB*) in this way because of his contribution, *Reflections upon Ancient and Modern Learning* (1694), to the debate then current

over which was superior, study derived from the Classical Greek and Roman writers or study based on modern sources. See Nos 65 and 75 below for his work on Welsh law.

2   Probably *The State of Physick* (1718).

1719

34. SGS No 61: From Revd Joseph Sparke to Maurice Johnson.
Peterborough, 7 September 1719.
Apologises that he does not have a copy of Ordericus Vitalis;[1] thanks Johnson for books [unspecified]; requests the return of Tanner's *Notitia Monastica* and asks Johnson to send a transcription of a fine, or land agreement, between the abbots of Croyland and Peterborough in 1216, which Johnson has; also asks to borrow André du Chesne's *Collection of Norman Histories*.

1   Ordericus Vitalis (1075–c.1143), son of an English mother and Norman father, became a monk at St Evroul in Normandy but visited England, staying for a time at Croyland Abbey. His history of the Church, *Historia Ecclesiastica*, refers to the abbey.

35. SGS No 27: From William Stukeley to Maurice Johnson.
Ormond Street, London, 29 November 1719.
He has passed on Johnson's queries about genealogy to the SA; gives news of SA activities; comments on his correspondence with Lord Pembroke about Stonehenge; discusses social activities in London; provides news about their London acquaintances and his dinner with Sir Isaac Newton; discusses Kneller's painting techniques.
On outside: sketches of designs for theatrical motifs, perhaps by Maurice Johnson.

1720

36. SGS No 12: From Revd Francis Peck[1] to Maurice Johnson.
[King's Cliffe], 29 March 1720.
Apologises for writing as he has not yet met Johnson; asks for any information Johnson has on Stamford, in return for information on Spalding which Peck can send; explains that 'I shall publish the first of 5 small volumes I intend in 3 months' time'.

1   Revd Francis Peck (1692–1743): Curate of King's Cliffe (Northants), and from 1723 Rector of Goadby Marwood (Leics). Though a keen antiquarian and member of the SA, who corresponded with Johnson and was a friend of Stukeley's, Peck did not become a member of the SGS. In 1721 he published proposals for printing his history of Stamford, which appeared in 1727 as *Academia tertia Anglicana, or The Antiquarian Annals of Stanford*. In 1732–5 he published *Desiderata Curiosa*, a collection of documents and commentaries relating to the sixteenth and seventeenth centuries. See his entry in *ODNB*.

37. SGS No 13: From William Stukeley to Maurice Johnson.
Ormond Street, London, 7 October 1720.
Comments on the depressing effects of the South Sea Bubble losses; gives news of the death of Gale's wife and of the publication of Bentley's New Testament; discusses the dissection of an elephant at Sir Hans Sloane's house.

1721

38. From Thomas Gerard[1] to Maurice Johnson.
3 September 1721.
Gives an account of the case of Peploe v. the Bishop of Chester over Peploe's right to the Wardenship of Manchester.
[1]   It has not been possible to identify him.

39. From Dr Walter Lynn to Maurice Johnson.
London, 30 September 1721.
Begins with a detailed account of the discovery by the Czar's surveyors of a ruined building near the Caspian Sea, containing nearly 3,000 volumes written in an unknown language, of which they were only able to remove three and explains the Czar's intention to have them deciphered.
He then describes the new working methods in coalmines in the North which he had been discussing, with particular reference to a steam-driven pumping engine for which he had made improvements:
… my head is so very dark with being in a Coalpitt, for nearly a whole week that I am blind as a mole to every thing above ground but grown sharper sighte to any thing below. Not to amuse you, I have just now parted with one Squire Leger who has a Colemine of his own at New Castle; we have had divers conferences together within these few days, two at Colonel Blaxton's, where he lodges, and one at a Tavern near Billingsgate this day: he has not only let me into the Natural History, together with the course of the rivers, temperature of the air, buildings &c of those Climes, but into the manners of the inhabitants, their employments, laws, Politicks and intregues and what different views those may have who never see the Sun from those who but sometimes do. in short he has been extremely obligeing and communicative of what ever I desir'd to know of him. he is as great a Mechanick almost as myself and has a brother that is more so, they two together set up one of the fire engins[1] they had purchasd without the assistance of the Patentie's workmen and have been improveing it some years so that 'tis now esteemed much the best engin in the North and has thoroughly convincd me of the equal falsity of those persons judgments who gave out that this engin was perfect and had no defect, and of those who say it is so imperfect that it never can be made good and servisable. he allows with me that not only the Mathematicks or the understanding of Numbers but a general knowledge of all sorts of Mechanicks and of Natural Phylosophy is necessary to bring this Engin to perfection: in the first of these I shall readily own his brother my superior but shall contest the two last, and as I have the good fortune to hit upon the true and genuine meaning of many parts of my Author unknown [p.3] to him and others, I shall mentain still and prove my own improvements, most essential, and valuable for their use. You see what I am full of. But pray give my hearty thanks to all concernd in the two letters yours and the Captains.[2] Pray excuse my not writeing to him in the best manner you can and tell him that that [sic] 'tis not my custome to write two letters by one post; besides he desires to know how I go on with Dr Tayler &c. and he is not yet come to Town for I enquir'd but last night. Mr Wren[3] arriv'd on Wednesday stay'd but a night and went forward for Hampton Court I discoursd with him but a few minutes, he told me he shou'd return hither with

his father in some days for the Winter. Your lodgings are secur'd and the Captains request perform'd by

> both your
> Oblig'd
> Humble Servant
> W L

[1]   A pamphlet in the SGS Library, Pamphlets L627.1 1726, *The Case of Walter Lynn*, discusses Lynn's attempts to patent his improvements to a pumping engine, although it contains no technical details of the machine. It was a steam-powered engine designed to pump water from mines, not a machine for extinguishing fires, as its name would suggest. See Walter Lynn's entry in Appendix 2

[2]   Captain Francis Pilliod, a Swiss-born army officer, now living in Spalding and married, as second husband, to John Green's mother. He was an early member of the SGS.

[3]   This is probably Christopher Wren, son of Sir Christopher; his father was living at Hampton Court at this time.

40. SGS No 91: From J. Richards to Maurice Johnson.
9 October 1721.
Provides a transcription of prescription for cure for piles (in French) from M. Chirac, later royal physicial to Louis XV, received from him at Montpellier in 1700, for Johnson's 'very troublesome distemper'; attached: note by Johnson on Green's (Dr Edward Green's) methods of curing piles.

1722

41. From Thomas Howgrave[1] to 'the Revd Mr Sharp Schoolmaster at Horncastle'.[2]
8 March 1722 [or 1723?].
Asks for the scholars to have the rest of the day as 'holyday als playday' as it was a Church holiday in 'Queen Ann's time'[3] and it is also his birthday.

[1]   Perhaps to be identified with Thomas Howgrave of Horncastle, a successful merchant whose land purchases entitled him to the rank of 'esquire'. He was baptized at Horncastle on 8 March 1659 (see J. Clare Hudson (ed.), *The Second Register Book of the Parish Church of St Mary, Horncastle [1640–1683]* (Horncastle, 1896), 41; B. A. Holderness, 'The English land market in the eighteenth century: the case of Lincolnshire', *Econ.H.R.* second series 27 (1974), 565–6). He was not a member of the SGS.

[2]   Perhaps William Sharpe, licensed as a schoolmaster at Horncastle on 15 July 1715 (LAO, Sub V/6).

[3]   8 March was the anniversary of Queen Anne's accession to the throne.

42. From Browne Willis[1] to Maurice Johnson.
Whaddon Hall near Fenny Stratford, Bucks, 18 June 1722.
Sends a list of MPs for Lincoln and Stamford; offers to send a list of Lincolnshire MPs.

[1]   See his entry in Appendix 2.

43. SGS No 59: From Roger Gale[1] to Maurice Johnson.
London, 19 July 1722.
Enquires about the Domesday Book entry for 'Drayton in Marisco de Holand'[2] which was important in 1066 as head of a large soke but apparently no longer exists; explains that the enquiry relates to Gale's *Registrum Honoris de Richmond*,

then in the press, as it was land belonging to Count Alan and part of the Honour of Richmond.

1   See his entry in Appendix 2.
2   Johnson annotates its location as Drayton in Swineshead near Boston, having been informed by Thomas Sooley of Kirton.

44. SGS No 60: From Revd Francis Peck to Maurice Johnson.
King's Cliffe, 20 October 1722.

Sr   No 60   Kings-Cliffe, Oct. 20 1722
   I ought long ago to have thanked You for the Book & Papers you was pleased to oblige me with, & which I here return, attended with the kindest Acknowledgments of Your Favour & Their Usefulness. Some Things there are in them indeed which I do not yet rightly understand: – haply thro' the Transcribers Abbreviations, & my Want of being used to them. Those I have noted, & wrote over against them the Particulars, wherein, if it be not too much Trouble, You will add to your first Obligation to give me a little farther Information: But This I leave as much to your Leisure as good-nature.
   Since I had the Happiness of seeing You, I have been turning over my Collections, & find my Self already possessed of so many Particulars (& those, if I judge right, something curious) relating to divers Parts of the County of Lincoln, that I have been transcribing them, & intend to publish them next Spring, in a Separate Vol of the same Paper & Letter with my Antiquities of Stamford. Should You have any Thing more to spare relating to that County (without substracting from any better Design of your own, for which I would be no means rob you of any Materials) you would highly please & serve me to communicate them. I call mine, [p.2] some Antiquities, Ecclesiastical & Civil, relating to the Church & County of Lincoln, ranged alphabetically under the Names of the respective Places whereunto they relate, & gathered from Divers MSS. & other Evidences upon the Spot, none of them ever before published.
   You have certainly more Books, & better Means of Information from your Acquaintance, Fortune, Learning, & other Circumstances than I can pretend to, so that if You delight as much in these Enquiries as I presume You do, You may bring almost any Thing You undertake of this Nature to a good Degree of Perfection. However if I knew what You designed, I would try hard to find some good old Paper or other worthy of your Acceptance. For I wish heartily to preserve Your Favour & express My Gratitude, being ever
                              Sr
                              Your obliged &
                              most obedient
                              humble Servant
                                   Fr. Peck

1723

45. From Richard Middleton Massey[1] to Maurice Johnson.
[Wisbech], 13 January 1723.
Thanks him for election to SGS membership; promises to send a root of mint

when the weather permits; explains that his messenger is bringing bottles of oil and water; regrets that he does not know where 'Dr Tanners piece' is but Dr Tanner would like to know about account books of religious houses.

Annotated by Johnson: a Lr from Richard Middleton Massey of Oxford MD from Wisbeach upon his and Richard Lake of the Castle Esquire being admitted Members.

¹ See his entry in Appendix 2.

46. From Revd John Britain¹ to Maurice Johnson.
Holbeach, 30 January 1723.
He is revising and correcting Stukeley's plate of the drainage of South Lincolnshire,² particularly in relation to the former Bicker Haven and the distances between towns.

¹ See his entry in Appendix 2.
² This was subscribed to by the SGS who received a copy in 1724. MB1 fol.22A for October 1723 refers to seeing 'the proof plates of Dr Stewkly a Member of the Soc's Mapp of Holland & Adjacent Counties'.

47. SGS No 58: From Revd Francis Peck to Maurice Johnson.
[King's] Cliffe, 26 April 1723.
Discusses some [unspecified] papers which Johnson has sent to Peck but which Peck now cannot find: 'my collections are at present in so much disorder' as he is about to be translated to a new living;¹ responds to Johnson's invitation to 'bring a Cargo of my Collections' to Spalding; discusses an entry in Domesday Book relating to 'Portland', attributing it to Stamford not to Northampton.

¹ Goadby Marwood in north-east Leicestershire.

48. From Revd Timothy Neve to Maurice Johnson [in London].
[Spalding], 4 July 1723.
Discusses the recently-discovered Chichester inscription,¹ regretting the damage to it and offers a possible explanation of it from the latest SGS meeting, suggesting it was set up by Claudius at his invasion.

Johnson has used the reverse of this letter for notes of inscriptions he found in Lincoln.

¹ Several of the following letters (Nos 49, 50, 51, 427 and 432) also deal with this inscription which caused keen interest among antiquarians.

49. From Maurice Johnson to 'My Couzen'.¹
[London] Undated but attached to No 48 above.
Discusses the partly-damaged inscription found at Chichester and sends a copy for the SGS's discussion at their meeting; comments on a MS of the Gospels and a missal written in AD750 by the Abbot of Thorney, which has an Anglo-Saxon translation between the lines of Latin text.

¹ It has not proved possible to identify which of Johnson's many relatives who were members of the SGS is addressed here.

50. From Roger Gale to Maurice Johnson.
London, 18 July 1723.
Discusses in detail the Roman inscription found at Chichester; has found an

inscription in Gruter[1] which is helpful in understanding and translating it, especially the missing portion; lists and describes five medals of Carausius[2] and discusses what legions Carausius had in Britain.

[1]   He refers to Jan Gruter's published collection of Latin inscriptions, *Inscriptiones antiquae totius orbis Romani* (Heidelberg, 1603).
[2]   Maurice Johnson and William Stukeley had a particular interest in the Roman Emperor Carausius (fl.290); they hoped to prove that he was of British origin. Carausius was also the subject of debates at the SA.

51. SGS No 57: From Roger Gale to Maurice Johnson.
London, 16 August 1723.
Discusses a planned journey with Stukeley to visit Chichester; discusses the decipherment of the Roman inscription found at Chichester and compares it in detail with other inscriptions; explains that 'if you direct to me at The Excise Office in the Old Jewry you need not trouble any of your friends to frank your letters'.

1724

52. From Sigismund Trafford[1] to Maurice Johnson.
Lynn, 14 April 1724.
Apologises for not being present at Commissioners of Sewers' meeting; is concerned about problems for south Lincolnshire arising from the 'Arbitrary Practices of the Corporation of Adventurers' [in Bedford Level] relating to the Shire Drain; thanks Johnson for his efforts in opposing them.

[1]   High Sheriff of Lincolnshire; see his entry in Appendix 2.

53. Copy of letter from Maurice Johnson to Sigismund Trafford.
Spalding, 20 April 1724.
Discusses in detail the proceedings at the Court of Sewers; explains problems between the Court of Sewers and the Bedford Level Adventurers relating to the proposed alterations to the Shire Drain and requesting his assistance in opposing the plan to bring inexperienced members on to the Commission of Sewers.
Annotated by Johnson: 'A Copy of a Lr to Sigismond Trafford Esq Highshireev of the County of Lincoln' and on outside: 'April 1724 To Sigismund Trafford Esq. concerning the Shire Dreyne & the corporation of Bedford Levell.'

54. From Revd Timothy Neve to Maurice Johnson.
Ludlow, 29 May 1724.
MB1 fol.77B, 4 June 1724.
Discusses his hope of seeing some antiquities and paintings in Wales and Shropshire; describes a coin, now lost, which he has not been able to see, and part of a battering-ram; comments on the difficulty of observing the eclipse of the sun [in 1724] because of clouds.

55. Draft of letter from Maurice Johnson to Sigismond Trafford.
Spalding, 13 June 1724.
Explains the latest stages of the 'affair relating to the Shire Dreyne'; suggests

a meeting of local gentry affected by the proposed plan, to attend the View of Jury when the Commission of Sewers visits the site; lists suitable local people to attend.

56. [SGS No] 47: From Maurice Johnson to Mrs E. Johnson (for SGS President).[1]
London, Thursday 18 June 1724.
MB1 fol.78A, 2 July 1724.
Johnson has attended a SA meeting where the SGS's offer of help with their study of coins was welcomed; gives an account of the proceedings at the SA; comments on Mr Switzer's[2] new book on fruit trees and gives other items of London news.
Enclosed: printed sheet describing a memorial to Edward Seabright and Henry Mompesson, English travellers murdered by highway robbers near Calais, with an engraving of the monument.

[1]   The outside is addressed to Mrs E. Johnson; what is preserved here is the portion of the letter intended for the SGS, as the letter begins 'Rev. Sir', i.e. Revd Stephen Lyon, President of the SGS.
[2]   Stephen Switzer (1682–1745) was a landscape gardener and florist who kept a plant shop close to Westminster Hall in London; see his entry in *ODNB*. His new book was *The Practical Fruit-Gardener. Being the best and newest method of raising, planting and pruning all sorts of fruit-trees, agreeably to the Experience and Practice of the most eminent Gardeners and Nursery-men* (London, 1724). Johnson's papers include Switzer's catalogues of plants which could be ordered and dispatched to customers, and he appears to have patronised Switzer's shop when in London as he has underlined several plants and written details for their delivery.

57. SGS No 56: From William Stukeley to Maurice Johnson.
Ormond Street, London, 12 November 1724.
Discusses his plans for publishing the first part of his *Itinerarium Curiosum*,[1] about the Parts of Holland, Lincolnshire; requests a preface from Johnson and asks for information about Roman remains in Lincolnshire to include in the book; sends latest news from the SA.

[1]   Published in 1724; a copy of the second edition is still in the SGS library.

58. Draft of letter from Maurice Johnson to Sir Isaac Newton.
26 November 1724.
MB1 fol.68A.[1]

To the Honoured S[r] Izaack Newton PRS & Warden of his Majesty's Mint from the Secretary SGS 29 Novemb[r] 1724 <u>to Invite him</u> by order of these Gentlemen <u>to become a Member</u>
Honoured S[r]
    Not having the good fortune to be known to You or meanes of otherwise addressing ~~you~~ I entreat You to pardon my takeing the Liberty of ~~troubling you with~~ this Letter the Intent of which is ~~only~~ to acquaint you S[r] that the Gentlemen of the Parts of Holland in Your Native County haveing Twelve years agoe formd themselves into a Society for promoting knowledge and ever since met weekly at Spalding & been Countenanced therein by Several Men of Quality & distinguishd learning becoming Members & being extremely desireous of the Honour of ∧^adding
                    that they may have Your leave so to do Which is all They have to ask
Your Name to 'em commanded Me to begg the great favour ∧ By granting which S[r] you will much encourage Us in our Endeavours to become Wiser & oblige a

great many Gentlemen of your own Country S^r I should be proud of the Honour of receiving your favourable answer to our Request & desire I may wait upon you for It being Hon. S^r Y^r most devoted &

most obedient Servant

On reverse: My letter to Sr Isaack Newton to Invite him to become a Member of the Gent. Society of Spalding in Lincolnshire I sent this by my Man Wm Stagg on Saturday 21 Novr 1724 & Sr Isaack returnd me for answer that he desired to see Me the first time I could come that way.

[1]   MB1 fol.81A, 26 November 1724, gives an account of 'The Secretaries Conference with Sr Izaack Newton': 'Memorandum That pursuant to the Order made by the Soc. on the 22^d of October last, I had the pleasure to wait upon Sr Izaack Newton on the 24 of this Month November & He recieved Me Very courteously: when haveing acquainted that Great Man how Ambitious Wee were of the Honour of Enrolling his Name amongst those of our Members, & given him a full Account of the Institution & Designe of this Society: I added, That his condescending to accept of our Invitation would not only be a Lasting Honour to It, but likewise a good Example to Other Learned Men especially other Lincolnshire Gentlemen, & a great Encouragement to Us – to which he was pleased very gratiously to reply – S^r I highly commend your Society; & very readly accept of the Invitation – I desire You not to call It condescention, thô I am Declining all Things of a Publick nature, even the busyness of the Royal Society, & am not likely ever to be present with You, Yet I take It as an honour done me by the Gentlemen in having this Regard for Me.

  This is the Substance & as near as I can remember (who wrote It down immediatly after I went from him) the Very Expresssions Sr Izaack was pleasd to Use, & which for a Perpetual Memorial is here Entred by me Maur. Johnson jun^r Soc. Gen. Sp. Secr.'

59. From Maurice Johnson to James Jurin and reply from James Jurin to Johnson.[1] 29 No[vember] 1724.
Good Friend.
I pray peruse this & alter It as you think most proper & under [   ] How I may direct It & when transcribed my Servant shall carry It from your most faithfull Friend. MJ

Dear Sir
I think your letter needs no alteration. You may direct it to Sr. I. N. at his house in St Martin's Street, Leicester Fields.
I am,
Your very affectionate
humble servant
J. Jurin.

[1]   Johnson had sent Jurin the draft of his invitation letter to Newton (No 58 above) for his comments, before sending it to Newton. See Jurin's entry in Appendix 2

60. From Revd William Hannes[1] to Maurice Johnson.
Stamford, 18 December 1724.
Thanks Johnson for a book [unspecified]: 'the Person you sent the Book by brought it me wet with Raign but he has dried it'; thanks him for an invitation to visit Spalding with Mr Noel and Dr Coleby;[2] explains that his books are at Johnson's service and that he kept the book over a month as he heard Johnson was in London.
Annotated by Johnson: 'Reverend Wm Hannes MA of Stamford Sch w. his Latin Ode[3] to Dr Frampton. The Cover of this was directed to me.'

[1]   Born c.1681; educated Magdalen College, Oxford (MA 1704); Master of Stamford School 1723–1726. He was not a member of the SGS.
[2]   William Noel, MP, SGS member 1724; for Dr Dixon Colby, see Appendix 2.
[3]   The Ode is not present.

61. From Matthew Snow[1] to Maurice Johnson.

[London], 24 December 1724

To 'My dear Maurice'

Apologises for delay in replying; thanks him for his admission to the SGS; explains that he was to go out of town with Sir John Hobart; promises to send a book by Breval [unspecified] and drink Johnson's health.

[1]   See his entry in Appendix 2.

1725

62. From Matthew Snow to Maurice Johnson.

Queen Street [London], 1725 [no day or month].

Invitation to him to dinner.

On reverse, sketch of a plan for a proposed SGS museum and sketch labelled 'Moulton Chapel' by Maurice Johnson.[1]

[1]   This letter was probably kept by Johnson because of the plans for the SGS museum which was under discussion at the time. There exist among the SGS's papers today five plans dated around 1725 for a museum for the Society; this would have been a 'museum' in the eighteenth-century sense of a laboratory and workroom in which their collections could be studied.

63. From William Gonville[1] to Maurice Johnson

[Alford], 16 February 1724 [actually 1725, dateable by entry in MB1 fol.84B].

Discusses coins, perhaps Roman, found in urns dug up at Well (Lincs) during building operations there.

[1]   See his entry in Appendix 2.

64. No 4: From Dr James Jurin to Maurice Johnson.

London, 26 February 1725.

MB1 fol.84A, 4 March 1725.

Dear Sir,   [SGS] No 4

I intend, if possible to pay my respects to you & your Brother at your Lodgings, before you go out of Town but for fear I should be prevented, the Time being so short, I send you the remainder of the Phil. Transactions[1] as far as they ha[ve been][2] publish'd. Pray make my Service a[cceptable][2] to the Gentlemen of your Society & to the good Families at Spalding. I am,

                                        Dear Sir,
Lincoln's Inn Fields   Your very affectionate
Febr. 26th 1724/5   & faithfull humble Servant
                                        J. Jurin

Pray let me have a fresh direction how to send the Microscopes,[3] when finish'd, Mr Colepeper having lost the former.

On reverse: To Maurice Johnson Esq
                            at Mrs Nokes's in

Essex Street   these present

[1] Jurin was the Secretary of the Royal Society from 1721 to 1727. These volumes of the Royal Society's *Philosophical Transactions* are still in the Original Collection of the SGS library.
[2] A gap in the paper here, caused by the removal of a seal, probably at a later stage.
[3] The SGS's Account Book records: '31 Decr 1724 Paid for Microscop. With those 5 Gns   05.05.00 ... 13 May 1725 V supra fol.78. Recd & produced the Microscopes & opend & Examd at the Soc & performed in my presence'.

65. From Revd William Clarke to Maurice Johnson.
Buxted, 16 June 1725.
Sends thanks from Dr Wootton,[1] his father-in-law, for Johnson's offer to lend him his collection of legal documents relating to Welsh law; discusses Dr Wootton's work on the early Welsh laws and his difficulty in obtaining books and documents to help in this; asks Johnson to bring his papers to London for collection; is pleased that the SGS is in such a thriving state.

[1] Dr William Wotton or Wootton (1666–1727), linguist and Anglican clergyman. His Latin translation of the early Welsh law code of Hywel Dda (d.949/50) was published in 1730, after his death, by his son-in-law Revd William Clarke as *Leges Walliæ*. See his entry in *ODNB* under 'Wotton' and no. 75 below; see also Clarke's entry in Appendix 2.

66. From Revd Timothy Neve to Maurice Johnson in London.
Spalding, 17 November 1725.

SGS No 52
Sir
I've been prevented the 2 last Posts of returning you the Thanks of the Soc. for your obliging Letter to us, last Thursday we were a pretty full Soc. to partake of the Entertainment you were so kind to send us. I was of Opinion at the time of reading the Verses[1] that they were intended for the greatest Satyr upon the Persons to whom they are Inscrib'd especially from the first & last Stanzas, he being said to be too great a Lover of a Severe Joke, as well as his Ease. But as you observe, the greatest Burlesque is in the very Nature of the verse it self, in prostituting the noble Alcaics to the low & pitifull Employment of Lampoon. We had a good deal of Discourse about our Musæum, & I find things likely to go on without much Opposition, (tho' there was some thing mention'd by a hasty Member that had like to've spoiled all.) It will be proper to have a plan or 2 to offer the Gent. & then we may easily calculate the expense. I believe our Ground will not allow of more than 20 foot in Length; tho we are to be exact when a Committee is orderd to take a view of it.

We had nothing (but what you were so good to send us) communicated to us last Thursday, ᵇᵘᵗonly there were some Boston verses read, which I thought not worth the entering in our Minutes. There was a proposal made, but not entred, about what you mentioned in yours, of laying in a Stock of wine, but as I imagine our intended Building will exhaust all our Stock, both what we have in hand, & what else we can raise, it may be as well to omitt that Provision at present.

You desire to have an Account of the Numbers of the Books to be continu'd for the Soc.[2] We've only the first 3 of the New Memoirs of Lit. We Have the 1, 2, 3 & 4ᵗʰ of the Bibl. Biblica for the year 1724 ending with part of the 6ᵗʰ Ch. of Numbers. Bibl. Literaria ends with the Nᵒ 9.

I've collected some short Account of Bishop Hooper[3] from Burnett, Strype &

Fox, which has given me only a great Desire of knowing more about that great Man, especially relating to that Sharp Controversie about Ceremonies, he was the unhappy Occasion of in the very Infancy of the Reformation. I find no notice taken of this Book which I have in my Possession by any one of the Historians above. which makes me think they never saw it. Unless Strype has mentiond it in his Annals of the Reformation[4] (which I wish to see) & hope you'll bring down along with you for the Soc. as orderd.

Sir, our best wishes & Thanks wait upon you for the great regard you express and Care you shew for your Cell in Spalding, & the Honour you do us in mentioning our very names to the learned Societies above, what ever we do here worthy of their Notice you may justly challenge to your Self, tho' out of Modesty to your self, and affection for us, you are pleas'd to let us partake of your Credit. But we hope that even the lesser Herd of us shall take care to demean ourselves with such becomingness, as to avoid the Flouts of the Scorner, whose Talent only lyes in rallying things that [are] sacred and serious.

Our worthy Præsident gives his humble Service to you & desires that if it should be in Mr Staggs way, he would be so kind as to enquire for Mr Abra. Nickson at Monday House in New round Court in the Strand, for the Rev. Mr Waterhouse at Mr Tho. Pre[   ] next to St Magnus Thames Street, to desire either of 'em to pay M[r] Kneplock the eight Shillings that is due to him in Ingoldsby's Account.

Be pleased to excuse this Trouble from
                          Sir
                   Your most obliged
Spalding   and most humble Servant
Nov[r] 17 1725   T. Neve
To Maurice Johnson Esq
at the Widdows Coffea House in Devereaux Court Inner Temple
                   London

In Maurice Johnson's hand: Rev[d] Mr Neve 17 Nov 1725
          For the Comittee
          of the Musæum
          1 The Præsident
          2 Secr
          3 Treasurer
          4 M Johnson Sen[r]
          5 Cap[t] Pilliod
          6 Jn[o] Johnson Esq
          7 George Stevens sen[r]
Annotated by Maurice Johnson: 'The Rev[d] Mr Tim Neve MA Master of the Free School & Tr[s] of GS in Spalding about a Designe of building a Museum adjoining to the Schoolmasters House towards the East.'[6]

[1]   The 'Verses' were the Latin ode to Dr Broxholme: see Nos 67 and 68 below.
[2]   Johnson is buying books and the latest copies of serial publications in London for the Society's library.
[3]   Died 1552; Bishop of Gloucester and Worcester, Chaplain to Protector Somerset in the reign of Edward VI.
[4]   John Strype, *Annals of the Reformation and establishment of religion and other various occur-*

rences in the Church of England, during the first twelve years of Queen Elizabeth's happy reign
(London, 1709). The edition of 1725 is in the SGS library.
5   Neve was the Treasurer of the SGS at this time.
6   The SGS drew up a range of plans for this proposed museum and meeting-room, but faced too
much opposition from a member [unidentified] to be able to proceed with the building. The Society
had to use rented accommodation, moving to several different locations in Spalding. A permanent
building was finally erected in 1910–11, during the revival of the Society under Dr Marten Perry.

67. SGS No 93: From Maurice Johnson to SGS members: 'Messieurs'.
[London], 9 November 1725.
MB1 fol.90A, 18 November 1725.
A 'General Epistle': gives detailed account of current legal cases which he has
attended, one in the Court of Chancery relating to the grant of an estate which
was later revoked and two criminal cases in the Court of the King's Bench; gives
an account of an SA meeting, where his account of SGS activities was well
received 'being the single instance of such an union out of London'; mentions the
SA's publications; comments on RS meetings including a Latin ode to Dr Noel
Broxholme,[1] attributed to Michael Mattaire, which he quotes; hears that Newton
has agreed to publish his Chronologies; passes on other items of news including
a probable rise in the price of port because of a bad summer across Europe.
1   Dr Noel Broxholm or Broxholme (1686–1748): see his entry in *ODNB*. A physician and Latin
poet, probably born at Stamford; a fellow-student with William Stukeley at St Thomas' Hospital.
Michael Mattaire (1668–1747) was a collector and cataloguer of books.

68. SGS No 94: From Maurice Johnson to Mrs Elizabeth Johnson.[1]
[London], Thursday 18 November 1725.
MB1 fol.90A, 25 November 1725.
Discusses and quotes in full Sir William Young's verses on Dr Broxholme; lists
topics discussed at the most recent RS meeting, in particular Dr Blair's[2] water
cure for mental illness; lists topics discussed at an SA meeting; explains points
relating to current legal cases in the Court of King's Bench concerned with debt
and forgery.
1   This letter, like others addressed to his wife which are preserved in this collection, is mainly
intended to be passed on to the SGS members for use at their meetings during Johnson's absence.
Purely personal letters to her have not survived in this collection, though some personal messages
are included by Johnson in the surviving letters.
2   Dr Patrick Blair (c.1680–1728); see his entry in *ODNB*.

69. From Roger Gale to Maurice Johnson.
London, 9 December 1725.
He has bought a copy of 'Hearns Sprott, Charta mag.'[1] for Johnson, costing one
and a half guineas.
1   An edition by Thomas Hearne, the Oxford antiquary, of a chronicle of St Augustine's Abbey,
Canterbury, from its foundation in the sixth century AD to 1252/3, written by Thomas Sprott, a monk
of the abbey. It was printed in Oxford in 1719.

70. From Beaupré Bell[1] to Maurice Johnson.
Beaupré Hall, Norfolk, 10 December 1715 [sic, an error for 1725].
Sends a drawing of a coat of arms and inscription relating to the Haultoft family
from Outwell Church; requests the loan, 'by Woods's Waggon', of Johnson's copy
of Bishop Alcock's sermons.[2]

Signed 'your affectionate Relation'.

¹ The well-known numismatist and collector, and a relative of Maurice Johnson. See his entry in Appendix 2.
² John Alcock (1430–1500), Bishop of Ely; see his entry in *ODNB*.

71. SGS No18: From George Ault to Maurice Johnson.
Boston, 13 December 1725.
MB1 fol.90B, 16 December 1725.
Thanks Johnson for his legal advice on an intended purchase [not specified]; refers to a proposal to publish a plan of King's Lynn and says he plans to get a copy for the SGS; sends a transcript of the proposal, by Mr William Rastrick,¹ who explains that he needs subscribers as it will cost at least £30 to produce but that Walpole is the dedicatee and will subscribe, as will many local gentry and customs officials.
Annotated by Johnson: 'Lr from the Learned Mr Geo. Ault the Teacher of the Presbyterian Congregation at Boston.'

¹ William Rastrick (baptised 1697, died 1752; see his entry in *ODNB*) was born at Spalding. By this time he was a Presbyterian preacher at King's Lynn and was known for his mathematical skills. The plan was published in 1725.

1726

72. Draft of letter from John Johnson as Clerk of Sewers to Robert Vyner MP.
Spalding, 9 March 1725/6.
Asks for the Lincolnshire MPs' support in opposing the New Outfall to drain the Bedford Level because of problems it would cause for Lincolnshire.
On the same folio is a draft of a letter from Maurice Johnson to Sigismond Trafford: Spalding, 9 March 1725/6
Asks for his support in opposing the Bill for the drainage scheme; lists influential people whose support he aims to enlist to oppose it.

73. From Roger Gale to Maurice Johnson.
London, 15 March 1726.

SGS No 53   London, March the 15th 1725 [actually 1726]¹
Dear Sr
    It is no small pleasure to me that the Cell of Spallding is in so prosperous a Condition as you represent it, and I shall not be at all chagrined if so hopefull a Child outdo's it's mother, as it seems to promise to do, for I think we do little more that talk here,² and I beleive no great matter will be produced from all our Schemes, but every thing go on in the old way we have been loitering in ever since our Institution. Our Secretary³ is like to leave us in a few months, and as he is to be settled for the residue of his days at Grantham, you will in all probability have more of his Company for the future, than we. he is now there and so I doubt not but you will see him before his return. Rosse⁴ was sold yesterday at Mr Bridges's auction, I could not possibly attend the Sale myself so entrusted your Commission to a friend, but am sorry to tell you it would not reach the price by half that the book sold for. which was so enormous that I beleive you must for ever despair of being Master of it, except by some very lucky accident,

the summe it went for being no lesse than 06^{li} 08^s 00^d. I should be glad to have better successe with Harris Travels,[5] and shall lay out for them as well as I can, thou' I beleive they also go at a good round rate, being out of print, they consist of 4 volumes. My humble Service to all the Fraternity, and beleive me Dear S^r

>Your most faithfull
>humble Servant
>R. Gale

Annotated by Johnson: 'L^r from Roger Gale Esq FRS & a member of the A[ntiquarian] & G[entlemen's] Socc.'

[1]   This letter refers to William Stukeley who was about to move to Grantham; Stukeley's move allows the dating of this letter to 1726.
[2]   At the Society of Antiquaries.
[3]   Dr William Stukeley, who moved to Grantham from London that year in the hope of building up a more successful medical practice.
[4]   This presumably refers to the catalogue of Mr Michael Rosse's extensive collection of 'curious prints and drawings ... antique seals and medals and other curiosities' published for the sale of the collection in April 1723.
[5]   John Harris, *Navigantium atque itinerantium bibliotheca: or a compleat collection of voyages and travels, consisting of above four hundred of the most authentic writers* (London, 1705).

74. From Robert Vyner to John Johnson.[1]
[London], 19 March 1726.
Recommends the speedy submission of the Lincolnshire gentlemen's petition against the Bill for the drainage of the Bedford Level; he has gained a promise that the first reading will be delayed until he has spoken to them.

[1]   This is in answer to John Johnson's letter of 9 March (No 72 above). See Vyner's entry in Appendix 2.

75. SGS No 33: Draft of letter from Maurice Johnson to Revd William Clarke.[1]
Spalding, 10 June 1726.
MB1 fol.97B, 16 June 1726.
He has been looking forward to the publication of Dr Wootton's book on Welsh law, especially as Welsh law may have some relation to that of the pre-Roman Ancient Britons; offers to lend Dr Wootton his own collection of documents relating to ancient laws, if they would be helpful for his work and proposes to bring them to London.

[1]   Rector of Buxted, near Uckfield (Sussex) and son-in-law to Dr Wootton. See No 65 above.

76. From Maurice Johnson to the SGS.[1]
[London], 28 June 1726.
MB1 fol.98A, 30 June 1726.
Sends a copy of satirical verses, attributed by Johnson to Dr Arbuthnot, about Swift's household goods: 'An Oken, broken Elbow-Chair ...' and gives some other brief items of London news, including Aaron Hill[2] receiving a gold medal from the Czarina, and the performance of Mlle Violante, a rope-dancer.

[1]   The letter is addressed to Mrs Elizabeth Johnson but the contents are meant for an SGS meeting; there may have been a personal section for her alone, which has not been preserved.
[2]   Aaron Hill (1685–1750), writer and entrepreneur; see his entry in *ODNB*.

77. From Revd Benjamin Clements[1] to the parishioners of Long Sutton (Lincs).
Gresham College, London, 2 July 1726.

Discusses affairs related to the finances of their church.

[1] Revd Benjamin Clement (BA of Pembroke College, Cambridge) was appointed curate of Long Sutton in 1707; he was also schoolmaster there (Cole, *Speculum Diœceseos Lincolniensis* (LRS 4, 1913), 121).

78. From Revd Timothy Neve to Maurice Johnson in London.
[Spalding], 3 July 1726.
Gives an account of recent SGS meetings, including the display of some plaster of Paris busts brought in by members, and a discussion he had with Mr Day[1] about Classical antiquities.

[1] William Day, a Spalding chandler and merchant, became a member of the SGS in 1726.

79. SGS No 5: From William Bogdani[1] to Maurice Johnson.
London, 10 October 1726.
MB1 fol.101A, 13 October 1726.
Gives a very detailed description of 'Clouds of Light' from the north, observed 'last Saturday night between 7 & 8' until 10 p.m.; requests SGS's comments on it. Annotated by Johnson: 'abt Aurora Borealis; An Acct of & reasons for Aurora Borealis – Wallis's Miscell. Curiosa No.2.'[2]

[1] See his entry in Appendix 2.
[2] John Wallis, 'A discourse concerning the measure of the airs resistance to bodies moved in it. By the learned John Wallis', in *Miscellanea Curiosa* (2nd edn, London, 1708).

80. From William Bogdani to Maurice Johnson.
London, 22 October 1726.
MB1 fol.101B, 27 October 1726.

Dear Sir,

My Absence from the Office was the Occasion of my not answering the Favour of yours in due Time, which I receiv'd (as I do all from your Hand) with great Pleasure & especially your additional Remarks on the late Phænomenon,[1] but am sorry my familiar, ignorant & indigested Letters should pass the Censure of your Learned Society,[2] I being willing to have Collected my Thoughts with the Judgment of the Curious before I had taken the Liberty to have communicated them to so Ingenious a Set of Gentlemen, however I am oblig'd to them for their Approbation, & Esteem it designd as an Encouragement to my intended Endeavours. But give me leave S[r] to say I can't but observe in your Letters an Air of Flattery too great to be consistent with solid Friendship (for such I am willing to perswade my self you profess to me) were I vain enough to beleive your Praises to be the Result of your Judgement, a Man so much superior to me in all parts of polite Literature I should be unworthy your Conversation.

No one can be more pleased with the news of the Recovery of your Health[3] than I am & hope it [erasure] to Continue that I may ~~have~~ ^Enjoy the Pleasure of your company at the Time & Place appointed whither I shall if possible come on Horseback that I may have the Honour to Accompany you to London, being proud of all Opportunitys of convincing you of the Esteem & Sincerity wherewith I am

        S[r]

P.S.   Your most obliged & most obedient humble
My most humble   Servant   W Bogdani

Service attends your
Family & all Friends

London 22 Oct. 1726
To
Maur. Johnson Jun. Esq.
at Spalding
Lincolnshire

1   The Aurora Borealis, referred to in Bogdani's previous letter of 10 October 1726 (No 79 above).
2   This reluctance to have letters regarded as private read to the SGS compares with Beaupré Bell's letter of 18 March 1731 (No 141 below) on the same subject of correspondence.
3   Johnson's illness is not specified here. At this stage in his life he suffered intermittently from hæmorrhoids which made riding difficult, and like many Fen dwellers was subject to 'feavers'. It is perhaps a little early in his life for the onset of attacks of giddiness which troubled him in later life.

81. From Beaupré Bell to Maurice Johnson.
Trinity College, Cambridge, 10 December 1726.
MB1 fol.106A, 19 January 1727.
He has sent to Johnson some Cambridge commencement verses and a collection of engravers' marks; offers to exchange with Johnson the duplicates in their coin collections.

82. SGS No 10: From William Bogdani to Maurice Johnson.
London, 20 December 1726.
MB1 fol.103B, 22 December 1726.

Dear S^r   No 10
I doubt not but I suffer much in your Esteem for neglecting to acknowledge the Receipt of your last with your acceptable present but besides my being deeply engag'd in earnest business from the Moment I rise till Midnight (which I hope may plead some Excuse) I was willing to procure such Memorandums relating to the Affair you desired, as might be entertaining. But having talk'd with the several persons who were best able to inform me, find no certain Discovery of the Method the Impostor[1] made use of, thus to deceive the World & particularly the Adepti. Those persons whose Reputations suffer most by being so grosly imposed on, & foil'd I may say at their own Weapons, are very industrious to convince the Publick of the Suspicion they had of the Fraud from the Beginning but in what they have publish'd it does not yet appear but they were equally deceiv'd, nor has the Woman in her Confession clear'd up the whole intricate design completely, but grossly prevaricates; As the Narration would be too tedious for an Epistle, I shall procure all the Accounts publish'd, & add what I have heard, if any thing different from what Contain'd therein, & send them, together with the Verses you mention per next Coach.
   I was at the Antiquarian Society a Fortnight after you left London & introduc'd by Dr Massy Lord Hertford [2] being then present the Soc. resolved to meet after Christmas at Capt. Floyer's Chambers & Orders are given to provide the Necessarys accordingly. I receive so great pleasure in that Company, that as I propose to my self great Improvements therein I shall be a constant Attender [page 2] Tho' I am very sorry you was not so kind as to inform me you had paid my Entrance mony, that I might have repaid it to you. Mr Lynn[3] who promis'd to

afford me his company to the Royal Society, inform'd me they would not meet that night, since when he left London & I beleive by this time is with you, to whom if you please give my humble Service.

We are here in great Expectation of a War. Our Board [of Ordnance] have News (which, however current, wants further confirmation) that our Garrison _∧^{at Gibraltar} expects daily to be beseig'd, there is a Report that the Spaniards have orderd a Fort to be built with all Expedition near the Castle in order to annoy both that and the Shipping but according to the plan of the place in the Office I do not think it practicable, however 8 Ships are put in Commission & I expect 4 more to be commission'd who are to go thither, & They take with them a Detachment of 1 Regiment from Disney's, Newtons & Anstruther's Regiments to reinforce that Garrison & a Detachment likewise of Artillery Officers & Gunners, there is this day orderd by the Board a very large Supply of stores which will amount I believe to near £12,000 for that place. Notwithstanding these tremendous preparations for War,_∧ ^{Capt Kennisbee} one of our Captains of Artillery there, being drunk & <u>not having the fear of God before his Eyes</u> did inhumanely beat one of the Matrosses[4] who out of affection to ~~another~~ Lieutenant who was laid up of the Gout lodging in the same house with Kennisbee, offer'd his Service to sit up with the Lieut^t & in the night let Kennisbee in at the Door, who so mauld him that the poor Wretch, in the greatest Agony & Torture died the next Morning, leaving a poor Widow & 3 helpless young Children, Kennisbee being confin'd, we Expect an Account of the Court Martial to be laid before his Majesty by the next Express from thence.

Admiral Wager sets out this Week for Portsmouth to Command the Fleet, which seems to Confirm Jennings's Disgrace,[5] this however is but surmise Jennings being old & not desirous to venture his Carcass in Danger any more.

The Exceedings in the last Year's Expences are so great & the continuance of them so necessary that it is beleiv'd it will occasion an additional Supply on the Land Tax; whatever they do I hope we shall have the pleasure of curbing our Enemies & our Austrian Friends, the latter tis said would gladly quit the Ostend Trade to be quiet, but I hope our designs [*small gap caused by removal of seal*] more extensive.

The Season now calls for Mirth & Diversion, I therefore wish you & all yours the most exquisite your Hearts can desire. My humble Service attends all your Fireside & all Friends at Spalding & in particular the worthy Assembly of Literati.

I am with the greatest Respect
Dear Sir
London   Your most oblig'd humble
20 Decr 1726   Servant   W Bogdani

To
Maur. Johnson Junr Esq
at Spalding
Lincolnshire

[1]   The 'Impostor' is not specified here but seems likely to be the 'pretended rabbit Breeder' discussed in the following letter (No 83) from Bogdani: the notorious case in 1726 of a woman from Godalming, Mary Tofts, who claimed to have given birth to live rabbits on several occasions at Guildford. Her case was widely reported in the newspapers, and she and the rabbits are depicted in one of Hogarth's engravings. On her removal to London, she was found to be an impostor after medical examination; she was committed for trial but her case was dismissed.

² Algernon Seymour (1684–1750), Marquis of Hertford and later Duke of Somerset, President of the Antiquarian Society of London 1724. For Dr Massey see Appendix 2.
³ George Lynn senior (1696–1742), a member also of the SGS; see Appendix 2.
⁴ Soldiers who assist the gunners with the firing of cannon.
⁵ Sir Charles Wager (1666–1743): First Lord of the Admiralty 1733–1742; Admiral Sir John Jennings (1664–1743). Both have entries in *ODNB*.

83. No 4: From William Bogdani to Maurice Johnson.
London, 31 December 1726.
MB1 fol.105A, 5 January 1727.
He has sent by the Peterborough Waggoner a Latin poem and books relating to the 'pretended Rabbit Breeder'; gives news of the Spanish army's preparations to attack Gibraltar and the arrival of Spanish ships; encloses verses: 'Recipe for a Soup ... to Dean Swift' beginning 'Take a Nuckle of Veal, You may buy it or steal'.
Annotated by Johnson: 'Lr from Wm Bogdani Esq FRS with the detection of the pretended Delivery by a Woman of Godalmin in Surry of Several Rabbits. a R. for a Soup in Verse.'

1727

84. From George Lynn junior¹ to Maurice Johnson.
Southwick, 6 January 1726/7.
Passes on best wishes to 'Dear Couzen'; looks forward to meeting him and John Johnson [Maurice's brother] in London.
¹ See his entry in Appendix 2.

85. From E. Wingfield to Maurice Johnson, addressed to him 'at his Chambers in the Temple'.
29 January 1726/7.
Asks Johnson as a skilled genealogist to send him information on the descendants of Thomas Lord Cromwell¹ and to find out whether any connection with the Wingfield family is traceable; he cannot understand the pedigree of the Cromwells drawn up by Johnson.
Annotated by Johnson: 'Couzen Wingfeild abt Ld Cromwell's descendg.'
¹ Thomas Lord Cromwell (1594–1653) had a son Wingfield Cromwell (1624–65). See Thomas's entry in *ODNB*. Mr Wingfield, who was a distant relative of Maurice Johnson, was not a member of the SGS.

86. SGS No 37: From Maurice Johnson to Mrs Elizabeth Johnson.¹
Lincoln, 16 March 1727.

SGS No 37   Lincoln, March the 16ᵗʰ 1726/7
My dearest Betty,
    when I left you on Sat. for this place I had not a speck on my Boots throughout my Journey but what I got by the plashy waters on Brigg End Causey² which 3 Miles took an houre & an half under the Conduct of a Goose Grazier who is one of the directors to Travailers thro that tedious & perilous pass. I calld at Donyngton on the Schoole-Master & found him very much Engaged in Tuition

of his disciples. He presents his Service to the Gent Soc & thanks for permitting him to become an Honourary Member.[3] Haveing dind'd at Sleeford & accepted a present from my Landlady of some old peices she had layd by for Me whereof one is Copper as large as an half peny & has a Crown upon it of this Shape [sketch of crown] & round It these words in hon[our] of the Blessed Virgin +AVE.MARIA.GRASIA.PLENA – Hail Mary full of Grace
On reverse a Cross patence & fleury …
[Discusses coins and an Egyptian talisman he has seen]
[page 4] … We have had a very great Assizes here and Our old Acquaintance my Lord Judge has used us all very civily & was so obligeing as to invite me to dine with him, which I did, & at my Instance dismissed my poor Riotous Neighbours with only the small Fine of a Marke a Piece. His Lordship enquired very kindly after my Father & presents his Service to him.
I begun this Letter early in the Assizes & have continued writing till the End of It being Thursday night before which I thought to have finished It & sent It to you I thank God I am very well & Intend to return from Nottingham where the Assizes end on Monday. So that I hope to be with You by this Se'night in the Evening or if I be deteind upon the Road by my Friend Mr Darwin[4] with whom I shall returne his seat lying in my way home I would not have You under any apprehensions or Feares about It I pray present my duty to my Father & Love to Bro (the Enclosed deputation from the Shireve to my Broth[r]) & Love to your Bro. & sisters & all our Little Ones.
My Clyent Ned Walker brings you this packet home with his Wife who now with all the Rest of the Merry Wives of Spalding are delivered from this Tribulation[5] which I hope will be a Warning to Them & has given Me an Opportunity of being of Service to my Poor Neighbours in distress which is the truest pleasure I think a Rational Man can have
I am most affectionately yours
Maur. Johnson jun.

[1] While some of this letter is evidently intended for use at SGS meetings, there is more personal content than in some of the other letters in this collection sent to his wife.
[2] A causeway, originally maintained by the small Gilbertine priory of Holland Bridge, across a marshy section of the Donington to Grantham road (the present A52) at Bridge End.
[3] Thomas Mills, SGS member and schoolmaster of the grammar school at Donington (Lincs), founded by Thomas Cowley.
[4] Robert Darwin, a fellow-barrister, lived at Elston in Nottinghamshire. He was a friend of Johnson's from the Midland Circuit and became an SGS member in 1733. His son Erasmus Darwin was a leading member of the Lunar Society in Birmingham in the later years of the eighteenth century and was the grandfather of Charles Darwin.
[5] This refers to the court case which Johnson has handled on their behalf. No further details are available but it seems to be a local dispute between neighbours which had got out of hand.

87. From Major-General Robert Hunter to Maurice Johnson.
London, 30 May 1727.
MB1 fol.114B, 25 May 1727.
Thanks Johnson for his admission to membership; encloses a notification from the commissioners [of drainage]; explains that he will send Bayle's *Dictionary* or another book if they already have it; sends compliments to the Johnson family.
Annotated by Johnson: 'Sometime Governor of New York.'[1]

[1] See his biography in *ODNB* and his entry in Appendix 2. Maurice Johnson was the steward of Hunter's estate at Crowland, which explains the interest in drainage shown in the letter.

1728

88. Part of a letter from Maurice Johnson to William Bogdani.
[Spalding], 6 April 1728.
Read to the SGS on 11 April 1728 by Johnson.
Discusses the history of the invention of ordnance, with historical references and quotations.
Annotated by Johnson: 'Part of a Lr to William Bogdani Esq a Clerk of his Majesties Ordonance at the Office of Ordonance in the Tour of London 6 April 1728 Concerning that Sort of Artillery Wee call Ordonance.'

89. From William Bogdani to Maurice Johnson.
London, 12 April 1728.
MB1 fol.133A, 18 April 1728.
Thanks Johnson for his opinion on an unnamed young lady's legal case over an unhappy recent marriage to a Mr Bissey, which he discusses in detail; discusses the health of himself and his wife; wants to investigate the history of the Office of Ordnance but the archives at the Tower are in a confused state because of bad management; gives very detailed comments on Johnson's dissertation on the history of ordnance, also on the claims that Roger Bacon was the inventor of gunpowder[1] and that one of Pompey's battles took place in Spain.

[1]   This, and the preceding letter, provide a good overview of the accepted knowledge in 1728 of the history of gunpowder.

90. SGS No 76: From Browne Willis to Maurice Johnson.
Whaddon Hall, Near Fenny Stratford, Bucks, 27 May 1728.
Asks for Johnson's help for Willis's local minister Mr Clark who is visiting Lincoln and Peterborough to search for dedications of Lincolnshire churches, which Willis hopes to print; says that Clark may call on Johnson; thanks Johnson for sending him information on the dedications and patrons of churches in Holland deanery.

91. From Revd Timothy Neve to Maurice Johnson in London.
[Spalding], 17 July 1728.
Discusses controversy aroused by a pamphlet *The Spirit of the Ecclesiastics*;[1] gives a very full account of an SGS meeting, including the acceptance of the presentation of a preserved foetus and a visit to a member's garden; requests information on the age of the Alexandrian MS in the Cotton Library, which Johnson has seen.

[1]   It has not proved possible to identify this pamphlet.

92. From Roger Gale to Maurice Johnson.
London, 19 October 1728.

S^r   London, Octob.the 19th 1728
At my return to this place, from whence I had been absent near a month, I found myself indebted to you for the favour of 2 letters; the first I have not yet seen, being sent forward to Mr Wallis, whom it chiefly concerned, by the first post after it came hither: and he being in Herefordshire, as I find by one of his, it has

not yett been sent back to me. The inclosed Certificate for Wm Archer I shall take care of, as soon as it lyes in my power to send Orders for his Instruction in the Excise, but we shall give none out till Christmasse is past. The news papers, before this time, will have acquainted you with Sr Richard Manningham's[1] success at Bethlehem. I wish it had been better, having an acquaintance myself with, and a value for that Gentleman. Your Society at Spalding do's me a great honor to desire my name may be inserted among them as a Member. I should look upon myself as extreamly happy, could I have any prospect of enjoying their learned and agreeable conversation, but as I cannot hope for that in person, a correspondence must make up the defect of my wishes, and if they please to admit me as an Honorary Member, I shall not onely make my most gratefull acknowledgements for that mark of distinction conferred upon me, but whenever any thing occurs to me worth their notice, shall take care to communicate it by the first opportunity. As for the book due upon my admission, I shall have one ready when I am entitled to desire their acceptance of it, and the first time [page 2] I have the pleasure of seeing you here, shall confer with you what it shall be, least my present should happen to be a useless Duplicate. I shall obey your commands, if I have any possibility of doing it, inquiring after the Roll of St Guthlac[2], but as I have not the least acquaintance with my Lord Oxfords Library keeper, nor with anybody that knows him I almost despair of getting any information of it. I cant think your Society suffers from the paucity of it, I am sure ours here[3] is not advantaged by its numbers. Pauci Bonique[4] will carry on any work better than a multitude, who for the most part are onely a clog and dead weight upon the Industrious. We have now gott commodious Chambers in the Kings bench Walks as I am told; but the Town being very thin yet, we have had no meeting; and when we come together again I shall be glad it may be for the better than hitherto, especially the lst year, during which our Society seems to have been Turpi damnata veterno.[5] I hope, notwithstanding what you say in your letter, that some time or other we shall see some product of your curious Collections, and that you will begin soon to go to work, that you may have time to finish

Dum vires annique sinunt[6], and am Dear S^r

                    Your most obliged
                    humble Servant
                         R Gale

To Maurice Johnson Esq:
at Spalding in
Lincolnshire
Annotated by Maurice Johnson: 'Roger Gale Esq. FR & AS on being invited to be of the GS at Spalding.'
On reverse: annotation by Maurice Johnson listing the new members for that year:
'Keeper of the Records at the Tower
Alexander Pope Esq
John Gay Esq
Castle Deputy
Cotton Librarian
Rt honble Gerard de Courcy
Lord Kinsale'

1   Sir Richard Manningham (1690–1759) was a famous man-midwife and expert in obstetrics and the first to establish a lying-in hospital; SGS member 1724. See his biography in *ODNB*. He had presumably applied unsuccessfully for a post at the Bethlehem Hospital where mental conditions were treated; he published on nervous diseases.

2   An early thirteenth-century document depicting incidents from the life of St Guthlac, the seventh-century hermit of Crowland. At the time, it was owned by the antiquarian Edward Harley, second Earl of Oxford (1689–1741); it is now in the British Library (Harley MS, Roll Y6). Lord Harley accepted SGS membership in 1729 (see No 95 below).

3   The Society of Antiquaries of London. Several of its members compared it unfavourably with the Spalding society at the time as regarded enthusiasm and regularity of meetings.

4   'Few and good'.

5   'Condemned to shameful inactivity'.

6   'While strength and time permit'.

93. From William Bogdani to Maurice Johnson.
Tower [of London], 29 October 1728.
He hopes to meet Johnson at Hitchin the following month; discusses details of management of Bogdani's estate there; comments on Dr Pemberton's book on Newton;[1] praises the success of the SGS and looks forward to visiting it when business allows.

'... Tis a great pleasure to hear of the Success & Progress the Spalding Society have made, which ₍is₎ a very commendable thing, & is what is cheifly wanted in Country Towns to make their Scituation agreeable. To Man who is a sociable Creature all the advantages of Nature and Art may amuse & divert for some time, but still there remains the greatest pleasure of Life, communicating to an ingenious[2] friend ones Thoughts & Observations & at the same time receiving his, by this means we are insensibly & delightfully carried on to the most sublime Notions & most useful Conceptions. This advantage you have in Spalding (a Town separated from the rest of Mankind) & in so eminent a Degree, as to vye with those others establish'd in the Metropolis of England & other Countrys, & I do not doubt, but while assisted with your indefatigable & uncommon Industry, ~~their~~ your Journals will as deservedly gain the Esteem of the World as the Philos Collects, the Mem. de l'acad. de Seances & Acta Eruditorum[3] have already done. I own I should very readily accept your invitation of paying my Respects to that learned Body, tho' I blush to own the Motive, i.e. to receive improvement by their ingenious Conversation unable to return the Benefit. But the Business I am here Engaged in prevents my enjoying that Happiness, so must be contented to receive with pleasure (which I always do) your Epistolatory Discourses ...'

He plans to make impressions of some coins using Mr Homberg's technique.
Annotated by Johnson: 'Lr from W Bogdani Esq FR & A Societies London of the Use & Value of Socs & in Praise of that at Spalding.'

1   Henry Pemberton, *A View of Sir Isaac Newton's Philosophy* (London, 1728). The SGS library still has the edition given by Bogdani.

2   MS 'igenious'.

3   The Royal Society's *Philosophical Transactions*, the *Journal* of the French Académie des Sciences and the German *Acta Eruditorum* published in Leipzig.

1729

94. From Revd Samuel Wesley junior[1] to Maurice Johnson.
[London, week preceding 23 January 1729.]
MB2 fol.2B, 23 January 1729.
Sends Latin verses spoken by pupils at Westminster School.[2]

[1]   Samuel Wesley junior, the eldest son of the Revd Samuel Wesley of Epworth, was at this time a master at Westminster School. Like his father, but unlike his more famous brothers, he became a member of the SGS. See his entry in Appendix 2 and the paragraph about him in the entry in *ODNB* relating to his father, Revd Samuel Wesley senior.
[2]   The MB entry records that these verses were recited at the school on 17 November 1728.

95. From Edward Harley, Earl of Oxford,[1] to Maurice Johnson.
8 February 1728/9.
MB2 fol.3B, 6 March 1729.
He is pleased to accept SGS membership; explains that he is sending books to the SGS: '3 volumes of ecclesiastical writers' in the Paris edition, also a print of 'my Greek lamp' and others.

[1]   See his entry in Appendix 2.

96. SGS No 11: From Revd Samuel Wesley senior[1] to Maurice Johnson.
Epworth, 12 February 1728/9.
Explains that Johnson's letter to him had been delayed by being addressed via Bawtry instead of via Gainsborough; thanks Johnson for his 'kind offices for my son Lambert'[2] in helping to find him a Customs Service post; explains that he [Wesley] has been in Yorkshire working in 'Lord Maulton's'[3] library in connection with his book on Job, and thanks Johnson for his help with the book; discusses another author working on Job but is not concerned that this book will overlap with Wesley's; asks if a planned reprint of Pliny's 'Natural History' has been published.

[1]   Revd Samuel Wesley senior was a North Lincolnshire clergyman and the father of Revd Samuel Wesley junior (see No 94 above) and the more famous John and Charles Wesley; see his entry in Appendix 2 and his biography in *ODNB*. His book about the Book of Job in the Bible, *Dissertationes in librum Jobi*, was published in 1735.
[2]   This was his son-in-law John Lambert, a surveyor married to Wesley's daughter Anne. Wesley's signature is in a shaky hand; the text of the letter is in another, clearer hand, perhaps that of Lambert.
[3]   Thomas Watson Wentworth, Lord Malton, who had succeeded to the title in 1728, became Marquis of Rockingham in 1734 and died in 1750. His great house at Wentworth Woodhouse, near Rotherham, was partly completed at this time and was completed by his son, the second Marquis, who was briefly Prime Minister under George III.

97. From William Stukeley to Maurice Johnson.
Grantham, 15 February 1728–9.
Discusses his plan for forming a society at Ancaster, for which he has met several prospective members; explains that this location is preferred because of convenience and Roman antiquities; quotes the verses he has written in reply to a poem by Lady Hertford on the River Kennet.

98. Draft of letter from Maurice Johnson to Lord Coleraine.[1]
[Spalding], 28 February 1728/9.
Gives news of RS activities, especially the new extensions to the RS building;

gives an account of SA activities including a description of a Roman mosaic; passes on the respects of the SGS to their patron; explains that John Green has been appointed Second Secretary of SGS and that a garden of medicinal herbs is being prepared; explains that Johnson is preparing for the press a new edition of Serjeant Finch's *Institute of Laws*.[2]

[1]   Henry Hare, Lord Coleraine, was a keen antiquarian, a member of the SA and SGS member (1727), a 'beneficient member'. He was also a leading Freemason. See his biography in *ODNB*.
[2]   Sir Henry Finch, 1558–1625, was a leading lawyer, and a Puritan; see his biography in *ODNB*. There is no evidence that Maurice Johnson's edition of his legal works was printed.

99. SGS No 31: From William Stukeley to Maurice Johnson.
[Grantham], 13 March 1728–9.
MB2 fol.4A, 20 March 1729.
Apologises for being unable to meet Johnson at Ancaster as he was sent for to an ill relative of his wife's; invites Johnson to meet him at Grantham; encloses his discourse on Threekingham to be read at the Ancaster meeting.[1]

[1]   Stukeley hoped to establish a learned society to meet at Ancaster during the Quarter Sessions held there.

100. From Maurice Johnson to John Green.
[London], 3 July 1729.
MB2 fol.9B, 10 July 1729.
Gives a list of the portraits at the RS, which have been cleaned; comments on the high duty on spirits and the probable adulteration of gin which will result; discusses his visit, with George Lynn, to Lambeth Palace to present an invitation to the Archbishop of Canterbury[1] to become an SGS member, describes Lambeth Palace, its library and paintings.

[1]   William Wake, who had been Bishop of Lincoln from 1705 to 1716; he did not accept the invitation to membership. See his entry in *ODNB*.

101. SGS No 49: From Revd Samuel Whiting to Maurice Johnson [in London].
Spalding, 5 July 1729.
Gives a report from an SGS meeting where an Ode on the Earl of Winchelsea's[1] death was communicated; asks about 'the great Dr Bentley's Cause'[2] as nothing has been recently reported in newspapers about it; asks Johnson to choose a book for Whiting's gift to the SGS library.
On reverse: Diagram of the arms of the founder of Olney Church, Bucks, dated by Johnson 'July 1729'.[3]

[1]   Heneage Finch, fifth Earl of Winchelsea, died on 30 September 1726; this Ode may be the Latin eulogy *In Obitum Prænobilis Viri, HENEAGII FINCH, Comitis de WINCHELSEA, Epicedium et Apotheosis*, printed in the *Gentleman's Magazine* 53 (1783), 872. See *CP* xii. 780–1.
[2]   'Dr Bentley's Cause' was the difficulty caused by his modernist approach to philological criticism and analysis of the Bible, which was disapproved of by fellows of his college and led to a long-running dispute at Trinity College, Cambridge; see his entry in *ODNB*. The SGS were interested as Bentley had been Master of Spalding Grammar School, where Whiting was now teaching; see his entry in Appendix 2.
[3]   This is presumably by Johnson who was making notes on his journey back from London, to report later to the SGS.

102. From Revd Timothy Neve to Maurice Johnson.
Peterborough, 21 June 1729.
MB2 fol.14B, 25 September 1729.

SGS No 11   Peterborough June 21 1729
Sir,
    We return'd yesterday from our Norfolk Ramble; & was much concern'd when I
came home, that I should be so unfortunate as to be abroad just at that time, when
I might have had the Pleasure of an evenings Chat with you at Peterborough:[1]
I hope to contrive better against y[r] Return from London if you'll be so good as
to give me the least Notice when that will be. For since I remov'd hither, I've, in
order to amend a crazy Constitution, enter'd upon a course of Physic wich will
last me the whole Summer, that is frequently to make use of my Horse & Saddle
which is the Seat of Health, & therefore shall be oftener abroad, than otherwise
my own Inclination would lead me.

My Journey to Houghton was the pleasantest I ever had, we crack'd Jokes all the
way, and were as merry as good Roads, fine weather, cheerful friends & generous
wine cou'd make us. At Lynn we met with the Bishop & Chancellor[2] of Norwich,
who had an Invitation that day by the Prime Minister [3] to dine at Houghton,
where my old friend the Dean of Norwich was to meet them. We all din'd there
together & were truly much more agreeably entertaind by the conversation of
the Guests, than the delicacies of the Table, (for in good Truth the Provision
would have much better suited the plainest farmer's, than so great a mans, &
was unworthy the Hospitality of so grand a House). The Grandure of the out
and the elegancies of the inside, were worth a seeing. The apartments are nicely
finish'd, the furniture not rich, the Paintings those of the best Masters. There's a
vast Profusion of Marble, several Antique Busts, curious Carvings, guildings &c.

The model of the House does not please our Dean's Taste, it is an oblong Square
with a Dome of carved, or rather rib'd stone at each corner, which he says are
highly improper for a private Building, & look too heavy insomuch that the
House seems to groan under their wait. But as I pretend no critical knowledge
in the Science of Architecture, I must own I was struck with its Magnificence,
tho not a large Pile: its strength & plainness made me fancy it much beyond all
the finicalness of Gothic garniture, & to come up to the ancient Simplicity of
Greece or Rome.

Upon the Road the Dean gave me this Translation of the celebrated Epitaph in
the Tatler
                    Underneath this stone doth lye
                    As much Virtue as could[4] dye
                    Which when alive did Vigour give
                    To as much beauty as could live[5]

the two last of which are a little nonsence.
                    Quanta mori potuit Virtus, et vivere quanta
                    Forma potest, eheu! conditur hoc Tumulo.

We are now return'd to partake of the feasting of the Audit which begins to
morrow, the Dean[6] & Chapter are going to make great Alterations in our Library,

to which there have been of late 2 great Benefactors, the late Bishop Kennet[7] & Dr Carter our late Prebendary, who gave all his Latin & Greek Books to Peterborough. They were last night for engaging me in the troublesom work of a Librarian, that is to dispose those several thousand Books, that are lately given, & for which they have made new Classes[8] in their proper order. I so far have promis'd to give my helping hand but not to take the whole management upon my self. However so far I will consent in order to get a key to my self. I hope by the time you return from London, we shall have them in some forwardness.

And now, Sir, I hope you left your good Lady & all the family well at Spalding, whom I think to wait upon before you come back. I thank you very heartily for your generous presents to my Son & Daughter, I blush even at the mention of it, as not being conscious to my self that I've merited such rewards. I hope & desire the Continuance of yours & the friendship of the rest of the good family, to whom I am indebted for many favours – My Brother [*gap caused by removal of seal*] s in Service to your self & Mr John and likewise the compliments of the female part of this family. I am, Sir,

Y[r] most oblig'd
and most humble Servant
T. Neve

To Maurice Johnson Esq
at the Widows Coffea
House in Devereaux Court
    Inner Temple
        London.

Annotated by Maurice Johnson: 'L[r] from Rev[d] Mr Tim. Neve MA Secr SG Peterb. & of the GSS ab[t] <u>Houghton</u> hall; Latin transl. of epitaph in the Tatler written by Mr Waller.'

[1] Neve was now a Minor Canon of Peterborough Cathedral and was planning to found the PGS at this time, as Johnson's note indicates. See Neve's entry in Appendix 2.

[2] The Bishop of Norwich was William Baker (Bishop 1721–1733); the Chancellor was Thomas Tanner, the famous antiquarian. The Dean, mentioned a few lines later was Thomas Cole (Dean 1724–1731).

[3] Robert Walpole (Prime Minister, 1721–1742). This is a very early use of this title as other than a term of ridicule; it began as a satirical name for Walpole as the senior minister of the Government and later became the accepted term for the Leader of the Government. Walpole's great house in north Norfolk, Houghton Hall, had just been completed.

[4] MS 'good'.

[5] This is an early eighteenth-century version, in an essay in the *Spectator* (not the *Tatler*), of Ben Jonson's 'Epitaph on Elizabeth L.H.'

Underneath this stone doth lie
As much beauty as could die
Which in life did harbour give
To more virtue than could live.

[6] Dean of Peterborough.

[7] White Kennett, Bishop of Peterborough 1718–1728.

[8] Bookcases.

103. SGS No 50: From George Lynn junior to Maurice Johnson.
Southwick, 1 September 1729.
Provides details of the Sutton family of Knaith (Lincs); discusses his use of a

former family chapel at Southwick for his books and prints; comments on a mineral spring in his grounds; promises to send a cat to the Johnson family.

104. SGS No 75: From Beaupré Bell to Maurice Johnson.
Beaupré Hall, 12 September 1729.
MB2 fol.15A, 25September 1729.
Discusses the books and seeds which he is sending to Spalding for Johnson. Also sends the arms of Walpole and a paper of abbreviations to be included in the SGS volume 'Alphabet of Arts and Sciences'.[1]

[1]   This collection and explanation of artistic, scientific and legal abbreviations was begun but not completed. It is still at Spalding.

105. SGS No 98: From John Harries[1] to 'Rev. Mr Neeve' in Peterborough, 'per Captn. Pollexfen'.
Antigua, 25 September 1729.
Postscript added 2 October 1729.
MB2 fol.19B, 18 December 1729.
Expresses gratitude for SGS membership; explains that he is making a collection for Spalding of seeds, shells, 'Reptiles in Rum'; comments that he has plans for coming home to claim an estate in Herefordshire but may then settle in Antigua; gives a description of local rarities including an albino 'Negro girl' and a 'whirlwind', also 'petrifactions'.

[1]   See his entry in Appendix 2.

106. No 62: From Maurice Johnson to John Johnson.
Undated portion of letter, dateable from MB entry as [London] shortly before 29 November 1729.
MB2 fol.19A.
He has bought a print of a flowering aloe; discusses a case of medical treatment with cantharides, once banned but now prescribed; comments on the Royal College of Physicians' refusal to accept foreign qualifications; discusses the latest legal appointments; gives an account of a case relating to fire insurance.

107. SGS No 39: Copy of part of a letter to Lord Hertford, as President of the SA, from an unspecified person; Lord Hertford permitted Johnson to copy this section.
December 1729. No day specified, but copied and read to SGS by Maurice Johnson on 25 December 1729.[1]
MB2 fol.20A, 25 December 1729.
Provides a very detailed description of a Roman pavement discovered at Littlecote Park, near Ramsbury (Wilts).

[1]   It is an interesting tribute to the dedication of Johnson and the SGS that the regular weekly meetings continued even on Christmas Day; it also throws light on the nature of Christmas celebrations at the period.

108. SGS No 20: From Henry Johnson[1] to Maurice Johnson.
Panama, 15 December 1729. English postmark 17 AP [17 April 1730].

Panama Decem[r] the 15th 1729

Dear Maurice,
At last you see by the date of this that I am again got to my old Post after a

tedious Journey of 6 months by land and by Water from London, in which space of time I mett with various adventures too tedious to relate but when I publish my book of Knight errantry these will also appear, let it suffice for the present that this is the first time in my Life that I have known the want of Water for our voyage from Jamaica to Porto Bello was not performed in less than 7 weeks although the distance is but 180 leagues and is usually done in 4 days, judge you therefore of our necessitys, in short we had like to have perished. Nor are my fategues less on Shoar for the Spaniards now look upon us all as Poltroons, & since the wonderful feats of our Squadrons on these coasts they hold our Nation in the utmost contempt, in so much that here they refuse to comply with the Preliminary Articles, & we are no better than Prisoners at large; so God knows when this epistle will come to hand, for I write by way of an amusement to beguile the tedious hours of captivity. I lost my good Friend & companion Mr Rigby who dyed in Jamaica, so by his death I am come to possess the sounding name of President of the Royal Assiento of Great Brittain in these parts. [page 2] alas I have only the Title, the Substance is not with me, but I hope if affairs shall be a little cleared up to reap the advantage also.

I shall not tire your patience with tedious descriptions of which you have so often heard & read from me & others of these countrys. I shall only relate to you what happened here in this part of the world which to all [erasure] seemed wonderful & I know to a person so curious as yourself the story will not be unacceptable. One Senor Romero a native Spaniard, but inhabitant of Lima in very mean circumstances happened at last to cohabit with a young Indian Woman who by degrees contracted so great an affection for him that after some time she carried him to the inland country of Peru and shewed him an old Indian Grave which she told him she by tradition knew to contain great Treasure, and upon opening it appeared matter of Fact for the same man passed thro: this place last January in his way to Spain with 400,000 Dollars which he openly confessed & paid dutys for the same with other treasures which no doubt he concealed. in the same grave he also found the body entire & perfectly sound of an Indian Man his face hands & feet of the ordinary size of Men but the length of his Body no more than three quarters of a Spanish yard which is ⅛th less than ours,[2] his hair & beard perfect his eyes & mouth open & all his teeth sound, his Skin dry & hard like leather, of the same colour of all Indians here, Senor Romero carryed this body in order to present to the King of Spain in a little box wrapped up in cotton, the Lady in whose house I am had the care of the same during the time it was in Panama & used every day to expose it to the Sun, tho: it had not the least ill smell, the poor Indian girl[3] notwithstanding all her affection to the ungrateful Spaniard was left behind, & he is gone alone to Europe to spend their treasure – you may report their Story for certain truth, here are thousands who can avouch it, I am sorry no one had the Skill or curiosity to take a drawing of the said corpse with the exact dimensions which would have been a great curiosity & another thing no less wonderful is a living corpse I mean a Woman here in Panama of one hundred & forty two years of age has all her senses perfect, and her hair & teeth have grown again, I have not yet seen her, but intend it, that I may have satisfaction to report it from my own knowledge. I have now filled my sheet, so must conclude of force.

with affectionate Service to all the good family in Spalding from

Dear Maurice   Your truly Affectionate humble Servant
                      Hen. Johnson

To Maurice Johnson jun[r]
Esq at Spalding
in Lincolnshire
Annotated by Maurice Johnson: 'L[r] from the Honoured Henry Johnson Esquire
President of the Royal Assiento a member of SAL & SGS. State of our Trade
with Spain & in America. Strange History of Señor Romero & a Peruvian Lady
– Coins of an Ynca & Treasures taken out of his Tomb his Corps sent to the King
of Spain, a Woman at Panama 142 yeares old.'

[1]   Henry Johnson, a relation of Maurice Johnson and a traveller and merchant (see his entry in
Appendix 2) was at that time the President of the Royal Asiento of Panama, an organisation of
English merchants; the Royal Asiento of 1713–1750 was a concession by Spain granting Britain to
right to supply 'negro slaves' to the Spanish empire, initially for 30 years. His published work (1748)
was not an account of his travels but a translation of Piedra Lozano's account of an earthquake in
Lima in 1746, accompanied by his own account of the customs and natural history of Peru, *A true
and particular relation of the dreadful earthquake which happened at Lima*.
[2]   Note by Maurice Johnson: 'about 22 Inches'.
[3]   MS 'guirl'.

109. From Revd Barnaby Goche to Maurice Johnson.
[Crowland], 16 January [in 1720s; Goche became an SGS member in 1723 and
died in 1730].[1]
Provides the English version of a Greek epithalamion, supposed to be by Homer
but not found in any printed edition.

[1]   It is not possible to date this more precisely as no entry in the Minute Books relating to it has
been found. Goche, or Gooche, the incumbent of Crowland, dates his letters to Johnson with day and
month, but does not add the year. See Goche's entry in Appendix 2.

1730

110. SGS No 43: Copy of letter from Maurice Johnson on behalf of the SGS to
Academia Etrusca, Cortona, Italy.[1]
[Spalding], Calendis Januarii [1 January] 1730.
MB2 fols 23A and 23B, 15 January 1730.
In Latin; requests this Italian learned society to correspond with the SGS; lists
significant SGS members, gives a brief history of learning in Spalding and an
account of the SGS's current activities to indicate that the SGS is worthy to
correspond with them.

[1]   The letter was to be sent via Lord Coleraine who, on a previous visit, had been admitted to
membership of the Italian learned society, had discussed the SGS with them and obtained their agreement to correspond with the SGS.

111. SGS No 30: Copy of letter from Maurice Johnson[1] on behalf of SGS to
Johannes Kouwenhove,[2] Rotterdam.
[Spalding], Calendis Januarii [1 January] 1730.
MB2 fol.23B, 15 January 1730.
In Latin; invites him to accept membership of the SGS and to encourage Burman
and Boerhaave[3] to accept membership, so that the SGS could correspond

with learned men in Leiden; lists the English doctors who have studied under
Boerhaave at Leiden who are now SGS members: Robert Mitchell, John Dinham
and George Bolton; gives an account of the history of learning in Spalding and of
the SGS library, to indicate that the SGS is suitable for them to correspond with.

1   Some of this letter is the same as the previous letter to the Academia Etrusca, but Maurice
Johnson has given it a distinctive angle by emphasising links with Holland and with the University
of Leiden in particular.
2   Johnson notes in Latin at the head of the letter that this letter is to be taken by Johannes Weyman,
an SGS member who is Dutch; he adds personal greetings from the Johnson family to Kouwenhove,
a Rotterdam lawyer, who is related to Weyman.
3   Professors at the University of Leiden; Boerhaave was famous for his work in chemistry. Dr
John Green of the SGS studied at Leiden; see No 155 below for further references to Boerhaave and
Burman.

112. From Revd Timothy Neve to Maurice Johnson.
[Peterborough], 14 January 1729/30.
MB2 fol.23B, 22 January 1730.
Describes King John's Tower, Thorpe,[1] near Peterborough; gives a detailed
account of the wall-paintings and building; gives a full account of the anatomy
of a swan and explains how this is connected with the ability of birds to sing;
comments on the work of Revd Joseph Sparke[2] as librarian at Peterborough.

1   Now Longthorpe Tower, well-known for its mediaeval wall-paintings.
2   Sparke, a Peterborough clergyman, owned property in Spalding which he leased to the SGS for
its meetings during the 1720s and 1730s; see his entry in Appendix 2 and in *ODNB*.

113. SGS No 12: From Revd Samuel Whiting to Maurice Johnson in London.
'E cubiculo meo Spald.',[1] 23 February 1729 [actual date 1730: see MB entry].
MB2 fol.24B, 12 February 1730.
Letter in Latin. Explains that Whiting has been busy with his work as a
schoolmaster; he knows Johnson is less censorious of stylistic efforts in Latin
composition than Bentley[2] so he will not judge his letter too harshly; comments
that Johnson's letters are being communicated to the SGS on Thursdays; gives
an account of SGS activities, explaining that though there was a thin attendance
in Johnson's absence the level of activity has now revived; asks him to enquire
about Hutchinson's edition of Xenophon.

1   'From my bedroom in Spalding'.
2   Dr Richard Bentley, the Classical scholar. See note to No 101 above.

114. From Revd Timothy Neve to Maurice Johnson.
Weston, 5 March 1729/30.
MB2 fol.26A, 9 April 1730.
Discusses, in great detail, the content of the published pamphlet *Alkibla*[1] and its
author's views, especially on the origins of the practice of bowing towards the
east at the name of Jesus during Church worship, and on the Last Judgement;
comments on the success of the SGS and discusses the possibility of a history of
the society being produced.

1   A pamphlet by William Asplin, published in 1728, about styles of church worship.

115. SGS No 13: From John Green[1] to Maurice Johnson.
Tower of London,[2] 7 March 1729/30.
Refers to Colonel Chartres[3] who 'has been the buzz of the town', discussing

his trial and conviction and expecting that he will be executed; comments on recent poems including a poem 'to the Pretender on the Pope's death', 'The Rape' [about Col. Chartres], and 'An Epistle from Calista to Allamant supposed my Lady Abergeny[4] to my Lord by Lady Mary Wortley Montagu'.

[1]   See his entry in Appendix 2.
[2]   John Green was staying at the Tower of London in the spring of 1730, presumably as a guest of William Bogdani, a member of the SGS and a regular correspondent with Johnson. This London visit may have been in connection with Green's medical studies.
[3]   Col. Francis Chartres or Charteris (1665–1732): see his biography in *ODNB*. A notorious gambler, he was well known for his dissolute behaviour and is thought to figure in Plate 1 of Hogarth's 'The Harlot's Progress'; he was accused of rape several times, and in 1729 was tried for the rape of a maidservant and sentenced to death, but pardoned; he died soon afterwards.
[4]   Lady Abergavenny, wife of William Nevill, 16th Baron Nevill and Lord Abergavenny.

116. SGS No 135: From John Green to Maurice Johnson.
Tower of London, 10 April 1730.
MB2 fol.26A, 16 April 1730.
Has visited Windsor: gives an account of 'the late [Earl of] Codogan's Extravagance which the present [Earl] is destroying … at Cavasham a mile from Reading',[1] describing the house and garden with its statues, and regretting that the garden is to be ploughed up; discusses an inscription in Okingham Church; sends details of a bill of fare from the Tower, dated 28 October 1478, 'for the Worshipful Company of Wax Chandlers'; discusses a motto by Sir Robert Walpole written on a window in the Tower; discusses subscribing to a book by Sir Andrew Ramsay[2] and mentions the seeds which he has bought for Maurice Johnson.

[1]   Caversham Park, the Earl of Cadogan's house near Reading.
[2]   Andrew Michael Ramsay (1681–1743), SGS member; his book *Les Voyages de Cyrus* was published in 1727 and became a great success in France and England. See his entry in *ODNB*.

117. From Weaver Bickerton[1] to Maurice Johnson.
[London], Undated; date stamp 18 AP. [Dateable to 1730 by publication dates of books referred to and MB reference.]
MB2 fol.26B, 23 April 1730.
Explains that Dr Tindal has just published Vol. I of 'Xtianity as old as the Creation'[2] and the Bishop of Salisbury has published two volumes of Dr Clarke's sermons.

[1]   Bickerton was a publisher and bookseller in Devereux Court, London, near the coffee-house from which Johnson dated many of his London letters.
[2]   Matthew Tindal, *Christianity as old as the Creation, or the gospel, a republication of the religion of Nature,* Vol. I (1730).

118. From Revd Timothy Neve to Maurice Johnson.
[Peterborough], 29 April 1730.
MB2 fol.27B, 30 April 1730.
Discusses Tindal's *Christianity as old as the Creation* and the religious disputes in London; mentions other books which Neve and other benefactors are purchasing for the SGS; comments ironically on John Green's residence at the Tower and his study to become a physician: 'he has quite thrown off all those religious old-fashioned conceits that his uncle and I had years together taken pains[1] to inculcate on his mind, so that I believe he will make an excellent physician'.

[1]   As schoolmasters of Spalding Grammar School.

119. SGS No 28: From Major-General Robert Hunter to Maurice Johnson.
Jamaica, 1 May 1730.
MB2 fol.41A, 7 January 1731.
He has heard from 'Mr Johnston at Cartagena'[1] but not since he went to Panama;
thanks Johnson for the good account of the prosperity of the Crowland estate
which has yielded 'Nothing but trouble and Expens' previously; explains that Mr
Crawford is to pay £3 for a book for Hunter's donation to the SGS library, as it
cannot easily be sent from Jamaica.[2]

[1]   This was Henry Johnson: see his letter (No 108 above) from Panama, dated 15 December 1729.
[2]   Johnson's annotation states that Hunter's letter of 27 May 1727 had promised the best edition of
Bayle's *Dictionary* for the SGS. Mr Crawford was a gentleman living at Crowland (Lincs), who had
been an SGS member since 1727. Johnson was steward of Hunter's estate at Crowland.

120. From Beaupré Bell to Maurice Johnson.
London, 18 May 1730.
MB2 fol.28B, 21 May 1730.
Gives lengthy details of coins of Carausius;[1] encourages Johnson to print his own
work on this subject; wishes Johnson had explained his methods so Bell could
help; discusses family legal affairs relating to arrears of Lady Oldfield's annuity.

[1]   The coinage of the Roman Emperor Carausius was a particular interest to numismatists of the
time, especially as Carausius spent time in Britain, ruling there as a rebel Emperor, and died there
in AD 293, killed by his finance minister Allectus who succeeded him. Johnson and Stukeley, who
collected coins of his reign, hoped to establish that he was of British origins, though he is now known
to have come from Gallia Belgica. Johnson produced a draft of an account of the coins produced in
his reign and that of Allectus, which was amended by Beaupré Bell but it was never published; it was
lent to Stukeley who drew on it for his own publication about the coinage of Carausius, *The medallic
history of Marcus Aurelius Valerius Carausius, Emperor in Britain,* 2 vols (London, 1757 and1759).
A number of letters in this collection deal with coins from his reign: Nos 15, 50, 120, 141, 150, 160,
165, 167, 168, 197, 209, 226, 233, 234, 235, 236, 285, 295, 399, 452, 515, 558, 564 and 566.

121. From Revd Timothy Neve to Maurice Johnson.
[Peterborough], 20 May 1730.
MB2 fol.28B, 21 May 1730.
Discusses books to be brought from London which are presents for the SGS
library, including a Polyglot Bible presented by Mrs Deacon;[1] informs him
that John Johnson, as Treasurer, has requested copies of Newton's works from
Newton's nephew 'Mr Tompson';[2] requests a copy of the SGS rules to serve as a
foundation for a new society at Peterborough.

[1]   This is still in the SGS library with an inscription recording Mrs Deacon's gift. It is unusual in
being presented by a woman, who is recorded as being a generous benefactor in Johnson's list of
the SGS's benefactors. Mary Deacon, born at Spalding, was the widow of a Canon of Peterborough
Cathedral; her generosity and that of her husband are recorded on his memorial in Peterborough
Cathedral.
[2]   Carrier Thompson, son-in-law of Sir Isaac Newton's half-brother Benjamin Smith. Thompson's
wife Hannah, Smith's daughter, was one of the eight named heirs to Newton's fortune of £31,000 in
1727.

122. SGS No 38: From James Rowland to Maurice Johnson.
Bath, 3 June 1730.
MB2 fol.30A, 18 June 1730.

SGS No 38   Bath[1] June 3[d] 1730
Mr Secretary,
    Remember 'tis your own Order to a wandering unintelligent Member, that
occasions this impertinent Epistle, & draws upon you an unreasonable expence,[2]
it would provoke a Stoick to be charged two Groats for a Letter of intelligence,
which begins
S[r]   You must expect to find nothing here, but what you know much better
before; It wou'd be geat folly & presumtion in me to think of making any
Observations in my sudden short progress; that can have escaped the knowledge
of so Curious a person as the Ingenious Mr Johnson: I doubt not but when our
Society have duely consider'd that one penny more than the Expence of this
wou'd have purchased a Fowl noted to be much more clear sighted than your dull
Correspondent; they'll make a Bye Law that for the future no Letters be received
without Postage paid.
    At Hampton Court I saw two persons Copying the Cartoons in Peices full as
large as the Originalls & which I own to you pleased me much better: you see
what a Judg I am of Paintings: these are designed to be made into Tapistry. There
is a very fine Closset fitting up & Guilding for Her Majesty[3] adjoining to the
Picture Gallery at Winsor, & severall old Towers are repairing against the Court
comes there; I saw the Curious Amber Cabinet lately presented to her Majesty
and a Small Screen of the Princess Royalls own work. The Physick Garden at
Oxford is neglect & overrun with weeds & Grass like a Common Feild only the
Ever Greens are kept in order; the Greens in the Presidents Garden at Maudlin
[Magdalen College] are very Curious & fine; and the Maze at Trinity is pretty &
pleasant.
    The Antique Statues & inscriptions that formerly stood around the Theator are
now fixt about the Windows in the Picture Gallery; I saw those & the Bodleian
Library of a Holyday morning when the place was cleaning & in a Cloud of dust,
so that I cou'd distinguish nor understood but very little in that great Collection
of Learning & Antiquity; you see how luckily I happened of an Opportunity to
cover my Ignorance: I also saw the Museum, but all in confusion the Monsters of
the Deep & the Deserts lay quietly together in one common heap & the Curiositys
of the East & West Indies lay undistinguished about the Floor cover'd with dust.
Blenheim Pallace is kept nicely cleane, but to our great mortification the Fine
Brussels Tapistrys of the Dukes Battles are kept cover'd & not to be seen but
when the Duchess is there.

As to the Rarities of Bath perhaps you'll think I take the priviledge of some other
Travailours should I tell you; Here are Statesmen, Philosophers Beaux Ladies
Clowns & Conjurers, Singers & Dancers all inanimate yet each act their Severall
parts with a Graceful Air & Mein almost equall to St James's or Drurylane
Lincolns Inn or Deeping Fen. And here's a Road made for Carriages to pass
two Miles laden with Severall Tuns weight without any Cattle to draw them[4]; yet
require skilful Drivers, for if they get loose from their managers will outrun the
swiftest Greyhounds & give way to none it is well it happens to be a bye Post
road: The stone used in Building Greenwich Hospitall passes this way; Had we

the convenience of such a contrivance for carrying off our waters; I doubt not but it wou'd be adjudged a better & more certaine method for draining the Fens than that invented by Captain Perry:[5] This Road is made at a great Expence upon peices of Timber about a foot & an half distance & in many places shodd with Iron.

I was last week at Bristoll where is the finest & largest Parochial Church I ever saw, said to be built at the Expence of one Private Person; In the middle of the City many of the Streets are narrow, the Buildings Old & hanging over like London before the Fire; the Key & Square are fine & Large, the River narrow & by the Hot Well runs between very high inaccessible rocks, where are got the Bristol Diamonds[6] a peice of which I have procured to put into Spalding Museum.

To divert you a little after this stupid Account of my Travails I have sent you a New Song I met with here, tho perhaps by this time the Children buy the same in Spalding Market for a halfpenny, thus you see what a rarity I have found out at last to send the Society, to whom pray present my most Humble Service.

We intend to set out on Monday next for Stonehedge, & from thence by way of Salisbury & Winchester into Sussex and hope to be in London in about three Weeks time;
my Wife joines in due respects to all your Good Family from
   Sr Your Humble Servant
   J. Rowland

The Beau Monde, or the Pleasures of St James's; A Ballad[7]

Oh! St James's is a lovely place
Tis better than the City
For there are Balls & Operas
And every thing that's pretty

There's little Lady Cuzzoni
And bouncing Dame Faustina
The Duce a Bit will either Sing
Unless they're both a Queen-a

And when we've ek'd out History
And made them Rival Queens;
They'll warble sweetly on the Stage
And scold behind the Scenes.
 Oh! St James's etc.

When having fill'd their Pockets full
No longer can they stay;
But turn their Backs upon the town
And scamper all away.

The Belles & Beaux cry after them,
With all their might & main
And Heidegger is sent in hast
To fetch 'em back againe.
 Oh! St James's etc.

Then Hey! For a Subscription
To the Opera, or the Ball;
The Silver Ticket walks about
Untill there comes a Call.

This puts them into Doleful Dumps;
Who were both Blithe & Gay;
There's nothing spoils Diversion more
Than telling what's to pay.
   Oh! St James's etc.

There's Pope has made the Witlings mad,
Who labour all they can;
To pull his Reputation down
And man the little Man.

But Wit & he so close are link'd
In vain is all this Pother;
They never can demolish one
Without destroying 'tother
   Oh! St James's etc.

And there's Miss Polly Peachum lugs
Our Nobles by the Eares,
Till Ponder Well, by farr Exceeds
The Musick of the Spheres.

When Lo! to show the Wisdom Great
Of London's famous Town
We set her up above herself
And then we take her down.
   Oh! St James's etc.

And there's your Beaux with powder'd Cloaths
Bedaub'd from Head to Shin:
Their Pocket-holes adorn'd with Gold,
But not a Souse[8] within.

And there's your pretty Gentlemen
All dressed in Silk & Sattin;
That get a Spice of everything
Excepting Sence & Latin.
   Oh! St James's etc.

And there's your Cits that leave the [*section missing*]
In Finsbury so sweet
But costlier Tits they keep, God wot!
In Bond & Poultney-Street

And there's your green Nobility
On Citizens so witty,
Whose Fortune & Gentility

Arose from Londons City
   Oh! St James's etc.

We go to Bed when others rise;
And dine at Candle light;
There's nothing mends Complexion more
Than turning Day to Night.

For what is Title, Wealth or Wit,
If Folks are not Genteel?
Or how can they be said to live
Who know not what's Quadrille?
   Oh! St James's etc.

Annotated by Maurice Johnson: 'L^r from Mr J. Rowland SGS Curiosities in his Tour at <u>Hampton Court, Windsor, Oxford Un</u>. <u>Blenheim Castle</u> & <u>Bristol City</u>.'

[1]   This would be of interest to Johnson, who had made a journey to Bath as a young man in 1710. He recorded it in the *Iter Bathonense*, a series of letters in Latin to his former headmaster at Spalding, Revd John Waring; this MS is in the SGS's archives. See Rowland's entry in Appendix 2.

[2]   The recipient, not the sender, usually paid for the letter, unless the sender agreed to pay or it could be 'franked' by an MP, in which case no postage was payable. The 'groats' in the next line are a joking reference; the groat, worth 4d, had gone out of use as a coin in 1662, but it gives some idea of the expense of posting, usually borne in the SGS's case by Maurice Johnson as Secretary.

[3]   Queen Caroline, wife of George II, died 1737.

[4]   This was Ralph Allen's rail track, very recently built, which transported stone down from his quarries above Bath. 'Cattle' was a popular term for horses used for drawing vehicles. Allen was also responsible for organising the 'cross posts' or 'bye posts' which took mail along local post roads and thus delivered it more quickly. Previously all mail had to travel via London.

[5]   Captain John Perry, SGS member and internationally well-known drainage engineer, involved in Fen drainage schemes; see his entry in *ODNB*.

[6]   A form of rock crystal or quartz found at Bristol, polished and used in making ornaments.

[7]   This was written by Henry Carey (1689–1743) a song-writer and playwright, best known for *Sally in our Alley*. St James's Palace was the London centre of the Court and the fashionable area. This satirical ballad refers to the latest events in the arts, including references to popular rival opera singers Francesca Cuzzoni and Faustina Bordoni and to two famous members of the SGS, both joining in 1728: Alexander Pope the poet and John Gay, author of the current successful musical play *The Beggar's Opera*, first produced in 1729, with its heroine Polly Peachum. It indicates that the cult of celebrity and the pursuit of fashion are not only modern phenomena. The 'Quadrille' referred to in the last verse was a fashionable card game.

[8]   Souse: sol or sou, a small coin.

123. SGS No 53: From Maurice Johnson to Revd Samuel Whiting.
Devereux Court [London], 18 June 1730.

Gives an account of the latest learned news and gossip from London, including the death of Dr Rutty, Secretary of the RS, the possibility of Dr Mortimer becoming Secretary and the proposed publication by 'Mr Hornsby and Mr Ward'[1] of a collection of all the Roman inscriptions found in Britain; expresses satisfaction that the SGS continues to meet through the summer when the RS and SA have ceased their activities.

On reverse, Latin epigrams collected by Johnson.

[1]   Cromwell Mortimer, an SGS member, was Secretary of the RS; see his entry in Appendix 2. John Horsley published *Britannia Romana, or the Roman Antiquities of Britain* in 1732, dedicating it to Sir Richard Ellys, a member of the SGS; John Ward was a significant antiquary and librarian and Professor of Rhetoric at Gresham College (see his entries in *ODNB* and in Appendix 2).

124. From George Lynn junior to Maurice Johnson.
Southwick, 22 July 1730.
MB2 fol.32A, 23 July 1730.
Discusses plans for a family visit by the Lynns to their cousins in Spalding; gives the dimensions of the Royal William, given to him in October 1729: ' 'tis said to be the largest ship that has been built'.

125. From Roger Gale to Maurice Johnson.
London, 11 August 1730.
Explains about his donation to the SGS library,[1] to be brought by Mr Warlow, Supervisor of the Excise, who is coming to survey Spalding.

¹   Johnson's annotation states that the book is Maffei's *History of Amphitheatres,* translated by Alexander Gordon (1730). The following letter also refers to it. This book is still in the SGS library.

126. SGS No 47: From Roger Gale to Maurice Johnson.
London, 23 September 1730.
MB2 fol.35B, 1 October 1730.
Refers to a controversy about amphitheatres from Maffei's book, which he has presented to the Society; provides a long series of replies to five questions from Johnson, particularly about the existence of Roman amphitheatres in Britain, about Roman coins and also books, including one which he identifies as probably André du Chesne's *History of England.*[1]

¹   For further details of this letter, see John Nichols (ed.), 'Reliquiæ Galeanæ', printed in *Bibliotheca Topographica Britannica* (London, 1780–90), iii. 285–6 and 289.

127. From Sir Richard Ellys[1] to Maurice Johnson.
29 September 1730.
MB2 fol.35B, 1 October 1730.

To Maurice Johnson Esq
Dear Sir
   Business I have had & journies I have made, since I had the favour of yours; but I easily see it is in vain to plead any thing of that kind after so long a neglect. I will frankly own my fault, and ask pardon, only assuring you it was not from any want of regard or respect for you. The account you ~~gave~~ sent me of what pass'd at Cambridge, was new & very agreeable to me, & I had it since confirm'd to me by one that was there, with the same character you gave of the Master of Bennett Coll[2] & Dr Williams. But what must I say for my Self to the Rev^d Mr Wesley. I receiv'd the proposal[3], am not a little pleas'd with the design, & very desirous to give it all the encouragement, that lies in my power. If he still be with you, or within reach of you, pray let him know it, with my humble service. What fine subjects for <u>Dissertations</u>? What pleasure must they give, well handled? I am delighted with the very thoughts of it, after the character you give of the learned Author: that he is in every respect equal to the great undertaking.
   And now, Sir, give me leave to finish with assuring you I am very sensible of the honour of being enroll'd among so many Great names, and shall always do what lies in my power to serve so useful a design & am
             S^r your most faithful

humble servant
Sept. 29 [17]30   R.Ellys
Annotated by Maurice Johnson: 'L^r from Sir Richd Ellys Bartt on his being admitted a Member of the Gentlemens Society in Spalding.'

[1]   See his entry in Appendix 2.
[2]   Corpus Christi College, Cambridge, earlier known as Benet College.
[3]   Revd Samuel Wesley of Epworth, SGS member and father of John and Charles; this was the proposal to publish his book on the Book of Job, referred to in No 96 above (12 February 1728/9).

128. SGS No 52: From William Stukeley to Maurice Johnson.
Stamford, 9 October 1730.
MB2 fol.36B, 22 October 1730.
Provides a detailed discussion of clean and unclean creatures as set out in the Book of Leviticus; discusses the history of the practice of sacrificing; hopes Johnson will visit the Deeping society.[1]

[1]   One of a number of short-lived local societies of the early eighteenth century; Stukeley attended and encouraged it while he lived at Stamford, close to the Deepings.

129. From Revd Timothy Neve to Maurice Johnson.
[Peterborough], 19 October 1730.
MB2 fol.36B, 22 October 1730.
Offers a detailed account of the beginning of the PGS in 1730 and its early activities.

130. From Revd Timothy Neve to Maurice Johnson.
Peterborough, 26 November 1730.
MB2 fol.39B, 31 December 1730.
Provides an account of the recent PGS meetings; gives a full account of Roman coins found between March and Wisbech.

131. SGS No.57: From Maurice Johnson to John Johnson.
[London], 5 December 1730.
MB2 fol.37B, 24 December 1730.
Discusses the prologue to *Ignoramus* spoken by the Captain of Westminster School, quotes it, also the epilogue and a speech from the play;[1] gives the latest SA news including the examination of a mediæval pectoral cross and a coin of Vespasian; asks John Johnson to attend the Croyland Court Leet for him as he is detained by legal cases in London, and gives details of what is to be done there.

[1]   The quotations were provided by Revd Samuel Wesley junior, Usher at Westminster School and SGS member. *Ignoramus*, a Latin comedy which is a satire against lawyers, was written by George Ruggle (see his biography in *ODNB*) in 1615. It was very popular in the seventeenth and eighteenth centuries and frequently performed in the universities and schools.

132. From Maurice Johnson to John Johnson.
[London], 15 December 1730.

SGS No 74   Devereaux Court
Dearest Broth^r
    I wrote to You largely from Wellen & Hitchin hope You received that Long Letter & am forced to begin this early knowing I shall be much straightened

other wise. The New Tragedy of Medæa[1] is a Translation from the Greek, & hurry'd into the House by the Spirit of Spight to anticipat & prevent One written by an Ingenious Young Gentleman on the same subject, but not a Translation this peice of Spite has a good deal provoked the Grubean Dunces, against Colley Cibber[2] the new Laureat, but whom all the wreaths of Delos, though he were loaded with Them, could not make a Poet. One Epigram on him ends thus (I only heard It repeated where I dined on Sunday, by a Gent I've no Acquaintance with) as I remember

The New Yeares Ode whilest Cibber sings
Oldfield[3] lyes buryd with our Kings.

But a keener Satyrist whom you know gave us these
Or something like 'em

When Roguey Pope foretold in Rhime
The Reign of Dulness in our Clime
Eusden says he shall wear the Bays
Cibber be Chancellor of Plays
Eusden alas is Snatcht by Fate:
The Goddess to support her State
Bids Cibber now be Laureat too
Her own Outdoings to Outdo.

My Couz G.Lynn who got this Frank and intends to've used It to You last post but had not time & as he says the Noble Lord who franked It[4] at the Soc. of Antiq. & all Friends there where I could not be present their Services to You and greet the Cell[5] as do the Drs. Jurin & Massey whom he see at the Royal Soc: where the worthy Præsident Sr. Hans Sloan[6] made a good Solemn & Serious Oration to the Company which was very numerous Upon some indecent Liberties taken by ˄some of the Members of laughing at what was communicated there if It didn't happen to hit their Tast, or was less accurate than a Man would have printed It, & more particularly if the well meaning Correspondent mentioned the name of God, which they ought to hear as well as pronounce with reverence & all their Efforts in their Enquiries ought to be as their Charter proposes Ad majorem Dei Creatoris Omnipotentis Gloriam.[7] This was doing his Duty &[8] becoming a Great Physician Philosopher & Christian Man, & I could Wish the same sentiments were now & then inculcated at Every Society for the sake of those who fantcy themselves not under so great Obligations to the Allwise & ruling Providence of Allmighty God, as to speak of him or hear his Name mencioned with Awe & humble reverence, Or that they are So, knowing that many things are not worth their notics, & therefore instead of recieving them with attention of Even patient Civility, make a Jest, as farr a Sneer gos, of what they may when they think better, find conducive to some usefull End, and towards the Attainment of Knowledge though perhapps not in their own way. You can scarce go into any Company but Martials Complaint still remains Et Pueri Nasum Rhinocerotis habent.[9] Yet every Ape & Monkey has the faculty of contracting Its muscles with a Sneer, as well as these forward Young Gentry, but use It with more discretion, in that They can neither intend to make a Jest of Religion or any Branch of Learning.

The Soc. of Antiq. have orderd the late Rt Revd Dr Sharpe Lord Archbishop of Yorke's curious Tables of all our English Coins from the Conquest to shew their weight & value (not Impressions or Images) to be engraven for the Members, continued to his present Majesty by their Secretary Mr West of the Temple our Bro. Member, who kindly communicated & Lends them the MSS. The Sollicitor

General[10] has bought & taken down 2 Houses next his Grace the Duke of Ancasters in Lincolne Inns fields fronting the middle Grand Walk of that Societys Gardens & is building a Magnificent house in their Stead.

The White China Apes with Seales under their Pedistals in Indian Characters which stood on my Chimney Piece are presented Me – see how Elegantly I've drawn out one of those ludicrous Pagodas [*small sketch of china ornament*] the Object of the Worship of Egypt (for which Juvenal ridicules them Severely) as well as of China. I have taken my Wifes & your advice, but P. by his Hypocrisy & Designing to decieve them seemd to Me to've done us some Service with the Gent. last night where Wee stayd 'till 3 this Morning, to good purpose as I have from our Friend reason to hope.[11]

I am with duty to my Father & mother Love to my Wife with the Enclos'd & all the Little ones & Your Self my dearest Brother Yr most Affect. Brother & Sincere Friend

   Maur. Johnson junr

Wee are all well health better Man & Horse

To John Johnson Esq
at Spalding in Lincolnshire   Free Colerane

1 *The Tragedy of Medea* by Charles Johnson (no relation to the Spalding Johnsons), first produced in 1730.

2 Colley Cibber the dramatist, who had been educated at the King's School, Grantham, became the new Poet Laureate in December 1730, in succession to Revd Laurence Eusden, who had been equally criticised by the writers and journalists satirised by Pope under the name of 'Grub Street' (see Introduction above, p. 000). The verse 'When Roguey Pope' quoted in this letter refers to Pope's satirical poem *The Dunciad* in which he attacked current writers as subjects of the Goddess of Dulness. Neither Eusden, mentioned later in this letter, nor Cibber produced memorable poetry.

3 The actress Anne Oldfield (1683–1730) had recently been buried in Westminster Abbey.

4 Lord Coleraine had 'franked' the letter, as is shown at the foot of this transcription, thus removing the need for the recipient to pay postage. He had apparently franked a blank sheet for Lynn, which Lynn then passed on to Johnson to use for his letter rather than using it himself.

5 The SGS.

6 Sir Hans Sloane (1660–1753): President of the Royal Society 1727–41 and member of the SGS 1733. His collections formed the basis of the British Museum. See his entry in *ODNB*.

7 'To the greater glory of God the omnipotent creator'. The Royal Society's Charter had been given by Charles II.

8 MS '& and'.

9 A quotation from the *Epigrams* of the Roman poet Martial: literally 'And boys have the nose of a rhinoceros' meaning that they are full of conceit and turn up their noses, like a rhinoceros' horn, at everything.

10 Sir Charles Talbot (1685–1737): Lord Chancellor, 1734–37; see his entry in *ODNB*.

11 This incident cannot be clarified.

1731

133. SGS No 84: From Beaupré Bell to Maurice Johnson.
[Beaupré Hall], 20 January 1731.
MB2 fol.42A, 21 January 1731.
Thanks Johnson for sending duplicate coins from his collection; discusses coins, especially one of Johnson's Greek coins, probably from Rhodes; explains that 'Mr Blomefield, a friend of mine is now preparing an History of Cambridge'[1] and requests information from Johnson's collections towards it.

¹   Francis Blomefield (1705–1752), best known for his *History of Norfolk* 1739. See his entry in *ODNB*.

134. SGS No 23: From Roger Gale to Maurice Johnson.
London, 23 January 1731.
MB2 fol.42A, 28 January 1731.
Sends details of a Roman inscription from Riechester, otherwise known as [High] Rochester in Redesdale (Northumberland);[1] relates it to similar inscriptions already published, as an aid to deciphering it; hopes Johnson will come to London for the legal term.[2]

¹   The inscription, only described but not quoted in this letter, is illustrated in full in MB2 fol.42A, 28 January 1731; Gale must have enclosed a sketch of the inscription, now not kept with the letter.
²   Maurice Johnson spent the three short legal terms each year in London; see the Introduction.

135. No 39: From Revd Benjamin Ray[1] to Maurice Johnson [for reading at SGS meeting].
4 February 1731.
MB2 fol.43A, 4 February 1731.
Offers 'Reasons why I think learned and useful meetings ought to be esteemed and reverenced'; provides evidence from Classical and modern authors and from experience.
Annotated by Johnson: 'A Learned Discourse in praise of Literary Societies communicated by the Revd Mr Ray SGS 4 Feb.1730.'

¹   See his entry in Appendix 2.

136. SGS No 34: From Roger Gale to Maurice Johnson.
[London], viii Idum Feb 1731 [6 February 1731].
MB2 fol.43A, 11 February 1731.
Long letter in Latin, annotated by Johnson: 'Epistola de Plumbeis Numismatibus';[1] criticises the Latin of the recently-composed epitaph on Newton for his memorial in Westminster Abbey, composed by the Dean of Peterborough, Dr Lockyer, a member of the SGS; discusses Roman leaden coins, especially one that Johnson owns.

¹   'A letter about lead coins'.

137. SGS No 92: From Maurice Johnson to the SGS.
[London], 16 February 1731.
MB2 fol.43B, 18 February 1731.
Gives an account of current events in London, including the RS's approval of a commemorative medal of Newton, struck at the Tower; discusses the work of Samuel Palmer[1] on the history of printing; describes a silver coin of Henry VIII which he has seen; explains the current appointment of surgeons at St Bartholomew's Hospital.

¹   Samuel Palmer (d.1732) published his *History of Printing* in 1732; he is known as an early employer of Benjamin Franklin.

138. SGS No 86: From Beaupré Bell to Maurice Johnson.
Beaupré Hall, 19 February 1731.
Comments on the medal struck to commemorate Newton, on Newton's epitaph

which Dr Bentley is writing and on the meaning of 'generositas' in Latin; pays tribute to Hearne's[1] publications at Oxford and Dr Bentley who is now 'correcting Chaucer but I believe will be persuaded by his friends not to publish it'.

[1] Thomas Hearne (1678–1735): Oxford librarian and antiquarian, at the heart of historical scholarship in Oxford from 1700 to 1735, particularly significant for his printing of early English texts. See his entry in *ODNB*.

139. No 65: From Revd Samuel Whiting to Maurice Johnson in London.
Spalding, 20 February 1730 [actually 1731].
He has little news to communicate; discusses instead 'the Sublimity and Magnificence of the Sacred Scriptures in thought and Language', compared with 'profane Authors'; passages from Homer are compared with Biblical passages 'not to disesteem the Pagan ones' but demonstrate the Bible's superiority even to their best passages.

140. SGS No 82: From Revd Samuel Wesley senior to Maurice Johnson.
Epworth, 15 March 1730/1.
Thanks Johnson for his help with Wesley's book;[1] explains that his book is about to go to press and 'the Prolegomena are printed.'

[1] On the Book of Job in the Bible; see No 96 above.

141. From Beaupré Bell to Maurice Johnson.
Beaupré Hall, Norfolk, 18 March 1731.
Comments on Johnson's MS account of Carausius; gives very detailed discussion of inscriptions on coins of Roman Emperors, especially Diocletian and Maximian; would like to borrow coins of emperors missing from his collection 'to take casts from'; has had a request from Hearne for information on 'an antient Author called <u>Girardus Cornubiensis;</u>[1] he is surprised to find that his personal letters to Johnson have been read at the SGS and minuted, as these are written 'as I speak' to a friend and the style is therefore too informal for public reading. It is 'highly against my inclination'.[2]

[1] Gerard of Cornwall, a historian living around 1350. His works have not survived, but two books, *De gestis regum West Saxonum* and *De gestis Britonum*, are cited by other writers. Lydgate claimed to have used Gerard as his source for his poem on Guy of Warwick.
[2] This comment by Bell compares with a similar view expressed by Bogdani: see his letter of 22 October 1726 (No 80 above). Evidently a formal style was customarily used if the writer expected a letter to be made public; both of these correspondents are concerned that their letters, intended to be informally written to a friend, will be thought to be lacking the appropriate style of expression for public presentation.

142. No 16: From Beaupré Bell to Maurice Johnson.
Beaupré Hall, 15 April 1731.
MB2 fol.47A, 22 April 1731.
Congratulates Johnson on 'increase of your Family';[1] discusses coinage; comments on Dr Woodward's[2] *Method of Fossils* and its synoptical table drawn up by John Martin FRS and gives an account of Bell's own fossil collection; mentions Dr Middleton Massey's drawings of English coins; explains Bell's own methods in drawing up a catalogue of the Roman Emperors.

[1] Johnson's daughter Anne Alethea was baptised on 4 March 1731.
[2] See note to No 14 above. In addition to his antiquarian studies, Woodward was known for his work on fossils, publishing *Essay towards a Natural History of the Earth* (1695) and *Method of*

Fossils. The SGS was interested in collecting fossils. The table was drawn up by John Martyn (1699–1768), FRS 1727; see his entry in *ODNB*.

143. SGS No 85: From Beaupré Bell to Maurice Johnson.
[Beaupré Hall], 24 April 1731.
MB2 fol.48A, 29 April 1731.
Praises the SGS: 'an Elegant and Useful Entertainment to the most Ingenious Gentlemen in your Neighbourhood'; discusses Mr Hearne's[1] limitations as an author and Wood's[2] account (1672) of Dr Fell's negative view of John Wycliffe.

[1]   See note to No 139 above.
[2]   Anthony à Wood (1632–1695): Oxford antiquary, supported by Dr Fell, Dean of Christ Church, Oxford, in his work on the history of Oxford. See A. Wood, *Athenæ Oxonienses*, ed. Philip Bliss, 4 vols (London, 1813–20), I, p.lxxi. See also Wood's entry in *ODNB*.

144. No 18: From Beaupré Bell to Maurice Johnson.
[Beaupré Hall], 5 June 1731.
MB2 fol.49B, 10 June 1731.
Provides two Latin poems from an unnamed MS in Trinity College Cambridge library, one by Panormita[1] and one by an unnamed friend of Bell's.

[1]   Antonio Beccadelli (1394–1471), known as Panormita and famous for his risqué Latin epigrams.

145. SGS/WS/15: From William Stukeley to Revd Gregory Henson, Dean of Stamford.
Stamford, 5 July 1731.
Later copy of letter, not in Stukeley's hand.
Discusses the choice of warden for Browne's Hospital, Stamford.

146. SGS No 31: From William Bogdani to Maurice Johnson.
[London], 15 July 1731.
MB2 fol.52B, 5 August 1731.
Gives transcription by Bogdani of 'Description of the Honor of Windesor, Taken and performed. By the Perambulation, Views and Delineation of John Norden[1] In Anno 1607'; full notes and copies of entries on the history of Windsor from other books are added in Johnson's hand.
Annotated by Johnson: 'Windsor reassumed by King Wm I with the reasons thereof.'

[1]   John Norden (c.1547–1723): surveyor and cartographer; see his entry in *ODNB*.

147. SGS No 87: From William Bogdani to Maurice Johnson.
London, 19 October 1731.
MB2 fol.54A, 21October 1731.

                                        Tower of London 19 Oct 1731
Dr Sir   SGS No 87
    I presume now to acquaint you with mine & my Wife's safe Arrival last Saturday Night at this place, after a very pleasant Journey thro' the places I propos'd at my first setting out.
    After I left you (which I do declare was to me the greatest Concern imaginable) I went on directly to Burleigh but it being a little too late to See the House, it being almost 4 o'th'Clock, I enquird of the Gentleman of the Chambers, whether

I might be permitted to See the House next day being Sunday & especially for that I should be at Stamford. He could not answer me, but went to ask her Ladyship who was so kind to send me word, that in regard to my coming so far for that pleasure I should not be refusd, I therefore from thence went to wait on Dr Colby[1] who was then not at home, but as soon as he came in & receivd the Letter you favour'd me with which I left for him he came to me to my Quarters & was so kind to Spend the Evening with me there & invited us to dine with him the next day which we did & were very kindly & obligingly receivd by him & his lady; After Dinner he favour'd us with his Company to Burleigh, where by his Means I had an Opportunity of veiwing that fine Collection of Pictures with much more time & attention than is usually allow'd to Strangers on these Occasions, and indeed for the Number, their good condition & beautifull performance exceed any Collection I have yet seen; tho' I am much concernd to see those fine paintings of Signor Verrio[2] in Rooms so unfinish'd, where I think [page 2] it almost impossible but that they must be very much damag'd if not entirely spoil'd when they come to break down the Walls, & rebuild them & lay the floors agreeable to the propos'd Model. Dr Colby on our Return was so good as to spend the Evening with us, & was so very obliging that I cannot enough express my Thanks to you for bringing me acquainted with him. I was by him inform'd that Dr Stukeley was at Stamford & had not been at London as we imagin'd, I therefore sent to let him know that Dr Colby was with me to spend the Evening & that we should be glad of his Company, who sent me word he would come presently, but he not coming, an Hour after I sent again least there should have been some mistake, who then sent me for answer he never went any whither on a Sunday Evening; however I waited on him the next morning, but could not then stay to Enjoy his Company long. I find by his discourse that the people & particularly the Clergy at Stamford are not so obliging to him as they ought, & especially to a Man of his Worth, the Reason I learn from him is, that they imagine him to be of different political principles to them; party affairs running very high among them to the great prejudice of all social Qualities.

On Monday Morning I set out for Southwick, & after great difficulties In finding the Way which is very intricate, I arriv'd at Mr Lynn's at Dinner Time, where I staid that Night & was very obligingly receiv'd & agreeable entertain'd by the two Magi[3] & had the pleasure of seeing there Couz. Bold, Lynn & Patt. Johnson; On Tuesday Morning after paying a Visit to the Sun & admiring the patches on her Face (while the Ladies were busy about their Coffee, Tea & less necessary Employments) we took [page 3] our Leaves & set out for Hitchin, & were in great hopes of meeting Mr Johnson & his Lady[4] on the road, being informd at Southwick that they were expected there that Night, but we miss'd them I cant tell how, tho' we went the same way they must come (being guided by Mr Lynn's servant sent on purpose to shew us the way) & put in at the same Inn at Bugden[5] that we were told they would Bait at. On Wednesday we din'd at Hitchin & Thursday with Will Barker & his Lady but I have so much plague & vexation with those tricking Hitchiners[6] that I left them Friday Morning & din'd with my Nephew at Hatfield staid there that Night & reach'd the Tower Saturday Night.

Thus S[r] you have a Detail of my Expedition from Spalding to London. But when I would express my Gratitude for the favours I receiv'd at your House I am at a loss for Language suitable to the just Sense I have of them. The many

Favours I have receiv'd at your Hands as well as these last which I most gratefully
acknowledge, are sufficient to convince me, Friendship is a Virtue not entirely
forsaken our Regions, tho' I have been so weak to look for her in the Breasts of
those whom I thought I had bound to me by the most signal Services, the most
cordial Affection & the most sincere Fidelity; I assure you S^r I shall always retain
the most grateful memory of your favours, & think my self happy to be in a
Capacity to return them.

I am very much concern'd at the Indisposition I left your Lady & my dear
Jenny[7] in & hope by this time they are happily Recover'd to whom please to give
mine & my Wife's most humble Service & many Thanks for their great Civilities;
please to present the same to your good Father & Mother, my dear Betsy, Bro.
Maurice, Sister Kitty & all my Bros & Sisters, to my dear Aunts Mary & Gressy,
to Mr Lyon, his Lady & my lovely Graciana, to Capt. Pilliod, his Lady, Couz
Walter & his Lady, to Aunt Johnson, & to all my good friends at Spalding &
beleive me ever with the greatest Sincerity
Dear Sr Your most affectionate most obligd & most obedient friend &
            humble Servant W Bogdani
Annotated by Maurice Johnson: 'a Lr from Wm Bogdani Esq FRS on his having
seen <u>Burleigh</u>'

¹   Dr Dixon Colby, a member of the SGS. He is the author of No 404 below; his son is referred to
in No 196 below. See his entry in Appendix 2.
²   Antionio Verrio (1639–1707): Italian painter, working in England. Verrio's murals can still be
seen at Burghley House. See his entry in *ODNB.*
³   Presumably the two George Lynns, father and son, both SGS members and relatives of the
Spalding Johnsons. George Lynn senior was a keen astronomer, and it would be through his telescope
that Bogdani observed the sun, compared here to a fashionable lady wearing patches on her face.
⁴   It is not possible to be certain which of the many branches of the Johnson relatives this refers
to. Maurice Johnson's sons were not yet married at this time, and his brother John was a widower. It
may be Revd Walter Johnson, the 'Couz. Walter' of the final paragraph.
⁵   Buckden (Hunts).
⁶   Bogdani was Lord of the Manor of Hitchin and had an estate there, of which Maurice Johnson
was his steward.
⁷   Johnson's daughter Jane, later the wife of Dr John Green. Betsy, in the same paragraph, is Johnson's daughter Elizabeth; Bogdani's relationship with Johnson's family cannot be clearly ascertained.

148. From Revd Robert Whatley[1] to the President and members of SGS.
Toft near Lincoln, 23 October 1731.
MB2 fol.54B, 4 November 1731.
Appreciates his election to membership though he feels unworthy of the honour;
he can communicate via a Lincoln bookseller, Mr Wood, who goes to Sleaford
market; sends some unspecified items for the SGS.
¹   Rector of Toft by Newton; see his entry in Appendix 2.

149. No 55: From William Bogdani to Maurice Johnson.
Tower of London, 30 October 1731.
MB2 fol.54B, 4 November 1731.
Discusses how he and Johnson are to travel from Hitchin to London; gives RS
news including a very detailed account of experiments on dogs with a distillation
made from laurel leaves; offers a warning against using laurel water in cookery;[1]
gives an account of the fire in the Cotton Library and damage to its contents.[2]
Annotated by Johnson: 'Wm Bogdani Esq FR & AS of Lawrell Leave Water,

poisoning and repeated Experiments made thereof – Acct of the Fire and burning part of Cotton Library in Ashburnham House.'

[1]   These experiments were reported in the *Philosophical Transactions* of the RS, VI v 365–374.

[2]   The Cottonian Library, an important collection started in the early seventeenth century, had been given to the nation in 1700 by Sir John Cotton, a descendant of the collectors. Housed at first in Ashburnham House, it was damaged by fire in 1731, with the loss of some valuable books and manuscripts. It later became one of the nuclei of the British Museum and Library. See Nos 156 and 564 below for further references to it.

150. From Beaupré Bell to Maurice Johnson.
Beaupré Hall, 19 November 1731.
MB2 fol.56A, 16 December 1731.
He will send a transcript of extracts from Banduri on Roman coins;[1] describes coins of Carausius in his own collection to help with Johnson's work on Carausius; asks about the publication of Berewood's book on ancient coins.
Attached: long, detailed list of coins of Carausius and Allectus, annotated by Johnson as having been received on 24 October 1732.
Annotated by Johnson at a later date: 'Coines of Carausius in Couz. B. Bell's Collection. Since in Trinity Coll Library at Cambridge of his guift.' Bell's collections and papers went to Trinity College after his death in 1741.

[1]   Anselmo Banduri (1671–1743): Italian numismatist, published in 1718 two volumes on the Roman imperial coinage, *Numismata Imperatorum Romanorum a Trajano Decio usque ad Palæologos Augustos.* See No 120 above for note on Carausius.

151. From Revd Timothy Neve to Maurice Johnson.
Weston, 20 December 1731.
MB2 fol.56B, 23 December 1731.
Neve has sent Mr Thompson's present to the SGS on Sir Isaac Newton's behalf;[1] discusses 'the Medal affair';[2] cannot persuade Mr Hill to part with a set of medallions, but if he gets them he will offer Johnson his choice; explains that in Peterborough he has met Mr West of the Temple, who wishes to become a PGS member;[3] apologises for the quality of his writing paper: 'Sad paper but the best I have here'.
Johnson's Latin annotation on reverse records the donation of the books.

[1]   The present was a set of copies of Newton's books: see letter from Neve (No 121 above) dated 20 May 1730.
[2]   This relates to the commemorative medal of Newton. See previous letters relating to this, by Maurice Johnson on 16 February 1731 (No 137 above) and by Beaupré Bell on 19 February 1731 (No 138 above).
[3]   Neve's phrase is 'of our society' – James West was already an SGS member, elected in 1730; he was later Treasurer and President of the RS.

1732

152. From Beaupré Bell to Maurice Johnson.
Beaupré Hall, Norfolk, 16 January 1731[1] [actually 1732].
Sends comments on British coins and catalogue of his own collection of medals of Roman Emperors; sends 'my Annual Tribute to the Library'; asks to borrow Mr Lynn's Scale for 'understanding Hales's Vegetable Statics'.[2]

[1]   It is difficult to determine whether the dating of Beaupré Bell's letters in the first three months

of the year refer to 1731 or 1732, as these are sometimes not reported in the Minute Books; where there is no Minute Book entry to confirm the date, Bell's dating has been adhered to, but as in this case he mentions a book published during 1731, the letter has been re-dated to 1732. The lack of Minute Book references to his letters could relate to his letter of 18 March 1731 (No 141 above), in which Bell objects to having his private letters to Johnson read aloud at SGS meetings.

2   The catalogue is not now filed with this letter.

3   This is Stephen Hales' book *Vegetable Staticks* (London, 1731). George Lynn senior had compiled a logarithmic scale.

153. SGS No 41: Portion of letter from John Green to Captain Pilliod [his stepfather].

[Leiden, Netherlands], 13 February 1731/2 (New Style).[1]

Writes from Leiden to give details of Green's work and study there, especially his study of dissection with Albenus, Professor of Anatomy; discusses stones in the gall bladder and provides an annotated drawing of one in position, presumably as shown to him in his anatomy class.

Annotated by Johnson: '1731 at Leyden from Capt. Pilliod's Papers found 1737.'

1   Writing from Leiden, where he is undertaking further studies in medicine, Green uses the 'New Style' of dating, the Gregorian calendar in use on the Continent. At the time, Britain was still using the Julian calendar which was eleven days behind this, and did not reform its calendar by changing to the Gregorian calendar until September 1752. Maurice Johnson (son) also frequently uses the 'New Style' of dating his letters when he writes from the Continent. See Green's biography in Appendix 2.

154. SGS No 78: From John Harries to 'Rev. Mr Neeve' at Peterborough.

London, 20 February 1731 [actually 1732].

MB2 fol.62A, 6 March 1732.

Apologises for his previous silence; he had 'given up as lost' his West Indies collection but his merchant's wife had kept it safe; lists the contents: coral to make lime for sugar-boiling, shells, nuts and petrified hardwood; he is now embarking for Jamaica where the governor is an SGS member;[1] promises to send 'raritys'.

1   Major-General Hunter: see No 119 above.

155. SGS No 45: From John Green to Maurice Johnson.

Leiden, 25 February 1732 (New Style).

MB2 fol.61B, 9 March 1732.

He hopes to propose Professor Boerhaave[1] as an SGS member; but is doubtful of getting Burman as Green does not attend his 'colleges'[2] in which he deals with history, 'antiquity' and 'criticizes on the Classicks'; gives an account of the public whipping of a thief; explains local methods of executing gentry found guilty of crimes; discusses a coming auction of books and antique medals and provides very detailed and precise drawings of some medals.

1   The famous chemist, under whom many English doctors studied at Leiden. Johnson had hoped to secure him and Professor Burman as members by his letter of January 1730 (No 111 above), but this had been unsuccessful, and neither of these two joined the SGS.

2   Classes.

156. From Maurice Johnson to Richard Falkner.[1]

London, 26 February 1732.

London 26 Feb[y] 1731[2]

Our Mother (to whom You'll make my Duty acceptable) will be so[3] good to excuse my answering yrs. before I write to her Having as Yet not had the opportunity of Waiting on our Friends Mrs Blow & Captn Edgeworth which Wee shall (God willing) to morrow then I hope to Send her word they're well: In the meane time I thank You Dear Dickey for your kind Letter and will execute your Commands have bespoke the Water Colours & Brushes again, & will add to them the Lead pencells & Drawing Book you desire: of all these the Best use You can make for a while is the designeing after Human Figures, the Basis of Art, & noblest Patern to Copy after in the Academy way. Ad Imaginem Mentis divinæ creavit Deus Hominem, & illi subfecit Orbem Terrarum & quæcumque Animalia, Terram, Aerem, aut Aquas colunt[4] as Moses has told us, & as Several of the most antient Greek and Latin Poets from him by Tradition not obscurely hint. I remember in the antient MS of Genesis lost for the greater part in the late Fatal fire of the Cottonian Library this was designed in Limnings on Velom as old the writing of that Book universaly[5] (I think) agreed to be the oldest in the World, & an Inestimable Loss, the Parliament are now consulting about the future safety of that Publick Library and my Friend Mr Wyndham has proposed what all men of Learning like, to build a properer place for a Chappell at Whitehall than that which was the Banqueting House is with 2000l. & to have that Settled as the Books are on the Publick for the Library[6] the designe on the Plafond or Cieling being realy profane for a Christian Chappell being a Compliment from Sr Peter Paul Rubens the Painter when Embassador to King James the Ist. And representing that Kings Apotheosis or Translation into Heaven amongst a Crowd of Heathen Deities. Now[7] S^r as his Majesty was a learned Prince and in whose reign that Library was I believe chiefly collected, the fancy suits well enough for the purpose & use proposed to put It to. But It has given great disgust to all Sober and Ingenious people as apply'd to divine Service and is one of the Glareing Improprieties a Great Poet has lately Satyrised in his Poem on False Taste, a Fault also found in some Noblemen's Chappels – thus

> And now the Chappel's Silver bell You hear,
> That summons You to all the Pride of Prayr:
> Light Quirks of Musick, broken & uneven,
> Make the Soul dance upon a Jigg to Heaven.
> On Painted Cielings You devoutly stare,
> Where sprawl the Saints of Verrio, or Laguerre
> On gilded Clouds in fair expansion lie
> And bring all Paradise before your Eye. &c[8]

You'll oblige me very much in presenting my humble Service to Bro^r J Burton, Falconer[9] & their Ladies if you See or write to 'em before Wee meet and to Mr Whiteing, whom I should be much more sorry to lose but for his Own Sake. I assure You S^r i am gladd I have been of any Service to You, and shall be ready to do You all in my Power, having all imaginable reasons to endeavour to make returns for the daily favours done Me and Mine both by Your good Mamma and Yourself & I begg of You to be assured that I am with Sincere Affection

   Dear Dickey

P.S. I pray give my Love to y^r Chumm[10]   Your very much Obliged and
and all my Boys & Girles, tell   Faithfull Friend
Betzy I'll write to her by the next   Maur Johnson jun^r

[1]   Johnson's much younger stepbrother; see his entry in Appendix 2.

[2]   This must be February 1732, as the Cottonian Library fire occurred in October 1731 and Pope's *Epistle on Taste*, from which the quotation in this letter is taken, was published in 1732.
[3]   MS 'so so'.
[4]   'God created man after the image of the Divine mind and put under him the earth and whatever creatures the earth, the air and the water support.' Johnson is paraphrasing Genesis 1:27ff.
[5]   MS 'univeraly'.
[6]   The plan to create a public library in the former Banqueting Hall in Whitehall did not come to fruition. However, the remains of the Cottonian Library did become the nucleus of the British Library.
[7]   MS 'Now now'.
[8]   The quotation is from Pope's *Moral Essays, Epistle IV*, lines 141–148. Pope was a member of the SGS, though not an active one. See No 147 above for another reference to the work of the Italian painter Antonio Verrio.
[9]   Richard Falkner's brother-in-law and older brother.
[10]   Maurice Johnson's eldest son Maurice, of the same age as Falkner. The two were good friends; see Nos 196, 211, 219, 240 and 246 below.

157. SGS No 9: From Revd Thomas Marshall[1] to Maurice Johnson.
Peterborough, 21 March 1731/2.
MB2 fol.62B, 23 March 1732.
Thanks Johnson for his letter; comments that Johnson's conjectures about arms on a silver seal found in the wall of the Bishop's Palace, Peterborough, endorse his own; agrees they are the arms of the See of Hereford – probably either relating to Thomas Cantelupe, Bishop of Hereford, perhaps on a visit to Peterborough, or William de la Zouche, prebendary of Peterborough 1646 who had Cantelupe family connections.[2]
Annotated by Johnson: 'SG Petrib. Secr SGS, of the Noble Family of Cantelupe, & their Arms on an Antient Seal.'

[1]   Revd Thomas Marshall was Vicar of St John's Church, Peterborough (1726–1748) and a member of the PGS. He taught in the King's Grammar School, Peterborough, from 1738 (Longden ix. 143–5). See Nos 159, 162, 341 n.1 and 351 n.1 below.
[2]   Thomas de Cantilupe (c.1220–1282); see his entry in *ODNB*. William Zouche held the Third Prebend in Peterborough Cathedral from 1646 until1679 (J. M. Horn, *Fasti Ecclesiae Anglicanae 1541–1858 VIII* (London, 1996), 128–30).

158. SGS No 10: From William Bogdani to Maurice Johnson.
London, 28 March 1732.
MB2 fol.63A, 30 March 1732.
Praises the growth of the PGS and SGS; has sent paints ordered by Johnson and offers very detailed and full advice on suitable colours and methods for painting the woodwork in Johnson's house, recommending deep brown as the fashionable colour; sends congratulations on a family wedding;[1] discusses an article in the *London Journal* on Hungarian vampires and the origins of the vampire myth,[2] showing the errors in it and explaining the ranks of the Hungarian army.
Annotated by Johnson: 'Lr from W. Bogdani Esq FR & A Socc. Best Method of House-Painting. of the Hungarian notion of Vampyres. of their Military Officers.'
Letter also annotated by Johnson with references to vampires in several books.

[1]   It has not proved possible to identify whose wedding this refers to, but it is probably that of one of Johnson's elder daughters.
[2]   Johnson has consulted him on this topic because of Bogdani's knowledge of Hungarian language and society; see his biography in Appendix 2.

159. SGS No 13: From Revd Thomas Marshall to Maurice Johnson.
Peterborough, 31 March1732.
MB2 fol.63A, 6 April 1732.
Gives a lengthy and detailed account of the foundation of his parish, St John's, Peterborough, transcribed from the PGS Minutes dated 7 October 1730; asks Johnson's opinion about recovering the original tithes to increase the value of the living.

160. From Beaupré Bell to Maurice Johnson.
[Beaupré Hall], 10 April 1732.
MB2 fol.63B, 13 April 1732.
Discusses coins of Carausius; comments on the accuracy of Johnson's notes on Diocletian and Maximian, suggesting Diocletian was not as bad as is asserted; discusses Judge Elias de Bekingham,[1] a judge in the reign of Edward I and his connection with Beckingham, on the Lincolnshire-Nottinghamshire border near Newark.

1 See his biography in *ODNB*.

161. Draft of letter from Maurice Johnson to Francis Scott, Duke of Buccleuch.
Spalding, 22 April 1732.
MB2 fol.64A, 13 April 1732.
Requests the Duke, already an honorary member, to become Patron of the SGS. Annotated by Johnson: 'This Lr was transcribed by me and subscribed by the Reverend Stephen Lyon President & transmitted to Capt. Pilliod to London to present to his Grace.'

162. Draft of letter from Maurice Johnson to Revd Thomas Marshall.
Spalding, 29 April 1732.
Replies to Marshall's letter of 31 March 1732; thanks him for information on St John's Church, Peterborough;[1] provides a lengthy and detailed legal opinion on the endowment of St. John's, in answer to Marshall's question about possible means of increasing his tithes. He explains why 'personal Tythes have now ceased in this land' and have generally been replaced by the Easter offering.

1 No 159 above.

163. From John Green to Maurice Johnson.
SGS No 20: Leiden, 4 July 1732 (New Style).
MB2 fol.67A, 13 July 1732.
Explains that he has been spending 8 or 9 hours a day at 'colleges' but now has the 'great vacation' until mid-September;[1] he has been to Katwijk at low tide to look in vain for Roman ruins which are now just off the coast but has seen the two branches of the Rhine estuary; discusses plants he has found, epitaphs in local churches and a Roman inscription found near the Hague; praises the SGS; tells a scandalous story about Professor Burman.

1 Here Green uses the Dutch academic term 'colleges' and a translation of 'grote vacantie' rather than the English equivalents which he would have used during his studies at Cambridge.

164. From Richard Norcliffe[1] to Maurice Johnson.
[Friderickshald, Norway], August 1732 [no day specified].
MB2 fol.71A, 17 August 1732.
Gives detailed replies to Mr Butters' questions [not quoted] about Norwegian flora and fauna; provides information about Greenland and its indigenous inhabitants, particularly their religion, provided for him by a returned missionary.[2]

1   See his entry in Appendix 2.
2   This is probably Revd Andreas Bing, who became a corresponding member of the SGS; see No 397 below (20 July 1742).

165. From Beaupré Bell to Maurice Johnson.
[Beaupré Hall], 8 August 1732.
MB2 fol.71A, 17 August 1732.
He has returned from a visit to Rutland; discusses a coin of William I, minted at Lincoln and found under Lincoln Cathedral, which he has acquired; comments on Mr Folkes'[1] coin collection and his forthcoming history of English coins; comments on a drawing of a coin or medal of Carausius depicting his head and a female head, in Stukeley's collection.

1   Martin Folkes, President of the RS and the SA. See his biography in *ODNB* and his entry in Appendix 2.

166. SGS No 100: From Roger Gale to Maurice Johnson.
London, 8 August 1732.
MB2 fol.70B, 17 August 1732.
Discusses 'a little brasse Busto' – a curious and exquisite Roman head found at York, near Bootham Bar, and discusses whom it could represent, also comments on a coin of Faustina;[1] asks for a copy of the new engraved map of Spalding.[2]

1   Perhaps Faustina, the wife or daughter of the Roman Emperor Antoninus Pius.
2   This is the 1732 map of the town, framed by sketches of its principal buildings, drawn by John Grundy senior. A copy of it is in the SGS. It is reproduced as Illustration 2 in this volume, p. 206.

167. SGS No 99: From Beaupré Bell to Maurice Johnson.
[Beaupré Hall], 28 August 1732.
MB2 fol.71B, 24 August 1732.
Discusses Bell's work in making casts of Classical seals; lists some which he is sending to Johnson and asks to borrow some from Johnson's collection; mentions the medal of Carausius owned by Sir Richard Ellys; discusses his plans to print by subscription his Cæsarean Tables with engravings of coins; sends Latin verse about Burnet's History[1] by Dr Moss, late Dean of Ely.

1   Gilbert Burnet (1643–1715): Bishop of Salisbury, author of *History of his own Times* (1723–4); see his entry in *ODNB*.

168. From Beaupré Bell to Maurice Johnson.
[Beaupré Hall], 8 September 1732.
Sends detailed and critical comments on Maurice Johnson's MS account of Carausius and Allectus, 'Decennium Carausii et Allecti'; criticises the length of the title, Johnson's Latin verse and some historical points; asks to have conjectures distinguished from facts; includes a chronology of dates and events; asks to keep Johnson's paper on English coins to show to Mr Folkes.
Annotated by Johnson: 'Cousin BBell's Criticisms and Kind Corrections of

some of my Errors and Improprieties in my Decennium Carausii et Allecti Impp. submitted to him.'

169. SGS No 99: From Captain John Topham[1] to Maurice Johnson.
Gloucester Street, London, 7 October 1732.
MB2 fol.72B, 12 October 1732.

SGS No 99　　　　　　　　　　　　　　　　　　　　Glocester Street No.32
S^r　　　　　　　　　　　　　　　　　　　　　　　　　　　Oct.7 1732
　　I've sent you by the Peterborough Waggon some trifling curiositys which were the best I cou'd collect in my Voyage & hope they will be a little acceptable to the Worthy Society. I am sorry to hear Mr Neve[2] has parted from the Society (for this reason) having made my little Collection still Less. I hope the Gentlemen are all Well & desire they will accept of my humble Service.
I hope S^r your Lady & family are all Well & desire they will accept of my most humble Service which is the only Return I can make for the great Civilitys [page 2] I Received from You & Your Lady when at Spalding.
　　　　from　　S^r　　　　your
　　　　　　most Humble Servant
　　　　　　　　Jno Topham

[1]　See his entry in Appendix 2.
[2]　Revd Timothy Neve had moved to Peterborough; presumably Topham is sending some of his collection to the Peterborough society.

170. From Captain John Topham to Maurice Johnson.
[London, 7 October 1732.]
Provides a list of specimens sent by Topham for the SGS museum:
'A Tygers Head
Hogg Fish
Piece of a Rhinoceros Skin
Three Claws of a Tyger
Snout of a fish
Gentoo Girls Love Letter In a Bottle
Severall little Scorpions
D^o Centumpes
Sucking Fish
A large Insect which I caught Flying.'

171. From Samuel Massey[1] to Maurice Johnson 'by Mr Lynn'.
17 October 1732.
MB2 fol.73A, 19 October 1732.
He has sent to Johnson a cast of a Classical head which is either of Alexander or Pallas; asks Johnson for impressions [of coins and seals] from his collection, not those depicting coats of arms but 'anything else'.

[1]　This is possibly Samuel Massey MD, apothecary of Wisbech, perhaps related to Richard Middleton Massey.

172. SGS No.97: From Beaupré Bell to Maurice Johnson.
[Beaupré Hall], 19 October 1732.
MB2 fol.73A, 19 October 1732.
Thanks Johnson for lending his copy of 'Walker on Coins';[1] asks if Johnson will permit Mr Folkes to have a cast of Johnson's gold coin of Edward III in his collection; sends copies of his proposals for printing by subscription his 'Tabulæ Augustæ' [not included].[2]

1   Obadiah Walker, *The Greek and Roman History Illustrated by Coins and Medals* (London, 1692).
2   Bell's work on the coins of the early Roman Emperors was never published. On his death he left his papers to Trinity College, Cambridge, where they are now held in 12 MS volumes. As Trinity did not publish them, the SGS was anxious to do so, but could not afford the expense.

173. Fragments of a letter from Maurice Johnson, in London [unsigned, undated, but dateable by date stamp '18 Nov' and Bogdani's letter read on 14 December 1732, No 174 below].
Addressed to 'Mrs Johnson Junr. at Spalding.'[1]
MB2 fol.74A, 23 November 1732
Incomplete sentences because of its fragmentary nature; refers to fishes including 'the Catt Fish', also to events at the SA, to Beaupré Bell's planned history of coins and to Bogdani's intention to copy and send an inscription from a rock in New England.[2]

1   His wife.
2   See Bogdani's letter, No 174 below.

174. No 56: Extract of letter sent by William Bogdani to Maurice Johnson.
Undated, but communicated to the SGS on 14 December 1732.
MB2 fol.75A, 14 December 1732.
Bogdani sends a copy he has made of part of a letter which gives a detailed description, written and sent to the Royal Society by Dr Isaac Greenwood, Hollesian Professor at New Cambridge [Harvard College] in December 1730, of a rock in Taunton River, Massachusetts, New England, which has Native American carvings; Bogdani's letter includes a copy he has made of a drawing of part of the carvings 'taken by the Revd. Mr Danforth 1680' and provides discussion of theories in New England about the meaning of the inscriptions.[1]
Annotated by Bogdani: 'Extract of a letter from Dr Isaac Greenwood, Hollesian Professor at New Cambridge. Dat. at Cambridge N.E. 8 Decem. 1730.'
Annotated by Johnson: 'Copied & the Drawing made by Wm Bogdani Esq. FR & A Socs London & GS at Spalding.'

1   This was also communicated at the Royal Society and the Antiquarian Society (see the Royal Society's *Philosophical Transactions* V ii 167).

175. SGS No 14: From Maurice Johnson to Maurice Johnson (son) for an SGS meeting.
[London], 22 December 1732.
Sends a drawing by Bogdani of a Roman pot found at Canterbury, belonging to Mr Frederick of the SA;[1] gives an account of activities at the SA, including their study of a French MS of Boccaccio's 'Fall of Princes' from 1409 which contained a drawing of Boccaccio and Petrarch; refers to an RS meeting where cutlery magnetised by lightning was shown.

1   Later an SGS member; see his entries in Appendix 2 and in *ODNB*.

176. From John Green to Maurice Johnson.
SGS No 96: Leiden, 27 December 1732 (New Style).
MB2 fol.76A, 28 December 1732.
Explains that he has a holiday 'vacancy' for a fortnight; gives an account of a trip to Flanders; provides a drawing and description of 'Arx Vilfordiana',[1] an old moated castle built in 1375 'midway between Melains [Mechelen] and Bruxells' which 'something resembles our first court at St John's [Cambridge]', giving a long Latin quotation about it from Stockman's *In Decisionibus Curiæ Brabantiæ*;[2] comments on the severe frost which has frozen the Rhine and hopes that it will kill the insects which bore into the wooden sea defences; discusses the Roman inscription sent in his 4 July letter;[3] he is sending some seeds to Johnson by a Boston or Lynn ship; gives a story of a Dutch servant girl, wrongly accused and whipped for stealing her mistress's necklace which was later found; comments on the Duchess of Buccleuch's death and hopes that the Duke her son will now give the SGS land and funds for a museum.[4]

[1] A castle, now demolished, in the Belgian town of Vilvoorde.
[2] Pieter Stockmans, *Decisionum curiæ Brabantiæ sesquicenturia* (Brussels, 1670).
[3] No 164 above.
[4] This did not happen; the SGS did not achieve a purpose-built museum and library until 1910–11.

177. No 87: From William Bogdani.
Heading: 'To Preserve Peaches & Apricots in Brandy. Mrs Bogdani 1732.'
Recipes for preserving fruit in brandy.
Annotated by Johnson: 'as practised at Paris & Montpelier'.

1733

178. SGS No 98: From Beaupré Bell to John Johnson.
[Beaupré Hall], 15 January 1732/3.
MB2 fol.80B, 18 January 1734.
Returns some loaned coins, keeping one until he 'can experiment its specific gravity'; sends casts of a coin of Otho and a coin of Constantinus VI Porphyrogenitus; expresses thanks for Johnson's encouragement over his planned publication; will look for genealogical material on Johnson family in Caius College library when in Cambridge but says he 'cannot come into your notion that there is an Affinity between all families which bear the same name'.

179. No 42: Letter from Christopher Fairchild to Capt. Pilliod (given to the SGS 7 October 1736 by Dr John Green after the death of Pilliod, his stepfather).
Lowther, 24 March 1732/3.
MB2 fol.170A, 7 October 1736.
Thanks Pilliod for his support; explains that he is likely to be staying at Lowther for some time, working as secretary or steward to 'My Lord';[1] sends a collection of inscriptions from memorials in Palmyra, from 324 BC to the early centuries AD, originally in Greek but later translated into Latin.

[1] Henry, third Viscount Lonsdale (1694–1751), of Lowther Castle, Westmorland (*CP* viii. 133).

180. No 21: From Henry Johnson to Maurice Johnson.
Granada, Spain, 2 April 1733.
MB2 fol.86B, 24 May 1733.

No.21   Granada, April the 2^d OS 1733[1]
Dear Maurice,
    I date this Letter to you from a terrestrial Paradise, from Granada, which
for its Situation may be called the first city of the World, the ancient capital
of the Moorish Kings who here kept their principal place of Residence after
they had conquered all these mighty dominions. You will wonder perhaps how
in so short a time I came hither to this great distance from old England. I left
Portsmouth the 3^d of last month and sailed thence with three men of war bound
for the Mediterranean who in their way thither always proposed to call in at
Lisbon, the place where my Aim was cheifly directed, but the Winds who at
Sea are our Masters would not suffer such a deviation in our voyage so we
proceeded directly to Gibraltar which we reached in 8 days from Spitthead a
most prodigious passage this, & which was as fair as it was prosperous. I cannot
say I was sorry for the occasion which lead me thus unexpectedly to see so
famous a Fortress which of late has made so much noise throughout Europe,
& which for its natural Strength has deserved the name of being impregnable, I
tarryed here a week, and happening into company with an English Gentleman
who was come thus far out of curiosity and had resolved to travel into Spain, I
also took the same Resolution, and we embarked together in a Ship bound for
Malaga where we arrived in 17 hours from Gibraltar. In this city we spent the
holy week as that time is most remarkable there for the many processions which
are exhibited on that solemn occasion, from the adjacent mountains it is from
whence we have the famous wine we so deservedly celebrate in England, this
city has at present in hand two noble publick works, fitter for a Kingdom to
undertake than a private people, the one an Aqueduct of three leagues in extent
of Stone with Arches of the same, the other a Mould[2] run out to [page 2] the
Sea in 7 Fathom water, on which they have already erected a chapel of neat
architecture, and on the extreem point intend to build a strong Fortress, these
both of them are works worthy of the ancient Romans, and show the Spirit of the
Spaniards which can thus subsist under a most oppressive Tyranny. From Malaga
to Granada the journey by Land consists of 4 days which is the way of reckoning
in this country, as all manner of carriages travel at one & the same rate; the way
we went was in vehicles called Calashes drawn by two Mules the Driver riding
one of them, these the true Emblems of Spanish State & Gravity in solemn pace
march two short miles in one long hour, just as our English Waggons and like
them too attended with the harmonious sound of jingling Bells which are for
ever tinkling in ones Ears; tis true this is a tedious way of travelling but then the
carriage is very reasonable, for these calashes are contrived to load a vast weight
of Baggage and move as fast in bad roads as in good, and thus without altering
at all their pace with two mules only will hold out for twenty days which with
use in England with a sett of horses would be impossible. Our Inns throughout all
Spain are no other than one long Building of Stone & Mortar, seldom with any
Rooms above, so on one and the same Floor below Men Mules Hoggs Doggs and
Asses are alike accomodated & often times without any partition wall between,
in these places we meet with no other furniture than Baggs of Flees as for Beds

& Provision we have none but what we carry along with us. In the very first of these Inns from our setting out from Malaga happened a comical accident: this place was such a one as I have been describing with the difference only that it had one dark hole above where passengers sometimes took up their Residence, this Room was directly over our heads. at night the time of Repose each man after accomodating his Litter of Straw to his own mind began to compose himself thereon, but hardly [page 3] after encountring Armies of Buggs & Flees had we scratched our selves to sleep, when my old friend Swartz (who travels with me & whose Stall was next to mine) began to call forth amain with a loud complaining accent affirming that his Face and Mouth were full of Piss and all his Bedding wetted with the same, our Servants (who in this country never sleep as they have nothing to sleep upon) soon took the Alarm & with lights came rushing in to learn the cause of all this outcry, when behold from the ceiling of the dirty Room over us came issuing down in a most copious Stream a Flood of briny Element which some poor Females unable to resist the pressing calls of nature for want of a more convenient vessel had abundantly scattered on the floor, & which by easy penetration had found its way in one continued stream to the Phiz of my unfortunate friend who was unhappily sleeping with mouth extended in a perpendicular line under them.

But however after all the fategues of coming at it, the city of Granada well repays our pains, for nothing certainly can be more glorious than its situation, especialy the so justly renowned Palace of the Alhambra which stands conspicuous on the summitt of a prodigious Hill and looks down on all the spreading town beneath it; Providence sure formed this place for a royal station, & the earliest Inhabitants seem to have taken the hint, for here are both Roman & Gothick Ruins in great abundance which seem to speak this always the place of Soveregnty, here too a great Emperor Charles the 5th, began to build a Palace, the outward case is finished of Marble after the highest manner, this by his Successors has been neglected and in glorious Ruins speaks the negligence of the latter Kings of Spain; but the Moorish buildings here exceed imagination, & with amazement show the tast of these once mighty People whom we so unjustly style Barbarians; these consist of many courts & cloisters the Pillars & Pavements all of Marble, of the same materials too are [page 4] all their Halls & Chambers beautifully intermixed with inlaid Pebles of a thousand different colours, the Roofs are frett work and beyond imagination exquisite in their kind of a composition likest to China whare which strikes the fancy with the most agreeable vew in the world, in every hall & court are fountains some of Jaspar, these for ever spout their waters amidst groves of Roses of Oranges of Jessamine, & there Streems serve to water all the palace; innumerable are their Baths & Grottos, and the whole Fabrick seems designed on purpose for Scenes of Love and pleasure, to which also the Climate much induces for here there is one eternal round of Summer, and yet the Mountains at the foot of which the Palace stands are for ever covered with the whitest Snow, which helps to make the Prospect from this Royal Seat perhaps the most agreeable as it certainly is the most romantick in the World, by this the Air is always temperate, & the Horizon in a most charming manner serene; ones Scenses are perfectly transported amidst these continual noise of falling Waters and the delightfull scents of all the fragrant groves with which every court abounds especially those where the Women used to be kept. nothing can be more solemn than the silence of this place, no noise but that of waters can

affect it, in short words are wanting to describe half the Beautys of this earthly
Paradise, all seems inchantment & another world. I design from hence for Cadiz
there to embark for the South of France; I already find great amendment in my
state of health, though am not yet able to walk without pain & difficulty,
My affectionate service attends all the good Family from
    Dear Maurice   Your faithfull Affectionate & very humble
                    Servant
                      Hen. Johnson
Annotated by Maurice Johnson: 'L[r] from H. Johnson Esq President of the Asiento
FA & SG Societys.'

[1]   Henry Johnson preferred to date his letters from the Continent using the English Old Style dating.
[2]   Mould: a mole, pier or breakwater.

181. SGS No 28: From Revd Edward Saul[1] to Maurice Johnson.
Belvoir, 6 April 1733.
MB2 fol.84B, 19 April 1733.
Explains that he is now 'Chaplain in waiting' at Belvoir Castle and has been
discussing Melton Roos[2] part of the Duke of Rutland's north Lincolnshire land,
and the gallows newly re-erected there; asks if Johnson has any records of
antiquities there, and any explanation of why the Rutland family still maintains
these gallows.

[1]   Revd Edward Saul (d.1753) was Rector of Harlaxton (Lincs), a village close to the Duke of
Rutland's castle at Belvoir. He was known to the SGS as the author of *An Historical and Philosophical Account of the Barometer* (London, 1730). He had been a Fellow of Magdalen College, Oxford,
from 1698 to 1704 where he was a contributor to a group of experimenters in natural philosophy who
were developing scientific instruments.
[2]   Now Melton Ross near Brigg.

182. From George Lynn senior[1] to Maurice Johnson.
[Southwick], 7 April 1733.
MB2 fol.107B, 11 April 1734.
Encloses for SGS 'Abridgement of my 8 years Register or Diary [of the weather]
1726–1733'; provides very detailed notes on barometer and thermometer
readings, rain and wind as observed and recorded by him at his home in Southwick
(Northants).[2]

[1]   See his entry in Appendix 2.
[2]   This information was also communicated to the RS as part of their recording of weather; see their
Philosophical Transactions VIII i 604.

183. Draft of reply by Maurice Johnson to Edward Saul.[1]
Spalding, 16 April 1733.
MB2 fol.84B, 19 April 1733.
Replies to Saul's request for information about the connection of the Dukes of
Rutland with Melton Roos 'in Yarborough hundred in the Parts of Lindsey';
refers to relevant charters, explains the connection of the families of Trusbut,
Roos and Albini with the Manners family, now Dukes of Rutland, and their
ownership of land; explains that the gallows was erected as a warning after an
affray between the Tyrwhitt and De Roos families in 1412 about common land

there, which was settled by the courts in favour of De Roos, an ancestor of the present Duke.

¹ See No 181 above.

184. From William Bogdani to Maurice Johnson.
Tower of London, 10 May 1733.
MB2 fol.86B, 17 May 1733.
Gives an account of an entry in Dr Mandeville's papers relating to the institution of a Vicar of Moulton in 1705 and other problems relating to the living of Moulton; discusses a date in an inscription in Sutterton Church and the difficulty of reading it; thanks Johnson for the SGS's observations of the eclipse[1] in Spalding which he has sent and compares them with the London observations made by the Royal Society.
Annotated by Johnson: 'Lr from Wm Bogdani Esq. FRS. Inscr in Sutterton Ch. Robt Wilby instit. in Vicar de Moulton 30 Aug. 1705. Eclipse.'

¹ A partial eclipse of the sun on 2 June 1733: the SGS's report on it in the Minute Book is an important contribution to the study of eclipses.

185. SGS No 67: From Richard Falkner to Maurice Johnson, in letter to Mrs Johnson senior [the remainder is missing].[1]
[Lincoln College, Oxford: Undated but dateable to end July/early August 1733.]
MB2 fol.91A, 9 August 1733.
Thanks Johnson for 'your obliging letter'; will 'execute the Orders you gave me in your last'; encloses verses from the 1733 'Oxford Act'.[2]
Enclosure: Latin verses, 'Morbus Anglicus'.

¹ Falkner had just gone as an undergraduate to Oxford with the intention of becoming a doctor. He is writing to his mother, Maurice Johnson senior's third wife, and encloses material for SGS meetings. Only the section of these letters intended for the SGS was kept by Johnson in his archive of the Society's correspondence; presumably the more personal section was kept by Falkner's mother. See Falkner's entry in Appendix 2 and the family tree in Appendix 5.
² A celebration at the giving of degrees. The 1733 'Act', in which students read satirical Latin verses, was a famous and lively occasion, and proved to be the final one of this kind. Falkner, who appears to have arrived in Oxford in time to attend the 'Act', sent copies of some of these verses to Johnson in following letters for the SGS. The Latin verses enclosed with this letter are a humorous discussion of what Johnson called 'the Hipp' [abbreviation for 'hypochondria']: melancholy or depression, alleged at the period to be a typically English ailment.

186. No 24: From William Bogdani to Maurice Johnson.
Tower of London, 9 August 1733.
MB2 fol.93A, 16 August 1733.
Thanks Johnson for becoming godfather to his son, William Maurice Bogdani;[1] sends congratulations on Revd Walter Johnson's preferment;[2] regrets to hear that 'the young intended Doctor'[3] was prevented by illness from coming to London; discusses specimens of seahorses; approves of the horse races taking place at Spalding as encouraging exercise in young men, but regrets the modern profit motive for them and compares it unfavourably with Classical practice; describes and sketches a coin of Tiberius.
Annotated by Johnson: 'Lr from Wm Bogdani Esq FRS of the Hippocampus Fish. in Laudem SGSp. his Rom. Coins of Albinus &c. Drawing of a Tiberius with the Reverse the Altar ROMAE ET AUGUSTO.'

[1]   As an adult, William Maurice Bogdani became an SGS member and sent Latin poetry from King's College, Cambridge, where he was a student.
[2]   This was perhaps his appointment as Chaplain to the Duke of Buccleuch. He was instituted successively as Vicar of Leeke (Staffs) in 1735 and as Rector of Redmarshall (Co. Durham) in 1737. See *Admissions to the College of St John the Evangelist in the University of Cambridge*, 4 vols (Cambridge, 1882–1931), iii. 358.
[3]   This is presumably Richard Falkner. Bogdani wrote to Falkner at Oxford on 17 May 1735, as someone whom he already knew and who shared his interest in mathematics; see No 249 below. John Green had already lodged with Bogdani at the Tower in early 1730; see his letter, No 116 above.

187. SGS No 10: From Beaupré Bell to Maurice Johnson.
[Beaupré Hall], 3 September 1733.
MB2 fol.94B, 6 September 1733.
Gives details of some of the 40 or 50 seals he has sent to Johnson by Wood's Waggon; admits that 'I have not Tast to admire such rude performances as most of our English coins, especially the most Ancient, are; which give Light to no History, & are only standing proofs of the Ignorance and Inartifice of our Ancestors'.

188. SGS No 140: From Edward Tebb[1] to Maurice Johnson.
Horncastle, 5 September 1733.
MB2 fol.94B, 6 September 1733.
Gives news of the finding of 'a Pot of Old Roman Coynes' while digging a canal at Hainton (Lincs) for Mr Heneage.

[1]   He cannot be identified further. The Heneage family owned Hainton Hall.

189. From Richard Falkner to Maurice Johnson, in letter to Mrs Johnson senior [the remainder is missing].
[Lincoln College, Oxford: undated but dateable to early September 1733.]
MB2 fol.94B, 6 September 1733.
Sends verses composed on Handel's performance of the oratorio 'Deborah' at 'our Theatre';[1] gives news of the laying of the first stone of the new quadrangle at Magdalen College, which is to be 'a noble Square' and to cost £9,000.[2]

[1]   The Sheldonian Theatre, Oxford.
[2]   This quadrangle was never completed; only one side was built.

190. SGS No 69: From Richard Falkner to Maurice Johnson, in letter to Mrs Johnson senior [the remainder is missing].
[Lincoln College, Oxford, undated but dateable to just before 20 September 1733.]
See MB2 fol.95A for 20 September 1733.
Explains that he could not get the copies of poems that Johnson required as 'most of our College is out of Town' but sends verses on the Almanac; he has sent to 'Bro: Tho: Falkner'[1] a picture 'which I painted'; expresses sympathy that Mrs Johnson, Maurice Johnson's wife, has been ill.
Enclosed: Latin verses, 'Calendarium Oxoniense 1733 … Composuit Rdus. Grey DD e Coll. Linc.'[2]

[1]   His elder brother, Revd Thomas Falkner, incumbent of Saleby near Alford. See Introduction, p. 000.
[2]   Revd Dr Richard Grey, Fellow of Lincoln College and eventually Archdeacon of Bedford.

191. No 25: From Beaupré Bell to Maurice Johnson.
Beaupré Hall, 16 September 1733.
MB2 fol.95A, 20 September 1733.
Discusses a MS of Magna Carta which he has sent to Johnson and the best methods of cataloguing coins; explains his own method of cataloguing; asks for spares of any duplicate fossils from the SGS collection, listing those he most wants; comments on the quality of Romano-British coins.

192. SGS No 43: From Maurice Johnson to Richard Falkner at Oxford.
Spalding, 26 September 1733.
Discusses the nautilus, with a sketch of it,[1] and gives Oppian's[2] description of it as discussed at a recent SGS meeting; offers a translation of Oppian into English verse, presumably by himself.

[1] This sketch is a copy of one in the Minute Book, MB 2 fols 95B and 96A (20 and 27 September 1733); the verse translation is also transcribed there. See also No 195 below. The nautilus was discussed at the SGS on 20 and 27 September 1733.

[2] Greek poet (second century AD), who wrote a poem on fish and fishing.

193. On same sheet as previous letter, No 192.
From Mrs Ann Johnson Senior to Richard Falkner [her son].[1]
[Undated, but sent by same post (26 September 1733).]

I beleve you will think I have very mutch forgot you haveing deferred a post longer then ueshall but indeed you are always in my thoughts, Mr Neve told me that to his great satisfaction he found you close at your study which he sade gave him mutch more plesuer then if you had been in company he was sorry he had no more time with you, I yesterday parted with your brother & sister Burton who had been with me but two nights I carried her in the Coch to the fife bells in Gosbertown[2] & from thence she rid home your pappa has got a great could or elyse I had this week gon to Alford & took your sister & gerls with me but when I shall be able to goe now I cannot tell, I hope by this your tuter is comed home & that he will in a short time be soe kind as let you have a beater rume[3] for I fear yours is a mallancolly one Mr Johnson was very well pleased with your last versis & allways pays me for your Leter which I wish I could transfer to you; my Dear boy take great care of your selfe & if you think you want to take any Phisick doe not omitt it, poor Molly Sharp is I think past danger but exceeding weake, wee are now more healthy then wee have been but some peeple yet sick, Mr Whiting[4] is now gon for preests orders & as is sade will ether be Mr Neves Cuarat[5] at Weson or Cuarat to Mr Lyon in this town, your brother & sister Falkner has been at Thorganbee ∧ a fortnight ther litel boy very well, your papa gives his kind Love & blessing to you next time I write he & all the rest of the famaly desire ther complements to you, my sarvis to your tuter & to Mr Lott if in Collige he is so kind as expres a great regard for you, I pray god bless you beleve me allways your very affectinat & tender mother
      Ann Johnson

[1] These letters illustrate the complex relationships within the Johnson family. Mrs Ann Johnson, referred to by Maurice Johnson in his letter (No 192) as 'Our Mother', is Falkner's mother by her second marriage, to Thomas Falkner of Boston, and Maurice Johnson's stepmother by her third marriage, to Maurice's father (Maurice Johnson senior), referred to in this letter as 'your pappa'. Johnson and Falkner are thus stepbrothers, despite Johnson being a generation older than Falkner,

who was approximately the same age as Johnson's eldest son Maurice. This letter was presumably kept by Falkner and added to the SGS archive after Falkner's death.

[2]   The Five Bells Inn at Gosberton, a few miles north of Spalding, was open until very recently. Opposite the inn, the Boston road turns off from the Donington road.

[3]   'rume': room.

[4]   Samuel Whiting, the Master of the Grammar School at Spalding, who had taught Falkner there. He was ordained to the priesthood by Bishop Reynolds of Lincoln at Buckden on 23 September 1733 (LAO, Register 38).

[5]   'Cuarat': Curate. Revd Timothy Neve was Vicar of Weston from 1721 until 1748 when he was succeeded by Samuel Whiting.

194. SGS No 66: From Richard Falkner to Maurice Johnson in letter to Mrs Johnson senior [the remainder is missing].

[Lincoln College, Oxford: Week preceeding 4 October 1733 (postmark 29 September).]

MB2 fol.97A, 4 October 1733.

Sends Latin verses: 'Anthomania' on the current passion for new types of flower, including tulips.[1]

[1]   This would be of particular interest to Johnson, who was a keen gardener and flower-grower.

195. SGS No 101: From William Bogdani to Maurice Johnson.

Tower of London, 4 October 1733.

MB2 fol.96B, 4 and 11 October 1733.

Has sent, as requested, drawings of the nautilus, with descriptions by Classical authors; requests Johnson's comments on the drawings of an idol, possibly Egyptian, which he has sent; reports that Sir Hans Sloane would be pleased to become an SGS member;[1] sends genealogical details of the family of Wakefeild; discusses an inscription found during the rebuilding of the tower of St George's Church, Southwark; gives family news.

Annotated by Johnson: 'Lr from Wm Bogdani Esq FRA & G Socc with Drawings of Nautilus & Bicorpus Idol in my Collection. Family of Wakefeild. part of an Inscription found in St Georges Church in Southwark.'

[1]   MB2 fol.45B records his election to membership.

196. SGS No 68: From Richard Falkner to Maurice Johnson (son).

[Lincoln College, Oxford], 12 October 1733.

MB2 fol.97A, 18 October 1733.

Begins 'Dear Maurice'; gives a detailed account of life in College and a description of Dr Isham the Rector.[1]

Enclosed: Latin verses 'Hortus Botanicus'.

Also second letter to Maurice Johnson [the Secretary], above part of the poem: Thanks Johnson for sending the translation of Oppian (referring to the nautilus) explains that he has shown the inscription on the Egyptian statue to his tutor who says the letters are not Arabic and promises to show it to an antiquarian; says he is sorry to hear Dr Colby's[2] son is ill.

[1]   Falkner was a close friend of Maurice Johnson (son) who was very close to him in age, although the relationship between them was technically that of uncle and nephew, as Falkner's mother had married Maurice Johnson (son)'s grandfather; they attended Spalding Grammar School together. See No 156 above. Dr Eusebius Isham, the Rector of Lincoln College, died in 1755.

[2]   Dr Dixon Colby of Stamford, an SGS member; see No 147 above and Colby's letter, No 404 below.

197. SGS No 102: From Beaupré Bell to Maurice Johnson.
[Beaupré Hall], 15 October 1733.
MB2 fol.97B, 18 October 1733.
Discusses getting some medals from Dr Mead's[1] collection engraved; asks if Johnson can get leave from Sir Richard Ellys to have his coin of Carausius copied; quotes an amusing rhyming epitaph for John Bell of Brakenhow who 'ligs under this stean' and gives his translation of it into Latin verse.

1　Dr Richard Mead (1673–1754), physician and antiquarian. See his entry in *ODNB*.

198. SGS No 49: From Richard Falkner to Maurice Johnson.
[Lincoln College, Oxford], 22 October 1733.
MB2 fol.99A, 1 November 1733.
Discusses the inscriptions under the 'Egyptian Images'; the 'Arabick Professor' says they are not Arabic but 'some Conceit of a Semichristian'; discusses new buildings in Oxford, explaining that some old houses have been pulled down to make another 'Wing at Queen's' College for which the Queen has given money; no verses are included with his letter on this occasion, as he is busy with disputations in College.

199. Portion of letter[1] from Maurice Johnson to Maurice Johnson (son) for SGS
Devereux Court, London, 17 November 1733.
He has taken letters from Maurice Johnson senior and John Johnson to Mr Moreland who sends news of the progress of a legal case they are concerned with; gives an account of recent activities at the RS and SA.

1　MB2 fol.100A (22 November 1733) gives a summary of a missing portion of this letter, an account of the character of the Prince of Orange given by someone who has met him. The Dutch Prince was about to come to England to marry the Princess Royal and several letters in 1734 refer to this (Nos 207, 214, 216, 217 and 218).

200. Copy of a letter from Joseph Ames to William Bogdani.
London, 17 November 1733.
MB1 fol.186A, 17 November 1733.

Good S^r　　　　　　　　　　　　　　　　　　London 17 Novr 1733
In obedience to your Request as well as my own Inclination, to make known the Character of a Virtuous Stranger: I shall give it you, as I have received it both from himself & Others – know then S^r that Job the son of Abraham, the Son of Solyman, the Son of Abdula &c was born to Abraham by his first wife Tautamata About 31 Years agoe: his Father being a Mahometan Priest; and of Note in the Languages was chose to be Tutor to the present Governour Sambo the son of Galaga, when his brother Boub governed Foutrè in Affrica; at a Town called Bondo situate on a Branch of the River Niger or Senegal about the Latitude 13 and Longitude 8 from London Job was born. His Youth was taken up in Learning, so that he could repeat the Koran by memory at 15 Years of Age He hath Learned Three Languages Besides the Fuller which is his Mother Tongue: vizt the Arabic, the Ganna & the Gallumbo & since the English. In his more advanced Years he taught Youth Arabic & dealt for Negroes &c, & in one Journey went five Weeks from Home towards Egypt. He says that the Arabians come into his Country for a certain Root, ˄^contrayerva 1 by which they cause Poisons (Perhaps it might be of

Use to Us to know It.) That he hath 2 Wives, 4 Children, 18 Servants, 3 Houses, 73 Head of Black Cattle, besides Asses and other Things: That his time was spent in the Offices of the Priesthood, and taking care of his Plantation. He went at the desire of his Father to sell two Negro Boys with a Caution not to go beyond the River Gambia but not meeting with the Success he desired ventured further with his Servant and sold the Boys for 28 Head of Cattle; on his returne home with the Cattle, a People called Mandingoes watch'd an Opportunity and seiz'd Him; and sold Him & his Servant to one Capt: Pike in the Service of Mr Henry Hunt Merchant in London, to whome before he had offered his Boys; so that the Capt. remembring him, gave him leave to write for his Ransom Monday Tuesday Wednesday & Thursday in March 1731. But the time being too short, He was obliged to sail of Fryday & carryed Job to Maryland, and there delivered Him to Mr Vachell Denton (Factor to Mr Hunt) who sold him to Mr Alexander Tulcey of Kent Island in Chesapeach Bay a little to the East of Annapolis, who soon employed Him to keep his Cattle, where he wrote that Arabick Letter that was after sent over in Mr Hunt's Packet (which I took a Copy of and endeavoured to get it translated). He spent much time with Mr John Humphrys Minister of Annapolis to teach Him Arabick. It hapened that Mr Oglethorpe[2] whether out of Tenderness, or thinking he might be usefull, desired Mr Hunt to purchase Him & left Bond to be satisfied by the Honourable the Affrican Company: accordingly He was brought over in May last, & lodged at Lime-house, where he hath wrote all the Koran over twice. He speaks tolerable English, & waits expecting to be sent to Gambia by the first Ship that goes in the Companys Service. I might have enlarged but let this Suffice at present from

Your affectionate Friend J Ames

He was ransomed by Mr Brassey Member of Parliament for Hertford & some other Gent. for £40 & £20 charges of Air Board & Keeping.

Annotated by Johnson: 'Mr J. Ames. Secr of the Antiq Soc London.

Account of Job Jalla $_\wedge$Dgiallo[3] in a L^r to Mr Bogdani of the Office of Ordnance in the Tower of London Socc. Reg. Antiq. & Gen.S.S. where I Conversed with this African Mahometan Preist 23 May 1734 who then wrote the Arabick before & after the following Address to the Gent. Soc. The Gentlemen who subscribed the Proposeing him for a Member of SGS London, 17 November 173 were the Honble James West of Lincolns Inn London TRS & Member of SGS and George Holmes Esq Deputy Record Keeper of the Tower of Lond^n FR & GS Spalding assented to by the said Wm Bogdani Esq and me Maurice Johnson.'

On reverse: Maurice Johnson's retrospective comments in support of Dgiallo, dated August 1750, demonstrating Johnson's policy of reviewing and annotating his archived correspondence. He gives references to two books[4] which describe Dgiallo's experiences:

'In Astley Collection of Voyages published in 2° at Lond^n 1745 Vol II are Several Accounts of this Learned Priest Job Jalla called by Moore p.229 Job ben Solomon & Cap. VII p.234 is of the Remarkable Captivity and Deliverance of him, being a Mohammedan Priest of Bûnda, near the River Gambra in 1732 & of his Country of Futâ in Africa called commonly Sanaga, Bunda was built by His Grandfather Abraham in the Reign of Abubekir King of Futâ & [?]dos hereditarily as the Priesthood there belong to him. whos whole history taken from Mr Moores

Account who was with him there, & in the Service of the African Company. And from Mr Blets account of him in a book he publish in 8° Lond^n 1734 from Job's own Mouth with who he was intimate with him in Maryland in America When he was there Sold for a Slave as well as afterwards in England when redeemed, & sent back to his own Country. to which I refer the Reader, and Add of my own Knowledge who spent some time in his Company and had opportunity to ask and heard him asked many Questions relating to him Self and Countrie That I believe the Accounts therein given of Both to be True. He was an Open, Candid, humane & Good man Spake English well enough to be understood, was Skilful in and wrote Arabic well & fast or very readily and Six other Eastern languages Dialects thereof used in differing Kingdomes of Africa, wore the Alchoran of his own writeing in a ribband hung on his breast a White Cotton long robe & a White Muslin Turban the Capp Crimson Velvett. he could repeat the whole Alchoran mementer, & so thrice Wrote it Over here & presented those MSS to Nathaniel Brassey Esq Burgess for Bedford/ Hertford who ransomed him and then to his Grace the Duke of Mountague who introduced him to the King and Queen and all the Royal Family, & made him many Rich & Sumptuous Presents, worthy both their Dignitys, with Models of every Machine, Instrument & Implement he desird who was very Curious in Mechanism & carryd back with him many of ours & more in Modles. & the third to Sir Hans Sloan Bartt President of the RS for whom he translated several Oriental Inscriptions & Coins & MSS

M Johnson President of SGS

1 August 1750

[1]   *The Royal English Dictionary* (5th edn, London, 1775) glosses 'contrayerva' as 'In Medicine and Botany, a species of birthwort'.

[2]   This could be the colonial governor in North America, James Oglethorpe (1696–1785); see his entry in *ODNB*.

[3]   These are Maurice Johnson's two attempts to spell his name, the first a more phonetic version, the second perhaps added later after reading the two books referred to on the reverse of the letter. Job Dgiallo, or Job ben Solomon (Ayuba Suleiman Diallo, 1701–1773), an Islamic scholar from West Africa, underwent the adventures described in the letter. When Johnson met him, he had been ransomed and was in London awaiting transport back to Africa; he was a great social success in London, as Johnson's notes on the reverse of the letter indicate. He was elected to membership of the SGS in 1733.

[4]   *A New General Collection of Voyages and Travels* (London: printed for Thomas Astley, 1745); Francis Moore, *Travels into the Inland Parts of Africa* (London, 1738). There is also a full account of Job in Thomas Bluett, *Some Memoirs of the Life of Job, the son of Solomon* (London, 1734); its frontispiece depicts Job in the exact costume that Maurice Johnson describes above.

201. Postscript of letter from Maurice Johnson to his brother John Johnson, intended for a meeting of the SGS.
[London], 22 November 1733, annotated: 'Communicated at SGS 29 Nov 1733'. MB2 fol.100A, 29 November 1733.
Gives an account of a recent RS meeting he has attended which included: discussion of methods used by Topham the Strong Man;[1] an account of 'Muscular Motion' by Dr Desaguliers; a letter from Beaupré Bell with a specimen of a haycock 'vitrified by Lightning'; an account of observations of the transit of Jupiter's satellites; a machine 'to hold the Eye steady for Couching' by Dr Desaguliers; a drawing of two conjoined foetuses.
Also gives an account of an SA meeting, where a set of Hollar prints of Holbein's

Dance of Death was presented; two sets of these prints are promised, one for the SGS and one for Johnson's own collection.

¹   Thomas Topham was famous for his remarkable feats of strength, of which he gave public exhibitions. The Royal Society exhibition was in connection with Dr Desaguliers' talk on 'Muscular Motion'. See Topham's biography in *ODNB*. For Desaguliers, see No 226 n.1 below.

202. SGS No 19: From Richard Falkner to Maurice Johnson.
[Lincoln College, Oxford: Undated but dateable to shortly before 20 December 1733.]
MB2 fol.101A, 20 December 1733.
Explains that he has not written to Johnson in London because he is awaiting an explanation of the inscription;¹ sends a sketch of a silver medal with inscription 'C.Licinius Mag.'; promises to send verses on the Prince of Orange's wedding.

¹   See Nos 195, 196 and 198 above.

1734

203. From William Bogdani to Maurice Johnson.
Tower of London, 1 January 1733 [actually1734].¹
MB2 fol.103A, 3 January 1733/4.
Accepts the honour of being godfather to Johnson's son Henry, refers to Henry's baptism and thanks John Johnson for deputising for him there; discusses the serious illness of his own son, Maurice Johnson's godson, and the methods of treating him; encloses his ideas on 'the Antient Musick' at MJ's request; sends New Year greetings.
Annotated by Johnson: 'Lr from the Ingenious & Learned My Good Friend W. Bogdani Esq FR & A Socc. London & SGS. On Musick. Read at that Anniversary of the Institution of SGS.'

¹   Dated by the date of Henry Eustace Johnson's birth, 26 December 1733. Bogdani frequently used the 'old system' of dating.

204. SGS: From William Bogdani to Maurice Johnson.
Tower of London, 1 January 1733 [actually 1734; see preceding letter].
MB2 fol.103A, 3 January 1733/4.
Lengthy letter giving a full account of his ideas on the history of music.

205. From Richard Falkner to Mrs Elizabeth Johnson, wife of Maurice Johnson.
[Lincoln College, Oxford], 1 January 1734.
MB2 fol.103A, 3 January 1733/4.
Begins 'Madam': Thanks her for her letter; sends verses in English about two Oxford ladies, made by 'a Gentleman of this College who was with Mr Wesley at Spalding about 6 years ago & is now gon to be his Curate'.¹
Enclosed: English verses 'Bright Sally glowing in her full blown Charms ...'

¹   MB2 fol.103A notes 'Rev Mr Whitelamb late of Linc. Coll. Oxford'. This was Revd John Whitelamb of Epworth, a protégé of the Wesleys, who was a student at Lincoln College when John Wesley was a tutor there. After ordination he returned to Epworth, married Mary, daughter of Revd Samuel Wesley senior, and served as Rector of the neighbouring parish of Wroot from 1734 until 1769. It has been suggested that while Whitelamb was at Oxford, John Wesley intervened in a developing

relationship between Whitelamb and some young women whom Wesley regarded as unsuitable for a member of his circle of devout young men; perhaps these verses are Whitelamb's tribute to these women (V. H. H. Green, *The Young Mr Wesley* (London, 1961), 233–6).

206. SGS No 103: From Beaupré Bell to Maurice Johnson.
[Beaupré Hall], 26 January 1733/4.
Gives details of books and prints of coins sent to Johnson by Wood's Waggon; sends copies of his updated proposals to print his book by subscription.
Specimen copy of the proposals attached by Johnson.

207. SGS No 65: From Richard Falkner to Maurice Johnson.
[Lincoln College, Oxford], 28 January 1734.
MB2 fol.104A, 31 January 1733/4.
Sends verses on the Prince of Orange's wedding 'made by one of our College'.
Enclosed: Latin verses 'Dum plausu vario populus …'

208. SGS No 80: From William Bogdani to Maurice Johnson.
[London], February 1733 [actually 1734].
MB2 fol.104B, 21 February 1734.
Gives an account of a hydraulic machine and its operation.
Annotated by Johnson: 'To the Gent. Soc. at Spalding communicated from Wm. Bogdani Esq. a member of the Soc. & of the Royal & Antiq. Socc. Feby 1733. Effects of a Hydraulic Machine Invented by 2 Clergymen in Picardy.'

209. From Beaupré Bell to Maurice Johnson.
[Beaupré Hall], 9 February 1733/4.
MB2 fol.106A, 21 March 1734.
Explains that he has received a cast from Johnson's coin of Aelius; asks him to procure a drawing and engraving of Sir Richard Ellys's bijugate coin of Carausius, exactly to size.
Included with this: sketches by Johnson of the coin 'which I drew from the coin itself rubbd on the paper. MJ 28 Febr', also a sketch of Ellys's porphyry vase, in Ellys's library.[1]

[1] The letter does not specify whether this was Ellys's library in his house in Bolton Street, London or at Nocton (Lincs), though the London library is more probable as Johnson was frequently in London and there is no record of him visiting Nocton.

210. SGS No 60: From Maurice Johnson (son)[1] to Maurice Johnson.
Spalding, 9 February 1733 [actually 1734].
Replies to Johnson's letter; gives account of an SGS meeting[1] and sends drawings of the shellfish Blatta Bizantina, as discussed there, with a long Latin quotation discussing the origin of its name and its uses in dyeing and medicine; requests more oil and paints for his drawings.

[1] The eldest son of Maurice Johnson the SGS Secretary; see his entry in Appendix 2.
[2] An account of this meeting is given in MB2 fol.104B, 7 February 1734. There are two definitions of the Blatta Bizantina; the one most closely fitting the sketch is the shell of a freshwater shellfish.

211. SGS No 71: From Richard Falkner to Maurice Johnson in London.
[Lincoln College, Oxford], 20 February 1734.
MB2 fol.105B, 28 February 1734.
Expresses thanks for Johnson's offer of services in Town; has heard from Maurice Johnson (son) with 'a very pretty Drawing of Hippocrates's Head'; sends an epigram on the Prince of Orange's wedding, by Mr Young's son.
Enclosed: Latin verses 'Auriacus Batavis princeps festinat ab Oris ...'

212. SGS No 23?: From Maurice Johnson to Richard Falkner at Oxford.
London, 23 February 1733/4.
Thanks him for sending Mr Young's Epithalamium;[1] comments on current political upheavals in London; gives news of activities at the RS including Dr Desaguliers's 'New Astronomical Machine' and at the SA including Vertue's engraving of a medal of Mary Queen of Scots and Lord Darnley; gives Spalding news including the fact that 'Dr Dinham's married to the widow Browne and intends this summer to sash the front of his house'[2] and of Dr Green's planned course of study in Leiden and elsewhere.

[1]   See previous letter, No 211.
[2]   Dr Dinham's house in London Road, Spalding, still has sash windows. His portrait and that of his wife are in the upstairs room of the SGS's museum and library at Spalding. Dr Dinham was an early member of the SGS, elected in 1722; his son John became President in 1759.

213. No 25: From Beaupré Bell to Maurice Johnson.
[Beaupré Hall], 23 February 1733/4.
MB2 fol.106A, 7 March 1734.
He has sent Johnson a specimen of hay vitrified by lightning[1]; discusses different casting techniques for use with coins and medals; comments on criticism of his own handwriting.

[1]   Maurice Johnson's letter to the SGS from London on 22 November 1733 (No 201 above) records hearing this discussed at the RS.

214. SGS No 70: From Richard Falkner to Maurice Johnson in London.
Lincoln College, Oxford, 25 February 1734.
MB2 fol.106A, 7 March 1734.
Sends 'verses on Coines'; discusses preparations in Oxford for the Prince of Orange who is to visit the next day; explains that the verses about the wedding are to be recited.
Latin verses 'Nummus Historicus', with the explanation that 'R. Hoblin e CCC sup Ordin: Commensar. recitavit in theatro Jul 6 1733'.[1]

[1]   Robert Hoblyn (1710–1756): politician and book-collector; see his entry in *ODNB*.

215. SGS No.46: From Maurice Johnson for the SGS.
[London], February 1733/4 [no day specified, no salutation; probably the first portion of the letter was not kept for the SGS archive].
MB2 fol.105A, 28 February 1734.
Discusses the inscription on the tomb of Chyndonax,[1] giving a quotation in French from a book of 1623, with a drawing; comments on Desaguliers's planetarium, shown at the RS, and on the SA's activities; sends a copy of the picture of Boccaccio and Petrarch from the book in Mr James West's library, mentioned in a previous letter of 22 December 1732 (No175).

¹ The tomb of Chyndonax, a Druid, whose alleged tomb with an inscription in Greek letters was discovered near Dijon in 1598. It was described by Jean Guenebault in *Le Réveil de Chyndonax* (Dijon, 1621). It would be of interest to Johnson and Stukeley since this was the name adopted by Stukeley in the Society of Roman Knights, to which Johnson also belonged, using the Roman name of Prasutagus.

216. SGS No 87: From William Bogdani to Maurice Johnson.
Tower of London, 9 March 1733 [actually 1734].
MB2 fol.106A, 14 March 1734.
Has sent by the Peterborough carrier a box of 'oil colours' for painting pictures,¹ intended for MJ's son Maurice, which he lists in full with their prices; gives an account of the Prince of Orange's admission as a member of the Royal Society. Annotated by Johnson: 'a Lr from Wm. Bogdani Esq. FRS that Manner of the Prince of Oranges being admitted a Member of the Royal Society London & his Reception thereat.'²

¹ This indicates Bogdani's familiarity with painting as the son of a successful painter; see his biography in Appendix 2 and that of his father Jacob in *ODNB*.
² William Charles Henry Friso, Prince of Orange, was admitted a Royal Fellow of the RS on 7 March 1734.

217. SGS No 59: From Richard Falkner to Mrs Johnson senior.
Lincoln College, Oxford, 11 March 1734.
MB2 fol.106A, 14 and 21 March 1734.

Honoured Madam¹   SGS No 59
As the most remarkable ₍Thing₎ that has lately happen'd here, is the Prince of Orange's visiting the University, I suppose you will expect to have an Account of his being entertain'd, which I think was in as elegant a Manner as could be. he was presented with the Degree of Dʳ of Law & desir'd that all the Noblemen who attended him might have the same Honour, which were 7. The Theatre at the Time of his taking ₍it₎ was as full as at the Act, but not so many Strangers as then. Digby Cotes our Orator made him a fine Speech after which ~~he~~ ₍the Prince₎ address'd himself to the Vicechancellor in Latin, & thank'd him for the Honour the University had done him, & that it shou'd receive the first Marks of his Favour, this Solemnity was concluded with a fine Concert of Musick, vocal and instrumental. at his Return from Blenheim he was met by all the Companys of Tradesmen who conducted him to the Town-Hall, where the Recorder made him a Speech, & the next Morning sent him his Freedom in a gold Box. The great Street was illuminated quite through with above 100 Candles in a Window which ₍made₎ a glorious Show, and, as he is now a Member both of the City and University, the same will be observ'd at his Wedding. The Election for Members here runs very high, the opposite Partys have many Fights & it is thought there will be much Mischief done before it is over; most of the College Gates are lockt up at nine; lest the Gowns-men shou'd suffer by their Quarrells. The Judges came into Town on Saturday, if there be any executed, 'tis likely there will [be] some Mischief, for the Members of the University commonly endeavour to carry off the Body to the Anatomy School.²
Dr Dimock's Brother and Mr Hickman, Mr Brown's Winecooper, call'd on me the other Day and I shew 'em what I cou'd in the Time they stay'd. I shall not have kept Act Term, till the latter End of June, when I hope to see You & all Friends.

If you see or write to Bro: Tho: pray desire [him] to send me a Bill as soon as he can & the Books. As the University has regain'd its ill Character by this ^late Instance of their Loyalty, 'tis thought Prince Frederick[3] will come & make another publick Act this Year. I believe you are by this time tir'd, so with Duty to Pappa, & Service to the Family I conclude
Honoured Madam your most dutiful Son
        Richd Falkner   Oxon Mar. the 11 1734
I have sent Mr Johnson some
more of the Copy of Verses call'd
Pyrrho Redivivus which he received
long since; & will trouble him
with the remainder in my next.

Annotated by Maurice Johnson: 'L^r from the Learned Mr R^d Falkner of Linc. Coll. Oxf^d of the Pr. of Oranges reception there & being presented to the Degree of LL D. With Pyrrho Redivivus.'[4]
Also included for Johnson: a further part of a Latin poem 'Pyrrho redivivus', explaining that 'J. Whitfeild AM Æd. Xti composuit. Welbore Ellis, Johann. Roberts Æd. Xti Alumni recitaverunt in Theatro.'

[1] His mother, Ann, née Wood. The widow of a first marriage to Mr William Gonville and a second to Mr Thomas Falkner, a Boston merchant and Richard's father, she was now married to Maurice Johnson senior. See Falkner's entry in Appendix 2 and the notes to her letter, No 193 above.
[2] This would interest Falkner as he was studying for a career in medicine.
[3] The Prince of Wales, son of George II and father of George III, died in 1751 and so never became king. The promised 'Act' did not take place.
[4] This satirical poem in Latin was one of those recited at the 1733 'Act'. Pyrrho was a Greek Sceptic philosopher who lived around 300 BC and the poem, written and recited by undergraduates from Christ Church, takes an equally sceptical view of early eighteenth-century Oxford.

218. SGS No 49: From Maurice Johnson to Richard Falkner.
Spalding, 20 March 1734.

                             Spalding, 20 Mar 1733/4
    I'm now to thank You, Dear S^r both for the favour of Your Letter I received at London with the Verses on Crokers Medaglion[1] which I saw at the Tower when I had the pleasure to accompany his Highness the Duke of Lorraine through the Mint there and all the other Offices As also for so much of the Sequel of the Sceptick[2] which You sent Me in our Mothers last Post with an Account of his Highness the Prince of Oranges reception amongst Yee at Oxford and the Honours Yee very justly shewd him, I must with some sort of Satisfaction Acquaint You That on Thursday last which was his Wedding day The High Shireff of this County[3] Mr Buissiere invited Sir Edmund Probyn the Judge of Assize, the Senior Councell, Clerk of Assize, Masters of the Cathedral Church, and all the Nobility and Gentlemen of the Grandjury, then in Town to a Splendid Entertainment[4] at the White Heart Inn in the Bayle of Lincoln where Wee were sumptuously Feasted and had plenty of French Wine, Musick, and Fireworks playd off before the House, to Drumms and Trumpetts, the whole City gloriously Illuminated, 2 Boon Fires one on Each Side the Great Gates of the Inn and a Hoggshead of Ale there –
Haveing celebrated as They thought these Nuptials on the right day but being mistaken They stayd for a Confirmation of the News: And On Monday last had

an Assembly at the Town hall, with bonefire in the Mercat place: My Wife who is much yours being indisposd of a Violent Cold my Father, Mother, Aunt Johnson, my Couzen her Son with Sister Jackson and Wife and I celebrated at home with Quadrille[5] and Rost Oranges and wine and were merry drinking the Bride and Groom, the King, Royal Family, and all our Friends particularly Your good Health. And hope to see You here this summer that Wee may be merry together at this old house. Mr Bro, Wife and all ours present You with their Services, and I desire You'll believe me to be with sincere esteem

      Dear Sir   Your most affectionate Friend and
                              Faithfull humble Servant
                              Maur. Johnson jun[r]

[1]   John Croker, an engraver who made designs for coins and medals. See No 214 above.
[2]   The Latin verses 'Pyrrho Redivivus'; see No 217 above.
[3]   Lincolnshire.
[4]   To celebrate the Prince of Orange's wedding to the Princess Royal.
[5]   A popular card game of the period (not the dance, which was of a later date.) The game is referred to in the final verse of the ballad quoted in No 122 above.

219. On reverse of No 218: From Maurice Johnson (son) to Richard Falkner at Oxford.
[Spalding, 20 March 1734.]
Thanks him for the verses on the Prince of Orange; gives news of recent proceedings at the SGS[1] including discussion of the Blatta Bizantina and a red porphyry vase owned by Sir Richard Ellys, which he sketches.

[1]   An account of this meeting is given in MB2 fol.106A (7 March 1734).

220. No 57: From Richard Falkner to Maurice Johnson [probably enclosed in a letter to Mrs Johnson senior].
[Lincoln College, Oxford.] Around 9 April 1734 [dateable by post mark].
MB2 fol.107B, 11 April 1734.
Explains that he will send sketches of some altars in the Oxford Picture Gallery; has sent 'Epithalamion Oxoniense'; sends translation of one of Prior's[1] epigrams into Latin: 'Cupidinis Error'.
Annotated by Johnson: 'Cupid mistaken.'

[1]   Matthew Prior (1664–1721): poet and diplomat; see his entry in *ODNB*.

221. From Richard Falkner to Maurice Johnson.
[Lincoln College], Oxford, 22 April 1734.
MB2 fol.108A, 25 April 1734.
Explains that the picture gallery was shut last week as it was a 'time of Festival' so he could not send drawings; gives news of greenhouses to be built in the Physic Garden; comments that there are no plans for a further 'Act';[1] sends an epitaph from St John's College Chapel.

[1]   The 1733 'Act' was indeed the last one to be celebrated in this style; it was replaced by the more decorous Encaenia.

222. SGS No 38: From Dr John Mitchell,[1] on behalf of Sir Richard Ellys, to Maurice Johnson.
London, 25 April 1734.
MB2 fol.108B, 23 May 1734.

Explains that Mitchell has shown an impression from a gem,[2] sent by Johnson, to Sir Richard Ellys who cannot determine the meaning of the inscription; suggests a genuine gem but composite, probably antique but taken from an older gem; Ellys proposes a possible origin in York in the Emperor Severus's time.

[1]   See his entry in Appendix 2.
[2]   An entry in MB2 fol.108B (23 May 1734) says it was 'an intaglia in Mrs Johnson's possession'.

223. SGS No 9: From Richard Falkner to Maurice Johnson in London.
Oxford, 12 May 1734.
MB2 fol.109A, 6 June 1734.[1]
Sends a drawing of a vase from a tombstone in the gallery at Oxford; explains that he is taking a course of mathematical lectures with Mr Badley 'where he shows us a great many curious Experiments'; includes three drawings of Roman tombstones from the museum.

[1]   The Minute Book entry adds that the letter had included 'a witty poem on an Owl', no longer preserved with the letter but copied into Maurice Johnson's anthology, now in the Huntington Library, Yale University. The SGS has photocopies of the contents of this anthology, including this poem.

224. SGS No 106: From Maurice Johnson to Maurice Johnson (son), mainly for SGS.
London, 14 May 1734.
MB2 fol.108A, 9 May 1734.
Discusses a treatise by Bishop Cumberland[1] and recommends his son to study the 'Old everlasting Patriarchal Ll [laws]';[2] asks him to show to the SGS a copy of a page from the diary of Burchard, Pope Julius II's Master of Ceremonies in 1504, relating to the French objection to Henry VII using the title of King of France; quotes from it in Latin.

[1]   Richard Cumberland (1632–1718): Bishop of Peterborough; see his entry in *ODNB*.
[2]   At this stage, Johnson was still planning for his son Maurice to follow the family profession by studying law. MB2 fol. 86B (17 May 1733) states 'Proposed by Capt[n] Pilliod That Mr Maurice Johnson Son of M Johnson one of the Secretaries of this Soc. Be elected a Regular Member of this Society … having been admitted as a Student into the hon[ble] society of the Inner Temple', and Johnson's private notes about his plans for his sons' education, interleaved in the Society's ABC of Abbreviations, contain the comment '1730. Maurice 16 admittandus Soc in honorabilem Soc. Int. Templi 25.9[ii] 1731 p. prem.solut. 4l 5s 2d'. He clearly hoped his eldest son would follow in his footsteps by studying at the Inner Temple. The younger Maurice's admission there on 25 November 1731 did not mean that he began to reside in London to study law at that stage, simply that his name was already 'on the books'. Presumably he did not find the law a congenial study, as his career plans rapidly changed to preparation for a commission in the Army (see Nos 239 and 240 below). It was the second son, Walter, who later studied law at the Inner Temple like his father.

225. SGS No 27: From Maurice Johnson to Maurice Johnson (son).
[London], 16 May 1734.
MB2 fol.108B, 23 May 1734.
Headed 'for next Thursday';[1] sends Classical Greek verses from Chalcedon on the Bosphorus, about making offerings to Jupiter for a safe passage into the Ægean Sea, also translations of it into Latin and English verse.

[1]   i.e. for the next meeting of the SGS.

226. From Maurice Johnson to Maurice Johnson (son).
Devereux Court, London, 4 July 1734.
Begins 'Dear Maur'; asks him to show Dr Desaguliers's[1] application for
membership to 'our worthy President & to my brother Secr. & your Unkle
Treasurer & Mr Operator Cox' and keep it for proposal at the next meeting; he
has had Bell's bijugate coin of Carausius engraved by Vertue.
On reverse: note of astronomical observations; also application for membership
by Dr Desaguliers, together with a list of important SGS members with whom
Desaguliers is acquainted: he lists 'S[r] Izack Newton S[r] Hans Sloane Major
General Hunter His Grace the Duke of Buccleuch, Roger Gale, James West,
Robert Gay, Wm Green, James Theobald Esquire Edward Lawrence & John
Grundy mathematician members theirof, right Honbl. Ld Colerain, Dr Stukely
& Mr Serjt. Amyand Mr Hepburne & Dr Jurin.'

[1] Revd Dr John Theophilus (Jean-Théophile) Desaguliers (1683–1744): French Protestant refugee
as a child; natural philosopher and lecturer, encouraged by Newton and particularly interested in
electricity and astronomy. See his entry in *ODNB*.

227. SGS No 104: From Maurice Johnson in London to Richard Falkner in
Spalding.
6 July 1734.
Johnson is 'glad to heare you're well arrived in Froggland[1] from the Oxen-ford';
congratulates him on his election to SGS membership, discusses current SGS
activities; gives a description of a specimen of a bat from Carolina.

[1] This is a typical comment about the Fens, which were renowned for the number of frogs, also
ironically nicknamed 'Fen nightingales'. This letter is illustrated on p.213.

228. From Richard Norcliffe to Maurice Johnson.
[Frederickshald, Norway], 10 July 1734.
MB2 fol.112B, 25 July 1734.
Sends an explanatory note to accompany what he designs as a rough draft of his
attached report.

229. From Richard Norcliffe to Maurice Johnson.
[Frederickshald, Norway], 10 July 1734.
Provides a full report on the state of learning and antiquities in Norway and
Denmark; gives an account of his visit to the site of Charles XII of Sweden's
death; accepts SGS membership.

230. No 28: From Beaupré Bell to Maurice Johnson.
[Beaupré Hall], 15 July 1734.
MB2 fol.112B, 18 July 1734.
Explains that he has copied some coins from Johnson's cabinet in Johnson's
absence but with Mrs Johnson's permission; sends a catalogue of Roman Emperors,
requests the loan of some of Johnson's seals to make casts, explaining that 'if
you put the seals in a little box, and fill it with Tobacco' they will travel safely;
comments on Constantine's vision of the Cross in the clouds before the Battle
of the Milvian Bridge in AD 312, suggesting that it is a natural phenomenon.

231. From Charles Littlebury to 'John Johnson, Attorney'.
Lincoln Castle, 23 July 1734.
A client now in prison for an offence against Captain Pilliod[1] pleads for assistance, and sends verses, written in prison, expressing his repentance.

[1] Francis Pilliod (d.1735): a Swiss Protestant from the canton of Berne, who had served in the British army in Europe during the War of the Spanish Succession. He married Mary Green of Spalding, becoming stepfather of Dr John Green. He became an SGS member in 1719 and was a leading member of the Society through the 1720s, insisting on the need for a working museum and drawing up plans for it.

232. SGS No 4: From John Rowell[1] to Maurice Johnson.
Peterborough, 21 August 1734.
MB2 fol 115B, 29 August 1734.
Thanks Johnson for his dissertation on seals on documents; answers Johnson's question about an inscription on a seal, in a very long and detailed discussion on the use of seals in which he gives full evidence from Classical authors and also Biblical references, in compiling which he has had Mr Neve's help.

[1] See his entry in Appendix 2.

233. From Beaupré Bell to Maurice Johnson.
Beaupré Hall, 6 October 1734.
MB2 fol.119A, 17 October 1734.
He has just returned from Rutland; thanks Johnson for his present of an engraving of Sir Richard Ellys's coin of Carausius which is not unique, as the Duke of Devonshire also has one; sends 'two Botanic Essays by my friend Martyn',[1] also plants for Dr Green, of which 'the Skeletons are the Agrifolium.'

[1] John Martyn, author of *Methodus plantarum circa Cantabrigium nascentium* (London, 1729).

234. From Dr Kennedy[1] to Maurice Johnson.
London, 16 October 1734.
Discusses the tour Kennedy has just made to the west and north of England; he has come across a coin of Carausius which may throw light on the one Johnson has had engraved; discusses whether it shows a picture of Apollo; explains that he has other coins which he will show to Johnson when he comes to London for Term; asks him to bring his coins of Carausius.

[1] Dr Patrick Kennedy; see his biography in *ODNB*. He was a Scottish numismatist and coin-collector. His particular interest was in coins of the third-century Roman Emperors Carausius and Allectus who had connections with Britain; this interest was shared by Maurice Johnson, Beaupré Bell, William Stukeley and Sir Richard Ellys. For a modern view on these coins see P. J. Casey, *Carausius and Allectus: The British Usurpers* (London, 1994).

235. Draft of letter by Maurice Johnson replying to Dr Kennedy; written on reverse of No 234.
Spalding, 25 October 1734.
Discusses points made in Kennedy's letter about coins of Carausius and the representation of emperors, gods and their attributes on Roman coins.
Also: Notes in Latin by Johnson, dated 1749, on the 'ORIVNA' inscription;[1]

Johnson comments correctly that this inscription is read by some others as a damaged version of 'FORTVNA'.

[1]   Johnson has evidently re-read Kennedy's letter in 1749, at the time when Stukeley was working on his book on 'Oriuna' who, he claimed, was the wife of the Emperor Carausius: see Stukeley's letter to Johnson on 24 April 1752 (No 558 below). Stukeley's theory was based on one of the coins of Carausius which showed a crowned woman with an inscription round the slightly chipped rim, which could be read as 'ORIVNA'; Stukeley interpreted this as the name of Carausius' wife and empress Oriuna, though others preferred to see it as an incomplete word 'FORTVNA' indicating that this was a representation of the goddess of good fortune. Much of the debate centred on the types of crown worn by empresses and by divine personalities on Roman coins. Kennedy disputed Stukeley's reading and published *A Dissertation upon Oriuna* in 1751. Both Stukeley and Kennedy had to work from engravings of the disputed coin, which had been sold to the King of France, Louis XV. This is discussed by Casey, *Carausius* (1995), 80–183 (see No 234 n.1 above).

236. From Beaupré Bell to Maurice Johnson.
Beaupré Hall, 7 November 1734.
MB2 fol.121A, 14 November 1734.
Offers detailed discussion of Johnson's comments on coins of Carausius and on the representation of deities on coins of the period, including Ellys's coin; explains that no Roman lady is depicted with a radiate crown, so the figure is unlikely to be Carausius's wife; Bell has missed seeing Kennedy at Stamford but has heard from Stukeley about the rare Carausius coin; he will bring his Carausius coins to Spalding when he comes to visit Johnson.

237. SGS No 44: From Richard Falkner to Maurice Johnson [probably in a letter to Mrs Johnson senior].
Lincoln College, Oxford, 18 December 1734.
MB2 fol.123B, 26 Dec. 1734.
Thanks Johnson for sending him a 'prologue and epilogue'; sends verses from Mr Hart, by an Eton scholar about the custom of Montem at the school; has transcribed 'a short account of the Condour' from 'Capt. Cooke's voyage to the South Sea'[1] including page references and a reference to Derham's *Physico-Theology*.[2]
Latin poem about Montem enclosed.

[1]   This was not the famous Captain Cook of the later eighteenth century, but Captain Edward Cooke. Cooke was second-in-command of one of the ships led by Captain Woodes Rogers, involved in the naval activities of the War of the Spanish Succession. The ships attacked Spanish ships on a voyage lasting from 1708 to 1711 which was one of the early circumnavigations of the globe, probably the tenth by European ships. In 1712 Woodes Rogers published *A Cruising Voyage around the World* and Cooke published *A Voyage to the South Sea, and round the World, perform'd in the years 1708, 1709, 1710 and 1711*. The latter book was particularly popular for its descriptions of natural history and for its account of 'Alexander Selkirk his manner of living ... during the four years and four months he lived upon the uninhabited island of Juan Fernandes.' Selkirk was the original of 'Robinson Crusoe', having been cast away on an island where he lived alone for over four years until another ship found him. The voyage was also described in Robert Kerr, *A General History and Collection of Voyages and Travel* (1811). Cooke's account includes a description of the South American condor.
[2]   William Derham, *Physico-Theology* (London, 1713), the text of his Boyle Lectures in 1711–12. A copy of this book is still in the SGS library.

1735

238. SGS No 107: From Beaupré Bell to Maurice Johnson.
[Beaupré Hall], 3 January 1735.
He will send a set of 'Lincolnshire Prints' for his annual contribution to the SGS; asks if he may borrow books and casts of coins.

239. SGS No 7: From Maurice Johnson (son) to Maurice Johnson.
London, 15 March 1734/5.
He hopes his father is safely back from Lincoln and plans to see him in London next term; gives an account of his studies at M. Foubert's Academy, especially riding and French;[1] describes a visit with Bogdani to the SA including seeing a Roman silver pot, perhaps an incense-pot, which had been excavated near Glastonbury and which Vertue was engraving; sends a sketch of the design of Juno inside it.

[1]   Johnson's original plan seems to have been for Maurice Johnson (son) to study law at the Inner Temple (see No 224 above), but he is now studying at Foubert's to prepare for a military career. Major Henry Foubert's Academy was a well-known riding-school in London, which also offered other aspects of a gentleman's education such as French, necessary for Continental travel with the army as well as entry to fashionable society abroad. It was situated in Foubert's Passage, now Foubert's Place, near Carnaby Street, and was run by the Foubert family until 1778. An engraving of a portrait of Major Foubert, by John Faber junior after Thomas Hudson, is in the National Portrait Gallery's collection.

240. SGS No 105: From Maurice Johnson (son) to Richard Falkner at Oxford.
London, 21 March 1734/5.
Gives an account of his studies at Foubert's Academy: 'it will cost my Father a great deal of Money my being here', and of visits to an opera and play; sends a drawing of the silver incense pot from Glastonbury.

241. From Roger Gale to Maurice Johnson.[1]
London, 22 March 1735.
MB2 fol.130B, 27 March 1735.
Gives an account, to be read at an SGS meeting, of 'a silver Table', the recently-discovered Corbridge Plate, of which he has received a description in a letter from Newcastle-upon-Tyne but not yet a drawing; gives 'an account of this table' and promises to send fuller details when he receives them.

[1]   Part of this letter is transcribed in *Stukeley* iii. 110–114.

242. No 6: From Richard Falkner to John Johnson[1] [probably enclosed in letter to Mrs Johnson senior].
[Lincoln College, Oxford], March 1735.
Knows that John is 'well vers'd in that rugged science of Algebra' which Falkner is beginning to study; sends, for John's comments, a page of mathematical workings from Mr Bogdani, in relation to Muller's book[2] connected with 'finding out the Longitude'.
Attached: page of mathematical workings.

[1]   This is Falkner's much older step-brother, Maurice Johnson's younger brother John, who was Treasurer of the SGS.

[2]   John Muller was a mathematician and colleague of Bogdani's at the Tower; he became a member of the SGS later in 1735. See his entry in Appendix 2 and references to him in the following letters. This is the first of a group of letters concerned with mathematics, particularly the new mathematics of 'fluxions' or calculus developed by Isaac Newton.

243. SGS No 30: From William Bogdani to Maurice Johnson.
Tower of London, 5 April 1735.
MB2 fol.131B, 10 April 1735.
He has little to report as the holidays 'have drove everybody out of this filthy Town'; expresses interest in Orme's[1] barometrical experiment which he has not heard mentioned in London; discusses in great detail Mr Gray's[2] experiment on a patient with electricity, which he has observed; is pleased to hear that the SGS has accepted his recommendation of Muller as an SGS member, discusses Muller's mathematical work and encourages subscriptions to his forthcoming book; discusses the newly-discovered Corbridge Plate and its possible uses; refers to Grundy's forthcoming drainage work in the Spalding area.
Annotated by Johnson: 'Lr from Wm Bogdani Esq.FRS Of Ormes Barometer. Electrical Experim[en]ts. Muller of Conic Sects and Fluxs. Galt of the Corbrig. Plate.'

[1]   Charles Orme's improvements to the barometer were reported to the RS, as recorded in its *Philosophical Transactions* VIII i 455. See Bogdani's letter of 29 April (No 246 below). This shows the SGS actively contributing to the national communication of scientific discoveries.
[2]   Stephen Gray (1666–1736): experimental philosopher, especially known for being the first experimenter to work effectively on electricity. See his entry in *ODNB*. Gray's experiment was communicated to the SGS by John Grundy (MB2 fol.130A).

244. SGS No 22: From Maurice Johnson to Richard Falkner.
[Spalding], 'Good Fryday April 1735' [4 April].
Expresses pleasure at Falkner's continuing friendship with Maurice Johnson (son); gives news from Spalding including the SGS's discussion of the Corbridge Plate and Grundy's plans for fen drainage.
On reverse: copy of the proposals for publishing Muller's book on conic sections and fluxions.[1]

[1]   This book, *A Mathematical Treatise, containing a System of Conic Sections, with the Doctrine of Fluxions and Fluents, applied to various Subjects* was published in 1736 and a copy is in the SGS library. An account of it was printed in the RS's *Philosophical Transactions* VIII ii 30.

245. From Richard Falkner to Maurice Johnson.
[Lincoln College, Oxford], 8 April [1735].
MB2 fol.131B, 17 April 1735.
Thanks him for his account of recent SGS activities; agrees to subscribe to Muller's book on mathematics and asks for details; explains he has been to see the 'Bristly Boy'[1] and gives a description of him; asks, on behalf of the college, for Johnson's help in identifying four coats of arms painted in Lincoln College chapel windows as the college is interested in identifying possible benefactors.[2]

[1]   MB2 fol.112A records Mr Ambler's account of seeing the 'Bristly Boy', whose skin was covered with small bristles, exhibited at Stamford.
[2]   These arms can still be seen in the windows of the chapel at Lincoln College, Oxford. (The drawing of them is no longer attached to the letter.) The Minute Book entry notes the identification by Johnson of the arms as those of John Williams, Bishop of Lincoln 1621–41, later Archbishop of York, and the arms of the Diocese of Lincoln. This request for Johnson's advice gives some indication of Johnson's reputation and skill as a genealogist.

246. No 31: From William Bogdani to Maurice Johnson.
Tower of London, 29 April 1735.
MB2 fol.132B, 1 May 1735.
Thanks Mr Grundy for his information about Orme's improvements to the barometer;[1] requests further technical details about Orme's methods, discussing the problems they raise and the effects of heating mercury to remove the air, and providing a detailed evaluation of the validity of Orme's barometer.
Annotated by Johnson: 'Lr from Wm Bogdani Esq FRS & GS at Spaldg. on Mr Ormes improvemts on the Barometer.'

[1]   See also No 243 (5 April 1735), above.

247. SGS No 88: From George Lynn senior to Maurice Johnson.
[Southwick, Northamptonshire], 1 May 1735.
MB2 fol.133B, 22 May 1735.
Discusses Muller's mathematics; demonstrates how fluxions [calculus] operates by working out in detail a problem arising from Bogdani's letter;[1] comments on Bishop Berkeley's carping about fluxions in the *Analyst*.
Annotated by Johnson: 'Read SGS 22 May 1735 MJ SGS Secr.'

[1]   See No 242 above.

248. From Roger Gale to Maurice Johnson.
Cottenham [near Cambridge], 13 May 1735.
MB2 fol.133B, 22 May 1735.
Gives further discussion of the 'table', giving more precise description now he has seen it and correcting the errors in the first description which he sent on 22 March;[1] intends to get Vertue to make an engraving of it; comments that 'the sight of it raised in us all some scruple as to its antiquity' and discusses whether it is 200 years old, of Spanish work, from an Armada wreck, or late Roman work.

[1]   The Corbridge Plate: see No 241 above. The plate is an excellent example of late Roman silver work.

249. No 32: From William Bogdani to Richard Falkner.
Tower of London, 17 May 1735.
He continues to recommend Muller's book to Falkner; reminds him that he has asked for his comments on a problem in fluxions; asks Falkner to reply and requests the opinion of Falkner's Oxford tutor about the mathematical problem.

250. SGS No 88: From Cornelius Little[1] to Maurice Johnson.
19 May 1735.
MB2 fol.133B, 22 May 1735.
Discusses the jawbone of a fish and a 'spear from the Indies' which he has sent to Johnson; requests any duplicate Roman coins that Johnson has.

[1]   A Cornelius Little corresponded with William Stukeley on antiquarian matters from a Gosberton address; he is not recorded as an SGS member. Another letter from someone of the same name is dated from Boston, on 4 May 1740 (see No 355 below). He was married in Boston in 1728.

251. SGS No 86: From William Bogdani to Maurice Johnson.
Tower of London, 20 May 1735.
MB2 fol.133B, 22 May 1735.
Gives Muller's method for 'finding 2 Conjugat Diameters of an Ellipsis or Hyperbola containing a given Angle having any 2 conjugate Diameters given', showing that this method is shorter than the Marquis de l'Hospital's;[1] discusses Archimedes' burning glass; gives directions for cultivating vines and making wine; comments on Mr Neve's presentation to the RS of the transactions of the PGS and encourages Johnson to do the same for the SGS; formally proposes Muller as an SGS member.
Annotated by Johnson: 'SGS Read 22 May.'
[1] Guillaume, Marquis de l'Hopital (1661–1704): an outstanding French mathematician who worked on differential calculus.

252. SGS No 87: From George Lynn senior to Maurice Johnson.
[Southwick], 27 May 1735.
MB2 fol.134B, 29 May 1735.
Adds further mathematical clarification of fluxions to his previous letter.[1]
[1] See No 247 above (1 May 1735).

253. No 85: From William Bogdani to Maurice Johnson.
Tower of London, 29 May 1735.
MB2 fol.136A, 5 June 1735.
Thanks Johnson for sending Mr Lynn's comments on Bogdani's letter about fluxions; points out that he had no intention of criticising Newton, whom he admires; gives worked examples of Muller's algebraic methods.

254. No 29: From Beaupré Bell to Maurice Johnson.
[Beaupré Hall], 2 June 1735.
MB2 fol.136B, 12 June 1735.
Bell is promoting Muller's proposals to publish his book on fluxions; he requests a duplicated fossil from Johnson's collection; 'having Purchas'd Mr Hawkesby's Hydrostatic Balance' he plans scientific experiments on the density of medals to 'distinguish the Genuine from the Counterfeit'.[1]
[1] Francis Hauksbee junior (1688–1763): developed the hydrostatic balance. He was the nephew of Francis Hauksbee senior. See his entry in *ODNB*.

255. SGS No 40: From Beaupré Bell to Maurice Johnson.
[Beaupré Hall], 7 July 1735.
MB2 fol140A, 17 July 1735.
Bell is returning books and sends casts of coins; he sends a copy of an inscription about a clock, carved on a Roman stone built into the church of the Benedictines at Taloire[1] in France and discusses whether it used sand or water; notes that his passion-flower plant given by Johnson now has fruit.
[1] In Alpes-Haute-Provence, just north of the Mediterranean coast.

256. From Dr Cromwell Mortimer[1] to William Bogdani (to be forwarded by Maurice Johnson).

London, 9 August 1735.

MB2 fol.143A, 14 August 1735.

Gives a detailed description of the structure of the heart, based on the investigations of Dr Stuart,[2] and explains how to make a paper model of the heart in accordance with Stuart's work. Encloses a specimen paper model.[3]

[1]   Secretary of the RS. See his entry in Appendix 2.

[2]   Dr Alexander Stuart (1673?-1742): began as a ship's surgeon then studied at Leiden. He was elected to the RS in 1714 and became physician at the new Westminster Hospital and later a founder of St George's Hospital, London. See his biography in *ODNB*. He was an enthusiast for inoculation against smallpox. His major research was into muscular motion, hence his interest in the operation of the heart. The RS's *Philosophical Transactions* VI iv 131 contains 'A Short Account of Dr Stuart's Paper, concerning the muscular Structure of the Heart, by Dr Mortimer'. This explains how such paper models can be made.

[3]   The model survives in the SGS archive.

257. SGS No 108: From Maurice Johnson (son) to Maurice Johnson.

London, 18 August 1735.

MB2 fol.143A, 21August 1735.

Discusses a visit made by him to Vertue who is working on inscriptions engraved in a recently-excavated ring; he sends a drawing that he has made of them for the SGS's opinion on their meaning; says that Vertue is copying a portrait of Charles Brandon and his wife[1] and would like Johnson's opinion about a detail of the portrait; sends sketches of sphinxes in Dr Mead's collection; assures his father that he is working hard: 'I am & will continue diligent in the prosecution of my exercises to the extent of my Capacity'.[2]

[1]   Duke of Suffolk (c.1484–1545) and his wife Mary, sister of Henry VIII and widow of King Louis XII of France (1496–1533). After her death the Duke married his much younger ward Katherine Willoughby of Grimsthorpe (Lincs).

[2]   This may relate to his previous lack of interest in studying for a legal career and his awareness of the expense of his education, as he had commented earlier to Falkner (see No 240 above), as his father will have to purchase a commission for him as well as paying for the training at Foubert's. The military training appears to have been more congenial; he proved to be a successful soldier, rising to the rank of Colonel in the Guards and serving in several campaigns; see his entry in Appendix 2.

258. SGS No 43: From Roger Gale to Maurice Johnson.[1]

London, 19 August 1735.

MB2 fol.143A, 21 August 1735.

Offers further discussion and a very detailed description of the Corbridge Plate, of which he now has a print, including two small illustrative sketches of particular details, a pyramidal structure and an object held by a seated woman; attempts to identify the figures on the plate as specific Roman mythological figures.

[1]   Sections of this letter are published in John Nichols (ed.), 'Reliquiæ Galeanæ', printed in *Bibliotheca Topographica Britannica* (London, 1780–90), iii. 57, 62, 65.

259. SGS No 21: From Roger Gale to Maurice Johnson.[1]

London, 2 September 1735.

MB2 fol.144A, 4 September 1735.

Gives more details of the Corbridge Plate, explaining that he cannot send a drawing to Johnson until the legal debate over its ownership is settled; admits that Sir John Clerk[2] agrees with Johnson that the seated woman may represent Britannia but rejects this idea; makes positive comments on the SGS:

'... The Extract of your Minutes surprises me, for who could have expected such a learned correspondence to have been cultivated, and so many curious observations communicated to a sett of Virtuosi allmost out of the world and who would never have been known but by the emanations of theyr own light? You have infinitely the advantage of our Antiquarian Society here at London, which confines itself to that study and knowledge, whereas you take in, and very rightly too, the whole compasse of Learning and Philosophy, and so comprehend at once the ends and institution of both our London Societys ...'

Comments on a letter received from New England by the RS, which discusses claims that a rattlesnake can mesmerise its prey by staring at it, agreeing that the effect is probably produced by the poison of its bite: 'Before we reason upon any thing we ought to be certain of the truth of the fact.'[3]

[1] Part of this letter is transcribed in *Stukeley* iii. 128.
[2] The well-known Scottish antiquary, based in Edinburgh; he later became a member of the SGS. See Nos 334, 336, 374, 383, 385, 388 and 486.
[3] The report on the rattlesnake is recorded in the RS's *Philosophical Transactions* IX iii 54–5.

260. SGS No 136: From Maurice Johnson (son) to Maurice Johnson.
London, 6 September 1735.
MB2 fol.144B, 11 September 1735.
Sends a drawing of a carved Egyptian figure which he received from Sir Richard Manningham's son;[1] has passed on information to Vertue about the inscription on the ring,[2] which Johnson thinks relates to St Guthlac; is pleased that the SGS goes well.

[1] Perhaps Thomas Manningham (d.1794), SGS member in 1741.
[2] See No 257 above.

261. SGS No 87: From William Bogdani, intended for the SGS.
[Tower of London], 11 September 1735.
MB2 fol.147B, 11 September 1735.
Works out an algebraic problem 'to find any number of means Proportional between any Two Quantities as a,b.'
Annotated by Johnson: 'Commmunicated by Wm Bogdani Esq 11 7r 1735.'

262. SGS No 89: From John Muller[1] to Maurice Johnson.
London, 15 September 1735.
MB2 fol.147B, 11 September 1735.
Appreciates the honour of membership, apologises for his English; sends a demonstration of a theorem by M. de Moivre;[2] agrees to communicate 'the use of this problem' to the Society next time; explains that the first part of his book on conic sections[3] is printed.

[1] See his entry in Appendix 2.
[2] Abraham de Moivre (1667–1754): French mathematician famous for his work on probability.
[3] See No 244 n.1 above.

263. From Revd John Lynn[1] to Maurice Johnson at Spalding.
Devonshire Square [London], 21 October 1735.
MB2 fol.149A, 23 October 1735.
Replies on behalf of the Lord Mayor, Sir Edward Bellamy, accepting his membership of the SGS; has 'with my Cousin' visited Mr Bogdani; sends good wishes for Johnson's and his wife's recovery from illness; is disappointed not to have been able to visit Spalding; he and his brother hope to see Johnson 'in Towne very soon'.
Signed 'Yr most affectionate kinsman and humble servt.'

[1]   See his entry in Appendix 2; one of the Lynn family of Southwick (Northants) and a relation of the Spalding Johnsons; Chaplain to Sir Edward Bellamy, Lord Mayor of London. This indicates the wide kinship network which helped to support the SGS. In 1749 Maurice Johnson's son Col. Maurice Johnson married Bellamy's daughter Elizabeth.

264. From William Hancock to 'Right Honble Sir' [presumably Maurice Johnson].
14 November 1735.
Writes on Mr Bromley's instructions, to give details of an order for candles which will be delivered.

265. SGS No 73: From John Grundy senior to Maurice Johnson.
Congerstone [Leicestershire], 29 November 1735.

Honoured Sir   SGS No 73
                              The many Favours I have allways received from you and your Good Family engages me to Lay hold of this opportunity to return you my hearty thanks for the same. And since I have the Honour by your ~~appointment~~ approbation to be admitted a Member of your Honourable Society, I think myself in Duty bound to give you an Account of what improvements I have made since my Absence from the Society. In the first place I went to Chester and took a map of the Open Bay With the works that are carrying on there and have Drawn a Fair Map with my remarks upon the proceedings there, Anexed to the same, My Fair Map and thoughts have been at Chester 2 or 3 months and hath been shown to all Parties with Aplause. I have sent you my Rough Coppy of my remarks, but could not spare my Rough Map, since the Fair one is out of my hands, Sir if you ~~shall~~ think it will oblige, I shall take it as a Favour to have it comunicated to the Society. I have ordered Brother Sands[1] to deliver it to you, Sir I humbly conceive I have Invented a Frustrum[2] Hedgehog or Porcupine that will Tear away the Sands and gain a Channel in any open Bay, in nearly half the Time it can be done by any in use in your Countery. I have Invented a Method of Jettying with 5 Piles in each Jetty, that may be Placed in the most Flowing Sands without being Blown up, Nay I dare say that by this method I could gain a stated Channel below Fosdyke without having any of my Jettys ~~Blown up~~ Broke down by the Tides. I have made an Improvement in the Battering Ram for Driving down Piles, and that in such a Manner, that Eight men shall with ease work a Beetle of Twelve Hundred weight, and raise it Twenty Feet, at one Turn of an Axis, and by that means strike 5 strokes upon the Pile, whilst that made use of by Captain Perry,[3] or Mr Kinderleys[4] at Chester, can with a Beetle of 9 hundred weight make one stroke with 12 men. I am now making Experiments by trying what weights will seperate the Power of Cohesion in any given Cube of Earth from the strongest Water Clay to the lightest sand, hopeing theirby to rays such

Dati as shall inform me in a Universal Theorem, to make Banks of any manner
of Different Strata's of Earth to Resist and overcome any given Pressure. I am
likewise a writing a Manuscript of Algebra for the Benifit of my son. Pray Good
Sir [erasure] Pardon my Troubling you in this manner; and be Pleas'd to make my
Humble Servis Agreeable to your Good Family, and to all the Gentlemen of our
Society and all Friends; and Sir I am both yours, and the Rest of the Honourable
Brotherhood's Most Humble and Obedient Servant to command at all Times
Novem: the 29th 1735   John Grundy
Congestone Saturday 12 at Night[5]

[1]   The title 'Brother' may relate to a member of Grundy's family, or is more probably a Masonic
title. Sands is explicitly referred to as 'Architect and Free Mason' in No 508 below. Grundy was a
member of the Freemasons, and Maurice Johnson was probably also a member of the Spalding lodge;
he is known to have been interested in Freemasonry, perhaps under Stukeley's influence. The reference to 'the Honourable Brotherhood' in his closing salutation may also have a Masonic significance.
See John Grundy senior's entry in Appendix 2; for Sands, see No 508 below.
[2]   Otherwise known as a frustum: a truncated cone, here an instrument in that shape, used for
scouring out drainage channels. Keeping channels open was particularly important in a Fenland area
like Spalding, where the lack of contours made the rivers run slowly and tend to choke up with sedi-
ment and where the tides drove sand into the river estuaries, so making access difficult for ships. The
other names that Grundy uses suggest that his cone was covered with spikes to assist the process.
The 'Beetle' mentioned later is a pile-driver.
[3]   Captain John Perry (1669/70–1733): a member of the SGS in 1730, known for his work in
drainage, especially his work for Peter the Great in Russia in the first decade of the eighteenth century
and his closing of the Dagenham Breach caused by the flooding of the Thames, 1716–1719. See his
entry in *ODNB*.
[4]   Nathaniel Kindersley (1673–1742): drainage engineer.
[5]   Congerstone (Leics). Grundy had taught mathematics at Market Bosworth Grammar School,
where his family was still living.

1736

266. SGS No 6: From Richard Falkner to Maurice Johnson in letter to Mrs
Johnson senior.
[Lincoln College, Oxford], January 14 [1736].
MB2 fol.155B, 22 January 1735/6.
Two letters on the same sheet:
Letter to his mother which gives news of College matters, also thanks her for a
'very good' cheese.
Also letter to Maurice Johnson: Discusses two new white marble statues 'done
by Rysbroke'[1] including the statue of Queen Caroline 'her present Majesty' at
Queen's College; sends an inscription from the picture gallery and a drawing of
the exact size of a stone removed from a dog's bladder and now in 'our Museum'.
Drawings attached.
Annotated by Johnson: 'A Lr from the learned Mr Richard Falkner a Student
in Physick at Lincoln Coll. in Oxford & member of Gent Soc at Sp. Sepulchral
Inscription – there. Drawing of a Stone cut out of a Dogs Bladder – there.'

[1]   John Michael Rysbrack (1694–1770): sculptor, SGS member 1733; see his entry in *ODNB*.

267. SGS No 8: From Beaupré Bell to Maurice Johnson.
[Beaupré Hall], 7 February 1736.
MB2 fol.157B, 26 February 1736
Sends a list of Greek monograms taken from sculptures and gems, for Johnson's use in compiling the ABC of Arts and Sciences.[1]

[1]   This was a project undertaken by the SGS to assist their studies; it was a MS collection of abbreviations used by creative artists, natural philosophers, writers etc. in signing their work, and of abbreviations in Latin, Greek and other languages used in historical documents. The volume is still in the SGS archive.

268. From Richard Falkner to Maurice Johnson.
[Lincoln College, Oxford]: Undated, just before 26 February 1736.
MB2 fol.157B, 26 February 1735/6.
Thanks Johnson for information which he has sent on Juno; has just heard 'a very pretty Dissertation upon Jupiter' by Mr Spence;[1] hopes to take casts of coins for Johnson; sends drawings of more inscriptions from the Oxford gallery; has heard from 'your son'.[2]

[1]   This is perhaps Joseph Spence (1699–1768), at that time Professor of Poetry at Oxford; see his entry in *ODNB*.
[2]   Maurice, his contemporary and friend.

269. SGS No 62: From Richard Falkner to Maurice Johnson.
[Lincoln College, Oxford], 14 March [1736].
MB2 fol.159A, 18 March 1735/6.
Has been able to 'roll off some very neat Engravings' of coins which he plans to cast; he has been unwell; sends a sketch of 'an old Medal found in Northamptonshire' with an inscription, perhaps in Hebrew [sketch enclosed];[1] he has been ordered not to undertake any writing at present.[2]

[1]   The sketch is enclosed.
[2]   Because of illness. This is the first reference in Falkner's letters to ill health, although a letter from Bogdani to Maurice Johnson on 16 August 1732 (No 186 above) refers to a previous illness of Falkner's.

270. SGS No 37: From William Brand[1] to Maurice Johnson.
Northumberland House, 20 March 1736.
Thanks Johnson for his past hospitality; sends a letter for Mrs Ambler;[2] he was unable to come to Spalding as his horse was ill at York; sends a cure for piles, a 'Sympathetical Remedy' from Mr Elder;[3] discusses iron mining and describes in some detail a new steel mill at Newcastle.

[1]   See his entry in Appendix 2.
[2]   Presumably the widowed mother of Maurice Johnson's wife Elizabeth, née Ambler. The letter is not present.
[3]   Perhaps David Elder, a London surgeon in the early eighteenth century.

271. No 33: From William Bogdani to Maurice Johnson.
London, 15 April 1736.
MB2 fol.160A, 22April 1736.

No 33   Tower of London, 15 April 1736
Dearest Friend
    The misery which I suffer at present on account of my excessive Lowness of Spirits which incapacitated me for any Business whatever will I hope plead an

Excuse for my being so wreched a Correspondent to one who knows too well the dire Effects of that English Malady;[1] but altho' I am not able to entertain you myself, my hearty wishes for you and yours will never be diminished, as well as my profound Respect for your Society of which I am a most unworthy Member, and that I may not be an altogether useless one, I have engaged the promise of our very learned ∧friend Mr Professor Celsius to become a Correspondent, in order to which he is desirous of being admitted in to your learned Body, & I have accordingly drawn up a recommendation of him, signed by your Son and my self, & hope it will be agreeable to the Society to accept of him as a Member, I think I need not expatiate much on this Gentleman's Abilities to you Sir who are a much better judge of Men, especially the Literati; to attempt his Praise, would be beyond my capacity, let it suffice that all Men of Learning and Science admire & esteem him, and if this proposal proves agreeable to the Society I shall be pleased to be the happy Instrument of enlarging your Correspondence.[2] Please Sir likewise to present my profound Respects to the Revd & Learned President and the rest of my honoured [page 2] friends the Members of the Society.

I wrote some time ago to acquaint Mr Butters of having sent his Bassoon by the Peterborough Carrier, I shall be glad to know if it is arrived safe, and that it pleases.

Please to make my most humble Service acceptable to your Lady, Mr Johnson & his Lady & all the family, and continue to esteem me
      Dear Sir
               Your most sincerely affectionate
               friend & most obliged humble
               servant   W Bogdani
Mr Maurice[3] desires you will please to accept his humble Duty, who presents his Duty Love & Service to all where due.
Annotated by Johnson: 'Lr from W Bogdani Esq FRS Recommending Mr Professor Celsius to the Gent Soc. at Sp.'

[1] The 'Hipp', hypochondria or melancholy as it was known then; probably what we would call depression. The English were thought to be particularly susceptible to it. See note by Johnson on the Latin verses sent from Oxford on this subject, July/August 1733 (No 185 above).
[2] Anders Celsius (1701–1744): Swedish astronomer who worked out the Celsius temperature scale. No letters from Celsius to the SGS have survived; he was admitted to SGS membership in 1736.
[3] Maurice Johnson's eldest son Maurice, who was living in London at the time and who is referred to earlier in the letter.

272. SGS No 91: From John Grundy senior to Maurice Johnson.
Congerstone, Leicestershire, 30 April 1736.
Thanks Johnson for his offer of a house in Spalding; hopes the Adventurers will raise the money for the proposed Fen drainage so that he can become Johnson's tenant in Spalding; expects a 'Paper War' with Mr Badeslade[1] about his disputing a point made in Grundy's book on the drainage at Chester.
Attaches an account, with diagrams, of John Harrison's clock,[2] 'a very curious Machine for the measuring of Time more accurately than any Clock, Watch or other Movement that hath been as yet contriv'd, invented and made by a Lincolnshire Man, (a Joyner), and is now to be seen at the Ingenious Mr Grahams in Fleet-Street London'.[3]

[1] Thomas Badeslade: engineer, surveyor, engraver and map-maker in the first half of the eighteenth

century. In 1736 he published a pamphlet criticising Grundy's work on Chester, *The new-cut Canal,
intended for improving the navigation of the city of Chester, etc.*
2   John Harrison (1693–1776): the famous Lincolnshire clock-maker, connected with the first
successful attempts to establish the longitude. For Harrison's clock, see his entry in *ODNB* and Dava
Sobel, *Longitude* (New York, 1995).
3   George Graham (1673–1751): the best-known horologist of his time.

273. SGS No 173: From Edward Walpole[1] to Maurice Johnson.
London, 19 June 1736.

SGS No 173   London June the 19th 1736
S[r]
    You will perhaps be surprizd at a Letter from me from this place, and more
so when you know the occasion of it which is to inform you that I am about
to commence Author at least Translator which is indeed the lowest sort of that
kind of Animals. as most people take care to prefix to those kind of works some
name which, though their labours doe it no honour, may gain them a credit with
other people for this end I have taken the liberty to place before mine that of the
Society of Spalding as I did not care to put my own name to it so I have let it
goe without a dedecation only inscrib'd it on the Title page To the Society By a
member of it. If in this I have been too forward it is known but to few, and I desire
you'll consult my credit, keep it secret and I shall never be suspected of any such
thing if it pleases you may then use your own discretion but I now impart to you
as to a friend. [page 2] It was shown to Mr Pope[2] before the Printer had it who
did not make an unfavourable report of it if he had you should never have seen
it. After so much preamble your curiosity no doubt is raisd to know what this
mighty work is only a translation of three small books of Sannazarins de partu
Virginis[3] consisting of something less than fourteen hundred verse. It was sent to
London above a year agoe and intended to be printed last Christmas but obstacles
interven'd and is but now just printed at Mr Lewis's in Covent Garden. There are
two or three strokes of Popery in it but as the Author was one I hope you'll let
them pass unobserv'd if you please to let me know how I will send one or two of
'em to you. I have nothing more to add but to enquire after yours and my cosen's
Healths and whether you are soon for this Town where I should be very glad [to]
meet you the approaching Term. My Wife joins with me in humble service to all
your good family. We would have made Spalding in our way to London had not
more Company gone with us whom we could neither leave nor bring with us. I
hope youll accept this true excuse and believe me
                          Dear Sir
                          Your affectionate kinsman and most obedient
                          Humble Servant   E Walpole
Please to direct for me
att Mrs Warhams in Drake Street
by Red Lion Square Holborn London

To Maurice Johnson Esq Jun[r]
att his house in Spalding Lincolnshire.
Annotated by Johnson: 'a Lr from the Ingenious Edward Walpole of Dunstan on
the Heath in Lincolnshr Esq on Inscribing his Translation of de Partu Virginis

revised by Mr Pope: to the Gent. Soc. at Spalding – Whereof he was a worthy Learned & Beneficent member.'

1   See his entry in Appendix 2.
2   Alexander Pope, the poet, a member of the SGS.
3   Jacopo Sannazaro (1458–1530), Italian poet. This edition was *Sannazarius on the birth of our Saviour. Done into English verse. And humbly inscrib'd to the gentlemen of the learned society of Spalding in the county of Lincoln. By a member of the said society* (London: for W. Lewis in Covent Garden, 1736). A copy is still held in the SGS Library.

274. SGS No 112: From Beaupré Bell to Maurice Johnson.
[Beaupré Hall], 27 June 1736.
MB2 fol.162B, 1 July 1736.
Bell is sending to Johnson his dissertation on Callimachus,[1] which he does not intend to publish; asks to borrow a book by Dr Arbuthnot.[2]

1   It is not clear whether he means the fifth-century BC Greek sculptor or the third-century BC Greek poet of the same name.
2   The book is unspecified, but see No 279 below (dated 28 August 1736). It is John Arbuthnot (1667–1735), *Tables of ancient coins, weights and measures, explain'd and exemplified in several dissertations* (London, 1727); a copy is still in the SGS library.

275. From Sir John Evelyn[1] to Maurice Johnson.
Westminster, 10 July 1736.
MB2 fol.163A, 15 July 1736.
Discusses patronage issues for Mr Stagg;[2] gives details of an SA meeting on 9 July, referring especially to Gale's paper on the Emperor Constantine not being born in Britain.

1   Baronet and book-collector; see his entry in Appendix 2.
2   The housekeeper and gardener at the SGS.

276. No 36: From William Bogdani to Maurice Johnson.
Tower of London, 17 July 1736.
MB2 fol,164A, 22 July 1736.
Compliments Johnson on the success of the SGS; reports on recent SA activities, including Roger Gale's account of 600 brass coins of the later Roman Empire found at Chichester, discussion of a medal of the Emperor Constantine, a dissertation by Gale claiming that Constantine was not born in Britain and a display by Martin Folkes of a plaster of Paris globe which is an exact copy of 'an antient Celestial Globe', thought to be Roman, in the Farnese Palace, Rome; sends regards from Maurice Johnson (son) in London.
Annotated by Johnson: 'Lr from W Bogdani Esq. Coines found at Chichester of Diocletian &c. of Constantin in Coll. Rogeri Gale A & SRS & Antiq. Lond. That Empr not born in Britain. Copy of the Sphæra Farnes: in the hands of Martin Folkes Esq. FRS.'

277. SGS No 97: From Revd Robert Whatley to the President and members of the SGS.
Lincoln, 10 August 1736.
MB2 fol.168A, 19 August 1736.
Sends three items for the SGS's museum:
A piece of 'Crude Lead Ore from Winster in Derbyshire'; '2 pieces of Flint in

the form of Cockleshells', fossil imprints which 'I myself took out of the Devil's Arse';[1] '2 pieces of petrifactions' from the Dropping Fountain at Knaresborough 'took off by myself'.

[1]   The old name for the Peak Cavern at Castleton (Derbyshire); this earlier name is now being used again.

278. From George Lynn senior to Maurice Johnson.
Southwick, 23 August 1736.
MB2 fol.167A, 26 August 1736.
Gives a detailed account of a tessellated pavement, thought to be Roman, found in Cotterstock Common Field (Northants), close to his home; discusses the best means of preserving it.

279. SGS No 114: From Beaupré Bell to Maurice Johnson.
[Beaupré Hall], 28 August 1736.
Sends legal documents from his collection for Johnson;[1] returns a coin of Callimachus and a bust of Homer; asks for the return of his dissertation on Callimachus.
Added on 29 August: He has just received Bogdani's copy of Arbuthnot's book;[2] Sclater Bacon, MP for Cambridge, has died of 'the numb Palsie'.[3]

[1]   Annotated by Johnson: 'Dr Wm Welwood's Sea Laws'. William Welwood (fl.1577–1622) was Professor of Mathematics and Law at St Andrews University.
[2]   See No 274 above.
[3]   Thomas Sclater-Bacon (d.1736): a rich lawyer of Linton (Cambs) and MP for Cambridge 1722–1736.

280. SGS No 110: From Edward Walpole to Maurice Johnson.
London, 11 September 1736.
Thanks Johnson for sending good news of the SGS's increase; comments on the book he has sent[1] which he began for personal interest without planning to publish; Sir Richard Ellys may enquire about the book and its author;[2] Walpole may see Johnson in London if he comes up in Term; he will call on him on his return, 'If when I come down yr Roads are passable for us high country folks'.
Annotated by Johnson: 'Edward Walpole Esq. on his sending him Sannazarins de Partu BMV wch he was pleased to inscribe to the Gentlemens Soc. at Sp.'

[1]   See No 273 above. This book is Walpole's own translation of Sannazaro. It is still in the SGS library.
[2]   Walpole dedicated his translation of Horace's Sixth Satire (1738) to Ellys.

281. SGS No 23: From William Bogdani to Maurice Johnson.
Mitre [Tavern, London],[1] 21 October 1736.
MB2 fol.171A, 28 October 1736.
Expresses gratitude for Johnson's help [unspecified]; he has got home safely; he would like Mr Lynn's opinion of a design for an iron oven and if this is favourable he hopes Mr Johnson will order it;[2] sends regards to all the family.
On reverse: sends a sketch of lower part of a Roman tombstone found at Bath, with Professor Ward's[3] comments on the inscription, also a description by Mr Frederick[3] of a silver plate found at Corbridge in the summer of 1736.
Annotated by Johnson: 'Lr from Wm Bogdani Esq. FR.A.GSS. Equestr. funeral

Monument of L. Vitellius found at Bath and Corbridge Plate Acerra Argent. 1736.'

1 The Mitre Tavern in Fleet Street was the meeting-place of the Society of Antiquaries in London.
2 This refers to Maurice Johnson's father, the owner of Ayscoughfee Hall. The Johnson family ordered the iron oven; plans for fitting it at Ayscoughfee Hall still exist in the SGS's archives.
3 John Ward, Charles Frederick; see their entries in Appendix 2

282. From Sir John Evelyn to Maurice Johnson.
Duke Street [London], 23 October 1736.
MB2 fol.171B, 28 October 1736.
Discusses more fully possible patronage for Mr Stagg;[1] gives an account of the discussion at a recent meeting of the SA, especially regarding a carving at Bath.[2]

1 See No 275 above.
2 Perhaps the Roman tombstone referred to in No 281 above.

283. From Richard Falkner to Maurice Johnson.
Boston, 9 November 1736.
MB2 fol.172A, 11 November 1736.[1]
Wishes Johnson 'Fortune in the new Method'[2] which his son proposes; he plans to copy some drawings from 'Couz. Stenit'[3] who has been to Tattershall to draw some 'Antiquities'; congratulates Johnson on the birth of a grandson.

1 This is Falkner's last letter in this collection. Maurice Johnson records in the list of SGS members in MB1 fol.195A that he died in 1737. See his entry in Appendix 2.
2 Of making impressions of coins.
3 William Stennett: SGS member 1746, an artist and merchant from Boston, whose drawings of local churches were admired by Stukeley.

284. No 61: From Maurice Johnson in London to John Johnson.
[Undated portion of letter, dateable to just before 27 November 1736.]
MB2 fol.172B, 2 December 1736.
Sends information for the SGS about new map of London City and a note about a satirical poem, 'Modern Matrimony'; has an engraving of the Corbridge Plate; explains that Mr Pincke[1] is sending samples of drugs for the SGS; describes a cup made of nautilus shell, seen at the house of Mr Sadler, Deputy Clerk of the Pells, also a gold coin thought to date from Jerusalem in the Hellenistic period.

1 Edward Pincke: London apothecary, SGS member 1733.

285. From Beaupré Bell to Maurice Johnson.
[Beaupré Hall], 27 November 1736.
He has read Bogdani's 'curious Dissertation'[1] with pleasure; he hopes Johnson can persuade him to write about composition; discusses 'a small radiate head' on a gem from Palmyra; he has medals of Carausius, Allectus and Abgarus which he will bring; gives news that Mr Wise,[2] keeper of the Oxford Museum, has published a History of Abgarus, but Bell has not yet obtained a copy.

1 Bogdani's dissertation on the history of music, dated 1 January 1734 (No 204 above).
2 Francis Wise (1695–1767). See his entry in *ODNB*.

286. No 34: From Beaupré Bell to William Bogdani.
[Beaupré Hall], 3 December 1736.
Makes detailed comments on Bogdani's treatise on music, particularly his

definition of a clef and the derivation of the signs for the different clefs; asks him to write about composition.

287. SGS No 10: From William Bogdani to Maurice Johnson.
[Tower of London.] Undated; read at SGS 30 December 1736.
MB2 fols173A and B, 30 December 1736.
Sends sketches of details of the Corbridge silver plate and of a Roman catapult sketched by Mr Vertue in October 1736, also an inscription from a seal of St Cuthbert and an epitaph from Malvern.

1737

288. From William Bogdani to Maurice Johnson (son).
Tower of London, 8 January 1736 [actually 1737].
MB2 fol.175B, 20 January 1737.
Is pleased to hear of 'Dear Bessy's Recovery'[1] and sends thanks for her letter; expresses his conviction that gratitude is due to God for recovery from illness; sends Latin verses by Mr William Richards, 'a Cambridge man from Stamford',[2] on the marriage of Frederick Prince of Wales to Princess Augusta of Saxe-Gotha; sends compliments to Richard Falkner and hopes he is recovered.
On reverse: Latin verses, 'In Nuptias Frederici Walliae Principis'.

[1]   This could be either Maurice Johnson's wife Elizabeth or Maurice Johnson's daughter Elizabeth, also known as 'Madcap Bet'.
[2]   Perhaps William Richards (1714–1752) of Eton and King's College, Cambridge (BA 1737–8). He was baptised at Stamford Baron, 12 December 1714. See J. and J. A. Venn, *Alumni Cantabrigienses*, 2 pts in 10v (Cambridge, 1922–54), I.iii. 450.

289. SGS No 34: From Beaupré Bell to Maurice Johnson.
[Beaupré Hall], 12 February 1736/7.
He has sent a Sweet William and a campanula to Johnson, also some ink made to a Dutch recipe; requests some of Mrs Johnson's peppermint water; is engaged in weighing Roman 'as' coins and asks to borrow Johnson's examples.[1]
Enclosed: An account, in Latin, of Roman emperors from Theodosius II to Valentinianus III.

[1]   Bell mentions in his letter of 2 June 1735 (No 254 above) that he has bought a balance for weighing coins.

290. SGS No 52: From George Lynn junior to William Bogdani.
Southwick, 18 May 1737.
Sends detailed written description of an iron oven[1] to be made for Ayscoughfee Hall, on the model of one at Southwick.
Drawing of oven (at Ayscoughfee Hall) 'as drawn out directed & fixed by W.Bogdani Esq.'

[1]   This was proposed by Bogdani on 21 October 1736 (No 281 above) and is discussed further in letters from Bogdani on 17 December 1737 and 7 April 1739 (Nos 302 and 327 below).

291. From George Wallis[1] to 'Wm Dilamore Esquire at the Old Whithart in Spalding'.[2]
Long Sutton, 1 June 1737.
Writes by 'John Andrew my Tenant' asking the [Drainage] Commissioners 'not to put a Oath to him' as Christ commands his followers 'not to Swear at all'; he cannot attend court in Spalding himself but will see that the required work is done.[3]

[1]   He is not otherwise recorded: presumably he is a local farmer; may be a Quaker, as he uses 'thee' instead of 'you' and objects to oaths. Presumably this letter survives in connection with Johnson's work with the Court of Sewers.
[2]   The Old White Hart was the principal inn of Spalding; the building still exists.
[3]   The nature of the work is not specified.

292. SGS No 118: From Roger Gale to Maurice Johnson.
[London], 7 June 1737.
MB2 fol.182A, 9 June 1737.
Disagrees with Johnson's attribution of the coats of arms on Boston Vicarage to the Priors of St. John of Jerusalem, discusses details of the coats of arms belonging to these priors and attributes the Boston ones to the Priors of Bardney Abbey, following a suggestion by Browne Willis; discusses the arms of the Hussey family.

293. From Dr Cromwell Mortimer to Maurice Johnson.
London, 23 July 1737.
MB2 fol.186B, 28 July 1737.
Explains his reasons for refusing to let Mr Gay[1] purchase a piece of land; discusses human bones filled with lead, found at Newport Pagnell church (Bucks) in 1619; asks for a monthly copy of the minutes of the SGS for the RS; discusses Oliver Cromwell's coffin plate, quoting its inscription.

[1]   Robert Gay (1676–1738): a surgeon, FRS 1718 and SGS member, elected in 1724, not the better-known dramatist John Gay, also known to Johnson.

294. SGS No 117: From Revd Matthew Robinson[1] to Maurice Johnson.
Lutton, Lincolnshire, 9 August 1737.
MB2 fol.187A, 11 August 1737.

SGS No 117
S^r   Lutton Aug^st 9 1737
    I think there is not an Herodotus in your Library at Spalding, as you want to compleat the Greek Historians, I imagine that Book may be as acceptable as any other; you will perceive that it is not a New one, though indeed little worse for using; it came to me so extreamly cheap that I can't but still look upon myself as indebted to the Society some Additional Present: Publick Libraries are what can't be too much encouraged, every one (methinks) that has any Regard for Learning shou'd willingly contribute to them, as being of such great Use & Assistance to all those in the Neighbourhood that are studiously inclined: I wish it was in my Power to offer something Hansome; however at present I hope the Gentlemen will accept of This as a grateful Acknowledgment of the Favour they did me in

admitting me one of Their Members. Pray, S^r, my humble Service to all your Family.

> Your most obliged humble Servant
>
> Matt: Robinson

Annotated by Johnson: 'L^r from the Revd Mr Matt. Robinson MA SGS. Curate of Lutton his Donation with Herodotus Folio.'[2]

1   See his entry in Appendix 2.
2   This volume is still in the SGS library.

295. SGS No 38: From Roger Gale to Maurice Johnson.
[London], 23 August 1737.
MB2 fol.189A, 25 August 1737.
'I am now all most with my foot in the stirrop for a journey into Yorkshire', as he is moving to his estate and leaving London;[1] asks Johnson to continue writing to him there with the latest antiquarian news to keep him in touch; mentions an article by himself in the RS's *Philosophical Transactions* about a point of Roman law; discusses a coin of Carausius found at Alcester (Warwicks).
Annotated by Johnson: 'From my dear friend the hon. Roger Gale Esq on his retiring to his country seat Scruton in Yorkshire.'
Also a note by Johnson about Carausius's status as Emperor and the reflection of this in inscriptions on contemporary coins.

1   Gale had recently been dismissed from his post in the Excise by Walpole and was retiring to his estate at Scruton (Yorks NR). See his biography in *ODNB* and his entry in Appendix 2.

296. SGS No 39: Part of a letter from Alexander Gordon[1] to Maurice Johnson.
London, 24 August 1737.
MB2 fol.189A, 25 August 1737.
Sends thanks from the SA for a copy of the SGS minutes, March-August 1737, which have been read to the SA; gives information on a picture of the murder of 'King Henry Darnley',[2] gold medals of Chancellor Bacon and Edward VI and other extracts from the SA minutes; offers to send to the SGS copies of dissertations on mummies owned by Capt. Letheullier and Dr Mead.
[The lower part of this letter is missing.]

1   Secretary to the SA. See Appendix 2 and his entry in *ODNB*. Capt. Letheullier and Dr Mead also have *ODNB* entries.
2   The husband of Mary Queen of Scots.

297. SGS No 116: From Alexander Gordon to Maurice Johnson.
London, 16 September 1737.
MB2 fol.190A, 22 September 1737.
Thanks Johnson for his letter about his image of Egyptian provenance and for details about coats of arms; 'I was ordered to place your letter within the Register book of our Society'; explains that attendance at SA meetings is thin as it is summer; sends greetings to 'our brethren of the Cell' at Spalding; explains that he was not able to send five prints and two dissertations on Egyptian antiquities but will send them by Thursday's coach, for Johnson to show and read to the SGS for their entertainment.

298. SGS No 115: From Alexander Gordon to Maurice Johnson.
[London] 22 September 1737.
MB2 fol.190A, 29 September 1737.
Asks for 'a Draught of the little [Egyptian] Image' for the SA to discuss; has sent the Egyptian papers; promises to send extracts from SA minutes.

299. Note from Maurice Johnson to Joseph Smith.
[Spalding, after 18 November 1737.]
MB2 fol. 196A, 24 November 1737.
Requests Joseph Smith's observations on Jupiter.
Enclosed: Smith's notes on his observations of the occultation of Jupiter by the moon on 'the 18o of 9th 1737'.[1]

[1] The Minute Book entry states that Smith's observations 'exactly answered our observations here'. Joseph Smith was a local astronomer, living in the nearby village of Fleet, who collaborated with the SGS in astronomical observations, on one occasion bringing his telescope to Spalding for members to observe an eclipse (see No 332 below) but who does not appear to have become a member of the SGS.

300. Note from Joseph Smith to Maurice Johnson.
[Fleet, Lincolnshire], 14 December 1737.
MB2 fol.199A, 15 December 1737.
Announces the occultation of the star Aldebaran by the moon, next Friday [16 December 1737].

301. From Joseph Smith to Maurice Johnson.
Fleet, 15 December 1737.
MB2 fol.199A, 15 December 1737.
Discusses his calculations of the occultation of Aldebaran; it will be on the 22nd, not the 16th of the month [i.e. Thursday 22 December, not Friday 16 December].

302. SGS No 51: From William Bogdani to Maurice Johnson.
Tower of London, 17 December 1737.
MB2 fol.199B, 22 December 1737.
Discusses Bogdani's health problems and his deterioration in health since he returned to the Tower as 'there is continually administred to me fresh Cause of Discontent and Uneasiness' in 'this[1] accursed Place'; explains the delay in casting the iron oven for Mr Johnson senior which is now completed; has discussed the alleged portrait of Sir Philip Sidney, in Johnson's possession, with George Vertue; describes in detail a newly-discovered Roman pavement at Wellow, Somerset, and a gold coin of Edward III; describes his son, Maurice Johnson's godson; comments on the firing of the Tower guns for Queen Caroline's funeral that day.[2] Annotated by Johnson: 'Lr from W Bogdani Esq relating to an Oven to be cast which has been Cast all in one as a Peice of Iron Ordnance for the Kitchin Chimney at Ascough Fee Hall as projected by him & Geo. Lynn Esq. Portr. Of Sr P. Sydney by F. Zucchari[3] there.'

[1] MS 'thus'.
[2] Queen Caroline (wife to George II) died on 20 November 1737.
[3] Federico Zuccaro (1543–1609): Italian painter who visited England in 1574. The attribution of the portrait to him is not now accepted.

1738

303. From Dr Cromwell Mortimer to Maurice Johnson.
London, 2 January 1737/8.
MB3 fol.1B, 12 January 1738.

S[r]

I have received yours of Aug. 15 last, but it being then Vacation time I could not lay it before the Royal Society till November 10 following, when I read it to them, & they order'd me to return you thanks for your letter & promise of Correspondence; & as a token how much they approve[1] of the Design of learned Gentlemen associating together in the manner you do at Spalding, they have order'd me to send the Philos. Transact.[2] as they come out to your Society: & they desire you will favour us with a Transcript of your minutes (as a Society at Dublin formerly did) every 3 or 5 months, that so by knowing the heads of what comes before you, we may know what to enquire after in particular, & then the most remarkable & usefull things may be usher'd into the world in the Phil. Trans. which otherwise, as you print nothing yourselves, would always have lain dormant in your Registers. I thank you for the Short Account you give me of the child suckd in by the Mill Stream;[3] but as you give me commission I ~~shall~~ have written to Dr Green about it, hoping you will make an apology to him for me, who am an utter Stranger, for writing to him.
Wishing your Society all manner of Prosperity, & yourself in particular an happy new year, I am,

S[r] Your obliged humble Servant

Lond. Jan 2 1737/8   C Mortimer R.S.Secr
P.S. Pray let me know to whom I may deliver the Transact. here in London, that they may be conveyed safe to your Society. I desire you will tear off the annexed letter to Dr Green & give it to him with my service.
Annotated by Johnson: 'L[r] from Dr Cromwell Mortimer Coll. Med. S/ RS Secr to the Secr of the Gent Soc at Sp. Notifying that the Royal Soc. Lond[n] ordered their Philos. Trans. to be Sent as published to the G. S.Sp.'

[1]   Underlined by Johnson and 'NB' written in the margin by him.
[2]   The Royal Society's annual publication, *Philosophical Transactions of the Royal Society.* Several reports from the SGS to the RS were printed in it; these are noted as footnotes to the appropriate letters.
[3]   This account was sent by Dr John Green and was published in the RS's *Philosophical Transactions* IX iii 241.

304. From Dr Cromwell Mortimer to Dr Green as joint Secretary of the SGS.
[London], 4 January 1737/8.
MB3 fol.1B, 12 January 1738.
Mortimer officially regularises relations between the RS and the SGS and will be glad to keep up a correspondence with the SGS.

305. From Sir Christopher Hales[1] to Maurice Johnson.
Lincoln, 15 March 1738.
He is honoured to accept SGS membership and offers a copy of Terence for the library.

[1]   Third baronet; see his entry in Appendix 2. He presented a copy of Terence's Latin comedies (printed Amsterdam, 1686) to the SGS, where it still survives.

306. From Revd Timothy Neve to Maurice Johnson.
[Peterborough], 7 June 1738.
MB3 fol.8B, 8 June 1738.
Discusses books for the SGS and activities at the PGS, especially Mr Harries's[1] accounts of coffee-growing in Jamaica; explains that Dr Desaguliers has accepted membership of the PGS.[2]

[1]   A member of the SGS; see his entry in Appendix 2.
[2]   See No 226 above for Dr Desaguliers' application for membership of the SGS; he became a PGS member on 25 May 1738.

307. SGS No 89: From Maurice Johnson (son) to Maurice Johnson.
Kensington, 24 July 1738.
MB3 fol.12B, 27 July 1738.
Discusses a visit to George Vertue; gives a detailed account from him of a Roman pavement found in June 1737 at Wells and a painted cloth belonging to Lord Digby[1] of Warwickshire, showing Queen Elizabeth carried in a chair, with her court; passes on Vertue's request to Johnson to identify which of the Queen's progresses it represents.

[1]   William Digby, fifth Baron Digby (1661–1752); see his entry in *ODNB*.

308. SGS No 30: Copy/draft of letter from Maurice Johnson to Francis Scott, Duke of Buccleuch.
Spalding, 26 July 1738.
Replies to the Duke's enquiry, explaining that the SGS does not have Pine's new edition of the poems of Horace as it is an expensive edition, 'the most elegant and curious Edition that was ever published', but would like to have a copy;[1] refers to their schooldays together at Eton: 'you'll pardon me talking as a School Fellow ... which makes Eaton ever Remembred by me with much more pleasure.'

[1]   Nos 311 and 312 below refer to the Duke's donation of this book to the SGS library.

309. SGS No 47: From Musgrave Heighington to Robert Butter.
Yarmouth, 7 August 1738.
MB3 fol.13B, 13 August 1738.
Heighington is pleased to hear Butter's health has improved; he can attend the SGS concert and 'bring all my family'; he has 'a new Performance' and some 'fine Italian musick' just imported.[1]

[1]   MB3 fol.15A (15 August 1738) records that the Italian music performed at the Anniversary Concert in 1738 included arias (though it does not name the composers) and an unspecified piece by Locatelli. Maurice Johnson was an enthusiast for music, and the concert was an annual event during the late 1730s and early 1740s, celebrating the anniversary of the SGS, to which 'the Ladies were also invited'. The music was performed by a local orchestra, many of them SGS members (Mr Butter played the bassoon), who rehearsed in the Society's premises on Monday evenings, using the SGS's harpsichord. They were assisted by visiting musicians brought by Heighington; the soloists were Heighington, his wife and young son, who came from Yarmouth by coach for the occasion. See his biography in *ODNB* and his entry in Appendix 2.

310. SGS No 138: From Alexander Gordon to Maurice Johnson.
The Mitre, Fleet Street, 20 August 1738.
MB3 fol.14B, 31 August 1738.
Thanks Johnson for details of SGS minutes which he has communicated and says he will insert an abstract in the SA minutes; gives information on SA meetings including discussion of Swedish medals and coins brought by Mr Dillenius[1] and of Cromwell's autograph and his letter on the execution of the Portuguese ambassador's brother, the ambassador's objection and 'his being sent packing immediately by frigate'; also comments on the funeral monument of the first Earl of Oxford[2] at Hatfield and an inscription from Moneysend, Essex, for the SGS to decipher and comment on.

[1]   This does not appear to be the celebrated botanist of German origin, John Jacob Dillenius.
[2]   Robert Harley, first Earl of Oxford (1661–1724): politician and father of the second Earl, an SGS member.

311. From Francis Scott, Duke of Buccleuch[1] to Maurice Johnson.
London, 29 August 1738.
MB3 fol.15A, 31 August 1738.
He has sent Pine's Horace to the SGS by the Spalding wagon; he agrees to send new publications as they appear.

[1]   See his entry in Appendix 2.

312. Copy/draft of letter from Maurice Johnson to Francis Scott, Duke of Buccleuch.
Spalding, 9 September 1738 [kept with No 308 (26 July 1738) above].

My Lord

Spalding 9th September 1738

Upon receiving the Honour of your Graces Lr of Advice on the 31st last That you had sent us down Pines Horace,[1] & Commanding me to give the Gentlemens Society here (who glory in [your] Patronage) Your gracious Assureances of Your farther Favours as learned Works come out worthy their Acceptance, tho the Books were not come to Hand, I could not but with great Joy take the Occasion of Communicating the Contents of your Graces most obligeing Lr that very day happening to be the last Thursday in August, when (as usual) Wee celebrated the Anniversary of Our Institution with a Grand Consert of vocal & Instrumental Musick & an handsom appearance of Members, & other Gentlemen & Ladies who were greatly delighted therewith. The Manner of your Graces bestowing your Benefits on us greatly enhancing the Esteem They justly have for them, & bear towards your Grace their most liberall Benefactor; That you may be assured my Lord this Great Author is still in use amongst us; Wee had besides some English and much of the newest Italian Musick, Two Odes of Horace, & Two of Anacreon, performed in full Concert & sung by the Master who set them to Musick Dr Musgrave Heighington a Dr of Musick of the University of Oxford[2] & Organist at Yarmouth, a Member of our Society. The Beginning of this Week The Books, Ostro splendentes & Auro,[3] came safe to my Hands, which on Thursday (our Day of Weekly meeting) I carryd ^in to the Musæum of the Soc: when the Members then there present as also those at the Preceeding Ordered me as one of their Secretaries to return your Grace the Hearty thanks of the Society And to Express their Pleasure & Gratitude for so noble a Benefaction & so much Honour done to this Soc. which tho indeed no vast[4] Number, & for the most part of them who meet constantly at It compos'd but of private Persons, Yet such as have the highest Honour for your Grace and a true Sense of your Goodness in Patronizing their Love for Literature Arts & Sciences & assiduous Endeavours, now indefatigably carryd on for 28 Yeares without Interruption, for improving their own knowledge, promoting a good Understanding throughout their Neighbourhood, Cheifly your Graces Seignioury where Arts & Sciences have Ever had some Vogue & regard & perpetuating their Undertakings (which had the Approbation & Sanction of our late Great Countryman & Fellow Member Sr Izaack Newton) By raising a Publick lending Library & storing & fixing a Musæum to preserve to Posterity such like sumptuous and universaly useful & admired Benefactions as your Grace has been pleased to enrich us with Entreating you my Lord to accept of our humble Duty & hearty thanks, Especialy of my Fathers my Brothers, & your Graces most faithful & most obedient Servant's

Maur. Johnson junr.

Annotated by Johnson: 'A Copy of a L[r] to his Grace the Duke of Buccleuch returning his Grace thanks by Order of the Gent Soc in Spalding for his presenting their Museum with Pine's Edition of Horace[1] Engraven throughout wth Suitable decorations, Head and Talepiece

And Bound in Red Morocco curiously gilded.'

[1]   This fine copy 'bound in Red Morocco curiously gilded' is still in the SGS library.
[2]   Although Heighington claimed to have studied at Oxford, no record of this has yet been found. A MS notebook containing some of his music is in the library of Christ Church, Oxford. See his entry in *ODNB*.
[3]   'Resplendent in purple and gold'.
[4]   MS 'vast vast'.

313. SGS No 120: From Musgrave Heighington to Maurice Johnson.
Yarmouth, 18 October 1738.
MB3 fol.18A, 26 October 1738.
He has sent to SGS some 'carved work' from 'Sr John Falstaffs wainscot'[1] and some seashore pebbles; sends Latimer's sermons and recommends two of them; will send the history of Yarmouth.

[1]   This refers to Sir John Fastolf (1380–1459: see his biography in *ODNB*), a Norfolk landowner and soldier whose residence was Caister Castle, just north of Yarmouth. Shakespeare used a version of his name for the fat, drunken knight in *Henry IV Parts I and II*, but this portrayal of Falstaff bears little resemblance to the real Fastolf, who took an active part in the Agincourt campaign under Henry V.

314. SGS No 8: From Maurice Johnson to Mrs Johnson (for SGS).
London, [7 November 1738].[1]
MB3 fol.19B, 30 November 1738.
Gives news of a model of the Mansion House and an exhibition of three clockwork figures of a lady, gentleman and druggist which he has visited with Miss Bellamy;[2] also of pictures made out of insects by Dandridge,[3] all of which he has seen in London.

[1]   Date not given, but dateable from minute book; this is a section cut out of a longer letter, presumably for SGS use.
[2]   This is probably the Miss Elizabeth Bellamy whom Johnson's eldest son Maurice married in 1749.
[3]   Bartholomew Dandridge (1691–1754): portrait painter; see his entry in *ODNB*.

315. SGS 119: From Roger Gale to Maurice Johnson in London.
[Scruton, Yorkshire], 14 November 1738.
MB3 fol.20B, 7 December 1738.
Thanks Johnson for his letter but regrets he cannot help him by recommending
Bogdani to Sir A. Fountain[1] with whom he is not well acquainted; discusses a
flint arrowhead from the East Indies, comparing it with one from Carlisle which
he has; speculates on the low level of civilisation in Britain when the Romans
arrived.
Note by Johnson that this was communicated to the SA on 23 November 1738
and was followed by a discussion led by a Swedish visitor, Mr Dillenius, about
the ancient use of flint in Sweden.

[1]   Sir Andrew Fountaine (1676–1753): art collector; see his entry in *ODNB*.

316. Part of a letter from Maurice Johnson to John Johnson.
[London], just before 30 November 1738.[1]
MB3 fols.19B and 20A, 30 November 1738.

'It may be dubious as It depends on My Dear Boys abilitie to travel also the time
I may be deteind at my Hitchin Leet adjournment whether Wee may reach you by
this day Sevenight, so I may as well Send by You my dearest Bro myne, & his,
with Sʳ Richard Ellys, Couzen Walpooles, Mr Vertue, Captⁿ Wilson, Services to
the Rev. President & all Other the Worthy Members present at our next Society
& Acquaint Them, With my thanks to Son Green for his last, Sr Richard has
desired their Acceptance of a Print of his Ancestor the great Hambden, Libertatis
Vindex[2] which he himself caused to be Engraved by Audran[3] at Paris to which
place he carryd with him the Origional, well painted but by whom uncertain,
thought to be done by a Gentlemans Hand. Captⁿ Wilson has (as I understood
him) Subscribed for a learned Oriental Author on purpose to present It to our
Library;& from others Wee are promised e'er long farther Benefactions of good
& usefull Books. Sʳ Richard Ellys has at length gotten the House Next adjoining
to his Noble Library[4] and is about adding all the Rooms of the same floor which
is on the first Storey to It. It will become then the generall rendezvous of all his
Reading Friends and indeed the learned Owner not only uses & understands his
Treasures but freely allows the full use of them even to his Friends own houses
of such as they desire, & therefore deserves them well ...'

Johnson then gives an account of the activities at the SA, including the examination
of a gold cup from Latin America, described as the 'cup of Montezuma'; includes
a sketch of the cup.

[1]   Undated but dateable from Minute Book entry. Probably this was a section of a letter, the
remaining portion of which was on family matters and has not survived.
[2]   The defender of liberty. Ellys was a descendent of John Hampden (1571–1643), Puritan and
Parliamentary leader in the early days of the Civil War, killed at the Battle of Chalgrove Field.
[3]   Probably Jean Audran (1667–1756), well known as engraver to Louis XIV.
[4]   At his London house in Bolton Street; the two houses still exist.

1739

317. SGS No 41: From John Grundy senior to the Deeping Drainers.
[Spalding], January 1738/9.
MB3 fol.21B, 4 January 1738/9.
Explains his plan for taking the River Welland in a straight course, based on his observations and calculations, which should save money; estimates the increased capacities that will be needed in the rivers leading to the Wash if the proposed drainage is to take place; describes in detail his new drainage works.
Annotated by Maurice Johnson: 'Report by John Grundy Mathematician on the Chanell of the River Welland in a direct course from the angle between Spalding & Cowbitt to Brother House.'

318. SGS 41: From William Bogdani to Maurice Johnson.
[London], 27 January 1738 [actually 1739].
MB3 fol.25A, 1 February 1739.
Thanks Johnson for his present of six plovers; comments on his own recent ill-health; discusses the recent election at the SA, in which 'Mr Secretary Gordon' was re-elected despite Gordon's incorrect assumption that Bogdani was forming a party to oppose him, and Bogdani was elected Director by a majority of one vote; comments on a gold coin of Elizabeth I, shown at the SA; gives detailed account of RS activities including Dr Stuart's[1] lecture on 'Elasticity' and Dr Hales's[2] lecture on preserving water fresh by 'acidulating the Water ... with oil of Sulphur or Spirit of Vitriol' which could be of value to sailors, though Bogdani is sceptical about the amount of chemicals to be added.
Annotated by Johnson: 'Lr from W Bogdani Esq F.R.& A.S.D. Prst. Hales Method for freshning Water for Sea service.'

[1]　See Nos 256 above and 339 below.
[2]　This lecture is published in Stephen Hales *Philosophical Experiments* (1739). See also No 152 above.

319. SGS No 90: From Dr Thomas Manningham[1] to Maurice Johnson.
Jermyn Street [London], 22 February 1738–9.
Thanks Johnson for his letter and present of game; is glad to hear of 'the flourishing Condition of the Cell at Spalding, & the Concert'; has seen 'my uncle Johnson'; discusses a possible book to send for the SGS library: Revd Mr Baker's *Reflections on Learning*.[2]

[1]　See his entry in Appendix 2.
[2]　Thomas Baker, *Reflections on Learning* (1699), a popular book which went into eight editions by 1760. It devotes a chapter to each of the major branches of learning. Baker was a historian and bibliographer; see his entry in *ODNB*.

320. Printed list of the Members of the Society for the Encouragement of Learning, printed 1739.
Headed in Cromwell Mortimer's handwriting: 'For Dr Mortimer to be Secretary'. 10 names are underlined, including 'Sir Richard Ellys Bart. Bolton Street', presumably in the hope of obtaining their votes for Mortimer.

321. From Dr Cromwell Mortimer to Maurice Johnson.
[London], 27 February 1738/9.
MB3 fol.28B, 1 March 1739.
Requests the interest of members of the SGS in supporting Mortimer for the post
of Secretary of the Society for the Encouragement of Learning,[1] in the place of
Alexander Gordon who has gone to America.

[1]   This short-lived society was founded in 1736 to offer support to authors who were finding difficulties with book publishers in getting their works printed.

322. No 41: From Dr Cromwell Mortimer to Maurice Johnson.
[London], 10 March 1738/9.
MB3 fol.29B, 22 March 1739.
Thanks the Society and members for voting for him to be secretary of the Society
for the Encouragement of Learning.

323. From Sir Richard Ellys to Maurice Johnson.
15 March 1739.
MB3 fol.29B, 22 March 1739.
Thanks Johnson for his dissertation on King Ethelred,[1] discusses his life and his
founding of Bardney Abbey; refers to early eighteenth-century works on glass
painting.

[1]   King of Mercia, c.700.

324. Letter from Thomas Blix to Mr John Goodman, merchant of Spalding. [On
mourning paper.]
Friderickshald [Norway], 22 March 1738 [actually 1739].
MB3 fol.30B, 5 April 1739.
As Blix's brother Col. Peder Colbiornsen,[1] has died, Blix is willing to take over,
as his partner in the timber trade, and offers to supply deal and other sorts of
wood.

[1]   Col. Peder Colbiornsen was a local Norwegian hero who had, as MB3 f. 30B reported, 'very
deep in water defended a Pass against Charles XII King of Sweden in an Attack he made on that
City [Friderickshald]' and was 'one of the Principal Subjects in his [the Danish King's] Kingdom of
Norway'; at that time, Norway was ruled by Denmark.

325. SGS No 42: From William Bogdani to Maurice Johnson.
Tower of London, 31 March 1739.
MB3 fol.30B, 5 April 1739.
Discusses and describes in great detail a communication to the SA about a mosaic
pavement found in the parish of Weldon, near Kettering, on Lord Hatton's estate;[1]
the discovery was reported by reading a letter from Mr Thomas Eayre to Lady
Betty Jermain.
Annotated by Johnson: 'Lr from W Bogdani Esq. F.R.& D. of A.S. on the
Discovery of the grand Mosaic Pavemt discovered at Cotterstock near Oundle in
Northtonshire, after Drawn & illumined by him & presented to the Museum SGS
from the Mensuration of G. Lynn's Esquire SGS.'

[1]   For a full description of this pavement, see David S. Neal and Stephen R. Cosh, *Roman Mosaics
of Britain. Volume I: Northern Britain, incorporating the Midlands and East Anglia* (London, 2002),
240–5.

326. SGS No 47: Extract of letter from William Johnson[1] to Henry Johnson in London.
[Surat, India, 5 April 1739.]
MB3 fol.51B, 28 February 1740.
Gives detailed description of Nadir Shah,[2] 'king of Indostan', and his recent conquests in India, including the taking of 'Dilly',[3] and the enormous wealth he has obtained from them.
Annotated by Johnson: 'Extract from a letter from Mr William Johnson Merchant dated from Surat in the Territories of the Great Mogul in the East Indies 5 April 1739
To his Brother Henry Johnson Esq in London a Member of the Gent Soc at Spalding and by him communicated to the Soc 28 February following [1740].'

[1] See his entry in Appendix 2.
[2] Nader Shah Afshar (late 17th cent.–1747): Shah of Iran who conquered Afghanistan and Northern India. He was assassinated in 1747.
[3] Delhi.

327. SGS No 79: From William Bogdani to Maurice Johnson.
Tower of London, 7 April 1739.
MB3 fol.30B, 12 April 1739.
Bogdani has sent Johnson some books by water and will send others; he has given the extract from the SGS minutes to the SA secretary to be read out; gives further information on the iron oven; discusses a method of preserving armour by 'vernish' using the traditional recipe and technique as used at the Tower of London.

328. SGS No 26: From Robert Flower[1] to Mr Everard, Spalding.
Bishop's Stortford, Hertfordshire, 14 April 1739.
MB3 fol.34A, 7 June 1739.
Discusses the abacus he has invented; provides a diagram of the abacus and an account of its operation. Calculation attached, 'set & cast by Mr J. Grundy & Mr Robert Flower'.
Maurice Johnson's annotation indicates that Flower demonstrated his abacus at the SGS on 21 June 1739.

[1] A member of a significant family of mathematical instrument makers in the seventeenth and eighteenth centuries. One of the family, Robert Flower (who may be the same person) published in 1771 a book on logarithms, *The Radix*.

329. From Revd Timothy Neve to Maurice Johnson.
Peterborough, 5 May 1739.
MB3 fol.33A, 10 May 1739.
Gives detailed discussion of antiquarian finds on the Great North Road between Chesterton, Water Newton and Wansford, including urns, coffins and grave goods; gives a list of Roman coins found in the area.

330. From Maurice Johnson to Musgrave Heighington.
[Spalding], 4 June 1739.

An Ode
For the Celebration of the Anniversary of the Gentlemens Society in Spalding on

the last Thursday in August 1739[1] at Mr Everards, Set to Musick by Musgrave Heighington Dr of Musick a Member of that Society to be performed by him and the Gentlemen of the Consert there. The musick begins with an Overture or Præludio
then this Chorus for 3 Voices
To Love and Social Joys let's Sing!
　　may this returning Day
for Years unnumber'd with It bring
　　Pleasures Noble, New & Gay:

(1st Stanza sung by the Dr)
The Fairest Glory of the Blest Abodes,
Great Parent & Delight of Men & Gods!
　　Thro' different Ages here Address'd
　　under a Vary'd Name
has been Invoked as Patroness
　　Her Votaries the Same!

　　2 (sung by Mrs Heighington)
'Twas Love inspired them to Adore her power,
　　Love from which Friendship comes
　　as from the Genial Shower
　　The fragrant Blossom blooms:

　　3 (sung by Maister Heighington)
From foaming Waves when Beauty Sprung
　　Tritons with vocal Shells proclaimd
Her charms, which every Lyre has Sung
　　Thrô Greece, & thro' Britannia fam'd:
Where all who felt her Influence own'd her Sway
Which (as our Sires) their Ofspring must Obey.

concluding with the same Chorus with which It began
Sent to Dr Heighington at Yarmouth by Caxton Bagg 4 June 1739
Ansrd by him & rehearsed at the Gent. Soc. in Spalding on Thursday
& at the Consort there on Fryday 23rd & 24th Aug.1739.

[1]　The programme for the Anniversary Concert, including this ode, is given in MB3 fol.40A (30 August 1739).

331. SGS No 39: From Musgrave Heighington to Maurice Johnson.
[No address or date; dated from internal evidence and MB3 fols.35B and 40A to 20 June 1739; Yarmouth post stamp.]

No 39.　　Sr
Your most Elegant, and Obligeing Letter I received on the 24th Janry and am asham'd to be tax'd with so great neglect in not returning an answer sooner but I hope a tolerable apology may be accepted, viz. your Ditty ravish'd me so much that I imediately put pen to paper and Composd the enclos'd Tune[1] and parts that very night, and designd to send it the next post to surprise you, and this is that very Original as you may Judge by its Complexion; but as I was then Composeing another piece of Musick, viz. a new Overture to Alexanders Feast,

I deferr'd sending till I coud send you a taste of it, which I have likewise enclosd in parts, they are two Airs at the Conclusion of the Overture; your Drake[2] has not only surprizd but ev'n Ravish'd most of our Ducks here, and one particularly who sings very agreably has Eloped to London with a Drake, but I don't know but his tune might be more surprising and as Ducks will swim and we so near the Sea I don't wonder that they sometimes take the diversion by water. I am Glad to hear the Gentlemen Improve and Practise that sweet part of the Muses, Harmony, and likewise pleased to hear you will have so Convenient a place for it, as your fine Hall, will be when finish'd, My Spouse and I design, God willing, to pay our respects at the Anniversary, and Mr Porter a young Gent who plays, now, a fine fiddle and German flute has promisd me to come likewise, and another at Norwich will come; I have Got the History of Yarmouth transcrib'd[3] in the Size you desire but cannot send that so shall bring it with me, I am glad you have so satisfactorily and advantageously fixd your young Gentlemen[4]

I should rejoice to hear (as you have done hitherto) that you may have [page 2] the same satisfaction in disposeing of your Angelick Females.

We have had a Severe winter here, and yesterday and this day we have as Cold Snow & Hail as any in the winter, tho for this month past,[5] we have had fine weather, I have had a Card Assembly once a week by Subscription at my house, and is reckon'd the politest diversion they have had in Yarmouth, and much exceeding Norwich Card Assembly –

It is time Now S[r] to pay our respects for all yours, and your Good familys Civilitys to us, which I, my wife and family do with all Sincerity, and Likewise, to all the Gentlemen of the Society, Nay I think we may Include the whole town of Spalding, by your kind Influence, and hope we shall remain in health, to meet you and all the rest, blest with the same next August

      I am Dear S[r]

Your most oblidged humble Servant

      Musgrave Heighington

Annotated by Johnson: 'L[r] from Dr Musgrave Heighington SGS with his Overture to his Composition of the Musick of Dryden's Feast of Alexander on the Conquest of Persia.'

[1]   Unfortunately the music, like most of Heighington's compositions, has not survived.
[2]   This incident remains a mystery.
[3]   See No 313 above. The 'history of Yarmouth' referred to here is probably a copy of the MS history of the town completed in 1619 by Manship and recorded as being kept in 'the Town Hutch' at Yarmouth. It was eventually published in an edition by Charles Palmer FSA in 1854. The first published history of Yarmouth was Henry Swinden's *History and Antiquities of the Ancient Burgh of Great Yarmouth* (Norwich, 1772).
[4]   Johnson's older sons. The youngest, Henry Eustace, did not leave home until 1750.
[5]   MS 'pat'.

332. SGS No 44: Notes by Joseph Smith for the SGS.
[Fleet, 19 July 1739.]
MB3 fol.36B, 19 July 1739.
Gives very detailed calculations of the exact path for Spalding of a partial solar eclipse, with diagrams; suggests that Mr Grundy will explain any difficulties in understanding them.
Maurice Johnson notes that this letter was explained at an SGS meeting, 19 July

1739; the eclipse was observed by Smith and some SGS members, including Maurice Johnson, at Spalding with Smith's telescope on 24 July.

333. Copy/draft of letter from Maurice Johnson to Francis Scott, Duke of Buccleuch.
Spalding, 22 July 1739.
Invites him to the SGS Anniversary celebrations; explains that August is a good time to visit as local gentry are at home between the local Assizes and Lincoln Races, so the Anniversary is held then.

334. SGS 122: From Roger Gale to Maurice Johnson.
Scruton, 18 August 1739.
MB3 fol.39A, 23 August 1739.
A lengthy letter: Johnson's letter had arrived 'Just as I was putting my foot into the stirrop for Scotland …'; compliments the SGS on its progress; discusses a coin presented by Mr Ott[1] to the PGS; apologises for his own inability to make casts from coins and discusses a Roman coin of Geta which he owns; gives a very full and detailed account of his journey to Scotland with Dr Knight,[2] commenting on Edinburgh and its colleges, their visit to Sir John Clerk at Mavisbank and Penicuik and their journey with him to Roslin Chapel which had been repaired under Sir John Clerk's influence; gives details of their further journey via an ancient fort to the spa at 'Moffat Water'; explains his return to Carlisle via Burnswark hill forts and Middlebie, commenting that most of his return to Scruton was on Roman roads; refers to John Horsley's *Britannia Romana*.

[1]   Revd J. H. Ott (d.1743): from Switzerland; a member of the PGS, a prebendary of Peterborough and librarian to Archbishop Wake at Lambeth Palace.
[2]   This is possibly Dr Samuel Knight (1678–1746): canon of Ely, antiquarian and correspondent of Roger Gale; see his entry in *ODNB*.

335. From Revd Timothy Neve to Maurice Johnson.
[Peterborough], 29 August 1739.
He is unable to attend the SGS Anniversary; he agrees to send any duplicates of items in the PGS's medal collection that Johnson may want.

336. SGS No 148: Copy made by Roger Gale of a letter from Sir John Clerk[1] to Roger Gale.
[Sent from Gale at Scruton to the SGS for their information.]
Written 19 August 1739, sent to Johnson 4 October 1739.
MB3 fol.41B, 11October 1739.
Gives a detailed account of Clerk's continued journey to Bulness or Bowness on the coast, describing the Roman station there at the end of the Roman Wall; disputes Horsley's[2] identification of the site; gives details of a Latin inscription there and speculates on reasons for the building of the Wall; comments on oaks found under the surface of the ground at 'Drumcrief' with a layer of buried birch trees above them, regarding them as evidence 'that our World sometime or other has suffered a very great convulsion.'
Also Gale's comments on the Deluge which is seen as the cause of this.

[1]   See his entry in Appendix 2.
[2]   See Nos 123 and 334 above.

337. SGS No 31: Copy/draft of letter from Maurice Johnson to Revd Dr Richard Bentley, Master of Trinity College Cambridge.[1]
[Spalding], 17 September 1739.
Offers suggestions of books for Bentley to donate to the SGS library, since he had accepted SGS membership some time previously on Sir Richard Ellys's nomination.

[1]   See note to No 101 above.

338. No 42: From William Bogdani to Maurice Johnson.
Tower of London, 10 November 1739.
MB3 fol.43B, 15 November 1739.
Apologises for delay in giving news of 'this Republic of Learning, being very busy with state affairs';[1] discusses the contents of recent RS meetings, including a claim that olive oil cures rattlesnake bite,[2] and a Brazilian crystal which could be useful for lenses in reflecting telescopes; discusses SA activities including a very full and detailed report received there on the Roman antiquities excavated at Nîmes in 1738 and 1739; describes a 'Chariot Glass' which is being made for Dr Green.
Annotated by Johnson: 'Lr from the Learned W Bogdani Esq FRS&A. Sallat Oyle cure for Poysons. Brasil Christals. Remains of antient Roman Edifices & Inscription at Nismes.'

[1]   As Clerk to the Ordnance, he was involved in supplies for the War of Jenkins' Ear, 1738.
[2]   These were reported in the RS's *Philosophical Transactions* IX iii 54.

339. From Dr Cromwell Mortimer to Dr Green 'Secretary at the Gentlemen's Society at Spalding'.
London, 16 November 1739.
MB3 fol.45A, 29 November 1739.
Sends Redi's *Opera Varia*,[1] the most recent *Philosophical Transactions* of the RS and Dr Stuart's *Lectures on Muscular Motion*;[2] requests further SGS minutes for the RS, also requests for the SA a copy of Maurice Johnson's dissertation on documentary seals, as read to the PGS.

[1]   Francesco Redi, *Opusculorum pars prior; sive Experimenta circa generationem insectorum* (Amsterdam, 1686). This is still in the SGS library.
[2]   Published in 1739.

340. From William Bogdani to Maurice Johnson.
[London.] Fragment, date missing; received by Johnson on 26 November 1739.
MB3 fol.44B, 29 November 1739.
Gives an account of recent SA meetings, particularly a debate on the later Roman emperors, including a controversy between 'Mr Secretary Gordon' and Mr Folkes, disagreeing on the date of a Roman inscription found at Nîmes; offers to get copies of their papers for the SGS.

341. From Revd Timothy Neve to Maurice Johnson.
5 December 1739.
MB3 fol.45B, 6 December 1739.
Gives a very detailed account of local politics including the election in Huntingdonshire; comments on the financial problems of the PGS, which he

claims are caused by their Treasurer;[1] explains that he has himself resumed the PGS secretaryship.

[1]   The treasurer was Revd Thomas Marshall, Vicar of St John's Church, Peterborough. See also Nos 157, 159 and 162 above; Johnson refers to him in No 347 below.

342. SGS No 40: From William Bogdani to Maurice Johnson.
Tower of London, 15 December 1739.
MB3 fol.46A, 20 December 1739
Explains that Mr Gordon has sent to Johnson a copy of a letter from France about the Roman excavations at Nîmes and also Gordon's own views on them; Bogdani will send Folkes's reply to these when he can obtain a copy of it; conveys the SA's thanks for Johnson's letter which the SA has registered.
Annotated by Johnson: 'Lr from Wm Bogdani Esq. of the Amphitheatre discoverd at Nismes & Controversy between the Learned & Judicious Mr Folkes SA & RS & Mr Alex Gordon Secr of the AS thereabout.'[1]

[1]   See No 340 above.

343. From Revd Timothy Neve to Maurice Johnson
[Peterborough], 19 December 1739.
MB3 fol.46A, 20 December 1739.
Sends details of recent PGS meetings for the SGS, in particular information about documents relating to Cardinal Wolsey, a discussion of seals and their impressions, an operation performed by Mr Cox[1] and a language for the deaf and dumb invented by Dr Newcome;[2] thanks Johnson for material from the SGS.

[1]   The Operator of the SGS.
[2]   Dr John Newcome (d.1765): Master of St John's College, Cambridge, Professor of Divinity at Cambridge and member of the SGS, elected 1730.

344. From Roger Gale to Maurice Johnson.
'a few days before Christmas 1739' [dated by a reference in his following letter, No 350 below, to December 21 1739].
MB3 fol.48A, 27 December 1739.
Sends a paper [enclosed] for the SGS: 'Historical account of part of Yorkshire – North Allerton and Scruton' written by Roger Gale from his previous notes.
His letter comments on the ladies enjoying the music at the SGS anniversary concert and approves of the value of this concert as it keeps the arts alive at the SGS as well as the antiquarian studies; asks to have his letters directed via Bedale not Northallerton as they will arrive more quickly.

345. SGS No 2: From Thomas Sympson[1] to Maurice Johnson.
Lincoln, 26 December 1739.
MB3 fol.48A, 3 January 1740.
He has searched the Lincoln registers for Vicars of Spalding; the other registers are at Buckden; sends details of the dedication of the chapel at Cowbit in 1486; offers Christmas greetings; encloses a list of mediæval Vicars of Spalding from the Lincoln registers, for Johnson's History of Spalding.

[1]   Master of Works and Clerk of the Fabric of Lincoln Cathedral. He became a member of the SGS and corresponded regularly in the 1740s. See his entry in Appendix 2.

346. SGS No 38: From William Bogdani to Maurice Johnson.
Tower of London, 29 December 1739.
MB3 fols 48B and 49A, 3 January 1740.

Apologises for not writing because of pressure of work 'nor can I think before I write, which to one of your Taste, were you not possessed of the utmost humanity as well as the most generous friendship, would be almost unpardonable'; comments on the discovery of fossil trees at 'Drumcrief', discusses how they could have been felled by a flood and distributed as a layer of birches above a layer of oaks; dicusses views on the linguistic origin of the word 'TASCIO' on a British coin; discusses recent RS activities including accounts of hot-houses for grapes designed by Professor Friewald and Mr Miller,[1] and SA activities including a report on the discovery of a silver pot of Saxon and Norman coins at Dungeness and drawings of 'venerable peices of Antiquity at Mahon there called the Heathen Altars'; explains that he has been ordered to tour the army quarters and garrisons of England and Scotland with the Major of his regiment and requests introductions to Johnson's friends across the country; hopes to pass through Spalding 'but I fear at this Season of the Year no WheelCarriage or scarse fourfooted one can pass thro' your Country'.

Annotated by Johnson: 'Lr from Wm Bogdani Esq. F.R.A.& G.Socc. of Fossil Timber & other Trees. TASCIO Num. Brit. Silver Pot found at Dungness. Antient Altar-Stones at Minorca. Controversy abt. the Inscr. found at Nismes.'

[1]   Philip Miller (1691–1771): gardener of the Physic Garden at Chelsea. *ODNB*.

1740

347. SGS No 46: From Maurice Johnson to Mrs Elizabeth Johnson.
Stilton, 6 February 1739/40.
MB3 fol.51A, 7 February 1739/40.

SGS No 46   Stilton Wednesday 6th February 1739/40
My Dearest

Wee & our Horses are all Safe and well arrived here by 5 a Clock having had a very good and pleasant Journey hither. From the End of Constitution Bank to Croyland almost all the Way on the Ice. At Cowbitt the Sun shone so bright as to induce old Mr Malsom to sit at the door on a bench in the 90th Year of his Age whom we complimented on being[1] so hearty. At Croyland Wee waited on Mr Crawford and found him well: his Bro the Captain is at Bath & paralytick. As advised Wee went to Peterborough by Eye and met most part of that Village returning from the execution of their Neighbour Elizabeth Wincely aged about 40, who having sent for Arsenick in aboundance to poison Rats, gave it to her Child about 5 or 6 yeares old bidding her mix It with Pudding & dip for their Man Servant & to give It him when he came in for his Dinner and if he or any body should ask what She had done and who bad her do so, to say her Grandmother gave It her & bad her mix It so & give It to the Man to Eat being Sweet & good for him. So that this most abominable Wicked Wretch made her innocent Child perpetrate this Horrid fact and then on her Evidence would have had her own innocent Mother an Antient Woman hanged for a Murther by herself premeditated to save paying a Small Summe due to the Poor man for Wages. She hired a Coach & 4 of Blackbourn to be carryd in to and from Execution for a Guinea, the Revd Mr Marshall[2] attended at the Gallows & prayd with her, but She would make no Sort of Confession & is this Night to be buryd on Hangmans Hill [page 2] A Part of the Church Yard adjacent to the Minster where Felons have usually been interred. Wee not only met, but also Overtook vast Numbers of Men Women & Children of all the Neighbouring Townes even to this which is 5 long Miles from the Gallows. a Lad of about 15 who had been burnt in the Hand for Stealing 2 Silver Watches & 10L. in money, and lay in Gaol, for his Fees, to quit that Score with the Gaoler was her Executioner. a bold audacious Rogue who had been Post boy here but lately. Another Phænomenon extraordinary has [been] this Frost & still Continues to Appeare here Wittlesea Meer is quite Frozen all Over, about a Fourteen [fortnight] agone there were 2 Horseraces runn smartly upon It one for a Sadle, won by Mr Jennings of Fassett, the Other for 8 Guineas. And also a Bull baited by [a] Number of good Dogs – & some bold Butchers on Sketes with Goads in their hands –

With our Dutys Loves & Services as due, you may be pleased to Send this to be communicated to the Gent. with myne & Bro. Services to the Society after You have read It. And if Mr Richards or any Neighbour be left who comes up this Term send me sealed up all the Franks[3] you find in the uppermost left hand drawer in my Study which I forgot directed at Mrs Danyels in Devereux [court] for my Dearest

Your most affectionat Husband Maur. Johnson junr.

To Mrs Elizabeth Johnson
near the High Bridge in Spalding Lincolnshire

¹   MS 'benig'.
²   For Revd Thomas Marshall, see Nos 157, 159, 162, 341 n.1 above and 351 n.1 below.
³   MPs were allowed to 'frank' letters, i.e. send them free of charge; they often franked blank sheets of paper and gave these to friends so that they could write a letter on the paper and send it free of charge. Johnson has collected a store of these for his letters home from London to the SGS and his family, but has forgotten to bring them with him.

348. SGS No 45: From Maurice Johnson to John Green.
[London], 10 February 1739/40.
MB3 fol.51A, 14 February 1739/40.
Discusses a rhinoceros on exhibition in London and some new books: Dr Turnbull's history of 'the Paintings of the Ancients' and Somervile's burlesque poem *Hobbinol or Rural Games.*[1]

¹   George Turnbull (1698–1748), *A curious collection of Ancient Paintings* (London, 1741). William Somervile (1675–1742) was a poet concentrating chiefly on sporting subjects; *Hobbinol, or the Rural Games*, a burlesque dedicated to Hogarth, was published in 1740. See their entries in *ODNB*.

349. SGS No 36: From Maurice Johnson to Dr Green.
[London], 23 February 1739 [1740].
MB3 fol.52A, 6 March 1739/40
Written at foot of printed details of lying-in hospital and preface to Sir Richard Manningham's book on midwifery.[1]
Explains that Sir Richard sends this for the SGS; greets 'all Members of the Concert';[2] gives details of recent RS meetings, especially a paper on the planets, comparing ancient and modern descriptions of them, and an account of Dr Desaguliers's experiments on statics and elasticity.

Annotated by Johnson: 'Read to SGS 6 Mar. 1739/40.'

[1] This was *Artis obstetricariæ compendium*, published in 1739 and 1740. See Manningham's entry in *ODNB* and No 92 above.
[2] The musical society.

350. SGS No 121: From Roger Gale to Maurice Johnson.
Scruton near Bedale, 29 February 1739/40.
MB3 fol.52B, 13 March 1740.
Checks that his history of Northallerton has arrived by post;[1] comments on a coin of the Emperor Constantine, 'a valuable medal' with a rare inscription, and gives its full history, discussing the arguments between English and French antiquaries about inscriptions indicating the origins of Roman coins; Gale claims the coin shows an abbreviation for 'minted in Londinium' but the French scholars prefer 'Lugdunum'.[2]

[1] Gale's letter of 21 December 1739 (No 344 above) states that he is sending this.
[2] Lyon, France.

351. SGS No 34: From Maurice Johnson (son) to Maurice Johnson.
London, 24 March 1740.
Sends by the Peterborough carrier a parcel of melon seeds from the King's gardener at Richmond, Mr Thomas Greening, which his friend Mr Fairchild had been given, and also pear and plum cuttings; is sorry Mr Ray has not attended SGS meetings since he quarrelled with Mr Cox: 'he is not the only rong headed of that Cloath amongst you';[1] regrets to hear of the death of Captain Wilson's daughter.

[1] This quarrel in the SGS between the medical man, Cox, and the cleric, Ray, reflects a similar quarrel at the PGS between the dominant medical man, Dr Charles Balguy (the anonymous translator of Boccaccio's *Decameron*) and Revd Thomas Marshall of St John's Church, Peterborough. Johnson was able to hold the SGS together but the PGS diminished into a book-lending club by the 1750s.

352. SGS No 48[?]: From Roger Gale to Maurice Johnson.
Scruton, 25 March 1740.
MB3 fol.53B, 27 March 1740.
Gale is pleased that the dissertation on the history of Northallerton arrived safely and was approved of by SGS;[1] discusses Northallerton fairs, correcting earlier errors relating to the charters that established them; disagrees with Johnson's claim that 'PLN' on a coin of Constantine, described in Gale's letter of 29 February,[2] refers to its being minted at Lincoln rather than London, despite Johnson's 'zeal for the honor of his countrey'; discusses inscriptions on coins and refers to the increase in value of coins with mistakes in their inscriptions, on account of their rarity; refers to 'Mr Johnson's'[3] account of the revolt in India.

[1] Roger Gale's pamphlet, *An Historical Account of the Borough of North Allerton* (1739), was printed in John Nichols (ed.), 'Reliquiæ Galeanæ', in *Bibliotheca Topographica Britannica* (London, 1780–90), Vol. III.
[2] No 350 above.
[3] William Johnson's letter (No 326 above), written on 5 April 1739 and read at the SGS on 28 February 1740.

353. SGS No 43: From Henry Johnson to Maurice Johnson.

London, 5April 1740.

MB3 fol.54A, 10 April 1740.

Hopes that Johnson returned to the Fens safely; has 'Mr Aimes of our Society's' catalogue of English printers for Johnson;[1] has bought a portrait of 'the great Ben: Johnson' by Zucchero[2] which he describes; gives SA news including Samuel Gale's resignation as Treasurer; has bought an Albano ware dish. Maurice Johnson's annotation refers to 'family Pictures'.[3]

[1]   Joseph Ames (1689–1759) of the SA; see his entry in Appendix 2 and in the *ODNB*.
[2]   For Zucchero or Zuccaro, see No 302 above; it is not now thought that he painted Ben Jonson.
[3]   The Johnson family claimed Ben Jonson the dramatist as an ancestor, though without firm evidence.

354. SGS No 36: From John Grundy junior[1] to Maurice Johnson.

Stevenage, 3 May 1740.

MB3 fol.55A, 8 May 1740.

Grundy has visited Dr Desaguliers and requested his book for the SGS library; discusses Desaguliers' *Mathematical Lectures* and his course of lectures in London, at which Topham the strong man[2] demonstrated his strength; comments on mosaics from Venice shown to him by Sir Thomas Hanmer[3] and the methods used for making them; has been to inspect the methods used in constructing the new Westminster Bridge in London; is to give Wright's *Use of the Globes*[4] to SGS.

[1]   Son of John Grundy senior and, like his father, a drainage engineer. See his entry in Appendix 2.
[2]   See the previous reference to him in a letter from Maurice Johnson on 29 November 1733 (No 201 above).
[3]   Sir Thomas Hanmer (1677–1746): Speaker of the House of Commons, 1714–15.
[4]   This is presumably Joseph Harris, *The description and use of the globes and the orrery* (London: printed for Thomas Wright, mathematical instrument maker, 1731). Gabriel Wright's book of a similar title, printed in 1783, is of too late a date.

355. SGS No 9: From Cornelius Little[1] to Maurice Johnson.

Boston, 4 May 1740.

Offers to sell Johnson a fine set of foreign pistols in holsters and a medal of the De Witt brothers.[2]

[1]   See No 250 above. This letter is addressed from Boston; Little appears to be dealing in antiquities.
[2]   Jan and Cornelius de Witt, Dutch government leaders in the mid-seventeenth century. They were originally successful in bringing prosperity to the Netherlands but were attacked and killed by a crowd in 1672 during demonstrations against them at the time of a French invasion. Jan de Witt was a noted mathematician, publishing *Elementa curvarum linearum* in 1659; he also used his mathematical skills in national economics.

356. SGS No 126: From Revd Robert Smyth[1] to Revd Mr Neve at Peterborough.

Woodston, 18 May 1740.

Sends thanks to Maurice Johnson for information about the Irby family; would like information from Johnson on the Batt family and their connections with other Lincolnshire families, especially any inscriptions relating to them.

[1]   See his entry in Appendix 2.

357. SGS No 44: From Revd Samuel Pegge[1] to Revd Mr Benjamin Ray.
Godmersham, 2 June 1740.
MB3 fol.57A, 5 June 1740.
Sends an account from an English gentleman in Angers of an amphitheatre at
Angers 'near the garden of a convent of nuns called La Fidelité'.

[1]   See his entry in Appendix 2.

358. SGS No 129: From Roger Gale to Maurice Johnson.
Scruton, 17 June 1740.
MB3 fol.58A, 26 June 1740.
Discusses an inscription at York about which he has consulted Dr Drake; Gale's
views on it have been printed in the *York Courant* and he will send the relevant newspaper cutting in case Johnson has not seen it;[1] regrets that he has not
received Johnson's letter of 25 March which must have been lost in the post;
thanks Johnson for sending an account of the amphitheatre at Angers;[2] adds
humorous comments on a poem about a wedding, sent by Johnson, and explains
that Gale's son is about to marry.

[1]   The cutting was sent in a later letter; see no.399 below. Francis Drake wrote a history of York and
was an SGS member in 1747 (see No 396 below and his entry in Appendix 2).
[2]   See No 357 above.

359. SGS No 14: From John Anstis, Garter King at Arms,[1] to Maurice Johnson.
'Mortlake in Surry near London', 25 June 1740.
MB3 fol.83B, 23 July 1741.
Discusses and answers Johnson's query about an unspecified mediæval document relating to the Black Prince, the origins, spelling and meaning of the Black
Prince's mottos 'Houmout' and 'Ich Dien' and the Prince's crest; disputes the
view that these were taken from the arms of King John of Bohemia, claiming
that the King's crest was different.[2]
Attached: Note by Maurice Johnson that the document was a grant of a pension
by the Black Prince, dated 34 Ed.3 [1361/2] and was shown to the SA at their
meeting on 2 December 1736.

[1]   See his entry in Appendix 2.
[2]   Recent research indicates that Anstis was right to question the popular tradition connecting the
crest with the King of Bohemia; this arose after the mediæval period and was first printed in the
sixteenth century. The King of Bohemia's crest was 'the entire wings of a vulture'; no early tradition
connects the motto 'Ich dien' with the Bohemian royal arms.

360. From Revd Timothy Neve to Maurice Johnson.
[Peterborough], 6 August 1740.
MB3 fol.60A, 7 August 1740.
Gives details of the wills of Dr Lockyer, Dean of Peterborough and President
of the PGS, of Revd Joseph Sparke, diocesan librarian of Peterborough and of
Mr Baker the Cambridge antiquarian;[1] explains the disposal of Bishop Kennett's
books; gives details of fossils found locally in a 30-foot deep excavation in the
neighbourhood of Fletton.

[1]   Revd Thomas Baker: a non-juring clergyman well-known for his antiquarian studies; see his entry
in *ODNB*. Revd Francis Lockier was an SGS member in 1726; Sparke joined in 1722. All three men
died in 1740.

361. SGS No 43: From Maurice Johnson (son) to Maurice Johnson.
Tower of London, 22 August 1740.[1]
MB3 fol.62A, 28 August 1740.
Sends apologies for not attending the SGS anniversary; discusses an inscription on a gun at Woolwich from Henry VIII's reign, dating it from its Latin inscription to before Henry's breach with Rome; quotes a Latin verse from the wainscot of the Mitre Tavern, Hampton Court; sends a sketch of a vase which was Dr Massey's [not kept with this letter].

[1]   He was presumably staying with Bogdani who had a house at the Tower.

362. SGS No 36: From Mr Wise[1] to Mr Collins, Stamford.
Wroxton near Banbury, 10 October 1740.
Communicated to SGS on 29 January 1741: MB3 fol.73B.
Discusses a Roman coin from the consular period and its inscription, also a 'Spanish invasion coin'.

[1]   He was the 'Keeper of the Museum, Oxon' as annotated by Maurice Johnson; see No 285 above. This appears to be a copy of part of the original letter, sent to Johnson, presumably by Mr Collins, for communication to the SGS.

363. From Maurice Johnson to John Johnson (brother).
London, 25 October 1740.
Read to SGS 30 October: MB3 fol.66A.
Describes his visit to Revd Timothy Neve at Peterborough, including a musical entertainment and a visit to the Dean and Chapter's library where he has bought some of their duplicate books for the SGS library; gives a lengthy and detailed account of his visit to Cambridge, including a meeting with the Master of St John's, a description of St John's College library and portraits of patrons; comments on a call paid to Dr Bentley at Trinity, where he reminded him of the requirement for members to donate a book to SGS library; gives an account of visits to other colleges, particularly King's and Emmanuel, and to Pembroke where he describes in detail the harpsichords he saw there; explains his suspicions of alterations made to a date in an early printed Bible in the University library, dated 1463, which he was sure should be 1475; plans to discuss this with Mr Ames.[1]

[1]   This is important in being Maurice Johnson's own account of his celebrated detection of a forgery in an early printed book; a detailed account of the incident is given by Revd Dr John Taylor of Cambridge in a letter dated 26 February 1741 (No 370 below), demonstrating Johnson's depth of knowledge of antiquarian matters. For a discussion of the question of altered dates in early printed books, see Adrian Johns, *The Nature of the Book* (University of Chicago Press, 1998), 356ff.

364. SGS No 127: From Maurice Johnson to Dr Green.
Cambridge, 4 November 1740.
Gives further details of his visit to Cambridge, particularly new buildings at Gonville and Caius College and a device for raising water and a chimney-jack for roasting meat at Pembroke Hall; explains that Dr Long, Master of Pembroke Hall, is finishing his book on astronomy[1] and refers to Classical details and drawings he is including; refers to illustrations for a new edition of Godwin's *De Praesulibus Angliae* by Dr Richardson, Master of Emmanuel College, a member of the SA;[2] gives a detailed account of the library of Joseph Sparke, who had died in July, mentioning several volumes; discusses Roman fresco paintings on a wall

in the palace of Maximus at Rome and sends sketches of them; sends messages and greetings to family members.

[1] Roger Long, an SGS member, published vol.1 of his book *Astronomy in five Books* in 1742; see his entry in *ODNB*.

[2] Dr William Richardson (1698–1775): Canon of Lincoln and antiquarian, who published in 1743 his continuation of Francis Godwin's 1616 Latin catalogue of English bishops; see his entry in *ODNB*.

365. No 10: From William Bogdani to Maurice Johnson.
Tower of London, 20 December 1740.
MB3 fol.71A, 25 December 1740.[1]
Expresses his relief at his son's recovery from serious illness and his concern for his education, as he hopes to send him to Eton; comments on the good and industrious character of 'Mr Watty';[2] explains problems with his Hitchin tenants, who are 'Beasts who will not be drove, perhaps they may be led';[3] gives an anecdote 'for the season of Mirth' of an elderly clergyman's rapid marriage and a verse made about it.
Annotated by Maurice Johnson: 'Lr from W Bogdani Esq. SGS with Just reprehension by a witty Lady on a proud Motto VENI VIDI VICI assumed as poesy for a Wedding Ring.'

[1] This date indicates the remarkable regularity of the SGS's weekly Thursday meetings; in 1740 they met on Christmas Day and the following week on New Year's Day 1740/1.

[2] Probably Maurice Johnson's son Walter Johnson, studying at the Inner Temple, known as 'Wat' in the family. He may have been staying with Bogdani, as other young members of the family had done.

[3] Although his work obliged him to live at the Tower of London for part of the year, Bogdani had an estate at Hitchin, for which Maurice Johnson was steward.

366. From Thomas Sympson to Maurice Johnson.
Lincoln, 20 December 1740.
MB3 fol.71B, 1 January 1741.
Thanks Johnson for his dissertation on Lincoln mints and coinage, discusses its contents; appreciates the honour of the proposal to admit him as an SGS member. Detailed annotations by Maurice Johnson on Sympson's comments about English coins, signed 'M. Johnson 1741'.

1741

367. SGS No 130: From Browne Willis to Maurice Johnson.
Whaddon Hall near Fenny Stratford, Buckinghamshire, 16 January 1740 [actually 1741].
MB3 fol. 73A, 22 January 1741.
Discusses Willis's work on market towns and his collection of traders' tokens, especially from Lincolnshire and Leicestershire, from which counties he still lacks some examples; asks to exchange specimens for some from Johnson's collection.

368. SGS No 46: From Revd John Francis[1] to Maurice Johnson.
Billingford, Norfolk, 3 February 1740 [actually 1741].
MB3 fol.74A, 12 February 1741.
Francis has sent a Roman urn dug up with others in the North Elmham area; discusses his own investigations into these urns, referring to Sir Thomas Browne's[2] *Hydriotaphia*; asks Johnson to inter the ashes but keep the urn.

[1]   An SGS member; see his entry in Appendix 2.
[2]   Sir Thomas Browne (1605–1682): Norfolk doctor and antiquarian, author of *Religio Medici* (London, 1642) and *Hydriotaphia or Urne Buriall* (London, 1658); see his entry in *ODNB*.

369. SGS No 77: From Revd Dr Philip Williams[1] to Maurice Johnson.
[St John's College, Cambridge], 13 February 1740 [actually 1741].
MB3 fol.75B, 26 February 1741.
Discusses Johnson's detection of alteration of a date in a Bible printed in Paris, held at Cambridge and thanks him for detecting it;[2] praises Johnson's son John's 'improvements'[3] and sends compliments from the Master and Dr Rutherforth; encloses a copy of a letter from Revd Dr John Taylor about the altered date.
Annotated by Johnson: 'SGS 31 Oct 1740 vol.3.66.'

[1]   See his entry in Appendix 2.
[2]   Maurice Johnson gave his own account of this incident in a letter to his brother John (No 363 above) on 25 October 1740; a full explanation is given in No 370 below. See Williams's entry in Appendix 2.
[3]   Maurice Johnson's son John was an undergraduate at St John's at the time; it is presumably through this connection that several of the Fellows of St John's became SGS members.

370. SGS No 75: Copy of letter from Revd Dr John Taylor[1] to Edward Harley, second Earl of Oxford.
Read at SGS 26 February 1741.
Original is dated Cambridge, 20 December 1740, but this is a copy sent to Maurice Johnson[2] in February 1741 by Revd Dr Philip Williams (President of St John's College, Cambridge and SGS member), enclosed with No 369 above.
[The letter gives a long, detailed account of the detection of an altered date in an early printed book at Cambridge and of Maurice Johnson's assistance in determining this forgery; sections of it are transcribed below. Lord Oxford, a keen antiquarian and book-collector and a member of the SGS, had searched across Europe in vain for another copy of this supposedly 1463/4 printed edition of the Vulgate Bible; Taylor explains that the first printing press in Paris was known to have been established in 1470, which made this book rare and controversial since it appeared to have been printed in Paris in 1463/4. He describes how Maurice Johnson pointed out that the date had been altered by hand from '1476' and the final two lines of the verse giving the date had been covered over.[3]]

'Copy of a L[r] to the Rt Hon Edward Earl of Oxford.
SGS No 75
My Lord   Cambridge Dec. 20 1740
The following Account relating to the Paris Bible of 1463/4, will not, I presume be disagreeable to your Lordship, as it serves to <u>clear up a very</u> <u>great difficulty in the History of Printing,</u>[4] and as the Fame of this rare & very curious Edition (I very well remember) to have excited your Lordships curiosity. It will be no longer a subject of wonder, that your Lordships Comissions over all Europe for

a Copy of this Book were Returned without success as your Lordship will be convinced from the perusal of these papers, that it cou'd not have happened otherwise ...'

Taylor quotes French authorities, Chevillier and Naude, who fixed the date of the establishment of the first printing press in Paris as 1470, the generally accepted date. This created problems with the date printed in this copy, at Cambridge, of the Bible printed in Paris, which appeared to date that book to 1463, especially as no other copies from that date could be found.[5]

'... For besides the time which must be required in laying in Materials & setting up a Printing House, this very large Volume consisting of 240 sheets which was finished at Press but at the beginning of the Year 1464, must have required when the Invention was very young & the Press moved heavily, a considerable time longer than the Compass of one Year to bring it to Perfection. Upon shewing this Curiosity a little while agoe to Mr Maurice Johnson of Spalding, a Gentleman exceedingly well versed in Antiquities, he almost immediately cryed out that there had been an erasement, and that in those two Words which establish the date, semi my Lord, is a visible forgery, wrote with the Hand in printing Ink on a place that had been scratched with the Knife, but otherwise no bad imitation of the Type, &, except that it borders a little too close upon the following word, upon the whole a very ingenious Counterfeit. The other word lustrum (thus lustr) has undergone no alteration but in the last letter, which is very ill connected with the letter preceeding, & in a quite different manner from any other part of the Book where those two letters meet, Besides my Lord that part of the word which remains in Print & untouched betrays upon comparison & to a very ordinary attention the imposture at the end of it ...

For I will venture to pronounce that this is a Copy of the Edition of the Bible in 1476, which is what Mr Palmer alluded to in his tribus lustris;[6] an Edition pretty well known, & altogether reconcileable with the testimony of our Printers, & the History of Printing ... [Taylor suggests the alteration was made] ... either thro' wantonness, or perhaps an affectation of being thought to be the Master of a singular Copy, or, what is still more likely, out of Avarice, transformed into what it is at present, & what has puzzled the most inquisitive for above twenty years last past.'

Annotated by Johnson: 'NB this learned Lord had given Commissions to many Booksellers and Others to procure him this pretended, and till this Discovery of the fallacy realy supposed Edition of the Vulgate Bible of 1463 printed at Paris at any Price, & the Copy herein mentioned cost Dr Jno Moor Lord Bishop of Ely much money.'

[1]   See his entry in Appendix 2.
[2]   Annotation by Johnson: 'I find this Memorandum made in my Diary of this Yeare 1740 & written by me 21 Octr. 1740 in the Publick Library of Cambridge University When their old Bible was there shewn me by Mr Register Taylor in presence of the Revd Mr Timothy Neve and Mr Clark of St John's Coll. [Colophon] to St Jeroms or vulgate Bible printed at Paris in the publick Library in Cambridge, called the Kings Library there, late Bp Moors.
Which makes It 1463 as Lewis XI began 1461
Iam semi undecimus Lustrum
      Tribus   Lustris
but it should be 1475/6 which is 3 Lustra or 15 yeares compleat
& so I wrote my Bro. from London on 25 Oct 1740 from this Memorandum. M. Johnson.'

3   There are detailed notes on the detection of the forgery by Johnson, which occurred on 24 October 1740, on pp.100–101 of Johnson's copy of Samuel Palmer's *General History of Printing* (1732), held in the SGS library. See also Maurice Johnson's letter to John Johnson, dated 25 October 1740 (No 363 above), and Philip Williams' letter to Maurice Johnson, dated 17 February 1740 (No 369 above). This letter is important in showing the extent of Maurice Johnson's antiquarian knowledge and his reputation as an expert.

4   Maurice Johnson's underlining. The history of printing was a topic of considerable interest at this time.

5   The date was given in the colophon at the end of the book, as was common in very early printed books, in three lines of Latin verse. The form in which Johnson saw them was quoted by Taylor:

Iam semi undecimus lustrum Francos Ludovicus

Rex erat, Ulricus, Martinus itemque Michael

Orti Teutonia hanc mihi composuere figuram.

meaning that when Louis XI had been king of France for two and a half years, Ulric, Martin and Michael who came from Germany printed this.

A *lustrum* was a Roman term for a period of five years; so, since Louis XI came to the throne in 1461 it would date the book's printing to 1463 or the beginning of 1464, i.e. before the accepted date of the establishment of a press in Paris. Johnson detected that 'semi..lustrum' (2½ years) had been inserted instead of 'tribus ... lustris' (15 years) which would date the book's printing to the more probable date of 1476, 15 years after 1461[see note 2 above]. After Johnson had detected this alteration, Taylor then noted that the final two lines of the colophon, usually five lines long, had been cut off, a strip of illumination pasted in and the page backed with the thick paper usually used to mend a page which had been torn.

6   Palmer, in his *General History of Printing*, had assumed that 'semi ... lustrum' was a mis-transcription for 'tribus ... lustris'.

371. SGS No 47: From John Johnson (brother) to Maurice Johnson.

Cursiters Street [London], 14 February 1740 [actually 1741].

MB3 fols 74B and 75A, 19 February 1741.

He is pleased that Maurice Johnson's health has improved and discusses the value of Mrs Stevens' Medicine;[1] gives Dr Lynn's views on reform of medicine along Galenic lines; explains that Dr Lynn has written a lampoon on the Dean of St Patrick's[2] who refused to be Lynn's patron in publishing his medical views; describes visits to a clockwork musical machine and a horseless chaise reputed to travel at 10 mph; discusses Shakespeare's new monument in Westminster Abbey which is proving popular.

1   In view of the medicine suggested, a commonly used medicine for dissolving internal stones, this would appear to be an attack of the 'stone' or 'gravel' in the bladder, from which Maurice Johnson suffered from time to time. 'Mrs Stevens' was Joanna Stephens (died 1774), famous for a remedy for getting rid of bladder stones without the need for a surgical operation. Her cure was commented on by the doctor and philosopher David Hartley. Parliament raised a £5,000 subscription to buy the recipe for her medicine in March 1740. See her entry in *ODNB*.

2   Dean Swift.

372. SGS No 42: From Thomas Sympson to Maurice Johnson.

Lincoln, 18 February 1740 [actually 1741].

MB3 fol.75a, 26 February 1741.

Regrets that Johnson will not be visiting Lincoln;[1] gives news of Lincoln Chapter members and friends; asks Johnson to translate Domesday entries for Lincoln; gives very full details of documents in the Lincoln cartulary; asks for information about a coat of arms from a building in Lincoln.

1   Presumably because of the ill-health referred to in John Johnson's letter (No 371 above).

373. From Thomas Sympson to Maurice Johnson.
Lincoln, 19 March [17]40 [actually 1741].
MB3 fol.77A, 26 March 1741.
Discusses the Fee Farm rent paid by Lincoln in the past and the foundation of
Burghersh's Chantry[1] in Lincoln Cathedral and associated endowments, and also
the defeat of claims by the Earl of Rutland in 1572[2] to receive payments from
the city of Lincoln.

[1] Henry Burghersh (1292–1340): Bishop of Lincoln; Lord Treasurer 1334–37. See his entry in
ODNB.
[2] Edward Manners (11549–1587): third Earl of Rutland and Lord Lieutenant of Lincolnshire. See
his entry in *ODNB*.

374. SGS No 46: From Roger Gale to Maurice Johnson.
Scruton, Yorkshire, 15 May 1741.
MB3 fol.79B, 28 May 1741.
Comments with pleasure on the prospect that his friend Sir John Clerk will join
the SGS;[1] explains that he has given Maurice Johnson's address to Clerk and
supplies Clerk's Edinburgh address; explains Clerk's views that the sunspots
which he has observed by telescope are probably responsible for the current four
years of cold weather; discusses Mr Little's coin of the Emperor Otho which may
be a forgery and explains that Clerk also has one which he claims is genuine;
praises Morell's *Thesaurus of Consular Moneys*;[2] is coming to Stamford to stay
with Stukeley and his wife[3] and may be able to visit Johnson.

[1] Clerk was elected as SGS member in 1740 but the letter informing him was lost in the post; see
No 385 below.
[2] Andreas Morell, *Thesaurus Morellianus* (Amsterdam, 1734).
[3] Gale's sister Elizabeth, Stukeley's second wife.

375. SGS No 44: From George Tookie[1] to Michael Cox.
Chippenham [Cambridgeshire], 16 July 1741.
MB3 fol.84A, 23 July 1741.
Comments on the increase in his surgical practice; gives accounts of some
cases; had missed seeing John Johnson[2] when visiting Cambridge; describes
and sketches a doe's uterus containing the bones of a dead fawn which she had
carried for over two years.

[1] George Tookie, a surgeon of Ely, was perhaps the brother of Revd Clement Tookie, vicar of Chippenham.
[2] Maurice Johnson's son.

376. SGS No 26: From Revd Dr Thomas Rutherforth[1] to Maurice Johnson.
[St John's College, Cambridge], 16 July 1741.
MB3 fols.86B and 87A, 20 August 1741.
Refers to the SGS's interests: 'I suppose natural history and English antiquities
are the branches of science that you chiefly improve'; gives lengthy and detailed
discussion of a misunderstood passage in Plutarch about the lens used to rekindle
the Vestal fires in ancient Rome,[2] criticising Lipsius's diagram based on this
misreading and offering his own diagrams; suspects a mistake in the copying of
the Greek text, which he attempts to correct; encloses a bill for Johnson's son[3]
for his study at St John's College, Cambridge.

[1] See his entry in Appendix 2.

² MB2 fol.141B shows Bogdani's diagram of a similar lens.
³ John Johnson.

377. SGS No 139: From Henry Johnson to Maurice Johnson.
Berkhamsted, 22 August 1741.
MB3 fol.88A, 27 August 1741.
Thanks Maurice Johnson for his letter asking about Berkhamsted Castle; describes the castle and earthworks, gives the history of the town, its earlier prosperity and its decline; discusses his two law suits there with the local people whom he describes as having 'pride, knavery and Poverty, the very worst Lott of common people I ever yet met with in any part of the World';[1] describes his fine house which had cost its previous owner £1000 to build; asks Maurice Johnson's advice on his garden and on books to buy to help him as he is now a JP; invites Maurice Johnson to stay on his next journey to London.

¹ As his earlier letters (Nos 108 and 180) indicate, he had travelled extensively in Spain, the Caribbean and Central America.

378. SGS No 50: From John Grundy junior to Maurice Johnson.
Gotham, Nottinghamshire, 4 September 1741.
MB3 fol.90A, 10 September 1741.
Gives a detailed account of a Roman pavement recently discovered at Welden[1] (Northamptonshire) and the Roman coins found with it; will send a drawing of the pavement if SGS would like it.[2]

¹ Weldon, near Corby. For the discovery of this pavement, see No 325 n.1 above. See also *Stukeley* iii. 40–44.
² In MB3 fol.90A, Johnson notes that the pavement had already been drawn and the drawing published, so the SGS had declined this offer.

379. From Revd Samuel Pegge to Revd Mr Ray.
[Godmersham, Kent], 14 September 1741.
MB3 fol.90B, 17 September 1741.
Discusses his friend Beaupré Bell's recent death and enquires about the editing of Bell's papers as he would like to assist with this; sends a copy of a curious inscription dating from c.1100, the dedication of St Mary's Church in Postling, Kent, for the SGS's comments.

380. SGS No 35: From Thomas Sympson to Maurice Johnson.
Lincoln, 28 September 1741.
MB3 fol.92A, 8 October 1741.
Gives a very detailed description of the burial of a man sewn up in ox-hide at Lincoln Cathedral 'under the porch of the north side Door, at the west end of the Minster', discovered when a new grave was being dug; it had been seen by Sir Joseph Ayloffe[1] but was later dismantled by the crowd of sightseers, though he has a small sample of the hide; discusses Lincoln Cathedral appointments.

¹ An SGS member; see Appendix 2.

381. SGS No 35: From Thomas Sympson to Maurice Johnson.
Lincoln, 26 October 1741.
MB3 fol.94B, 29 October 1741.
He would have sent an impression of an inscription on a lead plate but it has been

broken; he will send a drawing of it; refers to Dean Honywood's[1] version of it; discusses legal issues relating to Lincoln Cathedral Chapter and regrets that there will not be a clerk's post there for Mr Oldfield;[2] explains that a book [unspecified] that the SGS had subscribed to will not now be published.

[1] Michael Honywood: Dean of Lincoln, 1660–1681, responsible for the rebuilding of Lincoln Cathedral Library at his own expense, to designs by Sir Christopher Wren. See his biography in *ODNB*.

[2] Johnson is presumably trying to find a post for Anthony Oldfield, a relative. One of Oldfield's letters (No 506 below) comments on his attempts to find employment.

382. SGS No 33: From John Grundy junior to Maurice Johnson.
Gotham, 28 November 1741.
MB3 fol.97B, 17 December 1741.
Comments on the mines discovered and owned by Sir Robert Clifton in Scotland; offers detailed discussion of the copper mines in Derbyshire and Staffordshire and the high quality of copper mined there; has a mineral specimen for the SGS collection; is coming to Spalding in the near future.

383. SGS No 128: From Roger Gale to Maurice Johnson.
Scruton, 28 November 1741.
MB3 fol.99A, 31 December 1741.
Explains that Sir John Clerk has not heard from SGS about his election to membership;[1] discusses a Roman altar at 'Boulnesse' in Cumberland,[2] found two years previously, enclosing a drawing of the altar and its inscription and relating it to others in Horsley's book.[3]

[1] This may point to some problems with the postal service to and from Spalding at this time, as several letters from Johnson are reported as not having been received. Clerk had been elected to membership in 1740.

[2] Bowness on Solway, at the western end of the Roman Wall.

[3] John Horsley (1675–1732), *Britannia Romana: or, The Roman Antiquities of Britain* (London, 1732).

384. SGS No 51: From Peregrine Bertie[1] to Maurice Johnson.
Leyton, Essex, 17 December 1741.
MB3 fol.98B, 24 December 1741.

'Dear S^r   Layton 17 Decr 1741
    My Brother tells me, He mentiond to you, the antiquitys my Son has Pickt up at Ambleside that you have Some of the Same Sort in Your Collection, but Doubts he gave you an Imperfect Description of em. As I Dont Know when You may see the Originals, He Tells me It will be Very Acceptable If I send You the best Copy I can. As You are so much a Conoisseur in these Matters, I Hope You will Favour me with your opinion of 'em, & If You Please, The Sentiments of your Worthy Society at Spalding of which You have Done me the Honour to Enter me a Member. These Arms were found alltogether in a kind of Bundle, Two foot Deep in a Peat Moss: I had 'em of the Person who took 'em Out of the Ground; They were then so sharp as to Cut their Fingers, But since, they have Tried the Metal of 'em so often on Every Oak Table in the Parish, That They have a Little Notchd & Blunted 'em. The Metal is a kind of Brass, but Its Weight & Toughness Inclines me to Think there is a great Mixture of Copper. The Romans had Fabricatures of Arms near their Great Stations, & This being near Keswick, where are

the Richest Copper Mines in the Island, Tis Probable They made a great Use of That metal. They are all Cast, & have some Marks of the Mould …'

Gives a detailed description of each of the six weapons, accompanied by precise sketches.

'… I Conceive, These Arms must be Roman. Amboglanna was a Great Roman Station, and That It is now calld Ambleside, Not only the Similitude of Names, the Situation from whence Baxter derives It, near a Lake, a River & a Bogg; But the Roman Camp, The Inscriptions & coins which have been found there & even these arms fully Prove. Few Roman Stations have so many Marks to fix 'em. Most of the Swords upon the Medals & Columns have indeed guards to 'em,[2] but a few may be found without, and tho the Learned Editor of Cambden, says the Romans had no Arms of Brass, I Presume That Point is Unquestionable. The Roman Arms seem to be generally Straight & broad like These, & Those which are Crooked of the Scythe or Sicle kind, I apprehend to be the Swords of the Enemy. The Scythians & Nations Derivd from 'em, You know, were so calld for using such Crooked Weapons. But now I am got among the Scythians I am too far out of my Knowledge. If they are Roman, why may we not Reckon It, A Happy Omen for Our Country, That at a Time when all Europe is upon the Brink of a War,[3] We who were the Last Nation in Europe They conquered (Intacti Britanni. Pestem in Britannos).[4] Have Found a Set of Arms that were Handled by a People Who were Invincible.
Accept Yrself, & Present to Yʳ Good Family, all the best
wishes of the Season, From, Dear Sʳ, Yʳ most sincere
          Freind &c – P.Bertie'[5]
Annotated by Johnson: 'SGS No 51 Lʳ from the Honᵇˡᵉ Peregrine Bartie[1] Esq SGS about Brass Swords & other Armes dug up at Ambleside, with VI Drawing of them by that of the Celt attending seem to me to be British.'

[1]   Johnson's annotation 'Lr from the Honble Peregrine Bartie' confirms the accepted pronunciation at the time. See Bertie's entry in Appendix 2.
[2]   The weapons depicted in his sketches do not have a guard for the hand.
[3]   The War of the Austrian Succession (1740–1748), in which Britain was involved.
[4]   'The untouched (or unconquered) Britons. A plague on the Britons.' The first phrase may be an adaptation of a quotation from Horace's Epode VII 'intactus Britannus', 'the unconquered Briton'.
[5]   Filed with this letter in the SGS archives is a copy of an article by M. C. Fair, 'Note on Bronze Age Swords and Daggers of Cumberland, Westmorland and Lancashire North-of-the-Sands', originally published in *Cumberland and Westmorland Antiquarian and Archæological Society's Transactions,* New Series 45, reprinted as a pamphlet in 1946, which discusses these implements, reproduces the drawings from Bertie's letter and confirms the identification of the weapons by Johnson as Bronze Age British, not Roman as Bertie proposes. Fair's article, drawing on information supplied from the SGS by Mr Bailey, then the Hon. Curator of the SGS, assumes that the weapons had actually been displayed at a meeting of the SGS rather than described in a letter read out there; Bailey presumably took his information from the entry in the Minute Book, which is less precise, rather from the letter itself. This entry summarises the letter and copies the sketches of the drawings, and includes a comment by Johnson that as the Romans had given up 'Brass' weapons by this stage and the weapons resemble British swords in shape, they are more likely to be British.

1742

385. From Sir John Clerk to Maurice Johnson.
Edinburgh, 5 January 1742.
MB3 fol.104A, 21 January 1742.

Dear Sir   Edinbrugh 5 Jan[r] 1742
I had yesterday the favour of yours of the 28 of the last, but that which you took the truble to write to me some Months ago, never came to my hands.

I am extreamly oblidged to your Society for the Honour they have done me. but I fear it will never be in my power to make them any other return, than my willingness to serve them and my sincere wishes, that their good endeavours for promoting of Learning and all useful knowledge may be always successful. We, in this Country, have just such a Society[1] as yours who meet at Edin. once a month or oftner as there happens to be occasion, but can seldom give ourselves sufficient entertainment, in the mean time we watch for discoveries & when anything happens worth your Society's while I shall not neglect to communicate it.
I am ever Sir
        Your most obedient humble
        Servant John Clerk
Annotated by Johnson: 'L[r] from the Honourable Baron Clerk on his being admitted SGS.'

[1]   The Edinburgh Philosophical Society, originally called 'The Society for Improving Arts and Sciences and particularly Natural Knowledge', lasted from 1737 to 1747. After some changes, it became in 1783 the Royal Society of Edinburgh.

386. SGS No 45: From Revd Dr Thomas Rutherforth to Maurice Johnson.
St John's College, [Cambridge], 19 January 1741 [actually 1742].
MB3 fol.105A, 28 January 1742.
Asks about conditions for SGS membership; comments on Pliny's description of the winds and the compass points from which they originate, explaining how this differs from Gellius's account;[1] provides a long discussion on references to winds and their points of origin in the works of commentators on Classical texts.

[1]   Aulus Gellius, 2nd century AD. See *The Attic Nights of Aulus Gellius,* ed. J. C. Rolfe, 3 vols (1927–28).

387. SGS No 131: From Roger Gale to Maurice Johnson.
Scruton, 19 January 1741/2.
MB3 fol.105A, 28 January 1742.
Discusses the urns found at Elmham[1] and their supposed Danish origin, claiming that nothing Roman had been found at Elmham; gives his opinion that bronze implements found in Britain[2] belonged to the pre-Roman inhabitants and suggests that the Britons at the time of Cæsar used bronze weapons, discussing the use of bronze for cutting stone; discusses early forms of writing, especially that of the Hebrews; comments on the value of the 'flourishing and industrious' SGS 'with my best wishes to the Society, and your own family, out of which so considerable a part of it is formed, that you seem to have taken care (as far as human prudence

can go) of perpetuating your Institution to posterity'; sends an impression of a Roman seal [not present].

[1]   In Norfolk; see Revd John Francis's letter of 3 February 1741 (No 368 above).
[2]   The discussion of bronze weapons relates to the Ambleside hoard: see Peregrine Bertie's letter of 17 December 1741 (No 384 above), about which Johnson had apparently informed Gale.

388. SGS No 55: From Sir John Clerk to Maurice Johnson.
Edinburgh, 22 February 1742.[1]
MB3 fol.109A, 18 March 1742.
Offers very detailed discussion of early English and Roman urns and crema-tion practices, and of a seal and some coins of Gallienus[2] found in an urn, on which Johnson has asked his opinion; discusses relationships between the Welsh language and the languages of the ancient Britons and the Anglo-Saxons; comments on stone circles and other early stone monuments.

[1]   Part of this letter has been published in *Stukeley* ii. 282–5.
[2]   Roman Emperor AD 253–268.

389. SGS No 65: From George Lynn junior to Maurice Johnson.
Lincoln, 18 March 1741/2.
MB3 fol.109B, 25 March 1742.
Discusses his father's[1] treatment for the stone with Mrs Stevens' medicine; sends news of legal friends on the Circuit; discusses a rare gold coin of William I shown to the SA.

[1]   George Lynn senior, a member of the SGS; see his entry in Appendix 2. For 'Mrs Stevens', see No 371 above.

390. SGS No 123: From Maurice Johnson (son) to Maurice Johnson.
Charing Cross [London], 19 March 1742.
MB3 fol.109B, 25 March 1742.

SGS No 123   Charing Cross March 19th
1741[1]
I was favored with Yours Honoured S[r] of the 15th and am very much pleased to hear my Grandfather is so much mended, but very sorry to hear my Grandmother continues in so very lingring a State pray God deliver her out of it one way or other, for even Death is much to be prefered to her Condition & more espesialy as she is so good a Woman, and so well prepared for another State. I am very glad to hear my Uncle got down so well (I hope he did not keep Couz Wilsby up too late o Nights upon the Road & so mistime him) he will tell you the reason why I sent you no Ink Glasses, & as to Bumber Glassis now Burnt Ale is out of fashion there are none to be met with, but those you have are very good & fashionable. I have not yet been able to meet with any Orange Trees but if any come between this & the Time of Capt Wilsons being down will send my Mother a couple to whome be pleased to present my Duty. I am very glad to hear sister Harryot[2] will come up to town with the Capt. who I am sure will take good care of her, but fear she is worse of her old Complaint again if so am sure It is absolutely necessary for her to come up, but will say no more of it. With my love to sister Butter & her Secretary pray let her know I will execute her orders but must know how much

she is willing to go to for you cant have one under £1 5s & please likewise to let Sister Green know her Chairs will be very soon done & her Necklace by Saturday but was forced to buy her 2 Rows of Perls for the love knots were worn out & quite out of fashion I desire she will let me know her Orders about the Dish she mentioned for I have either lost or mislaied her Letter which is full as bad. I am Sr with Duty where Due your Obedient Son M Johnson

I have got you a Catalogue of Lord Oxford's[3] pictures & Busto's with the prices fixt to them for which they sold.

P.S. I was yesterday at Chelse at Lord Rennelas Guardens where they are making very great improvements and have built a most grand Amphitheatre[4] which I have just sketched out without the help of ruler or Compass as you will easily se the thing is by no means finished so I may have made many Mistakes which otherwise I should not have done but none of the work men could tell me or would either the width or hight or any Think about it and I believe there are at the least five hundred about the building but They saw I was attempting to draw it out, and that they did not like it for there is to be a very grand print to come out the Next Weak of It, and they did not know but I should be beforehand with 'em.

To Maurice Johnson Jun[r] Esq[r]

at Spalding, Lincolnshire   These

The letter also includes sketches of the outside and of a cross-section of the amphitheatre, annotated by Maurice Johnson: 'The Musick Amphitheatre at the Earle of Ranelaghs in Chelsey erected in 1741.' This section of the letter is illustrated on pp. 214–15.

[1]   The entry in the Minute Book shows that the date was 1742; Maurice Johnson (son) is using the system of dating letters by what we regard today as the previous year until 25 March when the year changed.

[2]   His sister Henrietta (born 1718, died unmarried). Sister Butter, mentioned below, is his sister Elizabeth (born 1713), married to local merchant, musician and SGS member Robert Butter; the 'Secretary' is perhaps a 'secretaire' or writing desk that she wants her brother to buy for her in London. Sister Green is his sister Jane (1711–1754), married to SGS second secretary Dr John Green.

[3]   Edward Harley, second Earl of Oxford, SGS member, died 1741.

[4]   Ranelagh Gardens were created by the second Earl of Ranelagh on his Chelsea estate. The Rotunda at Ranelagh Gardens was opened on 23 May 1742 for concerts, masquerades and other public entertainments; it was very popular and successful until 1802, attracting so many wealthy patrons that their coaches were held up in traffic jams. It was 185 feet in diameter, with a central column which housed the orchestra and boxes round the edge in which tea and supper parties could take place. It is well described by a French visitor in the *Gentleman's Magazine* for 1742.

391. From Revd Timothy Neve to Maurice Johnson.

Peterborough, 7 April 1742.

MB3 fol.111A, 8 April 1742.

Sends news of the recent transactions of the PGS for the SGS, including the receipt of a selection of fossils from the Grantham area sent by Revd Mr Saul of Harlaxton,[1] gifts of books including a printed *Legend of St Anne* of 1497,[2] a detailed description of Lyveden New Bield in Northamptonshire including its Latin inscription and a list of local thermometer readings.

[1]   See Saul's letter, No 181 above.

[2]   Its first printing. Maurice Johnson was particularly interested in early printed books and owned many in his private collection. For an account of his private library, see Bernard Quaritch, *Contributions towards a Dictionary of English Book Collectors* (reprinted London, 1969).

392. SGS No 52: From Sir Joseph Ayloffe[1] to Maurice Johnson.
'Careystreet Ne[a]r Lincolns Innfeild' London, 9 April 1742.
MB3 fol.111B, 15 April 1742.
Apologises for his delay in replying because of ill health; sends the latest SA news, commenting that little is being communicated; explains that Bogdani is not attending after he was not chosen as the new Director; gives news of a tessellated pavement at West Dean, near Salisbury, a silver medal, perhaps from the reign of Philip and Mary and a set of 'curious drawings' from the sixteenth century showing Abbot Islip[2] of Westminster in the reign of Henry VIII; comments on the seal of Holy Trinity Church, Edinburgh, in the reign of James II of Scotland, and on Stukeley's drawings of Tickencote Church.
Annotated by Maurice Johnson: 'L[r] from S[r] Joseph Ayloff Bar[tt] FR &A Socc. & a Beneficent Member of the SGSp.'

[1]   See his entry in Appendix 2.
[2]   John Islip (d.1532): Abbot of Westminster; see his entry in *ODNB*.

393. SGS No 32: From Dr James Jurin to William Bogdani at his house in the Tower of London.
Austin Friars [London], 16 April 1742.[1]
MB3 fol.112B, 22 April 1742.
Prescribes soap lees for the stone, for 'Mr Johnson';[2] gives his meteorological observations for 1–8 April 1742.

[1]   This letter is transcribed in Andrea Rusnock, *The Correspondence of James Jurin (1684–1750)* (Amsterdam, 1996), 433–434.
[2]   Presumably this is Maurice Johnson, who has been suffering from 'the stone'; see John Johnson's letter to him of 14 February 1741 (No 371 above). This could also explain the comment by George Lynn junior about his father's health problems in his letter of 18 March 1742 (No 389 above).

394. SGS No 48: From John Hepburn[1] to Michael Cox.
Stamford, 22 April 1742.
MB3 fol.113A, 29 April 1742.
Sends a bladder stone for the SGS museum; describes the case and the removal of the stone from a child's urethra in Rutland in 1734.

[1]   See his entry in Appendix 2.

395. From Revd Timothy Neve to Maurice Johnson.
Peterborough, 16 June 1742.
MB3 fol.117B, 17 June 1742.
Sends an abstract of the PGS minutes from February to May 1742 and a list of the prints held by the PGS; gives an account of the recovery of a cartulary of Peterborough Abbey;[1] sends good wishes for Johnson's sons at sea and in Flanders.[2]

[1]   This was the collection of charters compiled in the late 13th century by Henry of Pytchley the younger (Peterborough, Dean and Chapter MS 5). For a description of the manuscript, quoting this letter, see Janet D. Martin, *The Cartularies and Registers of Peterborough Abbey* (Northamptonshire Record Society 28, 1978), 15–16.
[2]   Martin Johnson: Maurice Johnson's fourth son, born 1727, a midshipman in the Royal Navy; Maurice: his eldest son, born 1714, serving as an officer with the '1st of Foot' (the Grenadier Guards) in Continental Europe.

396. From Francis Drake to Revd Thomas Drake.[1]
Norham, 14 July 1742.
MB3 fol.123A, 19 August 1742.
Gives a very detailed and outstanding description of the remains of 'Mailross'
or Melrose Abbey in Scotland and requests that the SA should produce good
engravings of these.
Added explanatory notes are in the hands of Maurice Johnson and Roger Gale.

[1]   This letter was sent to Maurice Johnson by Roger Gale, enclosed with Gale's own letter of 9
August 1742. Drake, the York historian, was writing to a relative, Revd Thomas Drake, who passed
the letter on to Gale. This is a helpful illustration of a significant way in which knowledge was transmitted in the early eighteenth century. For Francis Drake, see Appendix 2.

397. From Richard Norcliffe to Maurice Johnson.
Frederickshald [Norway], 17 July 1742.
MB3 fol.120A, 22 July 1742.
Discusses the poor state of current learning in Norway; sends a copy of his trans-
lation of the *Account of Greenland*, recently published in Danish.[1]

[1]   *Det Gamle Grønlands Perlustration eller Naturel Historie* (Copenhagen, 1741). It was written
by the Norwegian Lutheran minister, Revd Hans Egede (1686–1758), the first Christian missionary
to the Inuit of Greenland. The SGS hoped to publish Norcliffe's translation of Egede's book but
this proved financially impossible. It was published in London in 1745, but without the name of the
translator. Dr John Green's account of the book was printed in the RS's *Philosophical Transactions*
IX iii 409 in 1743.

398. SGS No 23: Revd Andreas Bing[1] to Mr Norcliffe.
[Frederikshald, Norway] 20 July 1742.
From MB3 fol.126B, 23 September 1742.
Letter in Norwegian, with abstract in English by Mr Norcliffe. Sends a diagram
of the track of a comet in relation to the Pole Star and the constellation of Lyra,
18 March to 19 April 1742, observed by 'Natural Eye' without instruments.
Annotated by Maurice Johnson: 'L[r] from the Revd. Pastor of Frederickshald Mr
Andreas Bing abt the Comett in July 1742 Shewn to Mr Weaver[2] Astronomer 3rd
Sept 1740 [sic].'

[1]   Bing had been one of the first Lutheran missionaries in Greenland, following the pioneering work
of Revd Hans Egede; see No 397 above, Norcliffe's letter of 24 August 1742 (No 401 below) and
his entry in Appendix 2. The information about the comet was also sent to the Royal Society: see
the letter from Cromwell Mortimer on 13 July 1743 (No 415 below). Although his letter was written
at this date, it was not sent to Spalding by Norcliffe until 24 August, perhaps because he needed the
time to prepare his English abstract of it. It was enclosed with Norcliffe's letter of 24 August (No
401 below).
[2]   Edmund Weaver (1695–1748): land surveyor, astronomer and almanac writer, one of William
Stukeley's friends.

399. From Roger Gale to Maurice Johnson.
Scruton, Yorkshire, 9 August 1742.
MB3 fol.123A, 19 August 1742.
He is pleased to hear of Norcliffe's gift to the SGS;[1] he sends an account cut out
from the *York Courant* of 29 June 1742 relating to Roman antiquities recently
discovered at York near the Mount[2] and suggests that the bones referred to in the
cutting are those of the Jews massacred at York in the twelfth century; discusses a

coin of the Emperor Carausius; discusses Pluche's *History of the Heavens*[3] which he has greatly admired and intends to re-read.

[1]   MB3 fol.120B for 24 July 1742 records that Norcliffe sent fossils, minerals, metals and shells from Norway and also his translation of Hans Egede's *History of Greenland*; see Norcliffe's letter of 17 July 1742, no.397 above.

[2]   The cutting is still attached to the letter.

[3]   Noël-Antoine Pluche, *The history of the heavens* (London, 1740). This was his second book, following his very popular *Nature Displayed* 1732. Fr. Pluche was a successful French author of popular science books.

400. SGS No 64: From Maurice Johnson (son) to Maurice Johnson.
Ghent, 13 August 1742 New Style.[1]
MB3 fol.124A, 26 August 1742.

He is following up, as asked, inscriptions in honour of the English and also looking for information about a Fleming called Dortville; his regiment is likely to encamp or go into action with the Hanoverians.

[1]   This would be 2 August in the English calendar at that time, which was before the adoption of the Gregorian Calendar in England in 1752. Maurice Johnson (son) had been posted abroad with his Guards regiment, which remained in quarters throughout 1742. In June 1743 the regiment took part in the Battle of Dettingen, the last battle in which the English troops were led into action by their king (George II).

401. From Richard Norcliffe to Maurice Johnson.
Friderickshald [Norway], 24 August 1742.
MB3 fol.126B, 23 September 1742.

S[r]   Friderickshald the 24 Augt 1742
    I did my self the Honour of writeing you the 16 July by Capt Solomon Burroughs for your Port, which hope is come safe to hand.[1]
    One of the Curates in this place Mr Andreas Bing has given me the Enclosed Observations,[2] & will be agreable if are Satisfactory.
    He s been near 5 Years Missionary in Greenland, his abode chiefly at Disco in 69 degrees Latitude,[3] & made several Observations not taken notice of in imperfect Translation I sent you, written by the present Superintendant.
    Mr Bing is allowed in these Parts, (as his College Attests also shew) Knowing in Mathematics, & Astronomy, that if you are desireous of any informations concerning these Northern parts of the world, if please Correspond with him in Latin, or send me it in English shall persuade his giving an immediate Satisfactory answer.
    With kind salutes I conclude myself S[r]
    Y[r] Most humble Servant
        R Norcliffe
To Maurice Johnson Esqr
at Spalding
Annotated by Johnson: '23 Sept The Rev[d] and Learned Mr Andrew Bing 1742 above recommended by Mr Norcliffe was proposed to be elected & admitted Member of the Gent Soc in Spalding by me
Rob[t] Butter   Maur. Johnson SGS Secr.
Answered 4 June 1743'

[1]   Norcliffe's abbreviated style is that of a 'business' letter, which is the type of letter he usually writes as a timber-merchant.

2   This is Bing's letter of 20 July 1742 (No 398 above).
3   A cave in the mountains at Disko, Greenland, is still known as Bing's Cave.

402. SGS No 52: From Revd Dr Thomas Rutherforth to Maurice Johnson.
[St John's College, Cambridge], 2 September 1742.
MB3 fol.125A, 9 September 1742.
Explains his new edition of his scheme of lectures; discusses John Johnson's[1]
progress as an undergraduate at St John's.

1   This was Maurice Johnson's son John; Rutherforth was his tutor at St John's College.

403. From Revd Timothy Neve to Maurice Johnson.
Peterborough, 8 September 1742.
MB3 fol.125B, 16 September 1742.
Apologises for not attending the SGS Anniversary and comments on the current
difficulties at the PGS: 'we meet and drink a bottle and so go home again just as
wise as we met'; gives a detailed description of the Aurora Borealis as observed
by him at Alwalton near Peterborough.[1]

1   Neve's report of this observation is recorded in the RS's *Philosophical Transactions* VIII ii 551.

404. From Dr Dixon Colby to Maurice Johnson.
[Stamford], 17 September 1742.
Thanks Johnson for a gift of plants,[1] one of which he has sent to the Countess of
Exeter at Burghley; discusses plants for gardens, especially growing conditions
for newly-imported ones: '... neither the East nor the West Indies can confine
the imagination of a true Florist.'[2]

1   Johnson's annotation states that this was a 'Malva Horaria'.
2   At this period, 'florist' meant a plant-collector and grower of rare flowers. See Colby's entry in
Appendix 2.

405. Letter to the SGS from signatories including the Duke of Bedford and
Browne Willis.
Stony Stratford, 1 November 1742.
Requests help for the inhabitants of Stony Stratford after a fire there.[1]
Maurice Johnson's annotation records individual contributions from members and
states that Revd Arthur Bransby[2] preached 'an excellent sermon' to encourage
donations. No general SGS contribution as such could be made as no funds
existed for such purposes.

1   146 houses and the Parish Church of St Mary Magdalene were destroyed.
2   Revd Arthur Bransby (d.1752): curate of Spalding in 1730 and rector of Great Coates (Lincs) in
1733. In 1735 he married Grace, daughter of Revd Stephen Lyon, President of SGS.

406. SGS No 30: From Maurice Johnson to Dr Green.
[London], 30 November 1742.[1]
MB3 fol.133B, 9 December 1742.
Sends a sketch of a bas-relief of a Roman gladiator on a piece of slate from
Chester, found in 1740, belonging to Dr Mead and shown at the SA on 24
November, and discusses the representation of gladiators and their equipment;
describes an illuminated Latin missal belonging to Henry VIII, with his auto-
graph, which he had seen at Lincoln's Inn in Mr West's library; describes Mr
Baker's[2] new improved solar microscope which magnified a flea to four feet in

length, and explains the possibility of adapting SGS's microscope in the same way.

¹   This letter was written in three stages over several days.
²   Henry Baker (1698–1774): natural philosopher and teacher of deaf people, who wrote extensively about the use of microscopes; see his entry in *ODNB*.

407. SGS No 63: From Maurice Johnson (son) to Maurice Johnson.
Ghent, 29 December Old Style [*sic*] 1742.¹
MB3 fol.134B, 23 December 1742.
Thanks his father for representing him as godfather to John Green's child; says he is glad that Green is not moving to Boston and that Mr Butter's gout is better; sends a sketch of a gold coin owned by the regimental paymaster, for his father's opinion;² discusses the current cold weather.

¹   The dating of this letter is problematic. The postmark is 'DE[cember] 21' and the letter appears to have been written before Christmas as he states '… a merry Xmas attend you'. It was received in Spalding in time to be read at the SGS meeting on 23 December 1742. Is the dating a mistake for '19 December' or for '29 November'? Either is possible; Maurice Johnson (son) is busy on campaign and is coping with the New Style of dating in use on the Continent and also the Old Style still used in England.
²   A note by Maurice Johnson states that it is a coin of the Emperor Charles VI.

1743

408. From Revd Timothy Neve to Maurice Johnson.
[Peterborough], 23 February 1742/3.
MB3 fol.139B, 24 February 1743.
Gives a very detailed description of a stone coffin found buried in Peterborough Cathedral, containing a body presumed to be that of an abbot; attempts to identify him from the history of the abbey and decides that John de Caux¹ is the most likely candidate.

¹   John de Caux (c.1205–1263): Abbot of Peterborough, 1249 to1263; see his biography in *ODNB*.

409. SGS No 33: From Revd Samuel Pegge to Revd Benjamin Ray.
[Godmersham], 21 March 1742 [actually 1743].
MB3 fol.141A, 24 March 1743.
Publicises a printed sermon by Pegge; discusses other publications including a new edition of Justin Martyr¹ produced in France; comments on an early Greek inscription in Athens and explains how it was brought to England.

¹   Second-century AD religious writer, author of two 'Apologiai' and 'Dialogue with Trypho the Jew' in which he gave an account of his religious conversion to Christianity. He was martyred at some time between 163 and 167.

410. SGS No 56: From John Johnson (son)¹ to Maurice Johnson.
St John's College, Cambridge, 8 April 1743.
MB3 fol.142A, 14 April 1743.
Describes in detail the garden and greenhouses belonging to Dr Walker,² Vice-Master of Trinity College; has mentioned to him Johnson's request to copy the catalogue of Beaupré Bell's coins and books; thanks the SGS for admitting him to membership; discusses a passage in Virgil's *Eclogues* relating to the markings

on hyacinth flowers, comparing it with passages in Aeschylus' *Ajax* and Ovid's *Metamorphoses*.

1   Son of Maurice Johnson: later incumbent of Spalding and SGS President 1755. See his entry in Appendix 2.
2   Richard Walker (1679–1764): founded the Cambridge University Botanical Garden in 1762. See his entry in *ODNB*.

411. SGS No 58: From Joseph Ames,[1] as secretary to the SA, to Maurice Johnson. London, 16 April 1743.
MB3 fol.143A, 21 April 1743.
Thanks Johnson for sending an account of SGS activities, which has been shown to the SA; answers Johnson's queries about a book, *Union of Hearts*, which he cannot trace,[2] and about the provenance of Dr Green's Chinese pottery statue, a well-known figure called 'The Happy Man'; explains that he is going to complete and publish his history of printing; refers to the sale of Lord Oxford's books, from which he hopes to purchase a Tindal translation of the New Testament; gives news that Mr Vertue is ill.

1   See his entry in Appendix 2.
2   This may be John Cook, *Redintegratio Amoris: or A union of hearts between the king ... the Lords and Commons ... and every honest man that desires a sound and durable peace* (London, 1647).

412. From John Swynfen[1] to Maurice Johnson.
'On Board the Colchester Indiaman Capt Mickelfield at Spit Head 15 Ap. 1743.'
MB3 fol.143B, 28 April 1743.
He will contact Johnson's kinsmen if he meets them on his travels and will send a full reply by one of the [East India Company's] ships with information on anything worth the SGS's attention, and items for Johnson's private collection; thanks Johnson for his hospitality; they are about to weigh anchor, and will sail with 3 other Indiamen and 'the Woolwich Man of War of fifty Guns'.

1   East India Company merchant: see his entry in Appendix 2.

413. SGS No 43: From Roger Gale to Maurice Johnson.
Scruton, 28 May 1743.
MB3 fols.145A and B, 2 June 1743.

SGS No. 43
Dear Sr Scruton May the 28th 1743
    I have been indebted to you a month for the favour of your last, and having nothing to alledge in my defence but the great difficulty I am under of making payment. In August last I had a violent fall from my horse, which gave me a great contusion upon the ribs of my right side and breast; in about two months time I thought myself pretty well again feeling no pain upon the bruised parts, but was exceeding weak occasioned by the opening of the vein where I was blooded, when I was in bed, and loosing in all 40 Ounces of blood as my Surgeon conjectured. This, with confinement, and want of Exercise, brought upon me such an ill habit of body, that by the Symptoms I was in fear of a Dropsy, but, thank God they are intirely dissipated, and I began to think myself perfectly well again. However, a day or two after the receipt of yours, when I intended to have answered it, I fell ill of a new disorder, which continuing upon me 4 or 5 days, reduced me allmost to deaths door, and having had two relapses since I thought

I had conquered it, am so very weak that it is not without pain and difficulty that I wield my pen, and half an hours writing never fails to give me a fresh remembrance of my disaster upon the muscles so long ago contused. I should not have troubled you thus long with a disagreeable relation of my Infirmitys, had it not been to give the reasons why your's has layn a month unanswered, which I am confident you will not surmise to have proceeded from any slighting of your Correspondence, which I much value.

I have this Spring (for I began after Xmas) not been idle however when I could possibly work. Last summer I got up a very handsome room for a repository of my books, I wont call it a Library, tho [page 2] it contains above 2000 Volums; I have busyed myself in placing them upon the Shelves, and then making a compleat Alphabetical Catalogue of them; a labor, I believe, I should hardly have ventured upon, had I apprehended the tediousnesse and difficulty of the work would have been so great as it proved, especially under my infirmitys, but I have conquered it by indefatigable perseverance, and can now say I am master of what I possesse.

as to Correspondences.[1]

I think the method of Correspondence you have schemed out[2] is very well designed, tho it will be very Laborious to the Secretary that is to carry it on; Infant Societys, as you observe will be the most industrious to promote it, as wanting sustenance themselves, and therefore willing to be nourished, and gather subsistance from all hands, which they may very much hope for from the Spalding Society, so well supplied with matter literary itself, and so communicative of it to others. As for S[r] John Clerk I have not heard from him these 2 months till last Monday, neither had that letter any thing of learning in it, nor any other that I have received from [him] this twelvemonth; which makes me believe that nothing curious has occurred to him in that time, and that therefore you have not been favoured with a line from him. I know him so well that I vouch for him to be the most free of his correspondence, never grudging any pains to please and entertain his friends.

I can not but think you very happy in your children, and hope the Divine Providence that has given you a competent number of them, will make them all blessings and comforts to you, as those that you mention seem to promise.

Marmor Sandvicense[1]

What you mention of the Earl of Sandwich's perpendicular Inscription[3] is exceeding curious and makes me impatient for Dr Taylor's observations upon it. I should think it by the manner of writing to be older than the Sigæan Inscription,[4] except some circumstances in its contents reduce it to a later date. The Chinese bring down their lines thus to this day, and by the strict adherence to their old customs, and not any other way of writing appearing among them from the earliest times, it seems to have been the primitive manner of recording theyr thoughts, and action. It is not improbable that the characters upon the China cup with the aquatick plant are an account of its vertues. We often have papers putt up with Tea, imported by the East India Company, full of them, neatly printed, upon severall colours. I once had given me 7 or 8 sorts by a gentleman who had lived 6 years in China, and asking him the meaning of these characters he told me they were encomiums of the Tea, expressing its great vertue, like a Quack bill; he presented me at the same time with 2 or 3 branches of the Tea shrub, which demonstrated the Pico, the Bohea and 3 sorts of Green tea to be the produce of the same plant, and onely to differ in the age, as the bud the young leaf, and the old leaf, farther alltered by the manner of drying them, which has since been confirmed by the account Dr Kaempfer gives of the Tea in his History of Japan.[5] The Specimens that I had, I presented to the Royall Society. The Epidemick feavor has had it's run here, but without much slaughter, onely demolishing a few old people, and is now ceased. As for Fogger [?]horp,[6] the distance of above 40 miles from this place makes me an entire stranger to it, neither have I an acquaintance in that part of the country. My humble service and best wishes attend the Society at Spalding, I am very sorry I have been so useless of late to it, by my infirmitys, and want of matter to communicate, having met with nothing worth their notice for some months.

> I am D[r] S[r]
> Your most obliged
> humble Servant
> R Gale

To Maurice Johnson junr Esq
at Spallding in Lincolnshire
Turn off at Stilton.
Annotated by Johnson: 'L[r] from R Gale Esq FRA & GSS. Quoad Correspondencys
Perpendicular Inscription of Chineze. Marm. Sandvicense.'

[1] Annotation by Johnson.
[2] The details of this scheme were presumably set out by Johnson in his previous letter to Gale; it appears to be a scheme for learned societies to exchange information on their discoveries by letter. Johnson had suggested such schemes previously in letters to Stukeley. The SGS and PGS exchanged information regularly, and both sent reports to the RS and SA, but schemes of shared correspondence with other provincial societies do not seem to have been successful, probably because these societies tended to be short-lived, like Stukeley's Brazen-nose Society. See Introduction, p. xv.
[3] 'The Sandwich Marble': John Montagu, fourth Earl of Sandwich (1718–1792) had undertaken a tour of the Turkish Empire, including Greece, then ruled by Turkey, and Egypt; he had returned in 1739 with a number of antiquities, including a very early inscription from Athens, carved on a piece of marble, which proved to be an account of the contributions levied by Athens on her allies. It was presented to Trinity College, Cambridge. Dr John Taylor of Cambridge, an SGS member, wrote an account of it, *Marmor Sandvicense cum commentario et notis* (Cambridge, 1743); it is this publication that Gale is looking forward to.
[4] A very early Greek inscription, the earliest known at that time, on a marble pillar found in the late seventeenth century, first noted by Dr William Sherard, British consul in Smyrna, brought to England by Lord Elgin in 1799 and now in the British Museum. An account of it was published in 1721 by Revd Edmund Chishill, chaplain to the British merchants in Smyrna.
[5] Engelbertus Kaempfer *The History of Japan*, translated from German by J. G. Scheuchzer (London, 1727).
[6] Foggathorpe (Yorks ER), north-east of Selby. There is a hall and manor house there.

414. From Revd Timothy Neve to Revd Mr Whiting at Spalding.
[Peterborough], 15 June 1743.
MB3 fol.146B, 30 June 1743.
Discusses Neve's tour in the West of England, including a detailed description of monuments in Burford church, near Tenbury Wells, Shropshire; gives an account of the character of Edward Harley, second Earl of Oxford, whom he had visited.[1]

[1] The visit would have taken place before the Earl's death in 1741.

415. Note from Cromwell Mortimer to William Bogdani.[1]
[London], 13 July 1743.
Thanks Bogdani for sending the 'observation of the comett'; he has 'laid it before the RS who order'd thanks to you and Mr Johnson'; explains that the 'abstract'[2] has been corrected by Mr Zollman.

1   This was attached to the letter from Revd Andreas Bing (No 398 above) in the SGS archive.
2   This refers to a summary by Norcliffe, in English, of Bing's observations and comments. Philip Henry Zollman (d.1748), FRS 1727, was the RS's first Assistant Secretary for Foreign Correspondence.

416. Copy of letter from Dr Walter Lynn to William Stukeley, 'Dr Stewkly', forwarded to Maurice Johnson.[1]
Nottingham, 23 July 1743.
MB3 fol.149A, 28 July 1743.
Quotes Lynn's epigram on the English victory over the French, 'the French cock', at Dettingen on 16 June 1743, discusses the derivation of the name 'Galli' for the French.
Also extensive notes in Maurice Johnson's hand, in Latin, on possible derivations of 'Galli'.

1   Sent by Mr Walter Carruthers of Nottingham, with whom Lynn had been lodging, presumably for Johnson's views on the etymology of 'Galli'.

417. SGS No 42: From Musgrave Heighington to Maurice Johnson.
Yarmouth, Norfolk, 26 July 1743.
MB3 fol.149B, 4 August 1743.
Heighington has received a poem sent by Maurice Johnson[1] and sends his setting of part of it, 'All Hail the Day', which will be performed at the SGS Anniversary; he hopes the author will pardon some rearrangement of words 'euphonia gratia'; he will come a week before the Anniversary with another musician, 'Mr Porter, who plays a fine fiddle and German flute'.

1   This is 'Ode on St Cecilia's Day', annotated by Johnson as being by Mr Jackson 'Usher of the Petit School at Spalding'. As in previous years, Heighington is to provide the music for the celebration of the SGS's Anniversary, held at the end of August each year in the late 1730s and early 1740s. See Nos 309, 312, 330 and 331 above. Unfortunately, Heighington's musical setting of the poem has not survived.

418. From Roger Gale to Maurice Johnson.
Scruton, Yorkshire, 27 October 1743.
MB3 fol.187B, 3 November 1743.
SGS No 59
Dear Sʳ   Scruton Octob. 27ᵗʰ 1743
    As no one can be a more hearty well-wisher to the learned and industrious Society at Spalding than myself, so nothing can be a greater pleasure to me than to hear of its prosperity, advancement, and good progresses in every thing that may contribute to its ease and honor. Nothing could promote the latter more than the commodious Receptacle and Apartements[1] described in your last, which I hope will be not only a safe repository for all it's Collections against the injury of time, and a negligent dispersion that may happen, as it does too often, in things of this nature, but that the agreeablenesse of the place may encourage frequent and numerous meetings, to the increase of friendly conversation, learned

conferences, and improving correspondence. I write this to you from a room in which I take more pleasure than ever I did in any other during my whole life. Finding myself master of a good Collection of books, but almost useless by lying in undigested heaps,[2] and dayly in danger of perishing by dust and damps, I took a resolution about a year and a half since, to build an additional room to my house where I might rescue them from destruction and enjoy the Company I delighted in, according to my mind, retired and uninterrupted, whenever I chose to be alone, and I can now truly say Nunquam minus solus, quam cum solus.[3] When I had got the case up which is 21 ft. in length by 17 I was allmost deterred from furnishing ∧it by the unpleasant dry piece of drudgery that I perceived was coming upon me, and I must unavoidably submit to in ranging the inhabitants in due order. However the elegance of ∧the place, and the pleasure I promised myself from its being brought into order, made me determin to sett my shoulders to the work, and by the assistance of two neighboring Clergymen I divided the 4 sides into 13 Classes, twelve foot hight, marked on the Cornish over each of them with A.B.C. &c. under which every shelf is numbred I. II. III. &c. and where every book as it stands in order upon the shelf: 1. 2. 3. &c. and all of them digested as well as my compasse would allow into Classicks, Lexicographers, History, Divinity &c. Still there was wanting a Compleat Catalogue that might serve as an Index to the whole, this I also ventured upon and conquered in lesse than 3 months; my confinement, and long indisposition [page 2] not only much expediting the work, but being greatly alleviated by it, so that Aliquisque malo fuit usus in illo.[4] Here I never want company to my mind ∧nor have too much, here I never have the hours lye heavy upon my hands and be at a losse how to throw them away, that generall curse of the country; and instead of ale, wine, punch and Squires, I can entertain myself with Consuls∧ and Emperors, that have a little apartment to themselves and Historians, Philosophers and a whole Academy of the Literati. You will pardon me for this long detail of my contentednesse, since your account of your new Musæum, and the objects now agreeably disposed all round me naturally lead me into it, and there is certainly no greater happynesse in the world than to make our friends partakers of that which we enjoy ourselves. I dare say it is no small pleasure to you, that while the young Gentleman in the Army[5] is doing his King and Country service in the field, he has so much reguard for his father, that he can entertain him with such Literary observations as fall in his way at the same time, I believe there are few such instances among our many Legions. I cant find either of the two Inscriptions he has sent you from Worms in Gruter,[6] or any other of our Collectors of Inscriptions, which is strange, since they are placed so openly in a great City as he mentions the first is so much defaced that I cannot make out the cornets Name upon it. There seems a line at least to be wanting at the top of the 2d LICNUS perhaps is for LICINIUS, a Roman name common enough, the other I never met with. CLOST. I take to be for CLUSTumina tribu, and HELVESIUS for HELVETIUS, a Switzer Annorum 47, his Age, and STIP. stipendiorum XXVI. the years he had served in the Army. HS. Hic situs est. I believe the last line should be read TIBerius IVLius CAPITOLINUS, and that still another line is wanting for A.P.M. Amico ponendam curavit or something like it.

The Marmor Sandvicense[7] by Dr Taylor is a learned and curious piece. Dr Longs Astronomy I have not seen. The List of all the Sherifs I shall be glad to

have when publish: pray inform me when it comes out. I fear it will be some time before Mr Sympsons History will be in the presse. Browne Willis writes me that the new Edition of Dr Tanners Monast. Notitia will be finisht by the end of the month. as I hear will also be Junii Etymologicon Anglicanum.[8]
I have room to add no more than my best services to your Society
And that I am Dear S[r]

Your ever most obliged humble Servant

R Gale

Annotated by Johnson: 'L[r] from R Gale Esq FRA & GSS of his Library, the Inscription under the Equestrian Funeral Monument whereof drawings sent by Capt Johnson from Worms.'

[1]   The SGS's meeting-place was moving from the Abbey Rooms to rooms in Gayton (later Holyrood) House, the former home of Maurice Johnson's wife Elizabeth, née Ambler, next door to Ayscoughfee Hall where Johnson lived. Minute Book 1 contains a sketch by Johnson of the proposed layout of the rooms for the Society's use.
[2]   Gale may be quoting from Thomas Burnet's *Telluris Theoria Sacra* (London, 1681) which referred to the Alps as 'vast, undigested heaps of stone'.
[3]   'Never less alone than when alone'. Cicero, *De Officiis*, attributes this saying to Publius Scipio.
[4]   'Some good function came out of that evil'. Gale is quoting from Ovid's *Metamorphoses* Book II.
[5]   Maurice Johnson's eldest son Maurice, now a captain in the Guards and serving on the British campaign in Continental Europe. He had sent to his father a letter describing a funeral monument he saw in the German city of Worms, which appeared to be that of a Roman cavalry soldier. This letter has not survived in the SGS archive, nor has another by him from the same period which gave his account of the battle of Dettingen.
[6]   See No 50 n.1 above.
[7]   See Gale's previous letter, No 413 n.2 above. 'Dr Longs Astronomy' is Roger Long, *Astronomy* (Cambridge 1742). The list of county sheriffs was being compiled by Johnson: see Nos 436 and 465 below; his list was not published. For Tanner's *Notitia Monastica,* see Nos 430 and 435 below. This new edition was published in 1744, edited by the author's brother, Revd John Tanner, Vicar of Lowestoft.
[8]   Franciscus Junius (1591–1677): German philologist who lived for over 20 years in England and whose work, *Etymologicum Anglicanum*, on the etymology of English was finally published in 1743 by Edward Lye.

419. SGS No 60: From Maurice Johnson (son) to John Johnson.[1]
Spires [Speyer, Germany], 11 November 1743 New Style.
MB3 fol.157A, 3 November 1743.[2]
Gives news that 'Spires'[3] has been burnt by the French and the cathedral is damaged; gives news of his visit to Heidelberg, describing its antiquities and the damage done to the Elector's palace by the earlier French attack in the 1620s.

[1]   He was travelling down the Rhine. This letter is to his uncle John, not his brother, since he signs the letter as 'your very obed[t] nephew'.
[2]   Again, the dating of the letter is problematic. The Minute Book entry for 3 November states that the letter had been 'received last Monday' which was 31 October by the English method of dating in 1743.
[3]   Speyer.

420. SGS No 15: From Revd Benjamin Ray to Maurice Johnson.[1]
[Spalding], 26 November 1743.
Pays tribute to Johnson because 'you so kindly & so generously feast us, to our great satisfaction, with one fine entertainment or other, during your absence from us';[2] sends information from Mr Pegge about a Roman inscription on marble;

asks Johnson's opinion of the meaning of a Latin passage in Julius Firmicus Martinus, *De Errore Profanarum Religionum*,[3] quotes and discusses its meaning in detail; hopes Walter[4] is 'better much for his journey'.

[1] Addressed 'To Maurice Johnson Esqr at Mr Harlands a Perukmakers in Cursiters Street Chansery Laine' in London.
[2] This indicates that Ray has returned to meetings as a regular member; see Maurice Johnson (son)'s letter of 24 March 1740 (No 351 above). Johnson appears to have changed his London address for receiving letters.
[3] Julius Firmicus Maternus: fourth-century Byzantine Christian author; his book deals with the errors of pagan religions. It was reprinted frequently, including an edition in 1743.
[4] Johnson's son.

421. SGS No 14: From William Stukeley to Maurice Johnson.
Stamford, 27 November 1743.
MB3 fol.161A, 15 December 1743.
Sends a request for plants for his garden which he is preparing; describes a strange bat which he has seen.
Also detailed notes by Maurice Johnson about types of bats as discussed at a meeting of the RS, probably in preparation for his reply to Stukeley.

422. SGS No 134: From Maurice Johnson to Henry Eustace Johnson.[1]
London, 3 December 1743.
Sends a drawing of Roman carving of a 'plumming line' and two heads in profile, in the possession of Mr James West;[2] he will bring Boerhaave's prescription from Mr West for Dr Green; sends news that mahogany is now unfashionable, so he has bought a newly-fashionable Japanned tea-board; gives news from the RS of the shooting, in Canadian Arctic waters, of a polar bear, which was 14 feet long; refers to Egede's book on Greenland.

[1] Henry Eustace Johnson, addressed as 'Dearest Son', was 10 years old at this time. This letter is intended to be passed on for reading at the next SGS meeting, but also contains details to interest a young boy.
[2] See No 151 above.

423. From Martin Folkes,[1] President of the RS, to Maurice Johnson.
London, 9 December 1743.
MB3 fol.161A, 15 December 1743.
Thanks the SGS for election to 'a Company I greatly honour, whose prosperity I ardently wish, and that all their designs for the promotion of true knowledge may be crownd with their desired success'; regrets that distance prevents his attendance but he will communicate with the SGS; requests information on the SGS's formation, nature and membership.

[1] His signature is interesting, indicating Folkes's awareness that he is bestowing honour as well as receiving it: 'M Folkes Pr.RS. of the Royal Academy of Sciences at Paris, the Society of Antiquaries at London; of the Florentine Academy, and Academy of Painting and Sculpture here. Member of the Societys of Arts and Sciences at Edinburgh and now through your favour of the Gentlemans Society at Spalding'. See his entry in Appendix 2.

424. SGS No 94: Maurice Johnson (son) to Maurice Johnson.
Brussels, 10 December 1743 New Style.
MB3 fol.161B, 22 December 1743.
Regrets that he has not heard from the family; has been ill of fever at Westbaden;[1]

has travelled by Rhine boat and postchaises to Brussels; describes his visit to Bonn, especially the elegance of the Elector's palace, and gives an account of sightseeing in Cologne and Liège; sends a drawing of a picture of the decapitation of John the Baptist, from an Albano ware dish that he has seen which is similar to one that his father has; refers to the coming marriage of Prince Charles.[2]

[1]   Wiesbaden.
[2]   Prince Charles, Duke of Lorraine (1722–1780), married on 7 January 1744 Maria Anna, sister of Empress Maria Theresa and was made, with his wife, joint Governor of the Austrian Netherlands.

1744

425. SGS No 29, other No 31: From William Stukeley to Maurice Johnson.
Stamford, 5 January 1743–4.
MB3 fol.164B, 12 January 1744.
Explains his plans for a visit to Westmorland with Roger Gale to re-visit Druid remains; discusses the different types of bat, leading to comments on the hibernation of various creatures and disagreement with Warburton's views on a future state;[1] sends comments on his observation of a comet between the constellations of Andromeda and Pegasus.

[1]   This relates to Warburton's famous book *The Divine Legation of Moses*, 2 vols (London, 1738–1741), in which he claimed that the idea of a future life was not known to ancient peoples until it was revealed to Moses. Warburton, then a Lincolnshire clergyman and later Bishop of Gloucester, was an acquaintance of Stukeley's; see Warburton's entry in *ODNB*.

426. SGS No 40: From William Stukeley to Maurice Johnson.
Stamford, 18 February 1743–4.
MB3 fol.166B, 23 February 1744.
Thanks Johnson for his gift of trees for Stukeley's garden; sends a description of the comet which is currently visible and a diagram of the comet's orbit.[1]

[1]   Stukeley's diagram compares interestingly with that sent by Andreas Bing of his observations in Norway in March–April 1742 (see No 398 above).

427. SGS No 93: From William Bowyer[1] to Maurice Johnson.
[London] 3 March 1743 [actually 1744].
MB3 fol.168A, 8 March 1744.
Thanks the SGS for the honour of membership; claims that the reputation of the SGS is similar to that of a University; offers 'the Welsh laws' as his present of a book to the SGS library; discusses Roman coins of Nero and Drusus found at Chichester and claims that they validate the dating of the Chichester inscription;[2] compares Germanicus' victory in Germania to the recent British victory at Dettingen; says he is not breaking the SGS's rule forbidding political comment because it is a historical parallel; says he is just printing 'Folkes' Table of Silver Coins from the Conquest'.[3]

[1]   See his entry in Appendix 2.
[2]   See earlier letters about the finding of this inscription in 1723 (Nos 48, 49, 50 and 51 above).
[3]   Martin Folkes (1690–1754), *A Table of English Silver Coins from the Norman Conquest to the Present Time* (London: Society of Antiquaries, 1745).

428. From Thomas Birch to Maurice Johnson.
St John's Lane, Clerkenwell, London, 24 March 1743/4.
MB3 fol.169A, 29 March 1744.
Apologises for delay in replying, as Johnson's letter was kept at the Royal Society's premises instead of being brought to him; thanks the SGS for electing him to membership; promises to help to promote the SGS's aims by 'communication of the Occurrences in the Republic of Letters' in London.[1]

¹ He would be well placed to do this as Director of the SA. See his entry in Appendix 2.

429. From Revd George Ferne[1] to Maurice Johnson.
Wigtoft, 26 March 1744.
MB3 fol 169A, 29 March 1744.
Thanks the SGS for admission; will not be able to attend regular meetings but will send either 'Dr Robinsons Hesiod or Smith's Cure of Deism'[2] or another book if the SGS has these.

¹ See his entry in Appendix 2.
² An edition of the works of the Greek author Hesiod, *Hesiodou tou Askraoi ta Heuriskomena*, with parallel Greek and Latin texts, edited by Thomas Robinson (Oxford, 1737); *The Cure of Deism* by 'A country clergyman' (London, 1736) [Revd Elisha Smith, Rector of Tydd St Giles 1722–1740]. See No 447 below.

430. From William Draper[1] to Maurice Johnson.
Cecil Street [London], 3 April 1744.
MB3 fol.169B, 5 April 1744.

Sʳ   Cecil Street, April 3ᵈ 1744
    To excuse my self for not sooner returning an answer to your very obliging Letter I must partly blame the Season, which has made me so sensible of it's Severity as to confine me to my room for several days with a violent Cold, & partly too I must find fault with my own indolence, which would not suffer me to make use of some favourable intervals to acknowledge with greater readiness the favour I receiv'd from you.
I am oblig'd to lay aside the thoughts of waiting on you at Spalding from some necessary avocations my private affairs occasion at this season of the year, but I think my self greatly oblig'd to return many thanks for your & your family's kind invitation, & beg my very humble Service may be acceptable to you all.   I lie under yet further obligations to you & the worthy Gentlemen of your ingenious Society for intending me the Honour of receiving me a member of it, though so unworthy an addition to it; but I should be still less deserving of that Honour should I neglect to embrace it when offer'd me in so candid & engaging a manner. I shall be always ready to contribute, according to my poor abilities, towards the welfare & Promotion of so laudable a Society which has already ow'd it's Rise and Progress so much to your patronage & ingenuity, & is in so great a measure to ow its happy continuance & prosperity to your ingenious & unwearied application.   I cannot but greatly approve of that part of the model of your society which admits of Accessions to it free from the unnecessary Cavils about the Matters of differing Religions, as well as from the medling in so frequently intricate & dangerous impertinences of State affairs. Learning has a field extensive enough for all her followers without interfering with the Bounds of her neighbours, & admits of no one into hers who would not

promote the Good of all human Society. The Arts & Sciences have always been of all Ages, Sexes & Opinions.

That you may long live to enjoy the Satisfaction of contributing so generously to the Commonweal of Learning is one of the favourite

wishes of S^r   your very humble Servant

Wm Draper

P.S. I propose presenting to the Society for their Library, conformably to custom, by some speedy Opportunity, Bishop Tanner's Notitia Monastica improv'd & enlarg'd By J. Tanner A.M. & lately printed at the Expence of the Society for the encouragement of Learning.[2]

Annotated by Johnson: 'L^r from William Draper Esq. FAS on his being admitted & donation to SG Sp. Bishop Tanners Notitia Monastica'

[1]   See his entry in Appendix 2. The book is listed in the eighteenth-century SGS catalogue as given by him and is still in the SGS library.

[2]   Members of the SGS had been involved in supporting the election of Dr Cromwell Mortimer to be secretary of this society; see Nos 320, 321 and 322 above.

431. From W. Beecroft to 'Rev. Sir' [Stephen Lyon as SGS President].

[Great Steeping], 1 June 1744.

He plans to visit Spalding for the SGS Anniversary Concert; sends a drawing of an inscription on a grave burial at Faldingworth Church:

ALAUN.STOURS.GYT.ICI.DEV.DASA.ALME.EIT.MERCI+

and asks for the SGS's help in translating it.[1]

[1]   'Alaun Stours lies here; may God have mercy on his soul.' Faldingworth is situated between Lincoln and Market Rasen. William Beecroft was Rector of Driby and Curate of Firsby with Great Steeping (LAO, LC18B, 222–3). Although he states he will attend the SGS Anniversary, the Minute Books do not record his membership.

432. SGS No 61: From Roger Gale to Maurice Johnson.

[Scruton], 12 June 1744.

MB3 fol.177B, 21 June 1744.

Explains his ill health;[1] declines Johnson's compliments and claims he cannot compliment in return as he 'can only give you the plain thoughts of a sincere mind, without gilding or throwing of dirt'; praises the SGS and PGS for their plans to preserve their papers in case they cease to meet; hopes the Antiquarians will take equal care and gain a charter in order to benefit from legacies; discusses a coin of Caligula found at Chichester and also the inscription found there in 1723; gives full and detailed reasons for dating the Chichester inscription[2] to soon after the Roman invasion of Britain; defends his own views against criticism by Professor Ward[3] of Gresham College, as discussed in Horsley's *Britannia Romana* p.337, quoting other inscriptions as supportive evidence.

Included with this letter is an engraving of the Chichester inscription, annotated by Maurice Johnson.

[1]   See No 413 above. Gale died later in 1744.

[2]   See No 427 above.

[3]   See his entry in Appendix 2.

433. SGS No 92: From Joseph Ames to Maurice Johnson.
London, 13 June 1744.
MB3 fol.176B, 28 June 1744.
Returns Johnson's books used in preparing his history of printing;[1] thanks him for his help and for the subscriptions to the book which Johnson has organised; sends news of SA meetings and of the printing of Mr Folkes's book on silver coins; discusses Henry Baker's invention of a method for taking impressions of coins and medals which will help the SA in producing a series of 'our English Money'.

[1]   Ames, the Secretary of the SA, published his *Typographical Antiquities* in 1749. See his entry in *ODNB*. For further discussion of the history of printing, see Nos 406 and 427 above.

434. From Revd George North[1] to Maurice Johnson.
Codicote, 23 June 1744.
MB3 fol.176B, 28 June 1744.
Discusses North's work on coins of Henry III and requests information from Johnson regarding the Mint at Lincoln.

[1]   See his entry in Appendix 2.

435. SGS No 15: From Thomas Birch to Maurice Johnson.
London, 26 June 1744.
MB3 fol.177A, 28 June 1744.
Apologises for his lack of communication with the SGS; offers to present the new edition of Bishop Tanner's *Notitia Monastica* if the SGS has not got it;[1] gives latest news of recent events at the RS and the SA, including Evelyn's plan for rebuilding London after the Great Fire, as shown to the SA; comments critically on Mr Harris's treatise *On Happiness*[2] and on recently-published biographies of Pope; briefly comments on the Leibniz-Newton controversy over 'Newton's philosophy'.

[1]   A copy of this had already been presented; see No 430 above.
[2]   James Harris, *Three Treatises ... the third concerning happiness* (London, 1744).

436. From William Draper to Maurice Johnson.
London, 16 July 1744.
MB3 fol.178B, 19 July 1744.
Comments on the value of writing a history of the activities of county sheriffs and discusses problems of historical methodology; discusses the functions of wall-paintings in churches.

437. SGS No 31: From Jane Green[1] to Maurice Johnson.
Redmarshall, Co. Durham, 17 July 1744.
MB3 fol.179A, 26 July 1744.

SGS No 31   Redmarshall[2] July 17: 1744
Dear Pappa and Mamma
    I am now I thank God so farr recovered that we went yesterday to Spend the whole Day with Mr Davison Who has a very good Old house[3] & Gardens, one Noble Room the Entrance into Which is Just in the Middle att Each End are 2 very large Windows ~~very near~~ which have Of each side very fine Pictures of their

family (which is very antient) upon the Peer[4] at the Uper End there is a Monk upon his ∧^knees with a Crusifix before him finely done, & over that Sr Something Daws dead in bed, & strikingly Well done, at the request of his friends after he was dead, there are several more at that end of the room but not worth Notice, then there is on each side the door A large Chimney over the left our Saviour taking from the Crose there is a great number of figures & tis well done, all as big as life, Over the door Mr Davison his Present Lady & the son he has by her she is sister to the great Yorkshire Turner the Member, then over the other Chimney is a most Noble Picture of Gundimore[5] at full length, & of his right hand Mary de Medisa and on the left a Spanish[6] embasador all of a sise & at the lower End upon the Peer is a former Duke of Cumberland, these are all said to be Court Pictures over the opposite door which goes into the garden is the Appearance of Brutus to Cesar the room is hung with fine old Tapestry & the Chairs are handsome Crimson Velvet in the dineing room he has all his ancestors but they are mear Sinepost painting there is a great number more on the Stare Case but much about the same with those in the dining room, we had half a dozen sorts of Wine & were entertaind throuout in a hospitable Old fashon'd Way his Son (by a former Wife) & his lady & little Child are there upon a Visit, all this for ought I know you may have had before, but as I have seen nothing els, save the minister of redmarshall his good lady, & old house I think a discription of it may be as agreeable to You as seeing it was to me, this is 2 little miles from us this family tho good & hospitable are far from polite, as indeed they ought to be, to receive a chair loaded with 3 witches & led by the Man, & attended only by one undertaker, Well ~~so~~ I wrote so far before I expected the Post & laid my letter by, in hopes to have something to answer but to my great Surprise I have no letter nor has had one since Sunday was a senight in sort I think all my friend extreamly unkind to ∧^me to let me be a hundred & fifty miles from home keep a sick bed with many other inconveniences & hear nothing from a place where I shoud hope to have a great number of friends but now begin to fear that out of sight is out of mind I beg you Sir to present my love & Duty to all my friends pertickularly to my Dear Mr Green & tell him this & beg of him not to write the Bishop of Durham but to Stockton upon Tease my blessing Dear Madam to my Dear Children & believe

me to be Honoured S^r your most Duttyfull Daughter
       to command Jane Green

my heart is so brim full I think it will burst

this is beyond all I ever sufferd except my Childs Death bed.[7]

To Maurice Johnson Junr Esq

att his house in

Spalding Lincolnshire

turn at Stilton

---

[1]   Maurice Johnson's eldest daughter, wife of Dr John Green, who was visiting her uncle, Revd Walter Johnson.

[2]   This was the living of Revd Walter Johnson, half-brother of Maurice Johnson's father, an early member of the SGS and former schoolmaster of Spalding. Jane refers to him and his house later in the letter. His son George's correspondence with the SGS when an undergraduate at Oxford is calendared below; see Nos 529, 539, 545, 549, 551 and 554.

[3]   Maurice Johnson comments that the Rt Hon William Davison, an ancestor of the present owner, had been Secretary of State to Queen Elizabeth in 1587; see his entry in *ODNB*. In the 1740s Revd William Davison was rector of Scruton, Roger Gale's home. It has not proved possible to identify the

'very good old house' with certainty: perhaps it was Blakeston Hall north-east of Redmarshall and just north-west of Stockton on Tees, which was pulled down in the 1950s.

4   The wall between two windows, as in the expression 'pier glass'.

5   This may be the Count of Gondomar, Spanish diplomat and ambassador to England in the reign of James I. Jane Green's references to people and subjects of paintings are often vague, as in the case of 'Sir Something Daws', so making identification difficult. 'Mary de Medisa' is presumably Maria de Medici, Queen of France. Jane has learnt about art, however, like all Maurice Johnson's children; she distinguishes between the better portraits and those she dismisses as 'mear Sinepost painting', inadequate painting as though done by a painter of signposts.

6   MS 'Spaish'.

7   Jane Green's unhappiness may be due to intense homesickness; she appears to be paying a visit to her relatives without her children, has been unwell during the visit and is desperate for letters from home. Her husband has presumably returned home earlier; he is known to have visited Redmarshall in 1744 as the SGS possesses a sketch of the church there, brought back by him in 1744.

438. From Revd George North to Maurice Johnson.
Codicote, 1 August 1744.
MB3 fol.181A, 16 August 1744.
Continues his discussion of coinage and mints in the reign of Henry III;[1] requests help from Johnson and his local associates in supplying examples of such coins; offers a detailed explanation of his numismatic methodology.

1   See No 434 above.

439. SGS No 36: From Maurice Johnson to Mrs Elizabeth Johnson.
St John's College, Cambridge, 18 September 1744.
MB3 fol.183B, 20 September 1744.
Expresses relief and pleasure at their son John's recovery from illness at university and discusses his medical treatment; comments on the history of Barnwell Priory, Cambridge, shown to him by Mr Jacob Butler, now living there; describes monuments at Fulbourn church;[1] discusses the garden of the Vice Master of Trinity College, Dr Walker, and the plants he has been given by Dr Walker; has a drawing of an Albano ware dish, sent by Maurice Johnson (son).

Also a note from their son John Johnson, assuring her of his recovery and explaining that they will return via Ely where they will 'accomplish my business'.[2]

1   For details of these, see Nikolaus Pevsner, *Cambridgeshire* (2nd edn, Harmondsworth, 1970), 221–2, 251 and 388–9. Barnwell Priory was an Augustinian Priory of which only a small church remains, though there is a 'picturesque house' nearby, perhaps Mr Butler's house.

2   This probably refers to his ordination as deacon, which took place at Ely on 23 September 1744.

440. SGS No 53: From Thomas Birch to Maurice Johnson.
London, 9 October 1744.
MB3 fol.184B, 11 October 1744.
Complains that the 'Republic of Learning has been so barren of Occurrences this summer'; he has heard from the Hague about a Greek medal from Smyrna and some recent Dutch publications; comments on the publication of Dr Mead's *Mechanical Account of Poisons* and mentions Mr Mallet's plans to write a biography of the Duke of Marlborough.[1]

1   Richard Mead's book was first published in 1702; the third edition, with large additions, was published in 1745. In 1744 the Duchess of Marlborough bequeathed £500 to David Mallet (1701/2–1765) to write a life of the late Duke; see Mallet's entry in *ODNB*. The book was never completed.

441. From Revd George North to Maurice Johnson.
Codicote, 16 November 1744.
MB3 fol.187B, 22 November 1744.
Accepts membership of the SGS; explains his numismatic studies at the Tower of London; asks Johnson to bring to their forthcoming meeting his coins of Henry III associated with putative mints at Lincoln and Newark.

442. From Maurice Johnson to Dr Green.[1]
Cursitor Street, London, 11 December 1744.
MB3 fol.188A, 13 December 1744.
Discusses Revd Dr Thomas Birch's donation to the SGS of 'Useful & Excellent Books elegantly bound': *Life of Robert Boyle* by Birch, published 1744, *Monumenta Vetustatis Kempiana* by Richard Aynsworth and John Ward, published in 1720 and the *Miscellaneous Works* of John Greaves, Professor of Astronomy at Oxford, published in 1738;[2] he also has a print of 'Baron Nieuwhoff, the King of Corsica'.[3]

[1] This letter is enclosed in a letter franked to Maurice Johnson but presumably intended for Mrs Elizabeth Johnson, as the annotation on it refers to 'son and daughter Green': 'Be pleased with my Blessing & thanks to Son & Daughter Green & their Children and Son's Johnson's and Walter's Loves to them, to give or send this and all enclosed save yʳ Lʳ to your Self, directly, being to be comᵈ to the Soc.'; this is a page meant for Dr Green, to be communicated to the SGS.
[2] These are still in the SGS library.
[3] Theodor, Baron Neuhoff (1694–1756), traveller and adventurer, came to Corsica in 1736 at the time of its struggles for independence from Genoa and offered to help if the Corsicans would make him king; his rule lasted only six months and he was then forced to leave the island.

1745

443. Draft of letter from Maurice Johnson to George Holmes.
Spalding, 4 January 1745.
Thanks him for his notes on coins 'de Moneta Aurea'; offers his own comments on English gold and silver coins from Anglo-Saxon times to the reign of Edward III, refuting the claim that there were no gold or silver coins before Edward III's reign and referring to a gold coin in his own collection; gives other notes on English coins.

444. No 54: From Revd Manwaring Laughton[1] to Revd Mr Whiting.
Lutton, 5 February 1745.
MB4 fol.7B, 21 March 1745.

No 54
Worthy Sʳ　　　　　　　　　　　　　　　　　　　Lutton Feb. 5ᵗʰ 1744–5
　　I take this oportunity of sending You the Mineral I mention'd to you when last att Spalding; but whether or no it is worthy of a Place in the Society Room I leave You to judge The Name of this Mineral is <u>Sparr</u>, and is never found (as I am inform'd) except where there is a Vein of Ore, tho' the Vein is sometimes so small as scarcely to be call'd <u>swearing Ore</u>, which (as my Correspondent expresses himself) considering the Conscience of a Miner You'll say must be small indeed. Swearing Ore is the Term the miners constantly use for these small Veins. The

Nature of these Veins is such, that they generally run forward in plains perpendicular to the Horizon, except that now and then they split into two and continue to lie at the distance of 6, 7 or 8 yards from one another for a considerable Way. But it seldom happens but one of these divided Veins unites at last into the same plain again. The thickness of these Veins is very variable and it is reckond to be a very good Vein that continues to be between [page 2] 3 and 4 Inches thick, tho' some have been known about Ashover (the Town from whence I had this piece of Sparr, about 4 Miles from Chesterfield in Derbyshire) to exceed a foot in thickness 'Tis the common opinion amongst Miners that these Veins are continu'd down as as far as the Centre of the Earth, it seldom, if ever, happening that they canfind them disappear under foot (the Water prevents them from sinking very low) tho it is common to hear of a veins dipping, which is when it disappears (& you get to the end of it) for want of Sparr, & proper Minerals[2] for it to lodge in. There are some pieces of Sparr which are very transparent, and will refract the Rays of all Colours, & shew as great Variety as the Prismatic Glass. Lord Malton,[3] I am told, has procur'd a great Quantity of Sparr & other the like Minerals to adorn a Grotto, which he intends shall exceed any we have yet in England. When Mr Johnson comes to your House I will beg you will let him see this Mineral and if he thinks it a Curiosity it is at the Society's Service. But you will hear his Sentiments of it before you make an Offer of it.

I am, Sir,

      Your most obedient

      Humble Servant

        M Laughton

P.S.Pray give my Service to all Friends.

To the Rev^d Mr Whiting

att Spalding.

Annotated by Johnson: 'Lead Spar – a large Specimen sent with this L^r and Account of the Lead Mine.'

1   See his entry in Appendix 2.
2   MS 'Minelals'.
3   Of Wentworth Woodhouse, Yorkshire; see No 96 above.

445. Copy of letter from Maurice Johnson to Martin Folkes.

[Spalding], 22 February 1745.

Annotated by Maurice Johnson: 'Copy of L^r. from MJ to MF of Saxon & English Coines & Medals'.

Expresses his satisfaction that the SA will have a set of English coins and medals drawn up by Folkes; gives a detailed history of Old English gold and silver coins and explains some current debates about them.[1]

1   See also Maurice Johnson's letter to George Holmes of 4 January 1745 (No 443 above). Folkes published his *Tables of English gold and silver coins* in 1736 and 1745.

446. SGS No 66: From Maurice Johnson (son) to Maurice Johnson.

Windsor, 25 February 1745.

MB4 fol.5A, 28 February 1745.

Sends a sketch of a medal of Socrates[1] and Latin verses made by the Captain of Eton; has had headaches and has met a physician, Dr Burton,[2] who was at

Leiden with Dr John Green but does not remember him; has duties with Marshal Bellisle[3] and will shortly be moving to London.

[1]   Maurice Johnson has interleaved this section with comments on Socrates.
[2]   Perhaps Dr Joshua Burton who studied at Leiden University.
[3]   Charles Duke of Belle-Isle, a French Marshal briefly imprisoned at Windsor in 1744–45 during the War of the Austrian Succession. He had strayed into Hanoverian territory while hunting and had been arrested by a Hanoverian official because he lacked an entry passport.

447. No 74: From Revd George Ferne, Rector of Wigtoft, to Maurice Johnson.
Wigtoft, 29 June 1745.
He is sending his donation of books to the SGS; he has sent Robinson's *Hesiod* and will send Smith's *Cure of Deism*[1] in a month or two when he has read it.

[1]   Both of these are still in the SGS library and are recorded as donated by Ferne. See No 429 above.

448. From Revd George North to Maurice Johnson.
Codicote, 10 July 1745.
MB4 fol.16A, 18 July 1745.
Discusses arrangements for his visit to Spalding; comments on a City of Lincoln charter of Henry II, which he has read in the Bodleian Library, Oxford.

449. SGS No 26: From Browne Willis to Maurice Johnson.
Lincoln, 12 July 1745.
MB4 fol.16A, 18 July 1745.
Discusses his collection of trade tokens; aims to get duplicates from Oxford University's collection; says that Dr Stukeley and Mr Banks[1] have promised tokens; requests Johnson to send duplicates, in particular from 'Holbech Dunnington Castor Tattershall Navenby Binbrook Folkingham Glanford Stanton Wragby'; Willis now has around 440 out of the possible 700 tokens from the English and Welsh market towns.

[1]   Two members of the Lincolnshire Banks family were members of the SGS. The complex Banks genealogy records four generations: Joseph Banks senior (1665–1727), FSA 1723; his son Joseph Banks junior (1692–1741), FSA 1718, SGS member 1722, FRS 1730; a relative William Banks (d.1761) who changed his name from Banks Hodgkinson to inherit Revesby in 1741; his son the famous naturalist Sir Joseph Banks (1743–1820), FRS 1766, SGS member 1768.

450. SGS No 24: From Browne Willis to Maurice Johnson.
Whaddon St James, [25 July] 1745.
MB4 fol.17A, 1 August 1745.
Thanks Johnson for sending trade tokens of Croyland, Spalding, Holbeach and Folkingham; has not received any from Banks or from Stukeley, who is in dispute with 'Mr Perkins';[1] discusses SGS activities.

[1]   This dispute was over Stukeley's views about an underground structure at Royston, containing carved images on the walls, and his claims that it was created as a chapel on the orders of the Lady Roisia, a local mediæval landowner. For details of the dispute with Charles Parkin over Royston Chapel, see William Stukeley, *Palæographia Britannica* (1743) and *Origines Roystonianæ* (1746), and Stuart Piggott, *William Stukeley: an eighteenth-century antiquary* (rev. edn, London, 1985), 120–121.

451. SGS No 25: From Revd John Johnson[1] to Maurice Johnson.
Ramsey, 26 July 1745.
MB4 fol.17A, 1 August 1745.
Wishes success to the Adventurers' schemes for fen drainage; plans to attend the

SGS anniversary; is unable to find a good history of Ramsey Abbey; discusses Ramsey grammar school and the government of the town.

[1] This is Maurice Johnson's son John, by now ordained (see his note to No 439 above) and serving as curate of Ramsey. See his entry in Appendix 2.

452. From Revd George North to Maurice Johnson.
Codicote, 23 September 1745.
MB4 fol.21B, 3 October 1745.
Discusses contents of Henry II's Lincoln charter[1] kept at Oxford; comments on his work on Roman coins, particularly those of Carausius, and asks if Johnson has any examples of Roman sestertii.

[1] See his previous letter of 10 July 1745 (No 448 above).

453. From George Shelvocke[1] to Maurice Johnson.
General Post Office [London], 5 November 1745.
MB4 fol.24A, 7 November 1745.
Apologises for delay caused by pressure of official business;[2] he is pleased to contribute to SGS activities and accepts the honour of nomination to membership; offers to send the SGS's foreign correspondence under his name without charge, as is already done for the RS.

[1] He was Secretary to the Post Office; see his entry in Appendix 2.
[2] This business pressure was caused by the 1745 panic over Prince Charles Edward Stuart's invasion.

1746

454. SGS No 68: Copy of letter from Thomas Savage to Richard Partridge.
Chester IImo 29th 1745.[1]
Gives a full and detailed account of the well-known skirmish between the Duke of Cumberland's forces and the retreating Jacobite forces at Clifton Bridge just south of Penrith, of which he was an eye-witness.
Annotated by Maurice Johnson: 'a Copy of Thos. Savage's Letter Relating to the battle of Clifton to Richard Partridge, Dated 29 of January 1745.'

[1] This is 1746 in one of the old forms of dating; see the explanation of this in the Introduction. The events described took place on 18 December 1745. The letter was presumably copied and sent to Johnson for the information of the SGS, though no details of how it reached him are given.

455. SGS No 24: From Maurice Johnson (son) to Maurice Johnson.
London, 18 February 1745 [actually 1746].
MB4 fol.31B, 20 February 1746.
He has been too busy to write; describes his journey to London with Wat;[1] sends a drawing of a sword found in the Thames at the new Westminster bridge; discusses the SA's proposal to publish engravings of all English gold and silver coins from William I to the present; has read to Wat a new satirical poem, 'Henry and Blanche'.[2]
Also a note by Maurice Johnson on London ceremonial swords and the probable date of this example.

[1] The family name for Walter Johnson, Maurice Johnson's second son.
[2] The origin of this poem is *Henry and Blanche: a Tale taken from the French of Gil Blas* (1745),

by Moses Mendes (1690–1758); see his entry in *ODNB*. It is possible that the Johnson brothers were enjoying a satire on this original.

456. SGS No 58: From William Stukeley to Maurice Johnson.
Stamford, 8 March 1745–6.
MB4 fol.33B, 13 March 1746.
Discusses his plans to revive the Brazen-nose Society at Stamford[1] and comments on the problems of running country societies.

1   Stukeley had run this society successfully from 1736 to 1737, but it declined on the death of his first wife, Frances (née Williamson), in the autumn of 1737.

457. From Timothy Neve junior[1] to Maurice Johnson.
CCC [Corpus Christi College] Oxford, 19 March 1745/6.
MB4 fol.38A, 27 March 1746.
Thanks the SGS for electing him to membership; sends a MS copy of the dedication of Dr Hickes's 'Saxon Grammar' which was not included in the printed book by the publisher because it was dedicated to Archbishop Sancroft;[2] explains his reason for refusing PGS membership, even though his father had founded the PGS, and discusses the current poor state of that society.

1   The son of Revd Timothy Neve and at that time an undergraduate at Oxford. See his entry in Appendix 2.
2   George Hickes (1642–1715): a non-juror, deprived of his position at the time for refusing the oath to King William III; see his biography in *ODNB*. His 'Saxon grammar', *Institutiones grammaticæ Anglo-Saxonicæ et Moeso-Gothicæ,* was printed in 1689.

458. From Revd John Johnson to Maurice Johnson.
Ramsey, Cambridgeshire, 30 April 1746.
MB4 fol.46A, 8 May 1746.

SGS No 30   Ramsey April 30th 1746
Dear & Honoured Sir,
    I've had the pleasure to receive two of the three, the second & last I presume, of your obliging Letters; to the former I promised myself that I should be able to have given You an Answer personally, but was prevented by my Master Whiston's[1] coming over to Ramsey, the Latter End of that Week; as I otherwise must have been, tho' then unknown to me, by the badness of our Roads at that time; to this latter I hope the pleasure of expressing myself more fully in a Fortnight or three Weeks when if I have the satisfaction of finding my Brother The Captain[2] with You, my Happiness must be greater, as I assure You it ever will be heightened to me, in meeting with You all, & all well together.
    the Season of the Spring being now gotten so very high, & the Summer advancing will be no small advantage, as I imagine, to our Gardens or your Plantations, where I think of spending a few Hours Cum quatuor voluminibus, non ita pridem, a Te memoratus.[3]
    [page 2] Of what Advantage your late Alteration may be in throwing of the Elmes from out the Gardens; I must profess myself afraid to see, being steadily attached to all my old Acquaintance & in Gratitude for its favourable Shade (so oft by Stealth, oft since with less of difficulty afforded me) obliged to regret the loss of a Variety so pleasing, a Retreat from the intolerable, midday Sun, so charmingly agreeable.

I with my humble Duty to the Gentlemen of our Society, congratulate them upon the Accession of so great a Strength, the lately elected, ingenious & very worthy Members, most of whom I have a good Acquaintance with & hope for (in its time) with the Rest.

I was a good deal at a loss in conjecturing who the proposed Gents (so many, & of my intimates) coud be, before the Receipt of your last: & shou'd have esteem'd it a real pleasure to've been with You, & given my little Interest in Favour of (& Justice to) 'em; tho' with the utmost Satisfaction must always acquiess in the Determination of the then present Members not more from the nature & Course of dispatching the Business of most Assemblies, than from the Experience I have long had of their indisputable Judgement.

I am entirely of your Opinion, in the Qualifications requisite to make a Member of a Society on the same Establishment with that of ours that [page 3] Application & Industry rather furnish a Man with those Attainments that are most desirable than Birth or Riches. & the Method of our electing of Them, will I hope always guard against those two fatal Extremes which both tend to subvert the best establish'd & most flourishing Assemblies. Both offsprings of the same despicable Parent Ignorance. How oft we see the Riches & Titles of a single Person abused by Pride to bear too great a Sway over the minds of others; & but too oft mean Creatures put in Power, thro' a Fondness of exerting it, tho' ignorantly; to entail a Scandal on their Institutors.

I have lately been reading over a Pamphlet, which I think wrote very ingeniously; 'tis a deep Piece of Metaphysicks, & as it gave me much Satisfaction in meeting with the following Head so clearly treated of I've flattered myself that You wou'd give it the reading & afterwards your Approbation. The pamphlet is an Answer & a very sufficient one I promise You to a philosophical Enquiry into the physical Rise & Spring of human Actions; in which Treatise, the Author weakly & wickedly enough attempts to prove Mankind, a piece of Mechanism actuated only by natural or material Causes; the fatal Tendencies of such a Doctrine are but too visible; & as an Answer to it had not been made by any person, this Gentleman who is now Curate of March in the Isle of Ely, whose Company I've had the pleasure of being in since at Ramsey; attempted it in a very modest ingenious & I dare to say, from having read it, very successful manner. after examining his Antagonists Essay very punctually, & answering it as particularly, He at last concludes his Answer with this proof of human Liberty. I give you this Hint that you many not be surpris'd at my beginning (as it wou'd otherwise seem) so abruptly to make a Copy of Him. the Examination of this philosophical Enquiry into the spring of human Actions is so metaphysical occasion'd from the Intricateness & very Abstruseness, not to say more of that Author; that twas not possible or worth while to attempt sending you that except I cou'd have bought the pamphlet, which I only borrowed. Nor had I indeed trouble You with this, if I had ever seen so conclusive Reasoning on the Subject, was the pamphlet common, or the Author much known, whose first publick Attempt I believe this to be.[4]

I am, Sir, with my Duty Love & Services to all Friends, particularly my Mother Grandfather & Molly Who, I hope, are much better.

Honoured Sir, your very obedient Son

J. Johnson

Enclosed with this letter are hand-copied extracts from a pamphlet, same date: 'On Human Liberty'; no author given.

1   This is not the famous William Whiston, the Cambridge philosopher and mathematician; it is possibly his nephew, Revd Thomas Whiston, perpetual curate of Ramsey 1745.
2   Maurice Johnson (son), John's elder brother, had returned home, perhaps after serving in the Culloden campaign in 1746.
3   'With four volumes not previously remembered by you.'
4   William Windle (born c.1707), curate of March (see J. Venn, *Biographical History of Gonville and Caius College, Vol. 2, 1713–1897* (Cambridge, 1899), 22). His pamphlet, *An Enquiry into the Immateriality of Thinking Substances,* was published in 1738 in response to Samuel Strutt's pamphlet *A Philosophical Enquiry into the Physical Spring of Human Actions* (1732). Windle attacked Strutt's totally mechanical explanation of human actions. Copies of both pamphlets are in the British Library.

459. From John Hill[1] to Maurice Johnson.
[London], 6 May 1746. [Dated from postmark.]
MB4 fol.46A, 8 May 1746.
Includes proposals for printing Theophrastus, *History of Stones, Gemms and other fossile substances*, which he has translated from Greek and annotated;[2] requests that the SGS should subscribe to it, sending subscriptions to 'John Hill, Apothecary in The Broad[way] Westminster'.
Included: printed proposals for publication.
Annotated by Maurice Johnson: 'Subscribed for on 9 May'.

1   See his entry in Appendix 2.
2   This was published in 1746.

460. SGS No 71: From William Stukeley to Maurice Johnson.
Stamford, 14 May 1746.
MB4 fol.47B, 22 May 1746.
He is busy preparing sermons for his church; discusses his attendance at Mr Griffis's[1] experimental philosophy lectures; explains the failure of the Stamford literary society; comments on activities at the Deepings club; discusses the visit of Maurice Johnson's daughter to Stukeley and his wife.[2]

1   William Griffis (1725–1766): itinerant scientific lecturer in the South of England.
2   Maurice Johnson's second daughter Elizabeth, known in the family as 'Madcap Bet', was staying with Stukeley and his second wife Elizabeth, née Gale, at Stamford.

461. SGS No 73: From Zachariah Brooke to Maurice Johnson.
St John's College, Cambridge, 14 May [1746].[1]
MB4 fol.49A, 22 May 1746.
Appreciates the honour of SGS membership; comments on the value of the SGS and the acquaintance of 'so many worthy and learned Men'; sends compliments to Maurice Johnson's son [John].

1   The letter is dateable from the list in MB4 of new SGS members. Brooke, Professor of Divinity at Cambridge, was proposed for membership on 27 March 1746 (MB4 fol.38A) and admitted on 10 April 1746 (MB4 fol.42A). See his entry in Appendix 2 and *ODNB.*

462. SGS No 27: From John Hill to Dr Green.
Broadway, Westminster, 20 May 1746.
MB4 fol.51B, 29 May 1746.
Sends thanks to the SGS for the honour of their correspondence on topics relating

to fossils and 'the fossile world' and to Maurice Johnson for his help; he will add to his book[1] the index suggested by the SGS if the size of the book allows this; gives precise and detailed answers to queries sent by Maurice Johnson and the SGS relating to gemstones and their formation, including accounts of his experiments on them; encourages the SGS to continue with 'fossile studys which are now universally growing into Repute and fashion'; promises to send fossil specimens for SGS collection.

[1]   See No 459 above (6 May 1746). Hill addresses this to Green as the SGS's second secretary, who was responsible for correspondence on matters of natural philosophy and medicine.

463. From Timothy Neve junior to Maurice Johnson.
Corpus Christi College Oxford, 25 June 1746.
MB4 fol.59A, 3 July 1746.
Compares the excellent organisation of the SGS with the poor state of the PGS; passes on Dr Charles Lyttleton's[1] request for membership; describes books in the Museum[2] and in the Bodleian Library; sends a transcription of a letter by Sir Thomas Herbert to Dr Samways[3] about his attendance on King Charles I the night before his execution, also copies of Crashaw's Latin 'Elegium Sepulchrale' on Nicholas Ferrar[4] and a Latin verse 'Te Deum' by W. Alsop.[5]

[1]   Charles Lyttelton (1714–1768): lawyer, priest and antiquary; made collections for the history of Worcestershire; SGS member 1746; became Bishop of Carlisle in 1762; see his entry in *ODNB*.
[2]   The Ashmolean or Science Museum.
[3]   Sir Thomas Herbert, first baronet (1606–1682); Peter Samways (1615–1693), royalist cleric; see their entries in *ODNB*.
[4]   The founder of the Little Gidding community; see his entry in the *ODNB*.
[5]   This is probably Anthony Alsop (1670–1726), a tutor at Christ Church, Oxford, well-known for his Latin poetry which was finally published in 1752 as *Ædis Christi olim alumni odarum libri duo*.

464. No 59: From Dr Samuel Hutchinson[1] to Maurice Johnson.
Batson's Coffee-House in Cornhill, London, 8 July 1746.
MB4 fol.59B, 10 July 1746.
Explains that he has been away from Cambridge so Johnson's letter to him was delayed; appreciates his election to membership of the SGS and will 'promote … the Honour and Improvement of the Society.'

[1]   See his entry in Appendix 2.

465. From Robert Smyth to Maurice Johnson.
Alwalton, 16 September 1746.
MB4 fol.74A, 18 September 1746.
He is sending this letter by Timothy Neve junior who is visiting Spalding; requests a copy of Johnson's lists of local MPs; offers help with Johnson's work on local MPs and sends notes on particular individuals.
Annotated by Maurice Johnson: 'Lr from the Revd Mr Robt Smyth of Woodston brought me by Mr Tim. Neve of CCC Oxf & by him received 18 Sepr 1746 with Lists of our Knts. [*illegible*] & Burgesses MSS.'

466. From Revd Robert Smyth to Maurice Johnson.
[Woodston, 16 September 1746.] Undated, but dateable from reference in MB4.
MB4 fol.74A, 18 September 1746.
Offers a list of Knights of the Shire for Lincolnshire from the reign of Edward I to Queen Anne, with notes on some individuals.

467. From Revd John Romley to Maurice Johnson.
Epworth, 23 September 1746.
MB4 fol.76B, 2 October 1746 and MB4 fol.103A, 21 May 1747.
Explains that an urn has been recovered from London and will be sent to Johnson; describes in detail a machine for dressing flax made by Mr Clegg of Haxey and sends diagrams of it;[1] has no information about a monastery at Mellwood, near Epworth; discusses a local Epworth resident, Mrs Knight, formerly a Drury Lane actress.

[1]   Joshua Clegg, who became an SGS member in 1747, was the Lincolnshire inventor of this machine; the diagrams are now kept at the SGS in Vol.III of 'Catalogue of Prints'. See Romley's entry in Appendix 2.

468. From Revd Robert Smyth to Maurice Johnson.
Woodston, 4 October 1746.
MB4 fol.78B, 16 October 1746.
Thanks Johnson for his list of MPs; makes suggestions for improving the listing, particularly by consulting Browne Willis; offers a further list of MPs for the Borough of Lincoln and for Lincolnshire boroughs, listing those for Lincoln City from the reign of Edward I to George II, Boston from Edward III to George II, Grantham from Edward IV to George I, Stamford from Edward I to George II and Great Grimsby from Edward I to George II.
Annotated by Maurice Johnson: 'Lr from the Revd & Learned Mr Robt Smyth MA FSG & Peterb. Socc. conteining Historical & Heraldic Observations on Lists of Lincs Shireffs & Members of Parliament in answer to the Lists of Woodston such sent him by MJ SGS Secr.'

469. From John Ward[1] to Maurice Johnson.
G[resham] C[ollege, London], Saturday 4 October 1746.
MB4 fol.77A, 9 October 1746.
Expresses his appreciation of his election to SGS membership and thanks for Johnson's letters containing transcripts from the SGS minutes; is willing to contribute to 'subserve your curious and instructive inquiries'; explains that Johnson's letters have been communicated to the SA; comments that a 'plate of antient weights and measures' is now finished and distributed to members.
Annotated by Maurice Johnson: 'Lr from the learned Mr John Ward Professor of Rhetorick in Gresham Coll. FR & A Socc. London.'

[1]   See his entry in Appendix 2.

470. From Emanuel Mendes da Costa[1] to the Gentlemen's Society, Spalding.
London, 8 November 1746.
MB4 fol.80B, 13 November 1746.

Gentlemen
    My Esteemed and Learned Friend Maurice Johnson Esqr: a Worthy Member of your Society, Who Honours me with his Acquaintance, and pleasured Me so far as to View my Collection of Natural Curiosities;[2] having Mentioned to Me your Learned and Laudable Society, immediately made me desire of becoming a Member of it. the Love I bear for the Sciences could not Assure me of a Greater Pleasure than in knowing a set of Gentlemen Unanimously United and with

their Utmost Efforts persuing so indefatigably Learning in General, As it is well known your Society does. I hope Gentlemen, the boldness I have taken in thus desiring to become a Member of your Learned Body, will by your goodness be passed over in Silence; As it was done with a thought for the benefit of the Sciences; and beg to refer the Love I bear to Learning, to the Character My said Esteemed Friend Maurice Johnson Esqr: will give you of me, and hope a [page 2] Reliance on his Recommendation. I further beg leave to Assure you Gentlemen, that I also shall be proud and greatly desirous of becoming a Correspondent Member of your Learned Body, for Any Commands you may Want in these parts, and Wait with Impatience for the honour of your Answer, if I can be so happy as to Obtain one, till when shall refer sending you some papers, and also some Specimens of Natural Curiosities for your Museum and remain

> Learned Gentlemen,
> With all Esteem,
> Your devoted humble Servant
> Emanuel Mendes da Costa

London 8th November 1746
Annotated by Maurice Johnson: 'Lr from Mr Emanuel Mendes da Costa SGS NP [?Natural Philosopher] a General Linguist & diligent & learned Philosopher to the Secretary & Members SGS to be admitted.'

[1]   See his entry in Appendix 2.
[2]   Da Costa was a keen collector of fossils; he was also expert in preserving birds and animals.

471. SGS No 24: From Dr Walter Lynn to Maurice Johnson.
Undated, but dateable from MB4 reference to the week before 11 December 1746.
MB4 fol.84A, 11 December 1746.
Describes his visit to his friend Kilpatrick[1] in a poorly-furnished room which Lynn claims is suitable for a poet; asks Johnson's opinion on a disagreement with Dr Roper 'who always sat as President next to the fire at Child's Coffee House'[2] over a Greek inscription on a Roman statue; discusses Kilpatrick's pamphlet defending his practice of inoculation during the smallpox epidemic in 'Charles Town Carolina' where Lynn had met him; explains that a recent book by Dr Dodd of St Bartholomew's Hospital[3] about smallpox had caused Kilpatrick to reply, so gaining him the approval of Dr Mead and Dr Jurin, whom Dodd had criticised.
Attached: note in Lynn's hand about a proposed Latin translation by Kilpatrick of poems, presumably some of Pope's works which are listed in another hand.

[1]   James Kilpatrick or Kirkpatrick (1696–1770) physician and poet, living in Charlestown, Carolina, and then in London; see his entry in *ODNB*.
[2]   Child's was a well-known London coffee-house near St Paul's, popular with clergymen, lawyers from the nearby courts of Doctors' Commons and members of the Royal Society who met informally there. It has not proved possible to identify Dr Roper. For further information on the London coffee-houses, see Markman Ellis, *The Coffee-House: a cultural history* (Phoenix, 2004).
[3]   Dr Pierce Dodd MD FRS FCP (1683–1764).

472. SGS No 60: From William Stukeley to Maurice Johnson.
Stamford, 17 December 1746.
MB4 fol.86B, 25 December 1746.
Discusses the printing of his history of Royston[1] and dismisses the views of

his critic; describes a visit to Edmondthorpe church, near Melton Mowbray; comments on the origin of fossil shells embedded in stone there.

¹   See Browne Willis's letter of 1 August 1745 (No 450 above).

473. From Anthony Oldfield¹ to Maurice Johnson.
Petworth, 20 December 1746.
He is pleased to accept SGS membership; discusses his toothache and its treatment; sends Christmas compliments.

¹   See his entry in Appendix 2.

474. From Emanuel Mendes da Costa to the Gentlemen's Society, Spalding.
[London], 27 December 1746.
Expresses his thanks for SGS membership; sends a box of fossils, Turberville Needham's *New Microscopical Discoveries* and Watson's *Letters on Electricity*.¹
Enclosed: his detailed paper on fossils which he has found in Surrey and a list of the specimens of fossils he sends for SGS museum.

¹   These books are still in the SGS library. Turberville Needham (1713–1781) was an English Catholic natural philosopher whose book was published in 1745; William Watson (1715–1787) was a significant physician and electrical experimenter whose *Experiments and Observations tending to illustrate the nature and properties of Electricity* was published in 1746; see their entries in *ODNB*.

1747

475. SGS No 23: From Dr Walter Lynn to Maurice Johnson.
No date; read at SGS 7 January 1746/7.
MB4 fol.87B, 7 January 1747.
Discusses, though not in specific medical detail, a medical case which had caused controversy, and which had been written up in three pamphlets, one by the doctor concerned in the case, Dr Thomson, one by a country doctor [unnamed] and one by a Scotsman, Douglas; Lynn explains that he is concerned that Dr Thomson claimed to have been in error because Lynn's kinsman, Dr Broxholme,¹ was also involved in the case; believes that Thomson would have done better to quote Galen as more effective than Hippocrates to justify himself, despite Dr Green's preference for Hippocrates; discusses the abilities of Green's mentor Boerhaave compared with those of 'Dr Ratcliffe'.²

¹   The first is possibly Dr Thomas Thompson, royal physician, who died in 1763; Douglas is unknown. For Dr Noel Broxholme MD FCP (1686–1748), see his entry in the *ODNB*. Verses about him are referred to in Nos 67 and 68 above.
²   Dr John Radcliffe (1652–1714): physician who funded both the Radcliffe Infirmary in Oxford and St Bartholomew's Hospital in London. See his entry in *ODNB*.

476. SGS No 71: From Maurice Johnson (son) to Maurice Johnson.
Breda [Netherlands], 13 January 1747 New Style.
MB4 fol.93B, 5 March 1747.
Sends a sketch and detailed account of a Roman camp and caves near Maastricht;¹ he is enclosing a print of a monument to the Prince of Orange.²

¹ The Dutch town of Maastricht, called in Roman times 'Mosæ trajectum' [crossing of the Maas/ Meuse], has extensive Roman relics.
² The print is no longer attached to this letter.

477. From William Stukeley to Maurice Johnson.
Stamford, 20 January 1746–7.
MB4 fol.88A, 8 January 1747; MB4 fol.90B, 29 January 1747.
Explains 'my conjectures upon that elegant carving, over the west door of Crowland abby: accompanyed with a drawing of it',¹ describing and explaining the five carvings of scenes from the life of St Guthlac.
Letter of 9 pages with enlargement of one drawing of St Guthlac.

¹ The SGS archive contains an extensive file of Stukeley's drawings and reports on the ruins of Croyland Abbey, Crowland, Lincolnshire, of which this letter is a part. See also No 479 below.

478. SGS No 22: From Revd Morgan Powell to 'the Rev. Mr Johnston'.¹
Kirton, 22 January 1746/7.
MB4 fol.90A, 29 January 1747.
Gives a full and detailed account of a friend's experiments in electricity.

¹ John Johnson, Maurice Johnson's son. See Powell's entry in Appendix 2.

479. From William Stukeley to Maurice Johnson.
Stamford, 28 January 1746–7.
MB4 fol.91A, 5 February 1747.
Says he is 'sending you the drawings of the acts of S. Guthlac' which should have accompanied his letter of 20 January but were omitted from it.
Enclosed: set of drawings of the carvings of St Guthlac's life, over the west doorway of Croyland Abbey, dated 'W. Stukeley 1746'.¹

¹ See No 477 above.

480. SGS No 21: From Dr James Parsons¹ to Maurice Johnson.
Red Lion Square [London], 26 February 1746/7.
MB4 fol.93B, 5 March 1747.
Sends thanks for SGS membership, promises to send books to the SGS; asks for a copy of Dr Green's 'useful catalogue of the Water Fowles he is about'.²

¹ See his entry in Appendix 2.
² Green, as SGS Second Secretary, was responsible for the Society's work in natural philosophy. His catalogue is not in the SGS's archive.

481. From Benjamin Cook¹ to Maurice Johnson.
London, 3 March 1747.
Discusses the collections of serpents and insects currently on show in London.

¹ See his entry in Appendix 2.

482. From Benjamin Cook to Maurice Johnson.
London, 7 March 1747.
Sends more information on London collections of insects and on a Queen Anne farthing.

483. No 66: From Dr James Parsons to Maurice Johnson.
Red Lion Square [London], 14 March 1746/7.
MB4 fol.94B, 19 March 1747.
He is sending copies of his publications for the SGS library: his lecture to the RS, *Muscular Motion;* also *An inquiry into the nature of hermaphrodites*; *A description of the human bladder with animadversions on Mrs Stephens' medicines* and *The Microscopical Theatre of Seeds*;[1] sends full details of his current experiments on fossils with acids and lists his results; asks Dr Green to try the experiments; offers Mr [John] Hill's help with the organisation of the SGS museum.[2]

1   These are in the SGS library today. Members of the SGS are still expected to donate a copy of their publications to the Society's library. For Mrs Stephens or Stevens, see Nos 371 and 389 above.
2   See John Hill's letter of 24 March 1747 (No 485 below).

484. From Timothy Neve junior to Maurice Johnson.
Corpus Christi College Oxford, 18 March 1746/7.
MB4 fol.96B, 26 March 1747.
Discusses in detail a MS copy of the Qur'an which is known to Maurice Johnson;[1] sends a transcript of an ode on Dr Pococke[2] by Smith.

1   A copy of the Qur'an, which may be the same one, is still in the SGS Library. A letter (11 February 1746/7) from Maurice Johnson to Timothy Neve junior mentions an Eastern manuscript given to the SGS by Dr Musgrave Heighington, which could be the MS referred to here.
2   Revd Dr Richard Pococke (1704–1765): see his entry in *ODNB*; a traveller in Britain, Ireland, Europe and the Near East, particularly Egypt; his journeys included mountain-climbing in the Alps, then an unusual pursuit. He published accounts of his travels in 1743 and 1745. In 1756 he became Bishop of Ossory in Ireland. In 1746 he was elected to membership of the SGS.

485. SGS No 20: From John Hill to Maurice Johnson.
London, 24 March 1746/7.
MB4 fol.97A, 2 April 1747.
Thanks the SGS for election to membership; discusses editions of Pliny, including those by Hardouin, Salmasius and Daleschamps;[1] discusses the best method of arranging a fossil collection and offers his help in 'methodizing and naming' the SGS's collection if they send it to him; comments on fossil wood and offers to exchange the SGS's spare samples for some of his own Irish ones from Lough Neagh; refers to Dr Stukeley's views on a query relating to the Chaldean and Hebrew names for the turquoise.

1   Published in 1723, 1668 and 1615 respectively.

486. From Sir John Clerk to Maurice Johnson.
Edinburgh, 29 March 1747.
MB4 fol.99B, 16 April 1747.
Comments on 'troubles' caused by the [Jacobite] 'Rebellion' of the past two years which had forced him to move temporarily to Durham:

'… I am mighty glad to find that the Gentlemen of your Society continue their Love of learning & Enquiries into all parts of Sciences as formerly. happy had it been for many of the subjects of G. Britain, if for these two years past they had been oblidged to employ their thoughts no other way – our troubles had in this case, been fewer & our attempts towards Learning, Vertue & Industry had been more conspicuous. these troubles were, in part, the occasion of my intermitting to write to you, for I left this country when the Rebellion was at its hight in this place & retired for some moneths to Durham where I had often very learned & agreable company ...'

Regrets the death of their friend Roger Gale; responds to questions in an earlier letter from Johnson about antiquities, and expresses his doubts about the claims made by Dr Woodward about the age of his shield;[1] asks about the draining of the Lincolnshire Fens and whether this process can help with draining a bog in Scotland in his neighbourhood.

[1] See William Stukeley's letter of 4 January 1715 to Maurice Johnson (No 14 above), which expresses similar doubts.

487. No 60: From Anthony Oldfield to Maurice Johnson.
Petworth, 10 May 1747.
MB4 fol.103A, 21 May 1747.
Discusses his marriage[1] and sends a poem on love written by an [anonymous] Oxford gentleman.

[1] Oldfield's wife, a local tradesman's daughter, is not named. Anthony Oldfield and Susan Puttock were married in the Palace Chapel, Chichester, on 2 May 1747.

488. From John Ward to Maurice Johnson.
G[resham]C[ollege, London] 26 May 1747.
MB4 fol.104A, 28 May 1747.
Explains that Johnson's letter to the SA has been communicated and inserted in their registers; says that the SA approved Johnson's identification of a 'filius Abbatis Nigelli' mentioned in the Spalding Priory Cartulary as the abbot's godson, and quotes examples of this usage from other documents; gives news that their print of the 'Courts of Wards and Liveries' is now finished, completing Vol. 1 of the SA's works; gives news that the Vice-President, Mr Folkes, has found, in the Cottonian Library, coins referred to by Speed in his *Chronicle*,[1] showing that Cotton had lent them to Speed for his work.

[1] There was a copy of Speed's *Historie of Great Britaine* (3rd edn, London, 1632) in the Spalding parish library.

489. SGS No 19: From Anthony Oldfield to Maurice Johnson.
Petworth, 8 June 1747.
MB4 fol.106A, 18 June 1747.
Discusses his possible rights of inheritance of family property under a will which he asks Johnson to obtain; sends an extract from an anniversary sermon preached by Dr King, Bishop of Chichester,[1] on 30 January 1664, about a troop of women who had supported the Parliamentary cause in that city during the Civil War.

[1] Dr Henry King (1592–1669); see his entry in *ODNB*.

490. From William Jackson[1] to Maurice Johnson.
Boston, 22 June 1747.
MB4 fol.107B, 25 June 1747.
Thanks the SGS for his admission and praises the extent of their interests 'whether natural Curiosities or human Productions'; sends as a present the skin of a rattlesnake; he had hoped to send the skin of 'a Nute' but it was destroyed by 'carelessness of a Servant'; fears he may have little to communicate as Boston

is 'very little productive of Polite Literature'; thanks Johnson for past use of his library.

[1] Jackson was one of the SGS's poets; see No 417 above and Jackson's entry in Appendix 2.

491. SGS No 19: From William Jackson to Maurice Johnson.
Boston, 27 June 1747.
MB4 fol.109A, 2 July 1747.
Sends a joking account of 'a Passenger' coming to Spalding by barge, who is really a snake, almost four yards long;[1] relates this to the story of Adam and Eve; comments on the result of the recent election.

[1] This evidently refers to the rattlesnake skin discussed in his previous letter. A nineteenth-century engraving of the SGS meeting room in William Moore, *The Gentlemen's Society at Spalding* (1851) shows a snake, presumably stuffed or a mounted skin, suspended from the roof; it is possible that this is the snake referred to here. See Illustration 7, p. 211.

492. From Revd Timothy Neve to Maurice Johnson.
Alwalton, 5 August 1747.
MB4 fol.117A, 13 August 1747.
Discusses Lincoln diocesan affairs, the harvest and a current outbreak of cattle disease; criticises Stukeley's views on the etymology of 'Alwalton'.

493. From William Jackson to Maurice Johnson.
Boston, 9 September 1747.
MB4 fol.120B, 10 September 1747.
Discusses the provenance of a seal of Boston Hospital; is honoured by SGS membership and praises the SGS: 'For, if there is a happiness exalted above the common Amusements of Life; if there is a pleasure here worthy the Soul of Man, it is found in the Conversation of our Friends, Men of Learning, Virtue & of like Inclinations with our Selves.'

494. SGS No 69: From William Stukeley to Maurice Johnson.
Stamford, 21 September 1747. Stukeley adds 'Mauritii die', i.e. St Maurice's Day.
MB4 fol.122B, 24 September 1747.
Discusses the finding of a Roman pavement at Winterton near Crowle in north Lincolnshire on the land of Mr George Slovin and gives information from Mr Slovin about a preserved female body found while digging on the Yorkshire Moors, including a detailed account of the shoes she was wearing.[1]

[1] This discovery was reported to the RS by George Slovin. Stukeley's diary entry about this discovery is printed in *Stukeley* ii. 344–5.

495. SGS No 18: From Robert Butter[1] to Maurice Johnson.
Ripon, Yorkshire, 26 September 1747.
MB4 fol.124A, 1 October 1747.
Butter has been unable to write for two months because of gout in his hand; comments on taking the waters at Harrogate; discusses inscriptions in Ripon Cathedral and local customs in Ripon connected with moving house.

[1] See his entry in Appendix 2.

496. SGS No 70: From Revd Thomas Rutherforth to Maurice Johnson.
[St John's College, Cambridge], 20 October 1747.
MB4 fol.125B, 22 October 1747.
Discusses the preserved body found in Yorkshire[1] and whether the preservation was natural or deliberately done; comments on tools found with the body and whether they were what the Romans called 'celts'.[2]

[1] See letter from William Stukeley, 21 September 1747 (No 494 above).
[2] Defined by the *OED* as a prehistoric edged implement of bronze or stone, occasionally of iron; the word was first used in this sense in 1715.

497. From Revd George North to Maurice Johnson.
Codicote, 30 November 1747.
MB4 fol.135A, 10 December 1747.
Discusses an unsuccessful legal action which he has undertaken; gives a very detailed account of the contents of an MS register of the Abbey of Hyde juxta Winton which he has recently purchased.[1]

[1] This was the *Liber Vitae* of Hyde Abbey, Winchester (now BL, Stowe 944). See W. de G. Birch (ed.), *Liber Vitae: Register and Martyrology of New Minster and Hyde Abbey, Winchester* (Hampshire Record Society, 1892).

1748

498. SGS No 75: From Revd Thomas Rutherforth to Maurice Johnson.
[St John's College, Cambridge], 27 February 1747 [actually 1748].
Asks for the return of his paper on how the Vestal Fire was rekindled as it is needed for his book.[1]

[1] See his letter of 16 July 1741 (No 376 above); Maurice Johnson annotated No 498 with a note requesting the return of No 376 afterwards to the SGS.

499. SGS No 103: From Dr James Jurin to Maurice Johnson.[1]
Lincoln's Inn Fields, 5 March 1747 [actually 1748, dated from Minute Book entry].
MB4 fol.115B, 17 March 1748.

Dear Sir
At the time that I had the favour of your Letter[2] & indeed almost ever since, I have been so much incommoded with one severe cold after another, that I could not get to the Royal Society so much as once. But having desir'd a Friend to communicate it, I understand that the Society have ordered their thanks to be return'd to you for the communication, though the Instrument is not new, several of them having been made in London, & one in particular by Dr Mortimer, our Secretary. Who was the Author of this Invention is hard to determine, but if I am not mistaken the first thought of it came from Mr Harrison[3] Inventor of the Clock to find the Longitude at Sea, in which Instrument I saw something of this kind a pretty many years ago, & since that several Pendulums of clocks have been made upon this principle by Mr Graham.[4] But with all this I shall by no means pretend to derogate from the honour of Lincolnshire, especially as it has given birth to so usefull a Society as yours at Spalding.
                    I am, Dear Sir, your most affectionate

& most obedient Servant
Ja^s Jurin

Lincoln's Inn Fields
March 5 1747
To Maurice Johnson Esq
in Spalding   Lincolnshire
Annotated by Maurice Johnson: 'Lr from Dr James Jurin R & GSS ... in Ansr to the Plan & Acct of our Metal thermometer.'[2]

[1]   This letter is also reprinted in Andrea Rusnock, *The Correspondence of James Jurin* (1996), 494.

[2]   The RS's *Philosophical Transactions* X i 446 has the entry 'A letter from Maurice Johnson Esq: Pres. Of the Gentlemen's Society at Spalding, concerning a Metalline Thermometer in the Museum of the Society'.

[3]   For John Harrison (1693–1776), see No 272 n.2 above.

[4]   George Graham (1673–1751): inventor of clocks and astronomical instruments; see his entry in *ODNB*.

500. From Charles Jennens[1] to Maurice Johnson.
Gopsal, 23 May 1748.
MB5 fol.15A, 2 June 1748.
Accepts the invitation to membership of the SGS, given via Mr Grundy.

[1]   See his entry in Appendix 2.

501. SGS No 77: From William Stukeley to Maurice Johnson.
Stamford, 25 May 1748.
MB5 fol.15A, 2 June 1748.
He has sent a present of fossils and petrifactions to Johnson; Stukeley is about to move to London, having sold his house to Mr Noel;[1] explains his reasons for the move; discusses the activities at recent RS meetings and explains how he writes his memoirs[2] of these meetings afterwards; gives details of his Stamford garden; discusses Parkin's reply to Stukeley's article about Royston Chapel and dismisses his criticisms.[3]

[1]   This house, 9 Barn Hill, Stamford, was rebuilt between 1796 and 1802; traces of Stukeley's occupation remain (see Royal Commission on Historical Monuments (England), *An Inventory of Historical Monuments: The Town of Stamford* (London, 1977), 64).

[2]   The SGS archive still contains 5 volumes of Stukeley's MS minutes of the RS's meetings, sent by him for the SGS.

[3]   See Stukeley's letter of 17 December 1746 (No 472 above).

502. SGS No 16: From Maurice Johnson (son) to Maurice Johnson.
Eindhoven, 18 July 1748 New Style.
MB5 fol.19B, 14 July 1748.[1]
Sends thanks for his election as governor of the Free School at Spalding; describes his visit to Nijmegen, and sends sketches of Roman inscriptions there; recommends Anson's *Voyage Round the World* as a good book;[2] explains that the Duke[3] is to set out for England.

[1]   This anomaly, which suggests that the letter was read before it had been received, is caused by the difference in dating systems between England and Continental Europe; see the Introduction for a discussion of this.

[2]   George Anson's voyage round the world was completed in 1744 as part of the British Navy's role in the War of the Austrian Succession. His book, *A Voyage round the World,* was first published in 1748.

³ This presumably refers to the Duke of Cumberland; Maurice Johnson (son) was serving as an officer on his staff.

503. SGS No 12: From Calamy Ives¹ to Maurice Johnson.
Undated; read to SGS 11 August 1748.
MB5 fol.22A, 11 August 1748.
Gives a very full and detailed account² [eight and a half sides of foolscap] of his journey to Ireland, with full descriptions of towns passed through; Nottingham, Derby (where he remarks on Jacobite sympathies among the people), Uttoxeter, Burton-on-Trent, Newcastle under Lyme, Nantwich, Chester, Parkgate, Holyhead, Dublin, Athlone, Castlereagh, Ballinoha;³ describes a bad crossing and the illness of the passengers; comments on Ireland, especially Dublin, and the poverty of the country people, and describes a land journey through Wales on the return journey, especially the dangerous passes near Snowdon.
Annotated by Dr John Green: 'Mr Calamy Ives' Letter with an account of the Journey he took from Grantham to Athlone in Ireland. from thence to Ballinoha.'

¹   See his entry in Appendix 2.
²   The account occupies eight and a half sides of foolscap.
³   Ballinoha is the only place not recognisable; he may be referring to Ballina, County Mayo, NW of Castlerea.

504. From Emanuel Mendes da Costa to Dr John Green.
'Bois le Duc in Dutch Brabant'['sHertogenbosch/Den Bosch, Netherlands], 10 October 1748.
MB5 fol.26A, 13 October 1748.
He is travelling with the army in Europe;¹ sends details of a coin collection seen at Colchester; asks for details of fossils discussed at the SGS; has acquired a collection of Swiss fossils and other collections from German states; sends a catalogue of plants found in Brabant and Holland and details of medals he has collected, with drawings.

¹   At the time Da Costa had a quartermaster's administrative post in the British Army.

505. SGS No 23: From Revd Dr. Thomas Sharp¹ to Thomas Lloid at Rothbury, Northumberland.²
Durham, 23 November 1748.
MB5 fol.30B, 8 December 1748.
Sends an explanation of the Roman plate found at Corbridge in 1735;³ discusses an inscription at 'Richester' and comments on a local collection of over 30 inscriptions from stones found near Hadrian's Wall; asks for the letter to be given to Mr Salkeld.⁴
Enclosed: Diagram and detailed description of altar found at Corbridge, with inscription in Greek letters.

¹   See his entry in Appendix 2.
²   The Minute Book notes that this letter was forwarded to Maurice Johnson by his friend Mr Lloyd. MB5 fols.24B and 25A (29 September 1748) contain an account of a letter from Lloyd to Maurice Johnson, which has not survived, describing other Roman remains along Hadrian's Wall. For earlier correspondence about the Corbridge plate, see Nos 241, 243, 244, 248, 258, 281, 284 and 287 above.
³   This is no longer with the letter.
⁴   The Salkeld family had estates in Whitehall (Cumberland).

1749

506. SGS No 73: From Anthony Oldfield to Maurice Johnson.
Newmarket, 1 February 1748 [actually 1749].
MB5 fol.33B, 9 February 1749.
Discusses possible patronage for himself; he has gained a temporary post as assistant to the agent of the Duchess of Somerset[1] and her daughters; sends details of two prints and the epitaph of Henry Jenkins aged 169 from Swaledale, buried at Bolton Abbey;[2] sends details about Dr Mitchell of Chichester, an SGS member, and Mr Turnor of Stoke Rochford.

[1]   Frances (d.1754), wife of Algernon, seventh Duke of Somerset, who had succeeded to the title on 2 December 1748 (*CP* xii. 79–81).
[2]   For more on Henry Jenkins (d.1670), 'the modern Methuselah', see his entry in *ODNB*. A painting of him is in the Castle Museum, York.

507. SGS No 14: From Anthony Oldfield to Maurice Johnson.
Newmarket, 9 February 1748 [actually 1749].
MB5 fol.34A, 16 February 1749.
He has sent the two prints via Mr Bogdani and also a copy of Tindal's translation of the New Testament; describes a chantry chapel in Salisbury Cathedral; refers to a difficult 16-day crossing undertaken by Maurice Johnson (son) on his return from Holland: 'I give you Joy Sir on his safe Arrival in England after so dangerous a Passage as I find He had being 16 days on Board in coming from Holland.'

508. Draft of petition by Maurice Johnson to John, Duke of Montagu, Master General of his Majesty's Ordinance, from the President and members of SGS and other inhabitants of Spalding.
Spalding, 14 February 1748/9.
MB5 fol.37B, 16 March 1749.

To His Grace   The most Noble John Duke of Montague &c. &c. &c.
Master General of his Majesties Ordinance.
The Honourable the Lieutenant General and Other the Officers or Commissioners of his Majesties Board of Ordinance
The humble Petition of the underwritten President[1] and Members of the Gentlemens Society for Cultivating Friendship and Promoting Literature and all Arts and Sciences And also of Other Inhabitants of the said Town in Lincolnshire Sheweth   That your Petitioners out of a Sense they have of the Blessings of Peace and in Obedience to his Majesties Order in Councell of 1st February 1748 for the Proclaiming It,[2] Attended and Assisted the Sheriff's Officer of the said County on the 14th: when Pursuant thereunto He proclaimed the Peace at High Markett on the Stone Steps where Antiently a Sumptuous Cross stood in the midst of the Markett Place there: And afterwards that Evening Subscribed towards Erecting a Triumphal Arch thereon against the Thanksgiving for the same to be Illuminated with fixed fireworks Under the Directions of Mr Thomas Ives Chief Constable of this Wapontake of Elloe Holland, Mr William Sands Architect and Free Mason,[3] Mr John Grundy Master of Mathematicks Engineer and Agent for the Adventurers for Dreyning our Fenns and James

Wetherell Joyner and Operator in Fireworks Which if executed wee concieve will Yeild more Delight to the Spectators and do more Honour on the Occasion, than Sticking up Candles in Windows and be also much Safer than flying fires in a Town which has Twice severely Suffered by fire within these Thirty Six Yeares and wherein many Buildings are covered with Reed.[4]

Wherefore your Petitioners humbly request your Graces, or the Honourable Boards, Orders and Directions, with Warrant of Leave or Licence for the same, or other like fixed fireworks, to be made used and fired by the said beforenamed Persons, or any of them Authorized accordingly pursuant to the Statute in that Case made and Provided.

And your Petitioners shall ever Pray &c.

Tho. Ives	John Bullen	M Johnson President & Steward of
Wm Sands	Collector of the	the Mannor of Spalding cum Membris
	Subscriptions	
James Wetherell		John Green for himself and the Society
		by their Order

A Copy of the Subscription paper and Names of Subscribers hitherto.
Spalding the 4th of February 1748[5]
Wee the Underwritten Inhabitants for avoiding the Dangers which Happen by Setting Candles up in Windows, Do agree That Instead thereof Wee will Pay to Mr Thomas Ives Chief Constable the money against our Names respectively set to be employed in Erecting a Triumphal Arch upon the Cross, with Safe fireworks therein, in Honour of the Peace, upon the Day to be Appointed for a Thanksgiving On that Occasion by or under the Direction of Mr William Sands and James Wetherell
    Examined with the Original
    by me John Newstead[6]

A Copy of the Subscription paper within referred to in the Hands of Mr John Bullen collector thereof
Names of the Subscribers as set by them.

	s.	d.			
M Johnson	5	0			
J Dinham	5	0			
John Green	5	0			
John Dinham	5	0			
John Grundy	2	6			
John Hursthouse	4	0			
Stephen Bell	2	6			
Joseph Hill	2	6			
Thomas Ives	2	6	Michael Cox	2	6
John Rodgerson	2	6	Thos Day	2	6
Joseph Hinson	2	6	Wm Sands	2	6
Jas Thompson	2	6	John Kingston	2	6
J. Rowland	2	6	Jno Taylor	2	6
G.Stevens	5	0	Basil Beridg	5	0
Henry Boulton)			Jno Ingram	2	6

John Richards)	5	0	Jno Slight	2	6
Samuel Whiting	2	6	Eliz. Buckworth	2	6
Geo Worrall	2	6	C.Richardson	2	6
Evd. Buckworth	5	0	E.Graham	2	6
John Hinson	2	6	M.Ambler	2	6
Saml. Inett	2	6	M.Bold	2	6
Thos Hebblethwaite	2	6	M.Weyman	2	6
Th. Gates	2	6	Ann Thompson	2	6
The Revd Mr Johnson	2	6			
Minister of Spalding[7]					

Examined with the Original
by me John Newstead

[Preserved with this letter is a drawing of the proposed arch, on a Classical model with a pediment and Ionic columns, and of the coats of arms planned to decorate it, including the Royal arms, the badge of the Duke of Cumberland and the arms of Spalding, and designs by Johnson and by George Vertue for 'Fire Potts' to hold the fireworks.]

[1] By this time Maurice Johnson had become President, taking over on the death (on 4 February 1747/8) of the long-serving Revd Stephen Lyon. (Lyon's monumental inscription in Spalding Church is printed in John, Lord Monson (ed.), *Lincolnshire Church Notes made by William John Monson 1828–1840* (LRS 31, 1936), 332.) Dr John Green, the Second (or assistant) Secretary, had taken over the secretaryship. As a trained lawyer, Johnson was experienced in drafting petitions in this elaborate format.

[2] This marked the end of the War of the Austrian Succession (1740–48), in which Britain had sided with Austria against France and Prussia. The date is actually 1749; see n.5 below.

[3] The Duke of Montagu was a leading Freemason. This is the 'Brother Sands' referred to in John Grundy senior's letter to Johnson (No 265 above). Ives, Sands, and Grundy were all SGS members. The reference to 'James Wetherell' without the prefix 'Mr' may indicate his lower status as a craftsman.

[4] This use of candles was a common method of celebratory illumination; see Richard Falkner's account of a similar illumination at Oxford (No 217 above). Johnson was aware of the fire risk from candles and from mobile fireworks or 'flying fires' such as rockets; Spalding had had a disastrous fire in 1714 which had destroyed many houses. His proposed 'fixed fireworks' under supervision are planned to avoid this risk.

[5] Actually 1749, as shown by the replies (Nos 511 and 512 below); see the Introduction for a note on dating of letters.

[6] Maurice Johnson's clerk. The list is of value in showing the main citizens of Spalding who could afford to subscribe.

[7] Maurice Johnson's son John, formerly curate at Ramsey; he was appointed to the living of Spalding on 6 June 1748 (LAO, Register 38, 561).

509. SGS No.78: From John Hill to Maurice Johnson.
London, 5 March 1748/9.
MB5 fol.38A, 16 March 1749.
Apologises for the lack of recent correspondence from him because of his wife's ill-health; Hill had recently written to Montesquieu[1] at Bordeaux for specimens of pyrites, which he has recently received and analysed to discover what traces of metals they contained; comments in technical detail about his analysis and the effect of the different metals on the shapes of the pyrites; hopes his analysis will be of use to miners in determining what metals they will find near the places where pyrites are found, since 'All our Researches into Nature ought to tend to

some usefull End'; requests 'Please hereafter to direct to me To John Hill Esq. over against St Georges Church in Bloomsbury'.[2]

[1]   Charles Louis de la Brède, Baron de Montesquieu (1689–1755), an almost exact contemporary of Maurice Johnson, was in England in 1729–31. His book *De l'Esprit des Lois* was published in 1748.
[2]   This move, and the 'Esq.' denote Hill's rising status. On his move to the newly-built Queen Square in Bloomsbury he now became a neighbour and friend of William Stukeley.

510. SGS No 13: From James Weeks[1] to Maurice Johnson.
Retford, [Nottinghamshire], 19 March 1748/9.
MB5 fol 39B, 23 March 1749.
Sends family news; gives an account of his visit to Welbeck on business; sends an impression of a seal; praises the artistic ability of 'my pretty black ey'd Pupil';[2] discusses an inventory from Leicestershire which lists 50 dogs among other unusual items, explaining that they were the property of Revd Mr Stagmore of Catthorpe near Lutterworth, who had bought items belonging to any local person who died poor, as a way of helping their families; sends greetings to the Johnson family, especially 'My Playfellow Miss Johnson, Miss Harriet my pupil and your sons'; says he had promised to see Walter Johnson.

[1]   See his entry in Appendix 2.
[2]   One of Maurice Johnson's daughters, presumably Henrietta, known in the family as Harriet; see the conclusion of the letter. Johnson was keen to encourage his children to learn to draw and paint. His daughter Anne Alethea, later Mrs Wallin, was a very able artist, some of whose drawings illustrate the SGS minute books.

511. SGS No 5: From Charles Frederick[1] to Maurice Johnson.
Berkeley Square [London], 25 March 1749.
Informs Maurice Johnson that the licence for fireworks is ready and will be sent; he is busy organising the Royal firework display.[2]

[1]   Frederick became an SGS member in 1751; see his entry in Appendix 2. This letter replies to the Spalding petition (No 508 above).
[2]   This Royal display on 27 April 1749 was accompanied by the performance of Handel's *Music for the Royal Fireworks*, composed for this occasion.

512. SGS No 5: From Charles Bush to Maurice Johnson.
Office of Ordnance [London], 27 March 1749.
MB5 fol.39B, 30 March 1749.
Sends the licence for the firework display and a covering letter.

513. SGS No 77: Copy of letter from Maurice Johnson to Dr Walker, Trinity College Cambridge, annotated as having been copied by Maurice Johnson's clerk John Newstead.
Spalding, 9 December 1749.
MB5 fol.51B, 14 December 1749.
Enquires whether the college will publish Beaupré Bell's tables of coins,[1] as they have had Bell's MS for some time and the SGS had subscribed to the publication sixteen years previously; if they have no such plans, he requests to have the MS and prepared engravings returned to him for the SGS to publish them.
Also Maurice Johnson's notes, made later, on this decision by the SGS, and a copy of a letter to him from John Harrison, at Cambridge dated 2 February

1749/50, saying he had delivered the letter to Dr Walker and was also concerned to have the MS published.

¹   Bell had left his papers and MSS to Trinity College at his death, with the intention of having his tables published. The SGS was keen to publish on several occasions but found the process too expensive. Bell's tables of coins have not been published.

514. SGS No 78: From William Stukeley to Maurice Johnson.
London, 20 Dec 1749.
MB5 fol. 51B, 28 December 1749.
Wishes that Beaupré Bell had left his papers to the SGS for publication; gives news of an enamelled shrine reputed to come from Croyland, exhibited by Stukeley at the RS; discusses his plans for printing the chronicle of Richard of Westminster;[1] plans to send his memoirs of RS meetings to the SGS,[2] and gives an account of recent RS meetings, including discussion of a stone axe; gives an account of the annual dinner at the RS; approves of Johnson's plans for fitting up his dining-room; has seen the Duke of Montagu's funeral procession.[3]

¹   See Stukeley's entry in *ODNB* for his involvement with this document, which was a recent forgery claiming to be the work of a mediæval monk at Westminster, Richard of Cirencester, describing Roman Britain; Stukeley believed it to be genuine. See also No 531 below.
²   See No 501 above.
³   John, 2nd Duke of Montagu (1690–1749), of Boughton House (Northants), was Stukeley's patron.

1750

515. SGS No 9: From William Stukeley to Maurice Johnson.
Queen Square, London, 16 January 1749–50.
MB5 fol.56B, 22 March 1750.
Thanks Johnson for information on the Johnsons from Boston who went to New England; regrets that Johnson does not plan to come to London; says he has sent his memoirs of RS meetings to Spalding for reading at SGS meetings and comments on how he records them; discusses coins of Carausius including the one formerly owned by Dr Mead which had an inscription which Stukeley read as containing the name 'ORIVNA'.[1]

¹   See Maurice Johnson's notes made in 1749, attached to his letter to Dr Kennedy (No 235 above).

516. From Maurice Johnson to Alexander Wilson[1] in Queen Street, Westminster.
Spalding, 19 January 1750.
Thanks him and Mr Raymond for a favour [unspecified] to his son Henry Eustace Johnson; discusses reports of courts of sewers in Essex and Kent relating to fen drainage, to compare them with those in South Holland, Lincolnshire, where Johnson has been Chairman of the Court of Sewers and his son Walter Johnson is Clerk to the Court.

¹   This letter is bound in Johnson's own volume of notes and papers relating to his work on Fen drainage. It may be connected with obtaining a post in the East India Company for his son. See Wilson's entry in Appendix 2.

517. SGS No 10: From Revd Benjamin Ray to Maurice Johnson.
[Cowbit, Lincolnshire, 20 January 1750, dated from MB entry.]
MB5 fol. 54A, 8 February 1750.
Explains that he is resolved to 'fix myself ... in my Cabin at Cowbite where I find more real pleasure from my Books and solitude than in the noise and hurry of Spalding, among the busy traders'; discusses items of Johnson family history; sends news from Mr Pegge about the Bishop of Coventry and Lichfield, Bishop Smallbrook,[1] who had criticised Dr Mead's *Medica Sacra* in which the death of Herod Agrippa was confused with that of Herod the Great;[2] encloses a halfpenny of Ray's grandfather's, coined at Spalding.
Also annotations by Johnson on this coin, stating that it was coined in 1666, and notes by Johnson on mercers, Ray's grandfather having been one, and on the deaths of the two Herods, presumably for discussion at SGS meetings.

1   Revd Richard Smalbroke (1672–1749). See his entry in *ODNB*.
2   Richard Mead, *Medica Sacra* (1749), a Latin commentary on the diseases mentioned in the Bible.

518. From Alexander Wilson to Maurice Johnson.[1]
Westminster, 28 February 1750.
Discusses details of fees payable to the undertakers of Fen drainage.

1   He addresses him as Maurice Johnson Senior, since his father, a founding member of the SGS, had died on 8 November 1747, aged 86. Until then Johnson signed himself, and was addressed, as 'Maurice Johnson junior'. The letter may date from 1751 but there is no other evidence by which this can be ascertained; if so, the following letter by Johnson is also 1751.

519. From Maurice Johnson to Alexander Wilson.
Spalding, 2 March 1750.
Replies to Wilson's letter; refutes complaints made at the Court of Sewers against fees levelled by the Spalding Commissioners; offers Wilson and his wife accommodation if he attends an SGS meeting.

520. SGS No 80: From William Stukeley to Maurice Johnson.
London, 9 March 1749–50.
MB5 fol.56A, 15 March 1749/50.
Explains that a volume of his summaries of RS meetings is being bound for the SGS, that Browne Willis has printed his book on MPs[1] and that an account of Druids in Cornwall by Revd Mr Borlase[2] is being printed; gives a description of an earthquake felt in London.

1   *Notitia Parliamentaria* (1750); a copy is in the SGS.
2   This book by Revd William Borlase (1696–1772), *Observations on the antiquities historical and monumental of the county of Cornwall,* was not printed until 1754.

521. From Robert New[1] to Maurice Johnson.
[London], 16 March 1750.[2]
Gives a very detailed account of the circumstances surrounding the SA's move to gain a charter and the meeting of the SA to vote on this; requests Johnson to send a draft of a coat of arms for the SA.

1   See his entry in *ODNB*.
2   As there is no Minute Book entry for this letter, the date could be either 1750 or 1751, since the letter was sent prior to 25 March. The SA actually obtained its charter in 1751, but discussion of it went on for some time previously. In view of Sir John Evelyn's letter (No 523 below), this letter is likely to be from 1750. See New's entry in Appendix 2.

522. SGS No 79: From Maurice Johnson to Dr Green.
Undated; dateable to 29 March 1750 by MB entry.
MB5 fol. 56B, 29 March 1750.
Discusses Green's onyx seal set in a ring, identifying it as ancient, probably of Classical origins, and explaining the Classical parallels to its design of a young man in a cap and cloak, carrying a trumpet.

523. From Sir John Evelyn to Maurice Johnson.
St James [London], 15 May 1750.
Sends thanks for Johnson's account to the SA of the onyx seal in Dr Green's collection;[1] discusses the origins of the broad arrow mark used by the Customs; gives an account of an SA meeting held to discuss obtaining a charter.

[1]   See letter from Maurice Johnson, 29 March 1750 (No 522 above).

524. SGS No 3: From William Stukeley to Maurice Johnson.
S George's, Queen Square, London, 15 May 1750.
MB5 fol.58A, 17 May 1750.
Explains his theory that earthquakes are caused by electrical vibrations; discusses his paper to the RS on this topic,[1] and his sermon on it, criticising other, more limited papers on earthquakes given at the RS; explains that the SA is getting a charter; gives news of informal meetings with his London friends such as John Hill;[2] comments that Handel's 'Messiah'[3] is to be performed for the Foundling Hospital.

[1]   The Royal Society's *Philosophical Transactions* X i 541 record a paper, 'The Philosophy of Earthquakes' by Dr Stukeley.
[2]   Hill's letter of 16 March 1749 (No 509 above), mentions his move to Queen Square.
[3]   First performed in Dublin in 1741 and in London in 1743.

525. From James Muscat to the President of the SGS.
Boston, 19 May 1750.
Sends a book as his donation to the SGS.
Annotated by Maurice Johnson: 'Dr Perry's View of the Levant'.[1]

[1]   Dr Charles Perry (1698–1780) published *View of the Levant* in 1743. This book is still in the SGS Library. See Muscat's entry in Appendix 2.

526. SGS No 80: From William Stukeley to Maurice Johnson.
S.Geo[rge's, Queen Square] London, 16 June 1750.
MB5 fol.59A, 21 June 1750.
Gives a detailed account of the Egyptian Society which met in the 1740s, of which he was a member, explaining that his activities there brought him into favour with the Duke of Montagu; explains that he now attends the RS only, as it is too demanding to go on to the SA on the same evening; discusses ancient Tyrian trading with Cornish tin mines; explains that his landlord in London is Samson Gideon.[1]
Also a note by Maurice Johnson on the origins of the word 'camisia', used by Stukeley to describe Egyptian costume.

[1]   Samson Gideon (1699–1762): a wealthy London financier of Portuguese Jewish origins, who helped to raise finance for the European wars in the mid-eighteenth century. He purchased the lordship of the manor of Spalding and owned estates there, around 1750; his son later gained a peerage as Lord Eardley. Gideon became an SGS member in 1751. See his entry in *ODNB*.

527. SGS No 67: From Dr Robert Mitchell[1] to Maurice Johnson.
Guildford, 29 June 1750.
MB5 fol.59B, 19 July1750.
Gives a detailed account of the antiquities in the Guildford area; has recently had a visit from Stukeley; describes Maurice Johnson as 'Source, support and life of the learned Spalding society'.

[1]   See his entry in Appendix 2.

528. Part of a letter from Maurice Johnson (son) to Maurice Johnson.
Annotated by Maurice Johnson: 'from London 31 July 1750'.
MB5 fol.60B, 2 August 1750.
He has copied from a letter received from Turkey by Sir James Foule[1] a description of Greek inscriptions and carvings on a vault; quotes the inscriptions and passes on a request from Sir James to Maurice Johnson for a translation of them.

[1]   Sir James Foulis (1714–1791) fifth baronet: a former Army officer and keen antiquarian.

529. SGS No 59: From George Johnson[1] to Maurice Johnson.
Brasenose College, Oxford, 3 August 1750.
MB5 fol.62A, 9 August 1750.
He has been discussing with Timothy Neve junior the possibility of visiting Spalding at the end of the month; gives a two-page catalogue of the pictures in the Oxford picture gallery; recommends a 'monthly miscellany' called 'The Oxford Student', which he will try to bring with him; asks for details of the London to Spalding waggon so that he can send his luggage in advance.
Postscript on reverse: His father has refused him permission to leave Oxford that summer, as he had visited Spalding four months previously.
Annotated by Maurice Johnson: 'A Catalogue of Pictures, Statues & Bustos in the Picture Gallery in Oxford.'

[1]   See his entry in Appendix 2.

530. SGS No 81. From Emanuel Mendes da Costa to Maurice Johnson.
London, 4 August 1750.
MB5 fol.62A, 9 August 1750.

Good Sir
I received your very Esteemed favour of June 23 last past, I am greatly thankfull to you for your kind Congratulation & wishes on My change of state[1] I hope the Almighty will attend it with his blessings.
    the letter you inclosed for the Revd Mr Giffard, (who lives in Queen Square in Holborn) after having perused it with the utmost Attention & pleasure, & admired it so Much as to wish to have a Copy of it, I deliver'd Myself to the said Gentleman who is greatly Obliged to you for it, and told me he would honour himself in Answering it. I have not seen him lately to know whether he has yet so pleasured himself. I have given Dr Green My thoughts in former letters on the Utility of Literary or Philosophical Correspondencies. My said thoughts Agree intirely with yours, & it is a pity such curious Correspondencies are not more Ardently persued by the Learned.
    I am greatly delighted at the regular Plan of our Society, which you proceed on, And As for Dr Grews Catalogue,[2] it is my Opinion no worthier nor better

choice of a Book to govern yourselves by in your Collection, could ever be thought of, since I Am Convinced it is As learned & Usefull a Work As ever was publishd. I am sensible your fens can add very little to your fossil Collection; but then Ample recompence is made you in the productions of the Animal & Vegetable Kingdoms, especially the former, which Abound with you. I hope you have a pretty Collection of preserved birds & fish; which Collections tho extremely Usefull & curious are but too Much Neglected. Mr Reaumur[3] has lately in our Phil.Trans. given the best method for preserving Birds: & Dr Gronovius[4] for preserving fish, in such a Manner as to place them in Books like Plants, his Way is also publish'd in [page 2] the Transactions which [I] refer you to; but I do not think he explains in a Clear Manner his Way, so that if on perusing of it you are in the least doubt on any thing, have recourse to Me: for when I was at Leyden I made my Apprenticeship thereto.

Your Correspondence is greatly Agreeable to Me, and what I Ardently desire, you had therefore good Sir no need to Apologies for the length of your Letter.

I am greatly Obliged to you for the description of the Pica Marina,[5] and the Accounts of the other Several Birds, but as for the Eagles you surprise Me, As I thought they cheifly frequented Steep Mountainous & Woody places: perhaps the Eagles you Mention, are the Ossifraga Ospreys or Sea Eagles. the other particulars of the Game Cocks, Horses &c I also thank you for, for they greatly pleased Me, I beg my Compliments to all my Brother Members, I am

> Good Sir
> Your much obliged & obedient humble Servant
> Emanuel Mendes da Costa

[1]   Presumably his marriage.
[2]   Nehemiah Grew, *Musæum Regalis Societatis: or a catalogue and description of the natural and artificial rarities belonging to the Royal Society* (1681). The SGS were cataloguing the collections in their museum.
[3]   René-Antoine Ferchault de Réaumur (1683–1757), FRS 1738: French scientist and entomologist, best known for his thermometric scale.
[4]   Jan Frederik Gronovius (1686–1762): Dutch botanist and patron of Linnæus.
[5]   The sea-pie or oyster-catcher.

531. From William Stukeley to Maurice Johnson.
Queen Square, London, 13 September 1750.
MB5 fol.64B, 20 September 1750.
Explains that a Roman coin offered to Kennedy for three guineas has been bought by Dr Mead for ten guineas and given to the French King; Stukeley has copied a 'sorry drawing' of it which he reproduces at the head of this letter, showing the inscription as 'ORIVNA';[1] comments sadly on the recent deaths of old friends and colleagues; explains that he is to preach before the College of Physicians; gives news that Dr Ayscough[2] has returned from Greece with many antiquities; discusses his work on the 'Richard of Cirencester' MS and his intention to publish it;[3] he has sent Johnson his book on earthquakes.[4]

[1]   See Nos 235 and 515 above for earlier discussion of this coin. Kennedy's letter to Johnson is No 234 above.
[2]   Perhaps the surgeon-apothecary Dr James Ayscough, who came from Holbeach.
[3]   See Stukeley's letter of 28 December 1749 (No 514 above).
[4]   William Stukeley, *Philosophy of Earthquakes, natural and religious, or an enquiry into their cause and their purpose* (London, 1750). See also No 524 above.

532. SGS No 4. From Revd Timothy Neve to Maurice Johnson.
Buckden, 25 September 1750.
MB5 fol.64B, 27 September 1750.

Dear Sir   Buckden 25 Sepr 1750
   Your favour of the 31 of Aug. past I did not receive till above a week after
date, & the week following was every day abroad, & last week was taken up with
my Examination of young Gentlemen for Orders, so that I could not conveniently
before now acknowledg the receit of it.
   In the first place I am glad to hear of the Health & flourishing Estate of your
family & send you my good wishes for the continuance & increase of it: And as
for the Society, I make no doubt, but so long as you so worthily preside over it, its
glory cannot fade, but its Riches & numbers must encrease And as you've made
so great a Collection of Books & valuable curiosities, I wish they could be put
upon so lasting a foundation as never to be liable to become a private Property:
a catalogue of all which being enter'd & annext to the parochial Library, with a
duplicate in the possession of the Society & another in the Hands of the Minister,
may possibly secure them from hazzard. But this I apprehend [page 2] may be
needless to mention to you, who have so much better Knowledge as well as
greater zeal for its safety & perpetuity. – As for my own part, I am asham'd I can
contribute so little to your amusement, who of late have been more conversant in
the modern than the antiquarian world. That which I think, makes the most noise
at present is the amazing treasures of Antiquity dug up from the subterraneous
city of Heraclea[1] by the King of the 2 Sicilies, beyond any thing that was ever
found before, & which have enrich'd his 2 fine palaces at Portici & Naples, with
the finest Statues, paintings &c some say the Equestrian Statue of Marble of
Balbus found there, is far beyond that of Antoninus in the Capitol, & the finest
in the world, the Inscription on the pedestal of the PR puzzles the learned
                    M.NONIO.M.F
                    BALBO
                    PR.PRO.COS.
                    HERCULANENSES
As for the paintings on the plaisterd walls or Stucco both for colouring, design
& drawing some of them they say are inimitably fine: & which they have found
means of taking off intire, & with a new invented varnish to preserve from decay.
That of Virginea is the best preserv'd & exquisitely beautiful, &c &c &c. There
is a little Book publishd in Italian by Marquis Don Marcello di Venuti & translated into English by Wickes Skurray,[2] with a particular Description of all these
curiosities, which probably you have [page 3] seen but F. Gori the famous Antiquarian is about to publish a full & more accurate account.[3]
   As to the Motto round Bishop Russell's[4] crest in the old dining room at
Buckden, it has puzzled every body here. the crest is a Dove with this Labell
IESUIS VERUS CELVY whether it be a conundrum upon his name RUSCEL
or what else I pretend not to know. His arms are upon another knot in the same
room, & upon the front of the great gate entring into the palace, blazond in
different colourd bricks within the wall.
   We have here the Bishop of London[5] & his Lady & the Dean of York who is
under great affliction for the Loss of his Lady, Mr Witchcoats Daughter a young
Lady of great Beauty & accomplishments. My son does not go abroad this year

as I expected:[6] the Bishop of Lincoln has been so good as to give him a small Living near Oxford consistent with his fellowship, & which he can serve from College, & I hope to prevail upon the Bishop of London to make him a Whitehall preacher, & then he will have a pritty income. Yesterday was Sennight[7] my wife & I & Dr Naylor made a visit to Southwick & found all the family there well, Mr & Mrs Lynn expected every post a Letter to summon them to London to meet their Brother Bellamy return'd from the East Indies. I beg my compliments to your good Lady & family, & I am, Sir,

Your most obedient Servant
Tim: Neve.

Since I wrote the within Legend of Bishop Russell's Crest, I've look'd at it again & find the Labell begins at VERUS & ends with CELVY the Dove in the middle of the ringlet, a rose betwixt his feet, & a Branch running up to his Neck.

[1]   Herculaneum, which was being excavated at this time.
[2]   *A description of the finest discoveries of the Antient City of Heraclea … Done into English,* translated by Wickes Skurray (London, 1750).
[3]   Antonio Francesco Gori published his book about Herculaneum in 1752 in Rome.
[4]   John Russell (c.1430–1494): Bishop of Lincoln 1480–1494; see his entry in *ODNB*.
[5]   Dr Thomas Sherlock (1678–1761); see his entry in *ODNB*.
[6]   No. 551 below, from Timothy Neve junior's friend George Johnson on 10 June 1751, says that Neve has gone abroad to Hamburg. The 'small Living near Oxford' mentioned by Neve was Easington, in the Diocese of Oxford, of which Neve became Rector in 1750.
[7]   That is, a week yesterday.

533. SGS No 17: From Henry Eustace Johnson[1] to his mother Mrs Elizabeth Johnson.
Gosberton, 3 October 1750.
MB5 fol.65B, 11 October 1750.

Honoured Madam   No 17   Gosberton, Oct[r] 3[d] 1750
    I am very much obliged to you for your kind Letter & am asshaimed I did not write to you before, it was not owing to negligence, but to a bad cut on my right Hand which is quite well. I am glad to hear Brother Johnson[2] is better hope you and my Honred Father Brothers and Sisters are well. I will send those Pens the first opportunity & the Monument[3] ear it be long. I have no News to let you know but what I think you must have heared, ^ tho you did not mention it in yours, makes me ^tell you that is a very sensible shock of an Earthquake[4] on Sunday[5] about half an Hour after 12, which was so great as to crack a strong House, the People thought the house would fall, I was a reading at that Time, heared a noise like thunder at a distance, I thought it was a Coach going past, got up to look through the Window & before I was well up I was in the Chair again, which surprised me, the House shook with a sort of tremor very odley. A Substantial Farmour told Mr Watson of Holbeck, he saw about 3 aclock on Monday morning a very strange lite N.West, forming a triangle 2 Points or Ends was red, the other the coulour of a Rainbow, this was as he toald us on tuesday about 8 a clock at night Mr Binks & I saw a most beautifull Phænomenan, which moved as it where near us tending N.West I have no more to add but duty Love & Service where due from your dutifull Son
          Hen. Eust. Johnson
Annotated by Maurice Johnson: 'This Account of the Earthquake read at SGS And Mr Operator Cox and Mr Sands & other Members present affirmed they were at the same 30 Sep[r] sensible of the same – by all Accounts it was strongly

felt at Croyland Deeping & Peterborough & very violently at Moulton Chapel & Whapload Drove Eastward. The President informed the Company that on the 2nd Inst being the Tuesday after John Griffin of Moulton Chapell Gate a Tenant of his assured him He was at the time mentioned sat reading in his house there & was Violently Shook in his Chair & his wife at the same time also extreemly disorderd.'

[1]   Henry Eustace, the youngest of Maurice Johnson's sons, was at the nearby village of Gosberton, probably at school. The letter shows elaborate penmanship such as he would have learnt in his handwriting lessons. He was preparing for a career with the East India Company; see his entry in Appendix 2.
[2]   Presumably his eldest brother Maurice; this form of title without the first name was commonly used for the eldest in a family
[3]   Unidentified.
[4]   This earthquake, one of a series in England in 1750, was widely felt. They were the subject of much comment and speculation among natural philosophers and were often reported at the RS; for Stukeley's interest see Nos 520, 524, 531 above and No 564 n.2 below.
[5]   Note by Maurice Johnson: 'the 30th of September'.

534. From Timothy Neve junior to Maurice Johnson.
CCC Oxon [Corpus Christi College, Oxford], 3 October 1750.
MB5 fol.65B, 11 October 1750.
Regrets he is unable to find either the pedigree of Dymoke[1] or Dr Platt's MS for Johnson; sends the epitaph of Mrs Mary Scott of Dalkeith who died in 1738 aged 125, and of Dr James in All Souls' Chapel; praises 'your kinsman here'.[2]

[1]   The Lincolnshire family holding the hereditary office of the Royal Champion.
[2]   George Johnson, son of Revd Walter Johnson, Rector of Redmarshall, Co. Durham and cousin to Maurice Johnson, who was an undergraduate at Brasenose College, Oxford: see his entry in Appendix 2 and his letters, Nos 529 above and 539, 545, 549, 551 and 554 below. The other people cannot be traced.

535. No 15: From Revd Samuel Pegge to Maurice Johnson.
Godmersham, 10 October 1750.
MB5 fol.65B, 18 October 1750.
Sends a very detailed discussion of the Aurora Borealis[1] as sighted in England and lists recorded observations of this before 1715, which had been claimed to be the first sighting in England; criticises assumptions, including those of Whiston,[2] that it was a predictive omen; refers to Hans Egede's account of the aurora in his book on Greenland.[3]

[1]   Pegge also sent to the SGS a dissertation in Latin on observations of the Aurora Borealis as recorded in Classical writers, including Xenophon, which was read to the Society on 28 March 1751, as noted by Johnson.
[2]   William Whiston (1667–1752): mathematician and natural philosopher; see his entry in *ODNB*.
[3]   For previous references to Egede's book, see Nos 397, 399 and 422 above.

536. From Revd Samuel Pegge to Maurice Johnson, attached in the SGS archive to his previous letter to Johnson, No 535 above.
[Godmersham], 11 October 1750.
Requests information on the SGS's list of Anglo-Saxon coins; refers to Dr Green whom he knew at Cambridge.

537. From William Dodd to Maurice Johnson.
Bourne, 28 October 1750.
MB5 fol.67A, 1 November 1750.
Asks Johnson to help him by lending a drawing by the late Beaupré Bell for inclusion in Dodd's translation of Callimachus[1] and by translating and commenting on some epigrams by that poet; discusses the possible locations of Bell's papers at Cambridge.

[1]   William Dodd's *The Hymns of Callimachus* was published in London in 1755. For Dodd's controversial life, see his entries in Appendix 2 and in *ODNB*. Callimachus was a Classical Greek poet (310/305 BC-240 BC).

538. SGS No 6: From George Shelvocke to Maurice Johnson.
General Post Office, London, 15 December 1750.
MB5 fol.70B, 20 December 1750.
Says he has forwarded a letter to a Norwegian correspondent;[1] agrees to help with a query from Johnson about the House of Anjou; discusses accounts of the recent excavations at Herculaneum, including his own account written at Naples in 1740, which he claims was the first in English.[2]

[1]   Either Richard Norcliffe or Revd Andreas Bing; see letters of 20 July and 24 August 1742 (Nos 398 and 401 above). Shelvocke's letter of 5 November 1745 (No 453 above) agrees to forward the SGS's foreign correspondence without charge.
[2]   Excavations at Herculaneum, buried by the eruption of Vesuvius in AD 79, were begun in 1738. See Timothy Neve's letter (No 532 above).

1751

539. SGS No 13: From George Johnson to Maurice Johnson.
Brasenose College, Oxford, 18 January 1751.
MB5 fol.71B, 24 January 1751.
Sends 'a little Peice'; has been concerned about Maurice Johnson's silence as he values his correspondence; has had 'a dull Xmas in College, nothing but Cards in the College Hall'; discusses the coming election of an MP for Oxford; gives news that Mr Neve junior has been unwell but has recovered.
Enclosed: Latin poem 'Pharmacopolarium' about an apothecary and his workshop.

540. SGS No 85: From Revd Edward Owen[1] to Maurice Johnson.
Kimbolton, 21 January 1750 [actually 1751].
MB5 fol.71B, 24 January 1751.
Thanks the SGS for electing him to membership; offers to send [unspecified] books for the SGS library.

[1]   See his entry in Appendix 2.

541. SGS No 88: From Revd Dr Thomas Sharp to Maurice Johnson.
Durham, 24 January 1750 [actually 1751].
MB5 fol.71B, 31 January 1751.
Appreciates his nomination as a member of the SGS; will send a book for the library; sends family news; discusses the artistic activities of Sharp's and Johnson's daughters.

542. From Robert New to Maurice Johnson.
26 January 1750 [actually 1751].
MB5 fol.71B, 31 January 1751.
Discusses the title and genealogy of the present Duke of Somerset[1] and Earl of Hertford, with comments on the Duke's politics; comments on the SA's new engraving of the death-warrant of Charles I.

[1] Edward Seymour, eighth Duke of Somerset, succeeded his distant relative Algernon, seventh Duke, in 1750 (*CP* xii. 80–83). New's letter is an excellent account of this very complex succession.

543. From Edmund Chapman to Maurice Johnson.
Grimsthorpe, 27 January 1550 [*sic*, actually 1751].[1]
MB5 fol.71B, 31 January 1751.
Sends thanks for his election to membership of the SGS and offers to send [unspecified] books.

[1] Chapman was elected to membership of the SGS in 1751; see his entry in Appendix 2.

544. SGS No 88: From Dale Ingram to Maurice Johnson.
Tower Hill, London, 9 February 1751.
MB5 fol.72B, 14 February 1751.
He is honoured to accept SGS membership; offers to send for the SGS library the books that he is publishing, including *Diseases of the American Climes* and volume 2 of *Practical Cases in Surgery*;[1] sends regards to 'the truly eminent Dr Green'.

[1] *Practical Cases and Observations in Surgery* (1751) by Dale Ingram is still in the library of the SGS. *Diseases of the American Climes* does not appear to have been published. See Ingram's entry in Appendix 2.

545. SGS No 5: From George Johnson to Maurice Johnson.
Brasenose College, Oxford, 11 February 1751.
MB5 fol.72B, 14 February 1751.
Thanks Johnson for his 'interest in procuring me a Demy at Magdalen'[1] but this could slow his gaining a Fellowship there; he is better off with his current scholarship;[2] explains that Mr Neve junior is now in London and plans to go abroad as a chaplain; gives details of curiosities and paintings in the Ashmolean Museum at Oxford; hopes to visit Spalding in the summer; will contact John Johnson; needs a receipt from Walter Johnson for £25 sent to him.

[1] A demyship was a scholarship equivalent to half the value of a fellowship. Maurice Johnson's private notes about his plans for his sons' education include the comment: 'Magdalen Coll in Oxf[d] founded by W[m] of Waynfleet Ld Bp of Winton Demys first then 5 Lincolnsh Fellows'. It is presumably one of the Lincolnshire awards that both of the Johnsons have in mind.
[2] This was at Brasenose College.

546. SGS No 82: From Dr Cornewall Tathwell to Maurice Johnson.
Hitchin, 20 February 1750 [actually 1751].[1]
MB5 fol.73B, 7 March 1751.
Thanks the SGS for his election to membership; discusses in detail a manuscript of Horace's poems belonging to Mr Drake of York, claimed to be 500 years old, and whether it throws light on the order of composition and dating of the poems; promises to write more on medical cases later.

[1] Tathwell was elected to membership in 1751; see his entry in Appendix 2.

547. SGS No 90: From William Stukeley to Maurice Johnson.
London, 13 April 1751.
MB5 fol.77B, 18 April 1751.
Sends an account of the Monday meetings of a discussion group at his neighbour Dr Hill's, recommends Hill's literary journal *The Inspector* for reading at the SGS[1] and comments on Stukeley's own contributions to it; refers to the death of the Prince of Wales[2] and those of a number of other noblemen; discusses the development of Stukeley's London library; promises more of his notes on RS meetings to come for the SGS; gives the latest London gossip.

[1]   Johnson evidently followed Stukeley's recommendation, since the SGS's collection of copies of *The Inspector* is still in the Society's archives.
[2]   Frederick, Prince of Wales, the son of George II and father of George III, who died unexpectedly on 20 March 1751.

548. From Nathan Drake to Maurice Johnson.
York, 20 April 1751.
MB5 fol.77B, 25 April 1751.
Thanks the SGS for electing him to membership and for their subscriptions to his publication [unspecified];[1] mentions his kinsman Francis Drake[2] being in Bath attending Lord Burlington.

[1]   This was most probably Drake's *View of Boston* which appeared in 1751; see his entry in Appendix 2.
[2]   Francis Drake was the author of *Eboracum*, his famous history of York, which was published in 1736 and dedicated to his patron the Earl of Burlington (1694–1753).

549. SGS No 83: From George Johnson to Maurice Johnson.
Brasenose College, Oxford, 13 May 1751.
MB5 fol.80A, 16 May 1751.
Apologises for his failure to reply; has had a cold and had to write verses as a College exercise on the death of the Prince of Wales; disliked writing Latin and Greek verses at school so he had asked his cousin John[1] to send any unpublished verses, but has now written his own Anacreontic Ode. He has not heard from his father and is concerned for his health; explains that Mr Neve junior has gone to Hamburg; he himself is preparing for his examination 'which I am told is but trifling'.
Enclosed: His Greek Ode.

[1]   Maurice Johnson's son.

550. SGS No 3: From Revd Robert Smyth to Maurice Johnson.
Woodston, 20 May 1751.
MB5 fol.80B, 23 May 1751.
Gives a very full and detailed description of the statues in the garden of Sir Francis St John's house at Longthorpe near Peterborough[1] and comments on the house and gardens; refers to the activities of the St John family in the Civil War.

[1]   Maurice Johnson's letter (No 23 above) also refers to these statues, which are no longer in Thorpe Hall gardens.

551. SGS No 83: From George Johnson to Maurice Johnson.
Brasenose College, Oxford, 10 June 1751.
MB5 fol.82A, 20 June 1751.

Dear Sir,   No 83   Oxford, Coll B-Nose, June 10, 1751
I am much obliged to you for your kind & expeditious Answer to my last touching my Father's late Indisposition. I received a letter from him soon after, wherein he told me he had had a lowness of Spirits occasion'd by being too closely confined, & not using any Exercise; which is a thing my Mama indulges herself in, & for that reason (I suppose) prescribes it to her Spouse. I am extremely obliged to you, dear Sir, for your kind endeavors in promoting my Interest at Magdalen,[1] the Fate of which depends on the 23^d of next Month: If I should not succeed, I propose to myself the Pleasure of seeing my good Friends at Spalding & Redmarshal till next Lent, & so stand at the next Election. [page 2] Our Epicedia Oxoniensia[2] were presented last week by Dr Brown the Vice-Chancellor, to his Majesty, & met with a most gracious reception. They were immediately published, as soon as we heard they were received. As I thought, Sir, the perusal of them would be not unacceptable, I beg leave to trouble you with a Copy of them: There are 140 Elegys in nine different languages,[3] reckon'd to be the best collection wrote in Oxford for many years. There is one copy in the Phonician language, wrote by one Mr Swinton of Ch.Ch.[4] a Man of great learning, but especially in the Antiquarian tast. I am told there are but two Persons beside him in Europe that understand the Language, which he has almost recovered from Oblivion, & will shortly publish a Grammer of it. I had a letter last Week from Mr Neve from Hamburgh, who tells me, he has got himself pretty well settled [page 3] to his Satisfaction, in regard to his Accommodation & Entertainment, tho he does not enjoy himself so well as when in England, as the Clergy at Hamburgh are so very much upon the Reserve, & he cannot speak Dutch, so that he is forced to converse by Signs. He comforts himself that it will not be of long continuance.[5]
I beg leave, to congratulate you, Sir, upon my Cousins promotion, which I am sure, Sir, he is in every respect worthy of: I beg my Compliments to your Lady & all the good Family, & to my Cousins Green, & am
dear Sir,
your affectionate & obliged Kinsman
G: Johnson
P.S. I beg my Compliments to Cousin John, & shall beg of him a Certificate of my birth, when he writes next.[6]

[1]   George Johnson was hoping to be elected to a fellowship at Magdalen College, Oxford, and Maurice Johnson was attempting to gain support for him.
[2]   These were a set of elegiac poems, in a variety of languages, lamenting the recent death of Frederick, Prince of Wales on 20 March 1751, and presented to King George II as the University's official commemoration of the Prince's death. See the Prince's entry in *ODNB*.
[3]   Maurice Johnson's annotation lists these as: '1.British or Welsh, 2 Hebrew, 3 Arabic, 4 Syriac, 5 Phænician, 6 Greek, 7 Hetrurian, 8 Latin & 9 English'. These are no longer archived with this letter and are presumably now lost, although Johnson annotated the letter 'From Mr George Johnson with that Universitys Elegys on the Prince of Wales's Death', indicating that he had received them.
[4]   Revd John Swinton (1707–1777): scholar in Oriental languages, who wrote articles on Phoenician inscriptions. At the time he was a Student of Christ Church, Oxford. See his entry in *ODNB*.
[5]   This is Neve's son Timothy, who had been at Oxford with George Johnson and was now a chaplain to the English community in Hamburg, despite his father's hope, expressed in No 532 above, that he

would not be going abroad. 'Dutch' was often used at this period to refer to the German language: 'High Dutch' for southern or standard German and 'Low Dutch' both for the speech of the Netherlands and the dialect of North Germany, 'Plattdeutsch'. See Timothy Neve junior's entry in Appendix 2 and in *ODNB* and his letters (Nos 457, 463, 484 and 534 above). He returned to Oxford to study theology, eventually becoming Lady Margaret Professor of Divinity there.

6   John Johnson, Maurice's son, had recently become minister of the church at Spalding (see No 508 n.7 above) and so would have the parish registers in which George Johnson's birth was recorded. It is John's elder brother, Maurice, whose promotion in the Army is referred to; presumably this was from Captain to Major, though he is documented either as Captain or, later, as Colonel.

552. SGS No 102: From Abel Smith junior to John Grundy.
[Nottingham], 15 June 1751.
MB5 fol.82B, 20 June 1751.
Explains that he has sent a copy of *The Antiquities of Nottingham* for the SGS library.[1]

1   Robert Thoroton (1623–1678), *The Antiquities of Nottinghamshire* (London, 1677). The book is still in the SGS library. See Smith's entry in Appendix 2.

553. SGS No 13: From Dale Ingram to Dr Green at Spalding.
26 June 1751.
MB5 fol.83B, 4 July 1751.
'A Cursory Examination of the Purpos, Porpoise or Sea Hogg By D. Ingram Surgeon.'
A detailed description of an examination of a specimen of a porpoise by Ingram.
Annotated by Johnson: 'Read SGS 4 July 1751.'

554. SGS No 1: From George Johnson to Maurice Johnson.
Magdalen College, Oxford, 2 December 1751.
MB5 fol.95B, 12 December 1751.
Apologises for his delay in writing; explains that his father is much improved in health and plans to travel next summer, perhaps to Oxford; compares Oxford and Cambridge, preferring the Sheldonian Theatre at Oxford to Cambridge's theatre, but admiring King's College chapel; notes that Oxford town hall is to be rebuilt; discusses the Earl of Orrery's published letters to his son, which contain comments about Swift[1] whom he had known; sends a list of the portraits recently put up in the newly-redecorated hall at Christ Church, Oxford; sends compliments to the family.
Annotated by Johnson: 'Catalogue of Pourtraits put up in Christ Church Coll. Hall.'[2]

1   John Boyle, Earl of Orrery (1707–1762), *Remarks on the Life and Writings of Dr Jonathan Swift* (London, 1751).
2   The list is still in the SGS archive.

555. SGS No 84: From Walter Johnson to Maurice Johnson.
Mortimer Street, London, 7 December 1751.[1]
MB5 fol.95B, 12 December 1751.

SGS No 84
Most honoured Sir   London Mortimer Street Decb[r] 7th 1751
    Am very sorry had it not in my Power to do my self the Pleasure before but really Mr Grindley Mr Walker Mr [*illegible*] Mr Hanbury & Mr 1000 other

Things Warehouses would not furnish any Thoughts worthy your Acceptance. I sent John pursuant to your Commands to Dr Hill's who will send you all his Papers that are in fruit but he says he doubts severall of Them are not to be had. Your Coal Bucket is gone to Mr Stevens's to go by Capt. Taylor when he next comes hither for he is not yet arrived. The Parchments are all stamped as you wished & safe packed up I paid for you at the Antiquarian Society Two Guineas as by Agreement in March last for which I have an Acquittal from the Secretary Mr Aimes the Treasurer being ill – I called on honest Robert New & wrote a Letter or rather concluded it in his Office & we went together to the Soc. Mr Tibbald was Vice president Mr Folks being so verry bad that tis not expected he will ever be his own Man again (This is the Test Expression on this Occasion). We had communicated a View or plan of the Savoy as it now stands with a full Discription of its age, Use &c – it being just now to be taken down And it is to be engraved.[3] We had a plan of the ~~Charity~~ Charter House[4] as taken from an Antient Drawing made in the 15th Cent By it the Topps of the Stonearched Doors entering into each of their Cells & which seem to be about 8 or 9 Feet high are at this Day just visible above the Ground this was a Remark made by two Ingenious Members then present who received their Education there. We had also communicated Two Prints or rather Impressions made by one Jackson[5] on Paper from Wooden Blocks They are [page 2] Most exquisite in their Way The One is of the Appollo Belvidere The Other Hercules slaying the Hydra They are done in the Same Taste & style as the Mezzitento's are from the Copper, but I think the Spirit is greater in These than in any Mezzitento I have yet Seen and the low or deeper Mussles expressed full as elegant & fine They are on Cartaridge Paper & the Colour blew. I know you have severall of Them that bro: Johnson brought from the Flemish School but None I think equall to These – They were not exhibited as if twas a New Light or Invention But as this Mr Jackson, being the First Man that ever executed in this Way in England he having been verry many Years abroad I suppose he is endeavouring to make his Blocks so large as to be able to execute any Part of History on the largest Paper for to line Rooms. then think how high this Tast may be carryed and at how easy a Rate thousands of Gent. may be furnished with the great Actions of their Ancestors or Princes ~~& in how elegant a Tast~~.

Wooden Church of Greenstead.[6] Wee had delivered in a Drawing made by Mr Virtue of the Antient Wooden Church at Greenstead near Ongar in Essex esteemed one of the most rare & out of the Way Parts of Antiquity Twas built Suddenly of Trees cut down & then Split in Two & in that rude Manner set upright with the riven Sides inwards which were drawn ^over with Mortar in Order to receive and Cover the Shrine of St Edmund which rested there in its Way for St Edmunds Bury where it remained The Trees are Oakes And seem to be by the Drawing about[7] 8 Feet high before the Covering – [page 3] but whether they stand any Depth in the Ground I cannot say or how they should have been preserved for now upwards of a Thousand Yeares I will not take upon me to conjecture – that is to be attempted at the Foot of the Print. Mr Vertue said twas too long to attempt at that Time The Steeple is all of Wood done in the Common Method as at Whaplode Drove of this the Revd Mr Dinham[8] ^to whom I beg my Compliments & to his better ½ can give you a more succinct & lively Idea You know I'me no Draftsman but I can express the rude Form of this rude Edifice almost as well as it is now in being.[9]

Mr Virtue presents his Service to you I called of him twice but could not find him at Home – he was at the Soc: Mr Bogdani is more jolly & buxom than he has been these 6 Yeares.[10] I am so often called upon that tis to no purpose to attempt writing any more especially as I have not yet wrote to the Dear ever present tho absent Fair. I beg you will make my duty acceptable to my Mother And Love to Bro. & sisters am ashamed to think they should all be so cruel as to let their Minds run a Wool gathering after a Sorry Assembly & not write me one Line to let me know how All Things stand at Spalding. I think there is some thing very musical in the Word Spalding it has no Asperates in it I hope to me although I find my Guardian Angels Sometimes sleep

I can no more, beg you will beleive me to be

> Your ever dutiful Son & obedient Servant
> Walter Johnson

I shall be at Home I hope Monday Night or Tuesday Noon.

P.S. With my love to Kitty[11] pray acquaint her that her Ticket as well as my own is in the Wheel I hope of Good Fortune and that I shall & must now be as ignorant as she of what Fortune intends us for they will not draw again whilst Monday 9 of Clock – I could sell her Ticket if she like of it for £18:10:0 which is a surprising Thing the wheel being extreemly poor – but such is the English Madness   My Love to Dicky & Nancy Wallin: I received much Joy in reading that Harriet was so well as to walk out & so good natured.

To Maurice Johnson Esq

at Spalding

Lincolnshire

[1]   Maurice Johnson's son Walter had now taken over the family's visits to London on legal business, on account of Maurice Johnson's increasing unwillingness to travel because of ill health. He has evidently been shopping on behalf of the Spalding family, hence his reference to the '1000 … Warehouses' he has had to visit. See Walter Johnson's entry in Appendix 2.

[2]   Ames, New and Folkes were all members of the SGS, as was Hill. 'Tibbald' was James Theobald, antiquary and merchant, not his contemporary Lewis Theobald, the Shakespeare scholar satirised by Pope.

[3]   This was the remains of the mediæval Savoy Palace in the Strand, London, pulled down soon afterwards. The modern Savoy Hotel is on the same site. Maurice Johnson added a note: 'this View was shewn to the Company at a Meeting of SGS 25 July last by the President. See [MB] Vol.5 fo.346 an Account thereof from GV [?George Vertue] a member'. The notes inserted by Maurice Johnson into this letter were probably done when he received it, to mark important sections to be read out at the next SGS meeting.

[4]   Note by Maurice Johnson: 'Antient Forme of the Charter House or Sutton's Hospital'.

[5]   John Baptist Jackson (c.1700–c.1773): woodcutter, printmaker and experimenter with woodblock printing of prints of famous paintings; he later specialised in wallpaper design. See his entry in *ODNB*.

[6]   Note by Maurice Johnson.

[7]   MS 'to be about'.

[8]   Revd John Dinham, a member of the SGS in 1749, was a leading member of the Society after Maurice Johnson's death, becoming President in 1759 on the death of Maurice's successor, his son Revd John Johnson. Dinham was the son of Dr Dinham, another regular member of the Society, whose portrait hangs in the SGS rooms.

[9]   Sketch of the church from the south and from the east. Note by Maurice Johnson: 'See a Picture of the like Fabrick with Hurdles to pargiter in Sir Henry Spelman Councells IV fol.11 & St Mary Stockys in Spalding the like Mins vol.4 fo.120.'

[10]   Bogdani's letters frequently refer to his ill-health and depressed spirits; see in particular Nos 271 and 302 above.

[11]   Maurice Johnson's third daughter Catherine, known in the family as Kitty, was born in 1715 and married Revd John Lodge. 'Dicky & Nancy Wallin' are Richard Wallin, a merchant in Jamaica, and

his wife Anne Alethea (née Johnson), Walter's sister; they were married in 1750. Harriet is Walter's sister Henrietta, whose ill health was mentioned in a letter from her brother Captain Maurice Johnson (see No 390 above). This letter shows the continuing closeness of Johnson's children.

1752

556. SGS No 45: From Thomas Birch to Maurice Johnson.
Norfolk Street, London, 17 March 1752.
MB5 fol.99A, 19 March 1752.

Dear Sir   No 45   London Norfolk Street 17 March 1752
    Your kind Letter, upon Occasion of the Honour, which the Royal Society has lately done me,[1] was so acceptable to me, that I should have been glad to have receiv'd it from your Son's Hands & to have return'd you my Acknowledgments for it immediately by him whom it would have been a great Satisfaction to me to have introduc'd to our assembly at Crane-court, as well as to our Brethren at the Mitre.
    I must now beg of you to make my Compliments to the Gentlemen of the Society of Spalding, & to assure them that I shall most punctually transmit to them a Copy of the Philosophical Transactions as soon as they shall be publish'd, & be ready to do them every other Service in my power, from the Regard which I owe to them & their Institution, & the Relation, in which I stand to them as a Member, & shall be extremely desirous of their correspondence for the Benefit of the Society, which I have the honour to serve.
    The Impression of the Transactions has been[2] [page 2] Suspended since the Death of my Predecessor on account of some new Regulations, which are making with regard to the Manner of their Publication. This had been hitherto left intirely to the Secretaries, but a Committee is now appointed, consisting of the Council for the time being, who have a power to call in any other Members of the Society occasionally to their assistance, & are to select out of the Papers, which shall be read, such as shall appear most worthy of the public.

[Gives a detailed list of what he considers to be 'the most considerable communications to the Society since I enter'd my Office' from 6 February to 12 March 1752.]

I am, Dear Sir,
The Society's and Your most humble & most obedient Servant
          Tho. Birch
Our Antiquarian Society cannot yet meet with an House to their Satisfaction. Dr Ward of Gresham College is their present Director.
[1]   Birch's promotion to Secretary of the RS.
[2]   MS 'been been'.

557. SGS No 2: From Robert Austin[1] to Maurice Johnson.
London, 23 April 1752.
MB5 fol.100A, 30 April 1752.
Written on blank page of a printed proposal to publish a treatise on cases in surgery and physic.

Discusses a proposal by his friend to design a device for a prize gold medal; asks for advice on it from Maurice Johnson and John Green; gives a long description of the proposed design.

1   See his entry in Appendix 2.

558. From William Stukeley to Maurice Johnson.
[London] 24 April 1752.
MB5 fol.100A, 30 April 1752.
Discusses SA affairs; does not want the SA to get a charter which he thinks will be 'a mean imitation of the Royal Society' and will be 'prejudicial to learning in general, by dividing the stream'; summarises his 24-page memoir on the history of the SA, where he is no longer an active member, since it meets on the same evening as the RS which he prefers to attend; explains that he is publishing his findings on 'ORIVNA'[1] whom he takes to be the wife of Carausius; his chief interest is the state of Christianity in Britain at the time; gives RS news and news of old friends; plans to visit Johnson in the summer; includes a very detailed drawing of a coin of Carausius and 'Oriuna'.

1   For previous correspondence on this topic, see Nos 235, 515 and 531 above. Stukeley's publication is *Palæographia Britannica: or, discourses on antiquities that relate to the history of Britain: Number III. Oriuna wife of Carausius, Emperor of Britain* (London, 1752).

559. From Dr Cornewall Tathwell to Maurice Johnson.
Stamford, 19 September 1752.
MB5 fol.108B, 21 September 1752.
Offers Dallowe's translation of Boerhaave's *Chemistry* as his gift for the SGS library;[1] sends a sketch of an altar put up by Philip Yorke[2] at 'Wrast near Silsoe', Bedfordshire, on the model of a Classical altar seen on Yorke's travels; will send a copy of the Greek inscription on the altar when Stukeley finds his copy of it and sends it to him; has had a letter from Stukeley, who plans a publication on Newton;[3] sends best wishes on Walter Johnson's wedding.

1   Timothy Dallowe, *Elements of Chemistry: being the annual lectures of Herman Boerhaave* (London, 1735). This offer was presumably refused, since the SGS already had, and still has, a translation by Shaw and Chambers, presented by Dr John Green.
2   Philip Yorke, second Earl of Hardwicke (1720–1750), married Jemima, Marchioness Grey (1722–1757) who owned Wrest Park, now an English Heritage property.
3   It was not published in Stukeley's lifetime, but see William Stukeley, *Memoirs of Sir Isaac Newton's Life*, ed. A. Hastings White (London, 1936).

560. From Maurice Johnson (son) to Maurice Johnson.
[No place specified, but probably London], 26 December 1752.
MB5 fol.111B, 28 December 1752.
He has sent a sketch of Mount Vesuvius in eruption, taken from a water-colour sent to his friend [unnamed].
Enclosure, dated Naples 15 May 1752: copy of sketch of the eruption, dated 25 October 1751, and copy of part of the original letter describing the eruption.

1753

561. SGS No 2: From Joseph Pole to 'the President & Secretary and Gentlemen of that Noble and Learned Body ...' [the SGS].
[Between 9 and 15 February] 1753.
MB5 fol.113B, 15 February 1753.
Acknowledges the honour of SGS membership;[1] sends a sample of rhinoceros skin, describes the rhinoceros from which it came; offers to send 'anything worthy'.

[1] MB5 fol.113B records that he was elected to membership on 8 February 1753, and that this letter was read at the SGS meeting on 15 February 1753. See his entry in Appendix 2.

562. SGS No 83: From Dr Cornewall Tathwell to Maurice Johnson.
Stamford, 15 March 1753.
Sent in two parts, on 22 February and 15 March 1753.[1]
MB5 fol.114A, 1 March and 22 March 1753.
Sends an inscription from the Wrest Park altar sent to him by Stukeley;[2] discusses the development of Greek and Phoenician writing and the forms of letters used by various Greek authors, comparing them with other scripts; gives Stukeley's views on the origin of the Wrest Park inscription, which uses the earliest forms of Greek letters and the 'boustrophedon' format.[3]

[1] This long letter occupies eight foolscap sides and is really a dissertation in letter form.
[2] See No 559 above and No 565 below.
[3] This early form of Greek writing was set out 'as the ox ploughs' with alternate lines reading from left to right, then right to left.

563. SGS No 116: From Thomas Birch to Maurice Johnson.
London, 31 March 1753.
MB5 fol.115A, 5 April 1753.
He has read to the RS Johnson's letter about floods at Yarm (Yorks NR), which will be reported in the RS's *Philosophical Transactions* 48; informs him that vol. 47 for 1751–2 is being printed and Birch will send the SGS's copy which contains an account, contributed by the SGS, of a waterspout in Deeping Fen; gives a detailed account of recent RS meetings; explains the planned move by the SA from the Mitre Inn to a house in Chancery Lane.

564. From William Stukeley to Maurice Johnson.
[London], 9 April 1753.
MB5 fol.116A, 19 April 1753.
Gives the news that Parliament has agreed to the setting-up of Sir Hans Sloane's Museum and £10,000 has been paid for 'the Oxford MSS, being 60,000 volumes and as many charters, & to these the Cotton library is to be joined';[1] discusses locations for this collection; gives news of Stukeley's daughter's marriage;[2] explains that the RS has had Johnson's paper on the waterspout which Stukeley suggests is an electrical phenomenon;[3] gives news of SA activities but complains of a general lack of interest in any serious study nowadays; provides news of the RS; asks for any unpublished coins of Carausius that Johnson has.

[1] The Cottonian Library had been damaged by fire in 1731 when housed in Ashburnham House

(see Nos 149 and 156 above); in 1753 it became part of the new collection, together with Sir Hans Sloane's collection, which formed the nucleus of the British Museum.

2   Frances Stukeley, born 1729, married Richard Fleming in 1752.

3   For the Deeping Fen waterspout, see No 563 above. At this period Stukeley was claiming electricity as the cause of many natural phenomena such as earthquakes; see No 524 above. The references to electrical experiments at the RS and elsewhere in letters by SGS correspondents (Nos 243, 474 and 478 above) show the interest in it during the eighteenth century.

565. SGS No 107: From John Ward to Maurice Johnson.
[London], 26 April 1753.
MB5 fol.117A, 3 May 1753.

Thanks Johnson for his letter; discusses Johnson's ideas for re-siting the SA and building a museum for their collections, but explains their impracticability; explains that they have taken a lease of a building in Chancery Lane, London; sends praise from the SA for the SGS; discusses SGS members' comments on the Greek inscription at Wrest Park,[1] but tactfully explains, to save SGS any further 'useless trouble', that the inscription was recently created 'by two or three Gentlemen of wit & learning for the amusement of themselves and friends'.

1   See Nos 559 and 562 above.

LETTERS RECEIVED BY THE SGS
AFTER THE DEATH OF MAURICE JOHNSON

1756

566. SGS No 63, other No 25: From William Stukeley to Dr John Green.
Queen Square [London], 2 October 1756.[1]
MB6 fol.24B, 21 October 1756.

Refers to Green's gold coin of Edward III; has sent back Maurice Johnson's volume on the coins of Carausius; explains that Stukeley's history of Carausius' coins is almost printed;[2] discusses the connection of Roman coin production with religious festivals.

1   This was written after the death of Maurice Johnson who died in January 1755. The SGS was continuing to meet successfully at this stage; its officers, Maurice's sons John and Walter and Revd John Rowning, took a leading part in keeping the Society active. After their deaths, it became a book club in the 1770s.

2   William Stukeley, *The Medallic History of Marcus Aurelius Carausius Emperor in Brittain,* Vol. I, was published in 1757. Vol.II appeared in 1759.

1760

567. From Revd Everard Buckworth[1] to Mrs Buckworth of Pinchbeck.
Rainbow Coffee House, Cornhill, London, 26 June 1760.

Asks her for legal details of an estate he has just sold.

1   See his entry in Appendix 2.

1761

568. Copy of letter from Thomas Hawkes[1] to 'The Gent[n] of the Spalding Society'. Norwich, August 1761.

A copy of this letter was sent to P. Colleson FRS at the Royal Society.

Discusses in detail the observation of the transit of Venus as observed at Norwich in [June] 1761; would like to have a copy of any observations of the transit made at Spalding.

[1]   Hawkes, a tinsmith and scientific instrument maker of Norwich, later moved to Spalding and became a member of the SGS. See his entry in Appendix 2. The SGS's papers contain a sales list of the goods he provided to customers. An orrery of his manufacture, acquired by the SGS at this time, is still in the Society's possession.

569. 6 June 1761

Observation of the Transit of Venus on 6 June 1761 made at Spalding in Lincolnshire [unsigned].

570. From John Grundy junior to Mr Danl. Jones Attorney at Law at Fakenham (Norfolk).

13 November 1782.[1]

Discusses payment of Grundy's claims for fees for harbour schemes in Norfolk.

[1]   This is a 'stray' letter which has somehow been filed with the SGS's early correspondence. John Grundy junior was an SGS corresponding member, though this letter is not addressed to, or intended for the SGS. See his entry in Appendix 2.

UNDATED LETTERS

The following letters are undated and cannot be given a date by reference to the SGS Minute Books or to their contents.

571. From Mr Cooke to Rev. Mr Jno. Britain SGS.[1]

No date or address.

Sends a very lengthy and detailed description of a visit to Durham, the town, cathedral and countryside, its products and the incomes of the Cathedral clergy.

[1]   There is no reference to this letter in the Minute Books. As Revd John Britain became a member of the SGS in 1714 and wrote a letter to Maurice Johnson in 1723 (No 46 above), it is likely that this letter dates from that period, a time when the SGS minutes were not being kept in full.

572. From G[eorge] Lynn.[1]

Note from G. Lynn about a Treatise of Colours enclosed. [Treatise not kept with this letter.]

[1]   See Appendix 2 for both George Lynns; it is not possible to decide which has sent this.

573. From Beaupré Bell to Maurice Johnson.

6 November[1] [no year].

Discusses exchanging coins, asks about Johnson's series of the coins of the Roman Emperors; has sent a catalogue of engravers' marks.

[1] No year is specified and there is no reference to the letter in the minute books. The contents are not related closely enough to any of the other letters to make a precise dating possible, but it is probably from the 1730s when Bell was an active correspondent. Following Bell's request to Maurice Johnson not to read out his informal letters at SGS meetings, as expressed in No 141 above, the letter may have been read privately by Maurice Johnson and so would not be referred to in the Minute Books. The letter must date from before August 1741, when Bell died.

574. Unsigned.
No date.[1]
Postscript of letter addressed to Maurice Johnson. Postmark Durham.
The writer encloses a set of queries from Dr Bedford for Dr Green whom he may already know, if he is the person 'who kept in the chambers with Edwards' at Cambridge. Also sends comments on some coins, and an impression of a coin done in isinglass.[2]

[1] As this is simply the postscript of a letter, no evidence of author or date has survived. There is no reference to it in the Minute Books.
[2] The queries and comments are no longer with the letter.

575. From C. Willes to Mr Jackson.
No date.[1]
He has transcribed as requested 'my Ingenious Friend's second letter' though 'the Fraternity of Ancient Spinsters are not renowned for complyance'.

[1] There is no reference to this in the Minute Books. Jackson was at Spalding in 1743 as 'Usher of the Petit School' and became an SGS member in 1746, moving to a Customs post in Boston in 1747. This letter could date from his residence in Spalding or could have been forwarded by him from Boston to the SGS. It has not proved possible to identify Mr Willes.

576. No signature or date.[1]
Postscript, in Beaupré Bell's hand, asking about 'the Enclosd Arms' [not present]. Note dated Jan. 13 'Mr Ray has just now insisted upon taking his Brothers medal so I have broke the Parcel open & given it to him'.
Annotated by Maurice Johnson: 'Mr B. Ray at the Soc. acknowledged he had read it'.

[1] Revd Benjamin Ray was active in the SGS in the 1730s and early 1740s. The note could have been from this period; the contents are not of the kind to merit mention in the Minute Books.

577. SGS No 10: From Revd Benjamin Ray to Maurice Johnson.
Undated.
Refers to 'the sarcasm upon the women' from the Greek of Xenarchus and a French translation.[1]

[1] As there is no reference to this in the Minute Books, it is not possible to date it more precisely. There are several Classical Greek writers called Xenarchus; the most likely is the comic poet and playwright living in the fourth century BC.

578. SGS No 10: From Revd Benjamin Ray to Maurice Johnson.
Undated.[1]
He has sent a dissertation on one of the subjects [unspecified] on which Johnson has recently given a paper to the SGS.

[1] The only recorded dissertation sent to the SGS by Revd Benjamin Ray is No 135 above, dated 4 February 1731, so this may be a covering letter to accompany it, which has become detached; there may, however, have been other dissertations by him which have not survived.

579. From John Green to Maurice Johnson.

Sunday Evening.

Requests the loan of 'Moufets Theat. Insect.'[1] as his own copy is defective. On reverse, a pencil sketch of a beetle.

[1]   Thomas Moffet (1553–1604), *Insectorum, sive Minimorum animalium Theatrum,* published post-humously by Sir Theodore Mayerne in 1634. See his entry in *ODNB* which suggests 'It has been supposed, on the basis of Moffet's interest in spiders, that his daughter Patience was the 'little Miss Muffet' of the nursery rhyme.' John Green was particularly interested in local Fenland creatures.

1. Coat of arms of the Spalding Gentlemen's Society, designed by Maurice Johnson and engraved by George Vertue in 1746.

2. John Grundy's map of Spalding, 1732.

3. Spalding Market Place, showing the Town Hall where the Society met on occasions during its early years. The Town Hall is the building with the clock and turret. Engraving by Hilkiah Burgess, 1822.

THE High Bridge Formerly
of three Stone Arches. with a View
of the Old Oratory and Society's
Museum &c

4. Sketch of the Society's meeting-rooms from 1727 to 1743, from the margin of John Grundy's map of Spalding, 1732. The Society's Rooms are in the building on the left (with four chimneys).

5. Gayton (Holyrood) House, Spalding, meeting-place of the Society from 1743 to 1755. Painting by Thomas Albin, 1872. The house was demolished in 1959 and the Council Offices erected on the site in 1962.

6. Mr Cox's Rooms, the meeting-place of the Society from 1755 to the 1880s. Mr Cox's Rooms are the white building just to the left of the bridge, behind two horses. Engraving by Hilkiah Burgess, 1827.

7. The Society's meeting-room in Mr Cox's Rooms, from *The Gentlemen's Society at Spalding*, printed by William Pickering, London, 1851.

Re-printed from the " Spalding Free Press," October 24th and 31st, 1911.

The Society's New Home, as photographed on the occasion
of the Opening.

8. The Society's new rooms and museum, opened in 1911.

Dear Sr

6 July 1734 London

Cos Rich. I'm glade to heare you're well arrived in Froggland, From the Oxen-ford, & hope You left all well there, & have brought some Curious things for the Speculation of oⁿ Society of wᶜʰ Sr I heartyly wish You Joy of being admitted a Regular Member. But by the Rules to pay nothing dureing Your residence at yᵉ University nor after unless You shalle choose Spalding for Your place of abode. Having layd so many obligations on that worthy Body & on me their unworthy Secretary by so longs Constant a good Correspondence we could do no less & You came in partly abᵗ the same time to a learned Mahometan Prelet from Africa & a Noble Peer of ye Realme my Lᵈ Visᵗ Falkland an old Frᵈ of Mine. I have, an Oddress from the famous Dʳ Desaguliers F.R.S. that he may have the like Hon. done Ricᵈ: Yousee Sr how if fame of our Social Virtues attract the dis—cerning from all parts of the Universe fo Elloc wᶜʰ is become the Seat of the Muses & Owes much of Its most elegant Collections to Your good Correspondence pray make my Duty Acceptable to oⁿ Mother & believe Me Your most affecᵗᵉ faithfull Tr Mᵗ Johnson Sen

9. Letter from Maurice Johnson in London to his stepbrother Richard Falkner, dated 6 July 1734 (no.227 in this calendar). Falkner, an Oxford undergraduate, had recently returned to Spalding for the vacation.

Charing Cross. March 19th 1741.

I was favored with Yours Honoured Sr. of the 15th and am very much pleased to hear my Grandfather is so much mended, but very sorry to hear my Grandmother continues in so very lingering a state pray God deliver her out of it one way or other, for even Death is much to be preferred to her Condition & more especialy as she is so good a Woman, and so well prepared for another State. I am very glad to hear my Uncle god does so well, I hope he did not keep Cousin Wiloby up too late o'Nights upon the Rode & so mistime him he will tell you the reason why I sent you no Ink Glasses, as to Bumber Glass, now Burnt Ale is out of fashion there are none to be met with, but those you have are very good & fashionable. I have not yet been able to meet with any Orange Trees but if any come between this & the Time of Capt Wilsons being down will send my Mother a couple to whome be pleased to present my Duty. I am very glad to hear sister Harryot will come up to Town with yr Capt who I am sure will take good care of her but fear she is worse of her old Complaint again if so am sure It is absolutely necessary for her to come up, but will say no more of it With my Love to sister Butter as her Secretary pray let her know but must know how much she is willing to go to for you Lady Babe one under 15/. I will execute her Orders, & please likewise to let sister Green know her Chairs will be very soone done & her Necklace by Saturday but was forced to buy her 2 Rows of Perls for the love knots were worn & quite out of fashion I desire she will let me know her Orders about ye Dish she mentioned for I have either lost or mislaid her Letter which is full as bad I am Sr. with Duty where Due your Obedt Son M. Johnson

10. Letter from Maurice Johnson (son) in London to his father Maurice Johnson in Spalding with his sketches of the new music room at Ranelagh, dated from Charing Cross, 19 March 1741/2 (no.390 in this calendar).

The MUSICK Amphitheatre at the Earle of Ranelaghs ᵃᵗ Chelsey It is I believe at least twenty yards high & will hold 2,000 men.

ᵉᶜted in 1741.

'tis slated with slate from Plymouth which looks Blew & shines — much

LG1
Nᵒ 123

ever countᵉ
number
Arches or
llers so —
ᵘ must not
ᵒin this to
ᵒrect for
ᵃs not mor
3 or 2
ᵘᵃker about it as Mʳ Brand will tell you who was with ᵐᵉ

of this part is not finished but I apprehend there is to be an arch between each of these pillars

believe there are elve Arches between ᵗ of the grand Entrance

Gallerys for people to walk in ?
Veranda above ?
Twelve Boxes in ?
each below & above

the Garden is very small, and will never come up to fox Hall, By reason of the narrowness and shortniſs of the Walkes

A large Circumference for People to walk in ?

The Orchistra

2

2

3

3

4

4

APPENDIX 1
LIST OF CORRESPONDENTS
in alphabetical order

The number in square brackets immediately following the name of a correspondent is the number of letters in the SGS archive written by that correspondent. The numbers in bold type indicate the number given to that particular letter in the calendar, followed by the date of the letter, in brackets. All letters are addressed to Maurice Johnson, unless another recipient is named for a specific letter.

Revd Samuel Addenbrooke [1]: **17** (1716) to Maurice Johnson senior
Joseph Ames [3]: **200** (1733); **411** (1743); **433** (1744)
John Anstis [1]: **359** (1740)
George Ault [1]: **71** (1725)
Robert Austin [1]: **557** (1752)
Sir Joseph Ayloffe [1]: **392** (1742)
Revd William Beecroft [1]: **431** (1744) to Revd Stephen Lyon
Beaupré Bell [37]: **70** (1725); **81** (1726); **104** (1729); **120** (1730); **133** (1731);**138** (1731); **141** (1731); **142** (1731); **143** (1731); **144** (1731); **150** (1731); **152** (1732); **160** (1732); **165** (1732); **167** (1732); **168** (1732); **172** (1732); **178** (1733); **187** (1733); **191** (1733); **197** (1733); **206** (1734); **209** (1734); **213** (1734); **230** (1734); **233** (1734); **236** (1734); **238** (1735); **254** (1735); **255** (1735); **267** (1736); **274** (1736); **279** (1736); **285** (1736); **286** (1736) to William Bogdani; **289** (1737); **573** (undated)
Peregrine Bertie [1]: **384** (1741)
Weaver Bickerton [1]: **117** (1730)
Andreas Bing [1]: **398** (1742) to Richard Norcliffe
Thomas Birch [5]: **428** (1744); **435** (1744); **440** (1744); **556** (1752); **563** (1753)
Thomas Blix [1]: **324** (1739)
William Bogdani [39]: **79** (1726); **80** (1726); **82** (1726); **83** (1726); **89** (1728); **93** (1728); **146** (1731); **147** (1731); **149** (1731); **158** (1732); **174** (1732); **177** (1732); **184** (1733); **186** (1733); **195** (1733); **203** (1734); **204** (1734); **208** (1734); **216** (1734); **243** (1735); **246** (1735); **249** (1735) to Richard Falkner; **251** (1735); **253** (1735); **261** (1735); **271** (1736); **276** (1736); **281** (1736); **287** (1736); **288** (1737) to Maurice Johnson (son); **302** (1737); **318** (1739); **325** (1739); **327** (1739); **338** (1739); **340** (1739); **342** (1739); **346** (1739); **365** (1740)
William Bowyer [1]: **427** (1744)
William Brand [1]: **270** (1736)
Revd John Britain [1]: **46** (1723)
Revd Zachariah Brooke [1]: **461** (1746)
Revd Everard Buckworth [1]: **567** (1760)
Charles Bush [1]: **512** (1749)
Robert Butter [1]: **495** (1747)

Edmund Chapman [1]: **543** (1751)
William Clarke, for Dr Wotton [1]: **65** (1725)
Revd Benjamin Clements [1]: **77** (1726) to the parishioners of Long Sutton
Sir John Clerk [4]: **336** (1739) copy of letter to Roger Gale; **385** (1742); **388** (1742); **486** (1747)
Dr Dixon Colby [1]: **404** (1742)
Benjamin Cook [2]: **481** (1747); **482** (1747)
Mr Cooke [1]: **571** (no date)
Revd Francis Curtis [4]: **4** (1712); **6** (1713); **7** (1713); **9** (1713)
William Dodd [1]: **537** (1750)
Francis Drake [1]: **396** (1742) to Revd Thomas Drake
Nathan Drake [1]: **548** (1751)
William Draper [2]: **430** (1744); **436** (1744)
Sir Richard Ellys [2]: **127** (1730); **323** (1739)
Sir John Evelyn [3]: **275** (1736); **282** (1736); **523** (1750)
Christopher Fairchild [1]: **179** (1733) to Captain Francis Pilliod
Richard Falkner [22]: **185** (1733); **189** (1733); **190** (1733); **194** (1733); **196** (1733); **198** (1733); **202** (1733); **205** (1734) to Mrs Elizabeth Johnson; **207** (1734); **211** (1734); **214** (1734); **217** (1734) to Mrs Ann Johnson; **220** (1734); **221** (1734); **223** (1734); **237** (1734); **242** (1735) to John Johnson; **245** (1735); **266** (1736); **268** (1736); **269** (1736); **283** (1736)
Revd George Ferne [2]: **429** (1744); **447** (1745)
Robert Flower [1]: **328** (1739) to Mr Everard
Martin Folkes [1]: **423** (1743)
Revd John Francis [1]: **368** (1741)
Charles Frederick [1]: **511** (1749)
Roger Gale [30] : **43** (1722); **50** (1723); **51** (1723); **69** (1725); **73** (1726); **92** (1728); **125** (1730); **126** (1730); **134** (1731); **136** (1731); **166** (1732); **241** (1735); **248** (1735); **258** (1735); **259** (1735); **292** (1737); **295** (1737); **315** (1738); **334** (1739); **344** (1739); **350** (1740); **352** (1740); **358** (1740); **374** (1741); **383** (1741); **387** (1742); **399** (1742); **413** (1743); **418** (1743); **432** (1744)
Thomas Gerard [1]: **38** (1721)
Revd Barnaby Goche [1]: **109** (1720s)
William Gonville [1]: **63** (1725)
Alexander Gordon [4]: **296** (1737); **297** (1737); **298** (1737); **310** (1738)
Charles Green [1]: **13** (1715)
Dr Edward Green [2]: **3** (1712); **32** (1718) to Mrs Johnson senior
Jane Green [1]: **437** (1744)
Dr John Green [7]: **115** (1730); **116** (1730); **153** (1732) to Captain Francis Pilliod; **155** (1732); **163** (1732); **176** (1732); **579** (undated)
John Grundy senior [3]: **265** (1735); **272** (1736); **317** (1739) to the Deeping Drainers
John Grundy junior [4]: **354** (1740); **378** (1741); **382** (1741); **570** (1782) to Daniel Jones
Sir Christopher Hales [1]: **305** (1738)
William Hancock [1]: **264** (1735)
Revd William Hannes [1]: **60** (1724)
Edward Harley, Earl of Oxford [1]: **95** (1729)

John Harries [2]: **105** (1729) to Revd Timothy Neve; **154** (1732) to Revd Timothy Neve

Thomas Hawkes [1]: **568** (1761)

Dr Musgrave Heighington [4] : **309** (1738) to Robert Butter; **313** (1738); **331** (1739); **417** (1743)

John Hepburn [1]: **394** (1742) to Mr Cox

John Hill [4]: **459** (1746); **462** (1746) to Dr John Green; **485** (1747); **509** (1749)

Thomas Howgrave [1]: **41** (1723) to the Revd Dr Thomas Sharp

Major-General Robert Hunter [2]: **87** (1727); **119** (1730)

Dr Samuel Hutchinson [1]: **464** (1746)

Dale Ingram [2]: **544** (1751); **553** (1751)

Calamy Ives [1]: **503** (1748)

William Jackson [3]: **490** (1747); **491** (1747); **493** (1747)

Charles Jennens [1]: **500** (1748)

Ann Johnson [1]: **193** (1733) to Richard Falkner

George Johnson [6]: **529** (1750); **539** (1751); **545** (1751); **549** (1751); **551** (1751); **554** (1751)

Henry Johnson [4]: **108** (1729); **180** (1733); **353** (1740); **377** (1741)

Henry Eustace Johnson [1]: **533** (1750) to Mrs Elizabeth Johnson

John Johnson (brother) [3]: **8** (1713); **72** (1726) to Robert Vyner; **371** (1741)

John Johnson (son) [4]: **410** (1743); **439** (1744); **451** (1745); **458** (1746)

Maurice Johnson [75]: **2** (1712) to Edward Green; **5** (1713) to Revd Francis Curtis; **10** (1714) to William Stukeley; **12** (1714) to William Stukeley; **15** (1715) to Richard Middleton Massey; **16** (1715) to Richard Middleton Massey; **18** (1716) to Revd Samuel Addenbrooke; **19** (1716) to Mr Jarvis; **22** (1716) to William Stukeley; **23** (1716) to William Stukeley; **29** (1718) to William Stukeley; **49** (1723) to 'My Couzen'; **53** (1724) to Sigismund Trafford; **55** (1724) to Sigismund Trafford; **56** (1724) to Mrs Elizabeth Johnson; **58** (1724) to Sir Isaac Newton; **59** (1724) to Dr James Jurin; **67** (1725) to the SGS; **68** (1725) to Mrs Elizabeth Johnson; **75** (1726) to Revd William Clarke; **76** (1726) to the SGS; **86** (1727) to Mrs Elizabeth Johnson; **88** (1728) to William Bogdani; **98** (1729) to Lord Coleraine; **100** (1729) to Dr John Green; **106** (1729) to John Johnson; **110** (1730) to the Academia Etrusca; **111** (1730) to Johan Kouwenhove; **123** (1730) to Revd Mr Whiting; **131** (1730) to John Johnson; **132** (1730) to John Johnson; **137** (1731) to the SGS; **156** (1732) to Richard Falkner; **161** (1732) to the Duke of Buccleuch; **162** (1732) to Revd Mr Marshall; **173** (1732) part of letter to Mrs Elizabeth Johnson; **175** (1732) to Maurice Johnson (son); **183** (1733) to Revd Edward Saul; **192** (1733) to Richard Falkner; **199** (1733) to Maurice Johnson (son); **201** (1733) to the SGS; **212** (1734) to Richard Falkner; **215** (1734) to the SGS; **218** (1734) to Richard Falkner; **224** (1734) to Maurice Johnson (son); **225** (1734) to Maurice Johnson (son); **226** (1734) to Maurice Johnson (son); **227** (1734) to Richard Falkner; **235** (1734) to Dr Patrick Kennedy; **244** (1735) to Richard Falkner; **284** (1736) to John Johnson; **299** (1737) to Joseph Smith; **308** (1738) to the Duke of Buccleuch; **312** (1738) to the Duke of Buccleuch; **314** (1738) to Mrs Elizabeth Johnson for the SGS; **316** (1738) to John Johnson; **330** (1739) to Musgrave Heighington; **333** (1739) to the Duke of Buccleuch; **337** (1739) to Richard Bentley; **347** (1740) to Mrs Elizabeth Johnson; **348** (1740) to Dr John Green for the SGS; **349** (1740) to Dr John Green for the SGS; **363** (1740) to John Johnson; **364** (1740) to Dr John Green for the SGS; **406** (1742) to Dr John Green for the SGS; **422** (1743) to Henry Eustace Johnson; **439** (1744) to Mrs Elizabeth Johnson; **442** (1744) to Dr John Green for the SGS; **443** (1745) to George Holmes; **445** (1745) to Martin Folkes; **508** (1749) to the Duke of Montagu; **513** (1749) to Dr Walker; **516** (1750) to Alexander Wilson; **519** (1750) to Alexander Wilson; **522** (1750) to Dr John Green

Maurice Johnson (son) [20]: **210** (1734); **219** (1734) to Richard Falkner; **239** (1735); **240** (1735) to Richard Falkner; **257** (1735); **260** (1735); **307** (1738); **351** (1740); **361** (1740); **390** (1742); **400** (1742); **407** (1742); **419** (1743) to John Johnson; **424** (1743); **446** (1745); **455** (1746); **476** (1747); **502** (1748); **528** (1750); **560** (1752)

Walter Johnson [1]: **555** (1751)

William Johnson [1]: **326** (1739) to Henry Johnson

Dr James Jurin [4]: **59** (1724); **64** (1725); **393** (1742); **499** (1748)

Dr Patrick Kennedy [1]: **234** (1734)

Revd Manwaring Laughton [1]: **444** (1745)

Cornelius Little [2]: **250** (1735); **355** (1740)

Charles Littlebury [1]: **231** (1734) to John Johnson

George Lynn senior [5]: **182** (1733); **247** (1735); **252** (1735); **278** (1736); **572** (undated)

George Lynn junior [5]: **84** (1727); **103** (1729); **124** (1730); **290** (1737) to William Bogdani; **389** (1742)

Revd John Lynn [1]: **263** (1735)

Dr Walter Lynn [4]: **39** (1721); **416** (1743) to William Stukeley; **471** (1746); **475** (1747)

Dr Thomas Manningham [1]: **319** (1739)

Revd Thomas Marshall [2]: **157** (1732); **159** (1732)

John Mason [1]: **1** (1710) to Mr Henley

Dr Richard Middleton Massey [1]: **45** (1723)

Samuel Massey [1]: **171** (1732)

Emanuel Mendes da Costa [4]: **470** (1746) to the SGS; **474** (1746) to the SGS; **504** (1748); **530** (1750)

Dr John Mitchell [1]: **222** (1734)

Dr Robert Mitchell [1]: **527** (1750)

Dr Cromwell Mortimer [9]: **256** (1735) to William Bogdani; **293** (1737); **303** (1738); **304** (1738) to Dr John Green; **320** (1739); **321** (1739); **322** (1739); **339** (1739) to Dr John Green; **415** (1743)

John Muller [1]: **262** (1735)

James Muscat [1]: **525** (1750)

Revd Timothy Neve senior [30]: **25** (1717); **27** (1718); **28** (1718); **33** (1718); **48** (1723); **54** (1724); **66** (1725); **78** (1726); **91** (1728); **102** (1729); **112** (1730); **114** (1730); **118** (1730); **121** (1730); **129** (1730); **130** (1730); **151** (1731); **306** (1738); **329** (1739); **335** (1739); **341** (1739); **343** (1739); **360** (1740); **391** (1742); **395** (1742); **403** (1742); **408** (1743); **414** (1743) to Revd Mr Whiting; **492** (1747); **532** (1750)

Timothy Neve junior [4]: **457** (1746); **463** (1746); **484** (1747); **534** (1750)

Robert New [2]: **521** (1750); **542** (1751)

Richard Norcliffe [5]: **164** (1732); **228** (1734); **229** (1734); **397** (1742); **401** (1742)

Revd George North [6]: **434** (1744); **438** (1744); **441** (1744); **448** (1745); **452** (1745); **497** (1747)
Anthony Oldfield [5]: **473** (1746); **487** (1747); **489** (1747); **506** (1749); **507** (1749)
Revd Edward Owen [1]: **540** (1751)
Dr James Parsons [2]: **480** (1747); **483** (1747)
Revd Francis Peck [3]: **36** (1720); **44** (1722); **47** (1723)
Revd Samuel Pegge [5]: **357** (1740) to Revd Benjamin Ray; **379** (1741) to Revd Benjamin Ray; **409** (1743) to Revd Benjamin Ray; **535** (1750); **536** (1750)
Joseph Pole [1]: **561** (1753) to the SGS
Revd Morgan Powell [1]: **478** (1747) to Revd John Johnson
Revd Benjamin Ray [6]: **135** (1731); **420** (1743); **517** (1750); **577** (undated); **577** (undated); **578** (undated)
J. Richards [1]: **40** (1721)
Revd Matthew Robinson [1]: **294** (1737)
Revd J. Romley [1]: **467** (1746)
John Rowell [1]: **232** (1734)
James Rowland [1]: **122** (1730)
John Russell, Duke of Bedford and others [1]: **405** (1742)
Revd Dr Thomas Rutherforth [5]: **376** (1741); **386** (1742); **402** (1742); **496** (1747); **498** (1748)
Revd Edward Saul [1]: **181** (1733)
Thomas Savage [1]: **454** (1746) to Richard Partridge
Francis Scott, Duke of Buccleuch [1]: **311** (1738)
Revd Dr Thomas Sharp [2]: **505** (1748) to Thomas Lloid; **541** (1751)
George Shelvocke [2]: **453** (1745); **538** (1750)
Abel Smith junior [1]: **552** (1751)
Joseph Smith [3]: **300** (1737); **301** (1737); **332** (1739)
Revd Robert Smyth [5]: **356** (1746) to the Revd Timothy Neve; **465** (1746); **466** (1746); **468** (1746); **550** (1751)
Matthew Snow [2]: **61** (1724); **62** (1725)
Revd Joseph Sparke [2]: **24** (1717); **34** (1719)
William Stukeley [33]: **11** (1714); **14** (1715); **20** (1716); **26** (1717); **30** (1718); **31** (1718); **35** (1719); **37** (1720); **57** (1724); **97** (1729); **99** (1729); **128** (1730); **145** (1731) to Revd Gregory Henson; **421** (1743); **425** (1744); **426** (1744); **456** (1746); **460** (1746); **472** (1746); **477** (1747); **479** (1747); **494** (1747); **501** (1748); **514** (1749); **515** (1750); **520** (1750); **524** (1750); **526** (1750); **531** (1750); **547** (1751); **558** (1752); **564** (1753); **566** (1756) to Dr John Green
John Swynfen [1]: **412** (1743)
Thomas Sympson [6]: **345** (1739); **366** (1740); **372** (1741); **373** (1741); **380** (1741); **381** (1741)
Dr Cornewall Tathwell [3]: **546** (1751); **559** (1752); **562** (1753)
Revd John Taylor [Kirkstead] [1]: **21** (1716) to Revd John Hardy
Revd John Taylor [Cambridge] [1]: **370** (1741) to Edward Harley, Earl of Oxford
Edward Tebb [1]: **188** (1733)
George Tookie [1]: **375** (1741) to Michael Cox
Captain John Topham [2]: **169** (1732); **170** (1732)
Sigismund Trafford [1]: **52** (1724)

Robert Vyner [1]: **74** (1726) to John Johnson
George Wallis [1]: **291** (1737) to William Dilamore
Edward Walpole [2]: **273** (1736); **280** (1736)
John Ward [3]: **469** (1746); **488** (1747); **565** (1753)
James Weeks [1]: **510** (1749)
Revd Samuel Wesley senior [2]: **96** (1729); **140** (1731)
Revd Samuel Wesley junior [1]: **94** (1729)
Revd Robert Whatley [2]: **148** (1731); **277** (1736)
Revd Samuel Whiting [3]: **101** (1729); **113** (1730); **139** (1731)
C. Willes [1]: **575** (undated)
Revd Dr Philip Williams [1]: **369** (1741)
Browne Willis [5]: **42** (1722); **90** (1728); **367** (1741); **449** (1745); **450** (1745)
Alexander Wilson [1]: **518** (1750)
E. Wingfield [1]: **85** (1727)
Mr Wise [1]: **362** (1740)
Unsigned [1]: **107** (1729) to Lord Hertford, copied by Maurice Johnson
Unknown authors [2]: **575** (undated); **577** (undated)

APPENDIX 2
BRIEF BIOGRAPHIES OF CORRESPONDENTS
who were members of
the Spalding Gentlemen's Society

Spelling of the names has been taken, as far as possible, from an original holograph signature on a letter from the person concerned.

The comment in inverted commas which forms part of some entries is Maurice Johnson's original description of that member, found in the papers of the Spalding Gentlemen's Society, and occasionally in the Grand Catalogue in which members were recorded. The term 'beneficient member' included in some entries is Maurice Johnson's, and was given to those SGS members who made a particular contribution to the Society, either by regular correspondence or by notable gifts of books or specimens for the Society's museum and collections.

ODNB at the end of an entry means that that member has an individual entry in the *Oxford Dictionary of National Biography* (2004). The better-known members are also mentioned in the group article on the *Spalding Gentlemen's Society* in the *ODNB*.

Ames, Joseph: (1689–1759) 'Secretary to the ASL [Antiquarian Society of London] 1741'; SGS member 1740; FRS 1743; London merchant and antiquarian collector, author of a significant book on the history of printing, *Typographical Antiquities, being an historical account of printing in England ... 1471–1600* 1749. *ODNB*.

Anstis, John: (1669–1744) 'Garter King of Arms', educated Exeter College, Oxford, 1685 and the Middle Temple, 1688; wealthy herald and antiquarian, MP for Cornish boroughs, assisted Walpole in the re-creation of the Order of the Bath; SGS member 1741. His son John Anstis junior (1708–1754) was also Garter King of Arms. *ODNB*.

Austin, Robert: (fl.1740s–1750s) of Vineyard, Peterborough; High Bailiff of Peterborough, PGS member 1738, SGS member by 1741; visited the SGS in 1745; antiquarian and clerk to the Commissioners of Navigation on the Nene.

Ayloffe, Sir Joseph: (1710–1781) 6th Baronet, London; educated Westminster School, St John's College, Oxford, 1726 and Lincoln's Inn; SGS member 1738, 'beneficient member'; FRS 1731, Vice-President; FSA 1732, Vice-President; antiquarian, Secretary to the Commission for Westminster Bridge 1731, Commissioner in the State Paper Office. *ODNB*.

Bell, Beaupré: (1704–1741) of Beaupré Hall, Outwell (Norfolk); educated Westminster School and Trinity College, Cambridge, to which he left his papers; SGS member 1726, 'beneficient member'; FSA 1725, PGS member 1731; second cousin to Maurice Johnson through his mother Margaret Oldfield; numismatist and antiquary, particularly interested in churches and Roman coins on which he was an expert. *ODNB*.

Bertie, Peregrine: (c.1688/9–1743) of Low Leyton (Essex), also had an estate near Ambleside; educated Charterhouse and Christ's College, Cambridge, entered 1704, and the Middle Temple 1705; FSA 1719; SGS member 1722, 'beneficient member'; barrister and antiquarian.

Bing, Revd Andreas: (fl.1730s–1740s) Norwegian Lutheran clergyman in Frederickshald, southern Norway, friend of Richard Norcliffe (q.v.); SGS member 1742 following Norcliffe's recommendation; had been one of the first Norwegian missionaries to the Inuit of Greenland, working for several years as part of Revd Hans Egede's team and based in Christianshaab, Disko Bay, where Bing's Cave is still known; while there, made astronomical observations, later communicated to the SGS. MB I fol.242 states 'The Reverend and Learned Mr Andrew Byng of Frederickshald in Norway Curate of the Church there STP Sometime Missionary in Greenland a Learned Divine Astronomer & Mathematician'.

Birch, Revd Dr Thomas: (1705–1760) of Clerkenwell, London; educated at a Quaker school in London. SGS member 1743; FRS 1735 Secretary of the RS 1752–65, FSA 1735, Director of the SA 1737–47; Trustee of the British Museum; editor and secretary, edited the English translation of Pierre Bayle's *Dictionary*; his patron was Lord Chancellor Hardwicke. *ODNB*.

Bogdani, William: (1699/1700–1771) Tower of London, 'one of the Clerks to the Ordnance'; Lord of the Manor of Hitchin (Herts); his wife Penelope (previously Bowell) was said to be a relation of Maurice Johnson; SGS member 1724, 'beneficient member' and visited the SGS in 1735; FRS 1730, FSA 1726; interested in mathematics and music; son of the London-based Hungarian Protestant artist Jacob Bogdani (1658–1724), referred to in Jacob Bogdani's *ODNB* entry. William Bogdani's son William Maurice Bogdani of Kings College, Cambridge, visited the SGS on 5 October 1752 and became a member in 1753.

Bowyer, William: (1699–1777) of London; educated Hadley (Surrey) and St John's College, Cambridge 1716–21; FSA 1736, Stationers' Company 1738; SGS member 1743; printer and editor; society printer to the SA 1736 and to the RS 1761; Printer of Votes for the House of Commons 1729–1777; printer to the Society for the Encouragement of Learning; his best-known apprentice, John Nichols, called him 'the most learned Printer of the eighteenth century'. *ODNB*.

Brand, William: (fl.1730s–1740s) SGS member 1746; steward to the Duke of Northumberland's estate at Cheveley Park, near Newmarket; he wrote from the Percys' London home Northumberland House and visited Newcastle.

Britain, Revd John: (c.1675–1723) born Sleaford, educated Oakham School and Christ's College, Cambridge, entered 1691; ordained deacon 1699 and priest 1700; Master of the Free School, Holbeach and perpetual curate of Gedney Fen; SGS member 1714, 'beneficient member'.

Brooke, Revd Dr Zachariah: (1716–1788) educated Stamford School and St John's College, Cambridge; Fellow 1739–1765, Lady Margaret Professor of Divinity, Cambridge 1765, Royal Chaplain; published *Defensio Miraculorum* 1748; SGS member 1746. *ODNB*.

Buckworth, Revd Everard: (1729–1792) lawyer and cleric; he was the son of Everard Buckworth of Spalding (SGS 1721) who had attended Eton just before Maurice Johnson. Educated Trinity Hall, Cambridge 1747 and Lincoln's Inn, entered 1747; Rector of Washingborough; Prebendary of Lincoln 1773 and of Canterbury 1775; SGS member 1753, SGS Secretary in 1756.

Butter, Robert: (fl.1730s–1740s) Spalding merchant and coastal surveyor, married Maurice Johnson's daughter Elizabeth, nicknamed by the Johnson family 'Madcap Bet'; SGS member 1730; interested in music (helped to organise SGS Anniversary concerts and played the bassoon there) and numismatics.

Chapman, Edmund: (fl.1740s–1750s), surgeon and teacher of music; Master of Music at Grimsthorpe Castle 1750; SGS member 1751. (Perhaps the son of Edmund Chapman, surgeon and man-midwife, developer of obstetric forceps, died 1738.) Visited SGS 31 August 1749 when resident at Grimsthorpe.

Clarke, Dr William: (1696–1771) born Shropshire, educated Shrewsbury School and St John's College, Cambridge; BA 1716, Fellow 1717–1725, MA 1719; SGS member 1718; rector of Buxted (Sussex) 1729–1768; prebendary of Chichester 1729, Canon Librarian of Chichester 1739; antiquarian and numismatist, assistant to his father-in-law Revd William Wotton (*ODNB*) in his linguistic and antiquarian research; an early enthusiast for sea-bathing at Brighton. *ODNB*.

Clerk, Sir John of Penicuik: (1676–1755) 2nd Baronet; Penicuik, Scotland; educated Penicuik Parish School, Glasgow University, Leiden University (law); Commissioner for the Treaty of Union between England and Scotland, 1707; Baron of the Court of Exchequer 1708; FSA 1725, FRS 1729; SGS member 1740, introduced by Roger Gale; coalmine owner, antiquary, advocate, musician. *ODNB*.

Colby, Dr Dixon: (1680–1756) born Kirton (Lincs); educated Merton College, Oxford 1696, BA 1700, MA 1703, BD and DD 1710; MD, Physician at Stamford; SGS member 1733; keen gardener and plant grower, interested in new varieties of imported plants.

Cook, Benjamin: (fl.1740s) Spalding; 'Register' (legal clerk) and personal assistant to Maurice Johnson; assistant to the Secretaries of the SGS; SGS member 1746.

Curtis, Revd Francis: (d.1717), educated Eton College and King's College, Cambridge 1700, Fellow 1703; assistant master at Eton, ordained priest 1709; Headmaster of Moulton Grammar School 1711–1717; early member of SGS, admitted 1714, one of the first corresponding members: MB1 fol.48A states: 'Admission of Extra regular members the Revd Mr Francis Curtis of Moulton 8 April 1714'. MB1 f.49 states 'Extra regular admission ... Revdus & Doctiss. Vir Franc s Curtis Admissus p. Soc. 8o Aprilis 1714'. Presented a folio Livy and a quarto Juvenal to the SGS; recorded as 'dead 1717' in list of members for 1720. Close friend of Maurice Johnson, often corresponded in Latin.

Dodd, Revd Dr William: (1729–1777), born Bourne (Lincs), educated Clare College, Cambridge, ordained priest 1753, LL.D 1766, one of the King's chaplains; theological author, charity promoter and fashionable preacher, popularly known as the 'macaroni parson'; visited the SGS 1750; SGS member 1751; published a translation of the poems of Callimachus 1755; condemned for forging a signature on a credit bill for £4,200 and was not pardoned despite the efforts of several thousand petitioners including Dr Samuel Johnson. *ODNB*.

Drake, Francis: (c.1696–1771) of York; apprenticed to a York surgeon and became City Surgeon of York; FSA 1735, PGS member 1735, FRS 1736; SGS member 1747; antiquary and author, publishing the history of York, *Eboracum* 1736. *ODNB*.

Drake, Nathan: (1726–1778) Born and educated at Lincoln, distant relative of Francis Drake (above); FSA 1743; SGS 1751; Fellow of the Society of Artists 1771; painter, specialising in landscapes. *ODNB*.

Draper, William: (fl.1730s–1740s) Cecil Street, London; [this may be William Draper of St John's College, Cambridge 1726, aged 17] antiquarian; FSA 1733; SGS 1743; visited the Society 1740; he donated the new 1743 edition of Bishop Tanner's *Notitia Monastica* to the SGS library.

Ellys, Sir Richard: (1682–1742) 3rd Baronet; of Nocton (Lincs) and Bolton Street, London, possibly also Place House, Ealing; SGS member 1730, 'beneficient member'; MP for Grantham, and later for Boston; book collector with extensive libraries at both of his houses; Calvinist, patron of the nonconformist chapel in Princes Street, London and biblical scholar, wrote *Fortuita Sacra* 1727, a study of disputed New Testament texts; patron of authors, notably John Horsley, William Stukeley, Edward Walpole and Thomas Boston. *ODNB*.

Evelyn, Sir John: (1681/2–1763) born Dartford (Kent); Balliol College, Oxford 1699; MP for Helston, Cornwall 1708–1710; 1st Baronet 1713; grandson and eventual heir of the diarist John Evelyn of Wooton (Surrey); FRS 1723, FSA 1725, SA Vice-President 1735–6; SGS member 1733; Tory Post-master General, Commissioner of Customs; letter writer, diarist, antiquarian and bibliophile, very extensive subscriber to books.

Falkner, Richard: (c.1715–1737) Oxford University medical student; born Boston, son and youngest child of Thomas Falkner and his wife Ann, who later married Maurice Johnson senior (the father of Maurice Johnson the SGS Secretary) as his third wife; moved to Spalding on his mother's re-marriage, which made him stepbrother of Maurice Johnson the Secretary though he was of the same generation as the Secretary's children. See genealogy in Appendix 5. Educated at Spalding Grammar School and Lincoln College Oxford, studying to become a doctor; SGS member 1734, assisted the SGS by helping to catalogue the library, building an air pump in 1735 and sending frequent letters from Oxford. The SGS's Loan Book records that he borrowed Chambers' Dictionary on 16 May 1737 but that by 6 June 1737 it was 'Returned after Mr Falkner's death per MJ'.

Ferne, Revd George: (c.1712–1790) educated Ely School and St John's College, Cambridge 1728; ordained priest 1735; SGS member 1739; usher at Peterborough School, then Vicar of Burgh and Winthorpe, later Vicar of Wigtoft and Quadring; Chaplain to the Earl of Kilmarnock; gave the SGS Robinson's edition of the works of Hesiod; visited the SGS in 1750 when living in Gosberton as Vicar of Wigtoft and Quadring.

Folkes, Martin: (1690–1754) educated privately and at Clare College Cambridge, entered 1706; inherited his father's extensive estate; FRS 1713, Vice-President 1723, President 1741; FSA 1720, President 1750, obtained a Royal Charter for the FSA; member of the Egyptian Society 1741; SGS member 1743, 'beneficient member'; Freemason, Deputy Grand Master 1725; foreign Fellow of the Académie Royale des Sciences; LL.D Oxford and Cambridge 1746; antiquarian, numismatist and mathematician, published on coins. *ODNB*.

Francis, Revd John: (?c.1695–1749) born North Elmham (Norfolk), educated at Walsingham and Caius College Cambridge, entered 1711; ordained priest

1719; Rector of Billingford and Brisley (Norfolk); SGS member 1741, sent to the SGS a burial urn excavated in his neighbourhood, near North Elmham.

Frederick, Sir Charles: (1709–1785) London, Berkeley Square; educated Westminster School, New College, Oxford, entered 1725, and the Middle Temple, entered 1728; FSA 1731, Director 1736 and 1740; FRS 1733; SGS member 1751; MP for Shoreham 1741–54 and for Queenborough 1754–84; Surveyor General of the Ordnance, active member of the Honourable Board of Ordnance for 36 years from 1746 under the patronage of the Duke of Montague, Master General of the Ordnance; responsible for the 1749 Royal Fireworks and for small arms during the Seven Years' War; an eminent antiquarian. *ODNB*.

Gale, Roger: (1672–1744) of Scruton (Yorks NR); educated St Paul's School, London and Trinity College, Cambridge, entered 1691, Fellow 1697; FRS 1717, Treasurer; FSA 1717, Vice-President; SGS member 1728; MP for Northallerton 1705–1713; civil servant, commissioner for stamp duties 1714, commissioner for excise 1715–1735; retired to his Scruton estate on losing his post under Walpole's reorganisation of Civil Service posts; antiquary and numismatist; brother of Samuel Gale, antiquarian (1682–1754), who was also an SGS member in 1733 and who sent at least one dissertation to the SGS; correspondence of the Gale brothers was published in *Bibliotheca Britannica Topographica* ii iii Reliquiæ Galeanæ, ed. John Nichols, 1782; brother-in-law of Revd Dr William Stukeley (q.v.); *ODNB*.

Goche, Revd Barnaby: (?1677–1730) born Bedfordshire, educated at Biggleswade and Peterhouse, Cambridge, entered 1693; ordained deacon 1698; Rector of Crowland and Chaplain of Cowbit; SGS member 1723.

Gonville, William: (d.1747) of Alford (Lincs); SGS 1727; drainage lawyer and Clerk to the Court of Sewers of Lincoln; a possible family connection of Maurice Johnson's through the marriage of Johnson's father, as his third wife, to Ann Falkner whose first husband had been a Mr Gonville.

Gordon, Alexander: (?1692–1754) born probably Aberdeen, educated Aberdeen University; his patron was Sir John Clerk; FSA 1725, Secretary 1735–1741; Secretary of the Society for the Encouragement of Learning 1736; Secretary of the Egyptian Society 1730s; SGS member 1737; member of the Society of Roman Knights; antiquarian, interested in Roman antiquities in Scotland and Egyptian antiquities, attempted to decipher Egyptian hieroglyphs; famous as a singer and musician, nicknamed 'Singing Sandy', who performed in Italy and Britain; Secretary to the Governor of Carolina, America, from 1741. *ODNB*.

Green, Dr Edward: (1665–1728) originally from Spalding; 'of Newgate London Surgeon of St Bartholemew & Xst Church Hospital Master of that ancient company'; educated Winchester School; the archivist of the Royal College of Surgeons confirms that he was the Master of the Worshipful Company of Barber-Surgeons in 1711; a significant subscriber to books.

Green, Dr John: (1708–1756) born at Spalding, son of John Green of Dunsby Hall and Mary Johnson who married as her second husband Captain Francis Pilliod, an early member of the SGS (see Appendix 5); his grandmother was a Lynn; educated at Spalding Grammar School (under Revd Timothy Neve), St John's College, Cambridge, admitted 1725 aged 17, Leiden University 1731 where he studied under Boerhaave; MD, physician; SGS member 1729, 'beneficient member', Second Secretary 1729, Secretary 1748; PGS member 1734;

FSA 1739; married 1736 Jane Green, eldest daughter of Maurice Johnson; a capable artist, also interested in natural history.

Grundy, John senior: (1696–1748) born Congerstone (Leics): 'of Market Bosworth in Leicestershire a Land Surveyor and Mathematician who made an Actual Survey of this Lordship [Spalding] & many others in this Neighbourhood & presented the Soc: with a Plan of this Town for an Ornament to their Museum' [1732]; lived at Congerstone and Spalding, taught mathematics at Market Bosworth Grammar School and Spalding Grammar School; surveyor of Charles Jennens' estate at Gopsall Park; SGS 1731, 'beneficient member', came to Spalding to survey the Duke of Buccleuch's estates; worked for the Deeping Fen Adventurers creating drains and experimenting with pumping engines; published pamphlets on drainage and wrote a MS 'Art of Drainage'. Mentioned in his son's entry in *ODNB* (see below).

Grundy, John junior: (1719–1783) son of John Grundy senior (see above), born Congerstone (Leics), family moved to Spalding in 1738, lived there and is buried in St Mary's Church, Spalding; SGS 1739, 'beneficient member'; consultant drainage engineer working in Lincolnshire, Norfolk and Yorkshire; Agent for the Deeping Fen Adventurers 1748–1764; founder-member of the Society of Civil Engineers 1771. *ODNB.*

Hales, Sir Christopher: (d.1776) 3rd baronet (baronetcy extinct in 1812); lived at Hackthorn (Lincs); SGS 1733, presented a copy of Terence's plays to the SGS library; regular subscriber to books.

Harley, Edward: (1689–1741) second Earl of Oxford; educated Westminster School and Christ Church, Oxford, entered 1707; DCL 1730; FRS 1727; SGS member 1728, 'beneficient member' who donated books and prints; MP, then member of the House of Lords; bibliophile, patron of antiquarians, writers and artists; built up an extraordinary library of MSS and books, especially early printed books; on his death his books were catalogued by Dr Samuel Johnson and William Oldys, and some were reprinted in the *Harleian Miscellany*; his family sold the MSS in 1753 to form one element of the original collection in the British Library. *ODNB.*

Harries, John: (d.1745) educated Lincoln's Inn; knew Revd Timothy Neve and was perhaps a former pupil of his at Spalding; SGS 1729; lived in the Caribbean and at the time of his death was of the Parish of St Andrew, Jamaica; in his will, dated 1742 and proved 1745, he stated : 'I also do hereby absolutely free my Negro woman named Betty and do order my Executors to pay her fifty pounds'.

Hawkes, Thomas: (fl. c. 1750–1760) of Magdalen Street, Norwich; is perhaps the Mr Hawkes who visited the SGS in 1753; may be the Thomas Hawkes who became a member in 1782, or else a relative; tinplate worker in Norwich and maker of mathematical instruments; astronomer, mathematician, land surveyor and mechanic; made an orrery or celestial sphere for the SGS in 1750, still in the SGS's museum and described in MB5 fol.64B, 20 September 1750; observed transit of Venus in Norwich in 1761, published details in the Norwich Mercury 13 June 1761 and sent them also to the SGS.

Heighington, Dr Musgrave: (1680–1764) born at Durham, 'sometime of Queen's College, Oxford'; musician and composer; organist at Hull 1717–20; performing in Dublin in the 1720s; City Organist and organist of St Nicholas' Church, Great Yarmouth, 1730s; SGS member 1736, 'beneficient member', organised the SGS's Anniversary Concerts 1737–1747, writing music for them, including settings of poems by SGS members, and performing there with his family; 1748 organist at St Martin's Church, Leicester, visited SGS from there in 1751; c.1756 organist at Dundee where he founded a musical society. Very little of his music survives; see Christ Church, Oxford library. *ODNB* and *Grove's Dictionary of Music*.

Hepburn, John: (?1685–1766) originally from Spalding; surgeon in the Army, later surgeon in Stamford; SGS member 1723; wrote to the SGS in 1742 about a case in 1734 when he extracted a stone from the urethra of a child.

Hill (Sir) John: (1714–1775) son of Canon Theophilus Hill, a PGS member; SGS 1740 PGS member 1747; MD St Andrews 1751; apothecary in London 1730; writer and natural philosopher specialising in botany and fossil collection; published *A History of Fossils* 1748, edited a journal *The Inspector* 1751–53; produced a 26-volume publication *The Vegetable System* between 1759 and 1775; maintained a correspondence with Linnaeus, awarded the Swedish Order of Vasa 1774; called by Dr Samuel Johnson 'a very curious observer'. *ODNB*.

Hunter, Major-General Robert: (1666–1734) born Edinburgh, educated as an attorney; FRS 1709; SGS member 1726; was ADC to the Duke of Marlborough in the early years of the War of the Spanish Succession, fought at Blenheim and Ramillies; prisoner of the French in Paris 1707–1709; became an effective Governor of New York and New Jersey 1710–1719; Controller of Customs under Walpole 1720–1727; Governor of Jamaica 1727–1734; Lord of the Manor of Crowland, where Maurice Johnson was his steward and was thanked for improvements. *ODNB*.

Hutchinson, Dr Samuel: (1721–c.1753) born Langton by Partney, son of Revd Samuel Hutchinson, SGS member 1729; educated Charterhouse and St John's College, Cambridge, entered 1738; Fellow in Physic at St John's 1743–1753; practised as a physician in Stamford; father and son visited the SGS in 1738; PGS member 1744; SGS member 1746; candidate for the Chair of Anatomy at Cambridge in 1746.

Ingram, Dale: (1710–1793) born at Spalding; worked as a surgeon in London; in 1733, according to MB1 fol.108A, 'Mr Dale Ingram chyrurgeon at Aleppo or in Turkey elsewhere' was listed as a member but crossed out and 'Neg X' written after his name; surgeon at Barbados 1743–1750; surgeon at Tower Hill, London 1750; became SGS member in 1751; published *Practical Cases and Observations in Surgery* 1751 and *Essay on the Plague* 1755; surgeon at Christ's Hospital, London 1759–1791. *ODNB*.

Ives, Calamy: (b.?1719,) possibly born in London; apothecary's apprentice in Spalding?; almost certainly an apothecary at Wisbech; SGS 1745; sent to the SGS an account of a journey to Ireland in 1747; visited the SGS 1748; described as being 'of Wragg Marsh' near Spalding, so perhaps had property there; leased property in St Martin's in the Fields, London, in 1745.

Jackson, William: (fl.1740s) schoolmaster, 'usher of the Petit School, Spalding' in the early 1740s, Customs official in Boston 1740s; SGS member 1746, sent a present of a stuffed snake for the museum; one of the SGS's poets, producing a translation of poems by Horace; his poem 'All Hail the Day', an extract from his 'Ode on St Cecilia's Day', was set to music by Musgrave Heighington and performed at the 1743 SGS Anniversary Concert.

Jennens, Charles: (1701–1773) of Gopsall Hall (Leics); born Gopsall, educated Balliol College, Oxford, entered 1716, member of Oxford Music Club 1718, as a non-juror did not take his degree; rebuilt Gopsall Hall in the neo-Palladian style; employed John Grundy senior (q.v.) who lived nearby, as his surveyor and water engineer; SGS member 1748; Shakespearean scholar and editor; art collector and patron of artists and sculptors; patron of non-jurors; musician, music collector and supporter of Handel with whom he worked as librettist for a number of oratorios, in particular *The Messiah*, *Saul* and *Belshazzar* and possibly *Israel in Egypt. ODNB.*

Johnson, Revd George: (1732–1786) born at Spalding, son of the Revd Walter Johnson, who was later Rector of Redmarshall (Co. Durham); cousin of Maurice Johnson; educated Spalding Grammar School, Durham School and Brasenose College Oxford, entered 1750, Demyship (scholarship) to Magdalen College, Oxford 1751, Fellow of Magdalen 1757–1765; SGS member 1753; wrote informative letters to SGS from Oxford; ordained priest 1757; Vicar of Norton (Co. Durham); Prebendary of Lincoln 1781, Rector of Lofthouse (Yorks), Rector of Frinton (Essex).

Johnson, Henry: (1689–1760) 'Henry Johnson of Westminster Esq Præsident of the Royal Assiento of Great Britain at Panama in America S Antiq. Brit. Lond S. Son of the honble Coll. William Johnson Governor of Cape Coast Castle etc in Africa'; his father was a relative of the Spalding Johnsons; referred to as 'cousin' by Maurice Johnson; President of the Royal Asiento in Central America, based in Panama; traveller in Central America and in Spain, SGS member 1724 and good contributor of letters about his travels; FSA 1720; owned an estate in Berkhamsted; Gamekeeper to Frederick, Prince of Wales; published an account of Lima, Peru, 1748; translated works by the Spanish Benedictine monk and scholar Benito Jeronimo Feijoo y Montenegro. *ODNB.*

Johnson, Henry Eustace: (1733–?) born Spalding, youngest surviving son of Maurice Johnson (q.v.) and his wife Elizabeth (née Ambler); educated Spalding and probably at a school in Gosberton; SGS member 1753; factor of the East India Company, EIC assistant secretary in Madras, India; wrote letters to the SGS from his travels, which have not survived; died at St Helena on a voyage back to England.

Johnson, John (brother): (1690–1744) born Spalding, younger son of Maurice Johnson senior by his first marriage to Jane Johnson and younger brother of Maurice Johnson (q.v.); educated Spalding Grammar School and the Inner Temple; barrister specialising in drainage law and interested in mathematics; a founder-member of the SGS, member 1712, Treasurer 1729–1742; FSA 1718. On his death, MB3 fol. 190A recorded: 'the death of John Johnson of the Inner Temple Esquire Clerk of the Court of Sewers for Elloe Holland & Steward of the Soke of Kirton and manners of Spalding, Bichar Beaumont, Croyland Holbeach Whapload and of the Mannor of Hitchin in Hetfordshire. Late the Prudent & Worthy Treasurer of this Societie & Great & liberal Benefactor both to that & the Concert here'.

Johnson, Revd John (son): (1722–1758) born Spalding, third surviving son of Maurice Johnson (q.v.) and his wife Elizabeth (née Ambler); educated Spalding Grammar School and St John's College, Cambridge, 1740; ordained deacon 1744, priest 1746; curate of Ramsey, then incumbent of St Mary and St Nicholas' Church, Spalding and Vicar of Moulton; SGS member 1742,

Second Secretary 1748, President 1755 following the death of his father Maurice Johnson (q.v.); unmarried.

Johnson, Maurice: (1688–1755) In his own words, from the SGS Grand Catalogue fol.21: 'Of the Inner Temple London Esq who founded the Gentlemens Society 12 Dec 1712 First Secretary thereof who compiled this Volume & the Catalogues of the Musæum, Librarys, etc. for the use of the sd. Soc. Soc. Antiqu. Brit. Lond. S. One of the Few Restorers thereof 1716/7, Law Reader in the Inner Temple Hall Steward of Spalding with the Members Holbeach Abbs. Croyland Hitchin in Herfordshire D. Recorder of the Boroughs of Stamford & Boston & of Councell by Chapter Act to the Revd. the Dean & Chapt. Of Peterb: Chairman of the Sessions of Sewers & of the Peace held at Spalding one of the IV Governours of the Royal free Grammar School there and in February 1748 Elected instead of the Revd. Stephen Lyon President SGS.'

Born Spalding, son of Maurice Johnson senior of Ayscoughfee Hall by his first wife Jane Johnson, educated Spalding Grammar School, Eton College and the Inner Temple; married, 5 January 1710, Elizabeth Ambler of Gayton House, Spalding, many children (see Appendix 5 for those who survived to adulthood, five of whom became SGS members); one of the re-founders of the Society of Antiquaries 1717; founder of the SGS, informally in 1710 and formally in 1712, Secretary 1713–1748, President 1748–1755; PGS member 1730; barrister specialising in drainage law, appearing before Parliamentary committees, antiquary, numismatist, collector of coins and books, especially early printed books, keen gardener and plant collector. *ODNB*.

Johnson, Maurice (son): (1714–1793) born Spalding, eldest surviving son of Maurice Johnson (q.v.) and his wife Elizabeth (née Ambler); educated Spalding Grammar School and Foubert's [military] Academy, London; SGS member 1733; contributed regular full letters from his army travels and London residence; officer in the First Regiment of Foot (the Guards), serving as Captain and later Colonel, travelled in Europe during the campaigns of the War of the Austrian Succession, fought at the Battle of Dettingen 1743, served on staff of the Duke of Cumberland, took part in the campaign against the Jacobites in 1745–46, perhaps present at Culloden; married Elizabeth daughter of Sir Edward Bellamy in 1749 and later married Mary Baker in 1755; gained an estate at Stanway, Essex, from his first wife; later returned to Ayscoughfee Hall after his father's death but took little part in the activities of the SGS in the second half of the eighteenth century.

Johnson, Walter: (1720–1771) second surviving son of Maurice Johnson (q.v.) and his wife Elizabeth (née Ambler); educated Spalding Grammar School and the Inner Temple; barrister in Spalding, lived at Gayton (Holyrood) House when he married Mary Fairfax; SGS member 1741; SGS Treasurer from 1742; active member in the 1760s (see Appendix 4); FSA 1749.

Johnson, William: (fl.1730s–1740s) brother of Henry Johnson (q.v.) and relative of Maurice Johnson; merchant with the East India Company in Surat, India; on the Council of the East India Company at Surat; reported on an invasion by Nader Shah in 1738; SGS member 1742.

Jurin, Dr James: (1684–1750) born London, educated Royal Mathematical School at Christ's Hospital, London and Trinity College, Cambridge; Fellow 1706; attended Leiden University; Headmaster of Newcastle Grammar School 1709; MD Cambridge 1716; FRS 1717, Secretary of the RS 1721;

SGS member 1723, a 'worthy & beneficient member' (MB1 fol.69); Maurice Johnson attended his lectures on mathematics and philosophy, perhaps in London, though William Stukeley claimed that 'Mr Johnson' had sent for Jurin to tutor his son before Jurin moved to London; Jurin helped Johnson in gaining Sir Isaac Newton as an SGS member; FRCP 1719, President of Royal College of Physicians 1750; physician at Guy's Hospital, worked on inoculation against smallpox; published a series of pamphlets in the 1720s, *The Success of Inoculating the Small Pox*. *ODNB*.

Laughton, Revd Manwaring: (c.1715–c.1789) born Yorkshire, educated at Chesterfield Grammar School and St John's College, Cambridge 1734; ordained deacon 1738 and priest 1740; SGS member 1739, gave the Society Sir Isaac Newton's *Treatise of the System of the World*; curate of Hose (Leics), then of Lutton (Lincs); later Vicar of Lyddington (Rutland) 1748; Rector of St Mary's Church, Stamford 1754; married Mary Goodhall in St Paul's Cathedral in 1751.

Lynn, George senior: (1676–1742) born Southwick (Northants), son of George Lynn of Southwick and Mary Johnson of Spalding; second cousin of Maurice Johnson; educated Inner Temple; Lord of the Manor of Southwick; married Elizabeth sister of Humphrey Bellamy of London and was father of George junior and John Lynn (q.v.); SGS member 1719, 'beneficient member', PGS member 1732; barrister, astronomer, mathematician who drew up a table of logarithms for the SGS, meteorological observer whose observations were communicated to the RS. *ODNB*.

Lynn, George junior: (1706/7–1758) born Southwick (Northants), son of George Lynn senior; second cousin to Maurice Johnson; educated Spalding Grammar School, St John's College, Cambridge 1721 and Inner Temple, entered 1722; barrister; SGS member 1723, 'beneficient member'; FSA 1726; PGS member 1730; married Anne Bellamy, sister of Elizabeth Bellamy who married Maurice Johnson's son Maurice; both were daughters of Sir Edward Bellamy; inherited Frinton Hall (Essex) through his wife; buried at Southwick with a monument by Roubiliac. *ODNB*.

Lynn, Revd John: (c.1710–1749) born Southwick (Northants), son of George Lynn senior and brother of George junior; second cousin of Maurice Johnson; educated Spalding Grammar School (under Revd Timothy Neve) and St John's College, Cambridge, entered 1726; ordained deacon 1733 and priest 1734; SGS member 1727; Chaplain to Sir Edward Bellamy, Lord Mayor of London 1734–35; Vicar of Southwick 1736–1749; Rector of Munslow (Shropshire) 1749.

Lynn, Dr Walter: (?1678–1762) born Southwick (Northants), son of George Lynn of Southwick and Mary Johnson of Spalding; brother of George Lynn senior (q.v.) second cousin to Maurice Johnson; educated Spalding Grammar School and Peterhouse, Cambridge, entered 1695; MB Cambridge 1704; medical writer and inventor; published *Essay toward a more easie and safe method of Cure in the Small Pox* 1714; early member of the SGS 1714; wrote *Nyktopsia* 1726, a satirical account of his invention of a candle-snuffer; published a pamphlet on steam-powered pumping engines in 1726 but it does not include any technical details; travelled widely, including a visit to Carolina, America; published *The Anatomist Dissected* 1740, opposing experimental surgery; died in Grantham. *ODNB*.

Manningham, Dr Thomas: The relationships of the Manningham family are difficult to sort out. The Thomas who sent a letter in 1739 lived in Jermyn St, London; he could be Thomas (1684–1750) educated Eton College and King's College, Cambridge, Fellow 1704, ordained priest 1709, Chaplain to the Speaker of the House of Commons and Prebendary of Westminster 1720–1750. He was the brother of Sir Richard Manningham (1685–1759, SGS member 1724), the famous man-midwife who established the first lying-in hospital for mothers in 1739 and published *Abstract of Midwifery for use in the Lying-in Infirmary* 1744, and whose wife was the sister of Henry Johnson (q.v.). Alternatively it could be Richard's son, also called Thomas (?1718–1794), who was MD of St Andrews University and practised as a doctor in London and Bath; SGS member 1741; LRCP 1765. He was also a leading Freemason.

Mendes da Costa, Emanuel: (1717–1791) born London of a Portuguese Jewish family; natural historian and merchant in fossils and shells; member of the Aurelian Society 1740; employed by the Army contractors in Europe in the 1740s; SGS member 1746, corresponded about fossils and the organisation of the SGS's collections in their museum; FRS 1747; FSA 1752; Clerk to the RS 1763, expelled 1768 for financial irregularities; published *Natural History of Fossils* 1757 and *British Conchology* 1778; *ODNB.*

Middleton Massey, Dr Richard: (1681–1743) born Cheshire, educated Brase-nose College, Oxford, entered 1697, non-juror so did not take his degree; 'he practised many years at Wisbeach & with Mr Rd. Lake put the Library there into very good Order & published some account & a catalogue of It'. MD Aberdeen 1720; practised as a physician in Wisbech, where he organised a learned society, then moved to London and finally practised in Cheshire, died at Rostherne, Cheshire; FRS 1712; FSA 1718, Secretary of the SA; SGS member 1721; subscribed extensively to books.

Mitchell, Dr John: (1685–1751) born in Scotland, studied in Padua, Reims and Leiden as a medical student; MD; librarian to Sir Richard Ellys (q.v.), prepared catalogue of Ellys' library which is now at Blickling Hall, Norfolk; SGS member 1733. [He is not the botanist Dr John Mitchell.]

Mitchell, Dr Robert: (1691–1771) 'sometime of Spalding, since of Guildford in Surrey ... he sometime practised at Boston and after that at Epsom'; medical student at Reims and at Leiden under Boerhaave; practised as a physician in Spalding, SGS member 1720; PGS member 1735; moved to Guildford, c.1728.

Mortimer, Dr Cromwell: (1693–1752) born Essex to a Dissenting family; MD Leiden 1724, a friend of Professor Boerhaave; LRCP 1725; MD Cambridge 1728; FRCP 1729; physician, secretary and antiquary, practising as a physician in London and as assistant to Sir Hans Sloane 1729–1740; FRS 1728, RS Secretary 1730–1752; FSA 1734; PGS member 1735; SGS member 1737; very active corresponding member of Paris Royal Academy of Sciences; supported by the SGS in his application to be Secretary of the Society for the Encouragement of Learning 1737. *ODNB.*

Muller, John: (1699–1784) born in Lorraine of German origins; mathematician in the ordnance office at the Tower of London and colleague of William Bogdani (q.v.); SGS 1735, 'beneficient member'; taught at the Royal Military Academy, Woolwich, 1745–1766 as a master then Professor of Fortification and Artillery; a significant mathematician, working on 'fluxions' or calculus; published *A Mathematical Treatise of Conic Sections and Fluxions* 1730 and *Rules and Orders for the Academy of Fortification and Gunnery* 1741.

Muscat, Revd James: (1708/9–1758) educated Merton College, Oxford, entered 1725 aged 16, then transferred to Corpus Christi College, BA 1729; schoolmaster at Boston Grammar School 1745–1759; SGS member 1746; probably the Revd James Muscat or Muscut who was Rector of Little Staughton (Beds) 1735.

Neve, Revd Timothy senior: (1694–1757) 'T.Neve MA Rector of Allwalton in the co. of Huntingdon Vicar of Weston & Chaplain of Wickham in Holland Linc. Canon of Peterborough & Chaplain to the Rt Revd Lord Bishop of Peterborough. Sometime the most worthy Master of Spalding School, Treasurer of the Gent. Soc & Dep. Librarian there to whose Ingenuity Industry & good Instance the Soc. Musæum & Library are greatly beholden. DD Archdeacon of Huntington Preb. of Nassington Founder of the Gents Soc at Peterborough.' Born near Ludlow, Shropshire; educated Ludlow School and St John's College, Cambridge, entered 1711; ordained priest 1718; Headmaster, Spalding Grammar School 1716–1729; SGS member 1718, Treasurer 1718–1729; minor canon of Peterborough Cathedral 1729–1745; Rector of Alwalton 1729–1757; Archdeacon of Huntingdon 1747; prebendary of Lincoln 1744–1757; founded the PGS on the model of the SGS 1730; Secretary and Treasurer of the PGS, author of articles on astronomy, published in the RS's *Philosophical Transactions* and the *Gentleman's Magazine. ODNB.*

Neve, Revd Timothy junior: (1724–1798) born at Spalding, son of Revd Timothy Neve senior (q.v.); educated Corpus Christi College, Oxford, entered 1737, Fellow 1747; SGS member 1746; PGS member 1747; ordained deacon 1747 and priest 1748; chaplain to the British community in Hamburg 1751; Rector of Middleton Stoney (Oxon) and Geddington (Northants); Bampton Lecturer at Oxford, lectures published as *Eight Sermons* 1781; Lady Margaret Professor of Divinity, Oxford, 1783; Prebendary of Worcester 1783. *ODNB.*

New, Robert: (d.1762) educated Middle Temple; barrister, legal officer, antiquarian and book collector; Clerk of the Papers to the King's Bench; FSA 1730; SGS member 1733.

Norcliffe, Richard: (fl. c.1730s–1740s) described by Johnson as a 'merchant, Kingston upon Hull' exporting timber from Scandinavia to England, based in Friderickshald (modern Halden) in south-west Norway, near the Swedish border; SGS member 1734; wrote letters describing Norwegian flora and fauna and sent geological and botanical specimens for the SGS museum; introduced the Revd Andreas Bing (q.v.) to the SGS; translated the Norwegian missionary Revd Hans Egede's history of Greenland, published London 1745 but without the translator's name.

North, Revd George: (1707–1772) born London, educated St Paul's School and Corpus Christi College, Cambridge, entered 1726, MA 1744; ordained deacon 1729, curate, then Vicar of Codicote and Welwyn (Herts) 1743, remained there for the rest of his life; well-known antiquarian and numismatist; FSA 1742, SGS member 1744.

Oldfield, Anthony: (born c.1710) descendant of Sir Anthony Oldfield of Spalding, and related to Maurice Johnson; assistant to the agent at Petworth House, Sussex, then assistant agent of the Duchess of Somerset; wrote from her house, Cheveley Park, south-east of Newmarket, a house later taken over by the Dukes of Rutland; SGS member 1746, corresponded about a family inheritance as well as his antiquarian interests.

Owen, Revd Edward: (1726–96) born Great Staughton/Kimbolton (Hunts), son of the Revd Edward Owen of St John's College, Oxford (1694–1751); educated St John's College, Oxford, entered 1744, BA 1748; perhaps curate at Kimbolton c.1750; gave to the SGS a copy of Marcus Hieronymus Vida, *Christiados* edited by his father (Oxford, 1725); Vicar of Southwick (Northants) 1754 to his death in 1796.

Parsons, Dr James: (1705–1770) born Ireland, educated Dublin and Reims, medical degree 1736; London-based physician, obstetrician and anatomist, opposed Joanna Stevens' treatment of internal stones by soap lees (see her entry in *ODNB*); keen antiquarian, friend of the artist William Hogarth; FRS 1741, foreign secretary of the RS 1751–1762, had 31 papers published in the RS's *Philosophical Transactions*; SGS member 1746; FSA 1748; see his entry in *ODNB*.

Pegge, Revd Samuel: (1704–1796) born Chesterfield, educated Chesterfield and St John's College, Cambridge; ordained priest 1730, Vicar of Godmersham (Kent) 1731, Vicar of Heath near Whittington (Derbys) from 1751 to his death; prebendary of Lichfield 1757–1796; SGS member 1730, introduced by his university friend Revd Benjamin Ray (q.v.); PGS member 1731; FSA 1751; keen and successful antiquarian, book-collector, numismatist and author, had 50 articles published in *Archæologia*; his letters in the SGS collection demonstrate his incisive mind. *ODNB*.

Pole, Joseph: (fl.1750s) 'a Berlin jeweller', seal-cutter and engraver.

Powell, Revd Morgan: (c.1725–1774) born Llanddeusant (Carmarthen), educated St Catharine's College, Cambridge 1742, BA 1746; University friend of Revd John Johnson (q.v.); ordained deacon 1745/6, priest 1746; Curate of Coton (Cambs) 1746, possibly curate at Kirton (Lincs); Vicar of Walsingham and West Barsham (Norfolk) 1756; Rector of Berwick St Leonard (Wilts) 1767.

Ray, Revd Benjamin: (1704–1760) born Spalding, educated Spalding Grammar School (under Revd Timothy Neve) and St John's College, Cambridge, entered 1721; University friend of Revd Samuel Pegge (q.v.); ordained priest 1729; Master of Sleaford Grammar School 1723–1736; Curate of Spalding 1727; perpetual curate of Cowbit and Surfleet 1729–1760; SGS member 1723, 'beneficient member', contributed several dissertations, including one on the benefits of learned societies; PGS member 1731.

Richards, John: (1699/1700–1767) born Spalding, son of a butcher, educated Spalding Grammar School and St John's College, Cambridge, admitted 1717; SGS member 1720.

Robinson, Revd Matthew: (d.1745) educated Lincoln College, Oxford, entered 1730, and Brasenose College, Oxford, Fellow 1736–1738; ordained deacon 1736, priest 1738; Curate of Sutton St Mary; Vicar of Kirton in Holland 1741; Master of Boston Grammar School 1737–1745; SGS member 1736.

Romley, Revd John: (c.1711–1754) born Burton (Lincs); educated Magdalen College, Oxford, 1735, and Lincoln College, Oxford; curate of Epworth; schoolmaster at Wroot; SGS member 1746.

Rowell, John senior: (d.1739) LL.B; Peterborough lawyer and perhaps also merchant; SGS member 1723; PGS 1730, President; subscriber to many books in the 1720s.

Rowland, James: (fl.1720s–1740s) bailiff of the Buccleuch family's manor of Spalding; SGS member 1720, important member and regular attender at SGS meetings.

Rutherforth, Revd Dr Thomas: (1712–1771) born Papworth St Agnes (Cambs), educated Huntingdon and St John's College, Cambridge, BA 1730, MA 1733, BD 1740, DD 1745; Fellow 1733–1752; ordained priest 1737; SGS member 1742, FRS 1743; Chaplain to Frederick, Prince of Wales, and to his widow after his death; Rector of Barley (Herts) and Brinkley (Cambs) 1751; Archdeacon of Essex 1752; Regius Professor of Divinity at Cambridge 1756–1771; Rector of Somersham (Hunts) 1756; Rector of Shenfield (Essex) 1767; keenly interested in natural science, which he taught at Cambridge, and in moral philosophy; published *Ordo Institutionum Physicarum* 1743, converted his course of lectures into a popular textbook *A system of natural philosophy, being a course of lectures in mechanics, optics, hydrostatics and astronomy* 1748 and published *Institutes of Natural Law* 1745 and 1746. *ODNB.*

Scott, Francis, second Duke of Buccleuch: (1694–1751) son of James Scott, Earl of Dalkeith and grandson of James, Duke of Monmouth and Frances Scott, Duchess of Buccleuch in her own right, who owned lands in Spalding for which the Johnsons were stewards; while he was Earl of Dalkeith he was educated at Eton College, at the same time as Maurice Johnson; SGS member 1722, Patron 1732, 'beneficient member'; presented the SGS with valuable books and maps; a significant Freemason, Grand Master 1723–24; FRS 1724; Knight of the Thistle 1725; succeeded as Duke of Buccleuch 1732; Lord Paramount of the Manor of Spalding.

Sharp, Revd Dr Thomas: (1693–1758) son of Rt Revd John Sharp, Archbishop of York, whose biography he wrote; educated Trinity College, Cambridge, graduated 1716, became a Fellow and later DD; Chaplain to Archbishop Dawes and Prebendary of Southwell 1716; Prebendary of York 1719; Rector of Rothbury (Northumberland) 1720; Archdeacon of Northumberland 1722; Prebendary of Durham 1732; antiquarian and book-collector; SGS member 1751; published numerous sermons and pamphlets which were collected and published posthumously in 6 volumes in 1763.

Shelvocke, George: (d.1760) son of George Shelvocke (1675–1742) privateer and author; sailed with his father round the world 1719–1722; Secretary to the Postmaster General 1742; FRS 1743; FSA 1744; SGS member 1745, agreed to endorse and send free of charge the SGS's overseas correspondence 1745; reissued in 1757 his father's *A Voyage round the World by way of the Great Sea*, originally published in 1726.

Smith, Abel junior: (fl. 1740s–1760s) of Nottingham, banker, merchant and MP for Nottingham, who created Smith and Payne's Bank in London in 1758; this merged with several others to become the National Provincial Bank in 1918 and is now the National Westminster Bank; his son was created Lord Carrington; SGS member 1751; he visited the SGS in 1752 and with his wife and son in 1753; he presented to the SGS Dr Charles Deering's *Nottinghamia Vetus et Nova or an Historical Account of the Ancient and Present State of the Town of Nottingham* 1751.

Smyth Revd Robert : (c.1700–1761) educated Westminster School and St John's College, Cambridge, entered 1717; ordained deacon 1722; chaplain to Catherine, widow of Sir John Leveson Gower; Rector of Woodston, near Peterborough, 1728–1761; SGS member 1726; early member of the PGS 1730 and its Secretary at one stage; historian who worked on listing all the Sheriffs of England; his MS account, with introduction by Maurice Johnson, is now lost; made voluminous notes on heraldry and monuments; assisted with Carter's history of the town and university of Cambridge, 1753.

Snow, Matthew: (c.1688–?1757) of Clipsham (Rutland), educated Eton, Trinity College, Cambridge, entered 1704, Fellow 1710, MA 1711, and the Middle Temple, entered 1706; Maurice Johnson notes 'Prothonotary of the Middle Temple'; a legal friend of Maurice Johnson; SGS 1724; one of his short letters has survived because it was used for sketch-plans of a projected museum for the SGS in 1725; presented to the Society in 1726 J. Breval's *Voyages through Europe with maps and prints.*

Sparke, Revd Joseph: (1682–1740) educated Peterborough and St John's College, Cambridge, entered 1699 aged 16, BA 1704; ordained deacon 1705, priest 1710; curate at Eye 1710; Librarian, Chapter Clerk and Master of Works, Peterborough Cathedral 1714; not a member of the PGS; FSA 1720; SGS member 1722; published *Historiæ Anglicanæ Scriptores Varii* 1723, a transcription of mediæval chronicles of Peterborough; owned premises in Spalding which he rented to the SGS as a meeting-place; see his entry in *ODNB.*

Stukeley, Revd Dr William: (1687–1765) born Holbeach, friend of Maurice Johnson from boyhood; educated Holbeach and Corpus Christi College, Cambridge, admitted 1703, MB 1709; studied under Dr Richard Mead at St Thomas's Hospital, London 1709; practised as physician in Boston 1710; practised as physician in London 1717; helped to re-activate the Society of Antiquaries 1717, FSA 1717, became Secretary; FRS 1718; became a Freemason in 1720; SGS member 1722; moved to practise as physician in Grantham 1727; ordained priest 1729 and became Rector and Vicar of All Saints, Stamford 1729; PGS member 1731; organised the Brazen-nose Society, Stamford, 1736–37; his wife Frances (née Williamson, of Allington, Lincolnshire) died in 1737 and in 1739 he married Elizabeth sister of Roger and Samuel Gale (q.v.); moved to London in 1747 as Rector of St George's, Queen Square; physician, clergyman, antiquary who began the systematic surveying and drawing of archæological sites; among many other books, published *Itinerarium Curiosum* in 1724 giving an account of his antiquarian travels, *Stonehenge* 1740, *Abury* 1743 and *De Situ Britanniæ* 1757. *ODNB.*

Swynfen, John: (d.1749) Merchant of Holborn, London, working for the East India Company; made regular voyages for the Company as overseer of cargo, particularly to Madras; brother of Revd George Swynfen, Vicar of Thornton by Horncastle; owned considerable property; visited the SGS in 1737, SGS member 1743; died on board the East India Company's ship *Onslow.*

Sympson, Thomas: (fl.1740s) Proctor and Master of Works at Lincoln Cathedral, antiquarian who undertook extensive research and transcribed the registers of Lincoln Cathedral for Johnson and the SGS; SGS member 1741.

Tathwell, Dr Cornewall: (?1723–1773) of Louth, educated St John's College, Oxford, entered 1741 aged 17, BA 1745, MA 1749, MB 1751, MD 1755; Fellow of St John's; physician in Stamford; SGS member 1751.

Taylor, Revd Dr John: (1704–1766) educated Shrewsbury School and St John's College, Cambridge, BA 1724, MA 1728, LL.D 1741, Fellow of St John's 1726, Law Fellow 1732; ordained deacon 1747; note by Maurice Johnson: 'Fellow of St John's Coll Cambridge, Registrar of that University & Deputy Keeper of the Publick Library there under Dr Middleton'; University Registrar 1731–1757, University Librarian 1731–1734; PGS member 1733; SGS member 1738; Chancellor of Lincoln Diocese 1744; Rector of Lawford (Essex) 1751, Archdeacon of Buckingham 1753; Prebendary of St Paul's Cathedral 1757; FSA 1748; called 'Demosthenes Taylor' by Dr Samuel Johnson. *ODNB*.

Topham, Captain John: (fl.1730s) 'of our country' i.e. a Lincolnshire man; sea officer sailing to China with the East India Company, porcelain expert, collector, particularly of specimens of natural history; SGS member 1729; PGS member 1732, knew Timothy Neve well so was perhaps one of his former pupils at Spalding; 'Thrice in the East Indies and is now going thither in the London Capt. Bootle Commander, who being present engages to become a Corresponding Member … that gentleman having been to China & several of those Eastern Countrys the Discourse at this Society ran much upon Porcellain'. (MB2 fol.12A)

Trafford, Sigismund: (1693/4–1741) of Dunton Hall, Tydd St Mary, High Sheriff of Lincolnshire, author of *An Essay on Draining* 1729 about the benefits of draining the North Level of the Fens and improving the Welland outfall to benefit the port of Wisbech; corresponded with Johnson during Parliamentary debates over the 1726 Bedford Level Adventurers' Bill; SGS member 1724.

Vyner, Robert: (1685–1777) of Gautby Hall, near Bardney; invited to SGS membership 1725; Independent Whig MP for Lincolnshire 1724–1761, involved in 1726 in the Parliamentary campaign against the Bedford Level Adventurers' Bill.

Walpole, Edward: (1702/3–1740) of Dunston (Lincs); a Roman Catholic landowner and poet; translated in 1736 *De Partu Virginis* by the Italian writer Jacopo Sannazaro into English verse and dedicated it to the SGS; also wrote *The Sixth Satire of the First Book of Horace, Imitated* 1738, which he dedicated to Sir Richard Ellys; SGS member 1733.

Ward, John: (1678/9–1758) of London; a Dissenter; clerk in the Navy Office, schoolmaster 1710 in London; Professor of Rhetoric at Gresham College, London 1720; FRS 1723, Vice-President 1752; SGS member 1727; FSA 1736, Director 1747, Vice-President 1753; Trustee of the British Museum 1753, LL.D Edinburgh 1751; antiquarian, numismatist and author, published *Lives of the Professors of Gresham College* 1740. *ODNB*.

Weeks, James: (fl.1740s–1750s) educated St Paul's School, London; 'limner and painter', artist and musician playing the harpsichord and violin; taught drawing and painting to some of Johnson's children; SGS member 1748, 'beneficient member', made a drawing of Lady Jane Grey (MB5 fol.17A) which still exists and a crayon sketch of Walter Johnson (MB5 fol.19A) now lost; worked at Welbeck Abbey for Lady Oxford.

Wesley, Revd Samuel senior: (1662–1735) born Winterbourne Whitchurch (Dorset), educated Dorchester Grammar School, a Dissenting academy in

London and Exeter College, Oxford; originally a Dissenter but became an Anglican; ordained deacon 1688 and priest 1689; curate of Newington Butts; Rector of South Ormsby (Lincs) 1691, Rector of Epworth 1695; married Susanna (1669–1742) also originally a Dissenter who became an Anglican; father of numerous children who included the famous Revd John Wesley the evangelist and originator of the Methodist movement and Revd Charles Wesley, the hymn-writer; SGS member 1724, 'beneficial member'; author of a poem on the life of Christ; his Latin account of the legal aspects of the Biblical Book of Job, *Jurisprudentia Jobi*, was published posthumously in 1735 with the support of the SGS and dedicated to Queen Caroline. *ODNB*.

Wesley, Revd Samuel junior: (1690/1–1739) born Spitalfields, London, eldest son of the Revd Samuel Wesley (q.v.) then curate of Spitalfields, and his wife Susanna; educated Westminster School and Christ Church, Oxford, entered 1711, BA 1715; head usher at Westminster School, helped to found the Westminster Infirmary; SGS member 1729, 'beneficial member'; headmaster Tiverton Grammar School (Devon) 1733; wrote poetry; like his father, a Tory sympathiser. *ODNB*, in the entry on his father, Revd Samuel Wesley senior.

Whatley, Revd Robert: (1691–1767) 'Rector of Toft, Prebendary of York'; admitted Inner Temple, 1711 and called to the Bar 1714; efforts to achieve patronage as a lawyer failed; ordained deacon 1728, priest 1729; Rector of Toft by Newton (Lincs) and Prebendary of Bilton in York Minster 1729; SGS 1731; Prebendary of Fridaythorpe, York, 1750; author of several argumentative legal pamphlets and pamphlets of sermons.

Whiting, Revd Samuel: (d.1757) born Boston; educated Clare College, Cambridge, BA 1727, MA 1730; ordained deacon 1731–32, priest 1733; usher at Spalding Grammar School 1729, then Master 1741–1757; incumbent of Wykeham Chapel near Spalding 1743, Vicar of Weston (Lincs) 1748–1757; SGS 1729.

Williams, Revd Dr Philip (1695–1749) Huntingdon School, St John's College Cambridge 1710, MA 1718, BD 1725, DD 1730; ordained deacon 1721, priest 1722; SGS member 1726, Fellow of St John's 1716–1741, University Public Orator 1730–1741, President of St John's College, Cambridge; Rector of Starston (Norfolk) 1729–1746, Rector of Barrow (Suffolk) 1740–1749, Vicar of Sutton St Mary (Long Sutton) 1746; published a number of sermons.

Willis, Browne: (1682–1760) of Blandford (Dorset); educated Westminster School and Christ Church, Oxford, entered 1700, and Inner Temple; MA 1720, DCL 1749; Tory MP for Buckingham 1705–1708; FSA 1717; PGS member 1746; SGS member 1747; lived at Whaddon Hall (Bucks); ecclesiastical antiquary and numismatist; published *Notitia Parliamentaria*, 3 vols, 1715 onwards, *A Survey of Cathedrals* 1727 and 1730 and *The History ... of Buckingham* 1755. *ODNB*.

Wilson, Captain Alexander: (fl.1730s–1750s) merchant; auditor and secretary to the Duke of Buccleuch; lived in Queen Street, Westminster; concerned in drainage of the Fens; SGS member 1738; frequent subscriber to books, especially those concerned with military fortification.

APPENDIX 3

THE ORIGINAL
EIGHTEENTH-CENTURY FILING SYSTEM
used by the SGS for its correspondence

As explained in the Introduction, the SGS originally listed and filed its correspondence in eight brown folio-size files of heavy paper. Later, most probably between 1890 and 1910, the letters were removed and organised alphabetically by author, thus taking them out of the original numerical filing system as explained below, and making it difficult to understand the numbering system used at the head of many of the letters. It is only on examination of the lists compiled in the eighteenth century for categorising the correspondence that the original system can be understood. The original lists and numberings have therefore been transcribed in this appendix from the brown files.

In the early eighteenth century, letters were sorted by the Secretary, Maurice Johnson, and his assistant Secretary, Dr John Green. The first division was into two groupings corresponding roughly to our modern Arts and Sciences, though with some overlap: 'Theological, Ethical, Juridical and Historical Topics' and 'Physical, Philosophical, and Mathematical Subjects' though 'physical' equates more closely to the modern 'medical' and 'philosophical' refers to 'natural philosophy' or science. The division is not always precise: some poetry and accounts of travels are filed in the second category, for example. A further division was then made on the basis of the size of paper on which they were written, the larger folio or the smaller quarto size. They were then divided into 'letters' or 'dissertations' for placing in the appropriate files. The files were given a Roman numeral from I to VIII. This produced the following organisation, quoting the titles they were given in Johnson's handwriting:

SGS I   Dissertations on Theological, Ethical, Juridical & Historical
          Topics MSS in Quarto   [50]
SGS II   L^{rs} on Theological, Ethical, Juridical & Historical Topics MSS
          in Quarto   [140]
SGS III   Dissertations on Theological, Ethical, Juridical & Historical
          Topics MSS in Folio   [59]
SGS IV   L^{rs} on Theological, Ethical, Juridical & Historical Topics MSS
          in Folio   [76]
SGS V   L^{rs} on Physical, Philosophical & Mathematical Subjects MSS
          in Quarto   [109]
SGS VI   L^{rs} on Physical, Philosophical & Mathematical Subjects MSS
          in Folio   [103]
SGS VII   Dissertations on Physical, Philosophical & Mathematical
          Subjects MSS in Quarto   [49]

SGS VIII SGS no.26. 5 bundles in Folio. Dissertations on Physical,
    Philosophical & Mathematical Subjects MSS in Folio   [58]
[The numbers in square brackets indicate the number of items in each folder.]

There was also a separate sheet X with a list of topics included in the SGS's correspondence:

Theology
Philosophy
Physick
Anatomy
Botany
Chyrurgery
Chemistry
Astronomy.

There is no surviving Sheet or Folder IX; some of the letters with SGS numbers which cannot be traced to the surviving lists may perhaps have been listed in Folder IX.

The title of each folder is in Maurice Johnson's handwriting, while that of the lists of contents inside is that of someone else. The writer is literate and familiar with the activities of the SGS, but on occasions mis-copies, especially the Latin phrases. It is possible that the straightforward task of copying or paraphrasing the headings, written on each letter by Johnson as Secretary, into the folders was given to the Society's Operator and curator, Michael Cox. As a surgeon-apothecary he would have had an education, but not to the standard of Maurice Johnson who had studied at Eton and the Inns of Court, or of the Second Secretary, John Green, with his University education at Cambridge and Leiden. The handwriting is not that of John Green, and no letters from Cox survive to permit a definite identification, but he was the SGS officer most likely to have been given this task. Each folder contains, on the inside of the cover, a numbered list of the correspondence originally filed inside it. These numbers were also written on the relevant letter or dissertation, as a method of filing and keeping a check on the contents of each folder. These are the 'SGS numbers' which appear at the head of many of the letters in this calendar; we have reproduced them as given, sometimes in the form 'SGS No 23' and sometimes simply as 'No 23'. Examination of the lists indicates a further attempt to categorise and group the contents, both by subject-matter and by author, though at times this system breaks down, perhaps as later letters were received or discovered among the Society's papers while the filing was taking place. The wording of the entries is restricted by the limited space available; it is mainly derived from the brief summaries of contents written at the head of the SGS's letters by Maurice Johnson and in some cases it is not easy to understand without reference to the contents of the letter.

In some cases the edges of the brown folders had become damaged in the course of time, so that some entries had become illegible. It has been possible to decipher some of these by reference to the letters to which they relate, though others cannot now be read. An illegible word or part of a word is indicated by [   ]. Some entries are self-explanatory; others are so brief as to give little, if any, indication of the contents.

Many of the items below are included in the calendar of correspondence.

Some are clearly papers or dissertations rather than letters, or are drawings or mathematical problems, so they have not been included in the calendar of correspondence, which is confined to letters. Others have not survived or are no longer among the Society's papers. It is possible to correlate some of the letters in the calendar with these original numbers listed below. These lists demonstrate the variety and extent of MS material presented at the weekly meetings of the SGS between 1710 and 1755, and provide a useful example of an early attempt to catalogue papers systematically.

I. *SGS Dissertations on Theological, Ethical, Juridical & Historical Topics*
MSS in Quarto

1.   The [ ] of Jno Walsh of Grimsby
2.   Roger Ascham's Epistle to Bransby
3.   Dr Stukely's account of the Carveing over the West door of Croyland abbey
4.   A List of Historical Subjects
5.   Dr Stukely's Explication of the Statues
6.   Indian Characters
7.   The Monument & Inscription of the Revd Mr Nich. Latham
8.   Papilio Pavo a drawing of B. Cooks
9.   A View of Lumley Castle by Dr Green
10. A Sketch by Mr Bogdani
11. Vasculum Ægyptiacum antiquissimum
12. Contract with the Emperor of Borneo
13. The Effigies of the Idol Thor
14. A Drawing of a Bottle Caskett
15. Tuscan Column in memory of Ed. 1st
16. Drawing of Cleopatra
17. from the Minute Book of the Antiq. Soc.
18. Pedestal found at York
19. Drawing of Antenna
20. "   of a Liquid Measure found in Gloucest[er]
21. Instrument of Brass found at Cotterstock
22. An Account of Spalding Fire
23. Dr Sharps Letter with the Roman Inscription
24. Account of an Emblematical picture of the Vision to St Barlaam
25. Dr Stukelys Letter to Dr Shaw Principal of Edmund Hall Oxon
26. Account of the Mannor of Spalding
27. Several Minute Figures by (?)Boverick Watch Maker
28. An Account of Melton Ross or Roos Lincoln
29. Granadilla folio tricuspid. flora parvo flav.
30. Letter from the Revd Mr J Johnson on Human Liberty
31. Impression of a Cleopatra Antiqua
32. [ ] from Orselius Numismatum
33. Dissertation on Cassibelin by the Revd Mr Ray
34. [   ]de Plumbeis Numismatibus
35. Of Bath & Batchelor Knights by [   ]
36. Letter from the Secretary at [   ]

37. Account of Physical Books at Warwick
38. Letter from Dr Mitchell Librarian to Sir Richard Ellys
39. A Learned Discourse in praise of Learned Societys. B. Ray
40. De Horologiis Antiq. B.Bell
41. A dissertation shewing the utility of studying the Fathers. B. Ray
42. Inscription at Palmyra from Mr Ch[   ]
43. Description of the Corbridge Plate R.Gale
44. Proposal for printing Fab[   ]
45. A Series of Eminent Painters
46. Proposal for printing the works of J [   ] Chief graver to [   ]
47. Theologia de uno tri[   ] et religion
48. Inscription on St Barth. Knife
49. A Machine for Turning
50. Mr Mason 1710 Character of the late Orator Henley then at Cambridge.

II. *SGS Letters on Theological, Ethical, Juridical & Historical Topics MSS in Quarto*

1. Mr G.Johnson's Catalogue of Pourtraits put up in Christ Church Coll. Hall Oxford
2. Mr Simpson's Letter de Vicaris Spalding
3. From Mr Smith of Woodston
4. Dr Neve's Opinion for Security of the Musæum SGS
5. A letter from Mr G. Johnson on different Subjects account of Pictures in the Ashmolean Library
6. From Mr G. Shelvock with account of Herculaneum
7. From Dr Mitchell with antiquities about Guildford
8. From Sir Jno. Evelyn out of the Charter of Incorporation for the Soc. of Antiq.
9. From Dr Stukeley with his Memoirs RSS
10. From the Rev. Mr Ray
11. Monkish Verses from Dr B. Willis
12. Mr Gerards Letter of the Tryall between Dr Gastrell Bishop of Chester & S. Peploe
13. From Mr James Weekes
14. From Mr Anth. Oldfeild antiquities
15. From Mr G. Vertue
16. From Capt. Johnson with Curiosities at Nimeguen
17. [   ] with Antiquities
18. [*Illegible because of damage to the folder*]
19. [*Illegible*]
20. [*Illegible*]
21. [*Illegible*]
22. [*Illegible*]
23. [   ] of a Sword dug out of [   ]
24. A Letter from Dr B. Willis
25. From the Revd J. Johnson de Ramsay
26. From Dr B. Willis

27. ⎫
28. ⎬ Three Letters from Mr G. North Antiquities
29. ⎭
30. A Letter from Mr Draper very Ingenious
31. Mrs Greens Letter from Redmarshall with some account thereof 1744
32. From the Revd Mr Beecroft with an ancient Inscription
33. From the Revd Mr S. Pegg
34. From Mr B. Bell Complimentary
35. From Mr T. Simpson account of a Nobleman Interred in Leather at Lincoln
36. From the Revd Mr Secretary Neve of the Interment of Dr Jno. Caux Abbot of Peterborough Justice in Eyre
37. A Letter from Mr Secr. Johnson at Lincoln 1726
38. From Mr George Lynn with the Dimensions of the Royal William man of War
39. From Mr B. Bell on coins
40. From Dr Neve his Tour into the West
41. From Mr T. Simpson with an Inscription
42. From D° on Episcopal Registers
43. From R. Gale Esqr. Marmor Sandvicense
44. From Mr Neve to Mr Johnson 1718
45. From Dr Green at Leyden with an account of inflicting punishments in the 7 Provinces with some very neat Drawings
46. From Mr Bogdani on the [*illegible*] Societys
47. From R. Gale
48. [*Illegible because of damage to the original folder*]
49. [*Illegible*]
50. [*Illegible*]
51. [*Illegible*]
52. [*Illegible*]
53. [*Illegible*]
54. [*Illegible*]
55. [*Illegible*]
56. A Letter from Dr Stukely on Publishing his Itinerary
57. From R. Gale Esq about the Chichester Inscription
58. From Mr Peck about the Annals of Stamford
59. From R.Gale Esq
60. From Mr Fr. Peck relateing to the Antiquities of Lincolnshire
61. From the Revd Mr Jos. Sparkes Concerning a Fine
62. A Letter from Dr Stukely 1718
63. From Dr Neve about fitting up the Musæum
64. About d°
65. A Letter from Mr G. Lynn
66. From Mr Secretary Johnson about Dunstable
67. From Mr Jos. Sparkes Incunabula Typ[*illegible*]
68. A Letter from Revd Mr Addenbrooke about Coins
69. From Mr B. Bell about armes & Family of Halltoft 1715
70. Mr Secretary Johnsons advice to Dr Stukely about studying British History
71. [*This number was not used.*]
72. Revd Mr Curtis's Opinion of a Book entitled Remarks on Free thinking

73. Mr Secretary Johnson to Dr Stukely De annulis
74. From D° about Indian & Chinese Seals
75. Letter from Mr B. Bell Armes of Wallpoles
76. From Brown Willis Esq Lincoln Minster
77. From the Rev. T. Neve about Worshipping toward the East
78. From D° about Founding Peterborough Society. the Plan of Spalding
79. Letter from Mr Neve with account of Mrs Deacons present the Polyglott Bible with the Lexicon. Cost eight Guineas.
80. Mr Neve's Letter to J. Johnson. his succeeding [*illegible*]
81. R.Gale Esq's Letter with Maffei's History of Amphitheatres
82. From Mr S. Wesley on his Publishing Dissert. in Librum Jobi
83. A Letter from R.Gale Esq about Richester Inscription
84. From B. Bell Esq of the Coins [*illegible*]
85. From D° in London Soc. Gen. Spalding
86. From D° about Sir Isaac's Medal
87. From Mr Bogdani on his seeing Burleigh
88. From Cornelius Little
89. From Capt. Johnson account of Paintings
90. From Mr Tho. Manningham
91. From the Rev. Mr G. North about coins of H3 and the Mint at Lincoln
92. From Mr J. Ames SA Secr. about his History of Printing
93. From Mr Bowyer Printer on his being SGS
94. From Capt Johnson at Brussells with a Drawing of an Albano Dish
95. From the Revd Mr Ray with an Inscription, Roman
96. From Dr Green at Leyden 1732 with a Neat Drawing Arx Vilford.
97. From B. Bell Esq proposals for Tab. August.
98. From D° of Otho before he was Emperor
99. From D°.
99. From Mr R. Gale account of His Brass Busto dug up at York
100. From Mr Bogdani an Inscription found in St Georges Church Southwark
101. A Letter from B. Bell Esq with a Latin Translation of a Humorous Epitaph on J. Bell
102. From Mr B. Bell of Coins Faustina
103. A Letter from Mr Secretary Johnson
104. From Capt. Johnson Incense Vessell Found at Walton
105. From Mr Secr. Johnson Diar. J. Buchard
106. Memoirs of the Manner of Hitchin Hertford
107. A Letter from Capt Johnson with Drawing of Sphinxes
108. From G. Lynn Senior Esq about the Cotterstock Pavement
109. From Mr E. Wallpole on Sending Sannizarius
110. From Sir Jno. Evelyn account of a Bass rel. At Bath
111. From B. Bell Esq Dissertation on Calimachus
112. From E. Wallpole dedicateing his Translation of Sanizarius to Spalding Society
113. From B. Bell Esq with Dr Wellwoods Sea Law
114. From Mr Alex Gordon SA Secr
115. From D°
116. From The Revd Mr Matt. Robinson Curate of Lutton with his Donation
117. From R. Gale Esq of Bar[dney] Abbey

118. From D° with an account of a Flint arrow Head
119. From Dr Heighington about Bishop Latimer
120. A Letter from Sir Richd. Ellys with an account of King Ethelred
121. From R. Gale Esq [*illegible*] ppell
122. Drawing of Ranelagh
123. From R. Gale Esq. on the seal of Constantine
124. A Letter from Revd Mr Neve with an account of Urnes and coins dug up at Chesterton.
125. From the Revd Mr Smith of Lincolnshire Families.
126. Mr Secretary Johnson Letter to Dr Green about Roman Painting
127. From R. Gale Esq of an altar found at Boulness Cumberland
128. From D° De Nexu Literarum in Inscript. Eboracens.
129. A Letter from B. Willis Esq. Town Obols.
130. From R. Gale Esq of antient British Armes
131. A Letter from R. Gale Esq with his Opinion of Antiq. Dug up at Michellgate York
132. From Mr G. Vertue Sentiments of our most antient Paintings
133. From Mr Secr. Johnson with a Drawing of an Antient Roman Plumbing Line.
134. From Dr Green an account of Lord Cadogan's seat at Cavasham
135. From Capt. Johnson with a Drawing of Orus Ægyptiacus
138 [*sic*] From Mr Secr. Gordon Monument with arms of Vere & other Minutes with an Autograph of Oliver Cromwell
139. From Mr H. Johnson about the Antiquities of Berkhamsted
140. From Horncastle account Roman coins found at Mr Heneages

III. *SGS Dissertations on Theological, Ethical, Juridical & Historical Topics*
MSS in Folio

1.   A Kalendar of Festivals & Sts. Days
2.   An Imitation of Horaces Integer Vitæ
3.   Of Going in procession or perambulation
4.   A Letter from Capt Johnson
5.   A Dissertation on Metalls Weights and Coins
6.   "   on the Coins of Cassibeline
7.   "   on Conturniate Medalls & their Marks
8.   A Dissertation on Julius Cæsars passage over the Thames by Samuel Gale Esq
9.   "   on the Armes of Cantolove in a Curious Seal found at Peterboro
10.   "   of the Ornaments and use of Painted Glass
11.   Concerning the Prebendary of Nassington
12.   A Dissertation upon a Gold Ducat of Ferdinand and Isabella King and Queen of Castile and Aragon
13.   History of St Jn° Baptists Church in Peterboro
14.   Garter King at Armes on Homout Ich Dien
15.   Of Nameing and assumeing or Changeing Names
16.   Of Contradictory Vows of Celibacy
17.   Of Architecture and Designing

18. Of Towns and Traders Ticketts &c.
19. Illustration of a Medallion of Clod. Sept. Alb. Cæsar
20. Dissertation de Ordinibus Sacris
21. Inscription on Dean Fotherbys Monument at Canterbury who was born at Great Grimsby
22. Drawing and dissertation of a China Vass
23. Of English Ecclesiastical Benefices
24. Sequel thereto
25. Of Discourse of Cutts, Prints, &c.
26. The Authority and usefulness of the Court of Sewers
27. View of a Romantick Villa at Cotherstock
28. A Curious Letter from Mr H. Johnson dated from Panama 1729 with a Discourse of the Secretarys on Sepulchres and of an Indian Woman 142 yrs. old
29. A Sketch of the King's Armes Tempo Jac. I
30. A Research into the Original of Idolatrous Corruption of Truth
31. Windsor Reassumed by R. Wm 1st
32. Orders of the Friendly Society of Spalding
33. LL. Cons. Brittannorum et Saxon
34. Johannis Anstis armr Aspilogia
35. A Rhapsody on ancient Ensignia
36. A Letter from Mr Wise of Oxford on Coins
37. A Daily Courant on 2 antient Medalls
38. On the Sovereignes Motto Dieu et Mon Droit
39. An account a Roman Pavement in Wiltshire
40. An Extract of a Deed poll belonging to the Vicars Fotheringay
41. Hypocausti apud Lindum detecti
42. A defence of this Crowns being Imperial
43. Inscriptions from Chichester
44. Dissertation on a Sepulchral Lamp
45. An Essay upon Equity MJ
46. Inscription found at Nismes in France
47. Dissertation on a Coin DN. VALEN. PP. AUG.
48. Dissertatio Philologica
49. Letter from Mr Bogdani Ordonance
50. De Officio Prothonotarii
51. The Antiquity of Funeral Orations
52. An Oration in Memory of Mr Sutton Founder of the Charter house
53. Dissertatio de Jurisprudentia Jobi S. Wesley
54. Letter from Dr Stukeley Concerning the progress of the Antiquarian Society dated 1718
55. De Sella Marmorea Votiva Divis Isidis
56. Extract of a Letter from Dr Isaac Greenwood Hollesian Professor at New Cambridge
57. Drawing of the Font in Ely Abbey
58. Account of Royston Cave in the Stamford Merc.
59. A Catalogue of Pictures Statues and Bustos in picture Gallery at Oxford from Mr George Johnson

IV. *Letters on Theological, Ethical, Juridical & Historical Topics*
MSS in Folio

1. A Long letter from Dr Stukely in defence of the Ancient Britains Boston 1714
2. From D° about Chronological Tables
3. Dr Neves Tour into Wales
4. Letter from Jn° Rowell Esq PP de Sigillis
5. From Dr Stukely with a Drawing of a King
6. From Mr G. Vertue about Coins of the Black Prince
7. From Coll. Johnson with a Drawing
8. From Mr Secretary Johnson to Dr Stukely on a Coin of Boadica
9. From Mr Secretary Johnson on D°
10. Account of Mr J. Sherlocks plan for the Rebuilding Spalding Markettplace
11. Dr Neves account of Houghton Hall
12. Letter from Mr Bogdani about pa[   ]
13. From Dr Green with account of Coll. Chartres
14. From Mr Secretary Johnson with drawing
15. Drawing of a Roman Urn dug up at Boston
16. Letter to Dr Massey
17. From Dr Stukely with an account of Telescopes
18. From Mr George Ault Presbyt. Minister at Boston
19. From Mr R. Falkner with a Drawing
20. From Dr Neve with account of Coins dug up at March
21. From R. Gale Esq Corbridge Plate
22. From Mr Secretary Johnson on D°
23. From Mr Bogdani on a Monument found at Bath of L. Vitellius
24. From Mr R. Falkner of Heraldry
25. From Mr Secretary Johnson of the abuse of Antient Gemms
26. A Letter from the Duke of Buccleuch with B. Langleys Antient Masonry
27. From Dr Stukely about Stone Henge
28. From His Excellency Major G. Hunter
29. From Mr G. Vertue of Shakespear
30. From the Duke of Buccleuch with Pines Horace with Mr Secretary Johnson answer
31. Letter from the Secretary to Dr Bentley
32. From Mr Bogdani about Amphit. at Nismes
33. From Dr Neve on his reassuming the title of Secretary to the Peterboro S.
34. A Letter from Dr Stukely on Bubble Schemes
35. From Dr Lynn MSS brought by Muscovites from the Coasts of the Caspian Sea
36. A letter from Dr Neve with some Minutes of the Peterbo[rough Soc.]
37. From D° dates at Ludlow 1724
38. From Mr Rowland account of Blenheim &c.
39. From Mr Alex' Gordon SA Secr.
40. From Mr Bogdani of the amph. at Nismes
41. A List of the Huntington G. Jury
42. A Letter from Mr Bogdani on the Cotterstock pavement with Dr Mortimers present Redi Opera

43. A letter from Mr Hen. Johnson with an account of a Picture Ben Johnson
44. From the Revd Mr Sam. Pegg amph[   ]
45. From the Honble. Peregrine Bertie at Angers
46. From the Revd Mr John Frances with a Roman urn
47. From Mr J. Johnson Treasurer SGS
48. From R. Gale on North Allerton Fair
49. From Mr R. Falkner
50. From Mr J. Grundy Junr. account of a [   ]
51. Letter from the Honble. P. Bertie about brass swords
52. From Sir Joseph Ayloft about Tesselated Pavs.
53. From Dr Neve with some minutes of Peterboro Soc.
54. From Mr Fr. Drake sent by R. Gale Esq.
55. From the Honble. Sir Jnº Clerk of Burning the Land
56. From Mr J. Johnson at Cambridge on admission
57. From Coll. Johnson dated at Worms Camp 175[?]
58. From Mr J. Ames SA Secret. Tindal New Test. 1526
59. From R. Gale Esq Inscription of an Equestrian Monument sent from ?Rome
60. From Coll. Johnson at Spires 1743 Heidelburg
61. From R. Gale Esq with Roman Inscription found at Chichester
62. From Mr Falkner with a Drawing
63. From Coll. Johnson at Ghent 1742
64. From Dº
65. Drawing of Red Marshall Church & Tucksford in Nottingham
66. A Letter from Coll. Johnson with rec. Of a medal of Socrates
67. From Mr J. Romley on his being elected
68. From Thos. Savage with a particular account of the Rebells at Chester
69. From Mr. G. Vertue relateing the State of AS
70. From Dº about Antiquities and Inscription on Mr [   ]s Villa
71. From Coll. Johnson at Breda with an account of a monᵗ of the Prince and Princess of Orange
72. From the Revd Mr John Romley account of curiosities at Epworth
73. From Mr Anth. Oldfeild with account of Ed. Jenkins monument aged 169
74. Dr Taylers Letter to Lord Oxford concerning the Paris Bible 1463/4
75. From Mr Vertue on a Late Aurora Borealis & Earth Quake
76. Dr Sharpes Critical Treatise of the [   ] of Our 3 Kings of the Name [   ]
77. The Societys propo[sa]ls for publishing Mr B. Bell Tabulæ Augustæ
78. A letter from Dr Stukely account of a Curious Enamelled Shrine
79. Dissertation on an Onyx Seal of Dr Greens
80. A Letter from Dr Stukely account of the Ægyptian Society London 1740
81. A Letter from Mr Neve about Sir Edward Seymours Claim to the title of D. Somerset
82. From Dr Tathwell Critical observat. on Horace
83. Several Letters from Dr Tathwell containing an Illustration of a Greek Boustrophedon inscription the Mithras
84. A Letter from Mr W. Johnson with account of Stockys Old Church in Essex

V. *SGS Letters on Physical, Philosophical & Mathematical Subjects*
MSS in Quarto

1. The Secretary's Letter to Mr Curtis & answer
2. D°
3. Mr Goche's Letter to the Secretary
4. Dr Jurin's letter with some account of the Microscopes
5. Mr Bogdani's account of an Aurora Borealis 1726
6. Mr Falkner's Letter from Oxford with inscriptions
7. Mr Prior's verses to Lady Harley
8. An account of the Front of St Paul's &c. in flies
9. A Letter from Cornelius Little
10. Letters from Mr Bogdani with Veni Vidi Vici with a Just reprehension on it by a Lady
11. Mr Bogdani's Letter with Swifts Soup
12. Mr Fr Peck's Letter
13. Dr Stukely's Letter 1720
14.   "   with an account of a Large Bat
15. Dr Birch's Letter
16. Letter from Mr B. Bell
17. D° from Mr M. Johnson
18. A Letter from Mr B. Bell. Poetry
19. D° from Dr Neve
20. Dr Green's Letter from Leyden
21. Mr H. Johnsons Letter from Granada
22. From Mr Bogdani with the Manner of admitting the Prince of Orange FRS
23. A Letter from the Secretary to Mr Falkner
24. Letter from Mr Bogdani with an account of the Hippocampus Drawings &c.
25. From Mr Bell on Fossills British Coins &c.
26. From D° with an account of Vitrified Hay
27. From the Secretary with the Seamans Vow
28. From Mr B. Bell with Catalog. Imp. Roman.
29. From D°
30.   } Letters from Mr Bogdani on the Barometer
31.   }
32. From D° to Mr Falkner
33. From D° recommending Mr Professor Celsius
34. From Mr B. Bell
35. Letter from Sir Jno. Evelyn on the Farnesian Sphere
36. Letter from Mr Bogdani on Coins found at Chichester
37. From Mr Brand with an account of Iron Ore &c.
38. From Dr C. Mortimer with some account of Cromwells being dug up again and hung up at Tyburn
39. A Letter from Dr Heighington
40. From Revd Mr Neve with Mr Harris's donation
41. From Dr Mortimer
42. A Letter from Mr Bogdani [   ] cure for poysons [   ] Chrystals &c.
43. From Col. Johnson with a Drawing enclos'd

44. A Letter from Mr George Tookie to Mr Cox with account of some Bones retained in utero of Doe 3 years
45. A Letter from Dr Rutherforth de Ventis
46. Mr Gales Copy of Sir Jno. Clerks Letter of acceptance to become a Member
47. A Letter from Mr Falkner with poem Cupidinis Error
48. From Mr Jno. Hepburn with an account of a Calculus extracted from the Urethra weighing [   ]
49. Letter from Dr Mortimer with [   ]
50. Letter from Dr Colby on Flowers
51. From Dr Neve with an account of Aurora Bor.
52. Letter from Dr Rutherforth with a promise of His Philosophy
53. A Letter from Dr Birch
54. From Mr Lawton with an account of Lead Mine
55. Letter from Mr Bogdani an account of the fire in the Cotton Library
56. Letter from [*erasure*]
57. A Letter from Mr Bogdani
58. From Dr Stukely
59. Letter from Dr Hutchinson
60. From Dr Stukely with Origines Royston.
61. A Morning thought an Ode by Mary Masters
62. Tripos Verses for 1756
63. A Letter from Dr Stukely some account of His Medal History
64. Mr T. Neve's Letter with an Ode on Dr Pocock
65. The Revd Mr Whiteing on the Sublime Stile of Holy Writ
66. A Letter from Dr Parsons
67. Dᵒ from Dr Neve
68. Letter from Anth. Oldfield with Poetry
69. From Dr Stukely account of Tesselated pavement
70. From Dr Rutherforth with an account of Celtes
71. A Letter from Dr Stukely
72. From Mr S. Wesley with an Epigram
73. From Dr Z. Brooks on being Elected
74. From the Revd Mr George Ferne
75. From Dr Rutherforth
76. From Mr John Swynfen
77. From Dr Stukely with a present of Fossills &c.
78. From Dr Hill Concerning the Pyrites
79. From Mr Bogdani with the Method of dressing Armour
80. From Dr Stukely on the Earthquake in 1749
81. From Mr Emanuel Mendes da Costa
82. A Translation of the last Will of an Indian Minister at Gay Head
83. A Letter from Mr George Johnson with an Ode on the Death of the Prince of W.
84. From Dr Sharp of Durham
85. From the Revd Mr Ed. Owen on being Elected SGS
86. From Mr Wm. Dodd with some account of his publishing Callimachus
87. From Rd Mr T. Neve with Epitaphs
88. From Mr Dale Ingram on his being Elected SGS
89. From Mr N. Drake on Dᵒ

90. From Dr Stukely with a Character of Dr Hill and his Literary Gazett
91. A Method of treating the Piles by Monsr. Chirac
92. A Letter from Mr M. Johnson London 1730
93. From D° with an Ode ad Noelem Broxolmium MD &c.
94. From D° with Sir Wm. Younges Verse to Mr Hedges Occasioned by the foregoing Ode
95. [*This number was not used.*]
96. Mr Hedges Letter from Germany to Dr Broxholme Translated for the Ladys assembly at Spalding
97. A Lettr from the Revd Mr Robt. Whatley with presents for the Musæum
98. From Mr Jo. Harris Late Antigua 7ber 25 1729 Very Curious
99. From Mr Jno. Topham with a Tygers Head and other Valuable Curiosities
100. Dr Broxholmes Answer to Mr Hedges ode
101. A Letter from Mr B. Bell on the difference between Stampt & Cast Medalls
102. From Mr Abel Smith Junr with his present of the Antiquities of Nottingham
103. From Dr Jurin on sending an account of the Metal Thermometer
104. Coll. Johnsons Letter with a Drawing of Mount Vesuvius
105. A Letter from Dr Birch Secret: to Royal Society with a promise of the Transact.
106. From D° with D° with further account of the Transactions
107. D° from Dr Ward of Gresham College
108. A Letter from Mr Da Costa with a present of Fossiles.

VI. *SGS Letters on Physical, Philosophical & Mathematical Subjects MSS in Folio*

1. Dr Hales Method of preserving Grain
2. A plan for Collecting cases in Physick &c.
3. A Letter from Dr Stukely about the Cause of Earthquakes
4. Of Petrified & Fossil Fish
5. Licence &c from the office of Ordnance for Exhibiting Fireworks at Spalding
6. A Discourse on the Learning and Politeness of the antient Britaines
7. Observationes Meteorolgocice [*sic*]
8. Proposals for Uranograhia [*sic*] Brittannica
9. Observationes Astronomicæ de Via Cometæ
10. Letter from Mr Bogdani with Method of House painting &c
11. A Very Curious Letter from Mr Da Costa from Bois le Duc in dutch Brabrant 1748 with Account of Fossils Vegetables Metalls &c.
12. Mr Calamy Ives Journey to Ireland
13. Account of St Winifreds Well
14. Mr Grundys Estimate for Water Works at Gopsall Leicestershire
15. Draught & Description of Boreing for Water
16. A Discourse concerning the Physitians Colledge and Surgeons Company
17. Letter from B. Cook
18. Letter from Mr Butter with some account of Rippon
19. Letter from Mr Jackson of Boston
20. Letter from Dr Hill on his being Elected
21. From Dr Parsons on D°

22. An Account of Electrical Experiments from the Revd Mr Powell
23. Heautontimoroumenos Dr Lynn
24. Another Long Letter from Dr Lynn
25. Letter from T. Neve Junr. with poem
26. Letter from Dr Rutherforth account of Kindleing the Vestal Fires
27. From Mr Jno.Hill apothecary in Broadway Westminster on his publishing Theophrastus
28. Mr Norcliff letter from Frederickshall about the Comett 1742
29. From Dr Stukely on D°
30. Letter form the Secretary with an account of Basso Relievo
31. Letter from Mr Norcliff
32. Letter from Dr Jurin with Directions for takeing Soap Lees
33. Letter from Mr Grundy Junr. on Copper Mines
34. Letter from Capt. Johnson
35. From the Revd Mr T. Neve senr on the death of Dr S[　]
36. Letter from Mr J. Grundy Junr
37. Letter from Mr Bogdani of Fossil Trees &c
38. Letter from Mr R. Gale with a Medal of Carausius
39. Lettr from Dr Stukely on his fixing in London 1717
40. Letter from Mr Secretary Johnson to Lord Colerain at Venice
41. Letter from Mr Bogdani with Dr Hales method of freshning Water for the Service
42. From Dr Heighington with Mr Jacksons anniversary Ode
43. Letter with a Draught of the Nautilus
44. Letter from Mr R. Falkner with account of the Condor
45. Letter from Mr Secretary Johnson
46. From D° dated at Stilton
47. From Dr Heighington
48. From the Secretary with an Epigram on Cheese Toasters
49. Letter from Capt. Johnson Blatta Byzantina
50. Letter from Dr Mortimer with an account of the Royal Society's ordering their Transactions to be sent us Jan 4th 1737/8
51. Letter from Mr Bogdani
52. From Dr Stukeley of Destiny [　]
53. Letter from the Secretary to Mr Whiteing
54. From Dr Stukeley with [　]
55. [*Number missed out in error*]
56. From Dr Stukely & Drawing of a Stuff Rat at Oxford
57. A letter from the Secretary MJ at London with Prologue & Epilogue to Ignoramus
58. Arbor Vitæ
59. Mr Falkners Letter from Oxford account of the Prince of Oranges reception
60. Limning of the Blatta bizantina
61. Account of Mr Sadlers Coll. of Shells
62. 　　" 　　of the Blowing Aloe et De Cantharidum usu
63. Descript. of Durham
64. Dr Lynn's Letter to Dr Stukeley
65. Mr Falkners Letter with Verses on Princess. Wedding
66. From D°

67. Letter from Mr Falkner with Verses. Morbus Anglicus
68. }
69. } Letters from Mr Falkner
70. Dᵒ with Verses Nummus Historicus
71. From Dᵒ
72. From Dᵒ
73. Letter from Mr Grundy on being SGS
74. with Chester Navigation Considered
75. Letter from Mr Norcliffs on being SGS
76. His Letter to Mr Butters Queries
77. An account of Mr Ormes Improvement of the Barometer
78. Mr Jᵒ Harris letter with account of present
79. Mr Lynns Observations on the Rain
80. Effects of an Hydraulic Machine
81. Letter from Mr G. Lynn
82. Aurora Borealis
83. An Ode from Horace
84. An Account of a Meteor 1715
85. Letter from Mr Bogdani on Fluxions
86. From Dᵒ
87. From Dᵒ
88. Letter from Mr G. Lynn Mathemat.
89. Letter from Mr Muller
90. Account of Building St Peters at Rome and St Pauls London.

VII. *SGS Dissertations on Physical, Philosophical & Mathematical Subjects*
MSS in Quarto

1. Sir Hans Sloans Musæum
2. Mr Poles account of the Rinoceros
3. Mr Cal[a]my Ives account of Frescati near Rome
4. Oratio in Ædibus Paulinis A. Oldfeild
5. Commendamus on the Chevalier Ramsay
6. On Chocolate Makeing
7. Concerning Corporate Bodys MJ
8. Secretum Sigillum Robert Com. de Ferrariis
9. A Sketch of Newcastle Light House
10. Advertisement of Salmon's Geograph. Grammar
11. Observationes Meteorologicæ P.Gabry
12. Mr Castell's directions for Breeding Canary Birds
13. Pharmacopolarium
14. Drawing of a Stickleback
15. Waxwork Anatomy
16. Wilks's Butterflyes
17. An account of a Course of Exp. Philosophy
18. An account of Deeping Fen Ducking
19. Dr Meads Rect. For the bite of a Mad Dog in his own hand
20. Of Arnotts dying yellow

21. Mrs Barker's case of a Jaundie occasioned by a [   ]
22. A Curious Limning of the Blatta Byzantina by Dr Green
23. Account of a Table Cloth burnt by lightning &c
24. Of Snuff Takeing and Smoaking by Dr Green
25. Of the Lavatera Africana
26. Size of the Great Diamond brought from [   ] to the King of Portugal
27. Account of the Indian King [   ]
28. The Anatomist Dissected by Dr Lynn
29. Dove & Bapth's course of Expr. Philosophy
30. Of Plants growing in to[   ]
31. Account of Matthew Buckinger very Cu[rious]
32. To preserve Peaches &c in Brandy
33. Dr Desaguliers Course of Philos.
34. Bishop Patrick's Epitaph
35. on Dr Harvey
36. Omni laude dignus cens[   ]atur by Mr John [   ]
37. Proofs of our Saviours Miracles
38. Dissertation on Musick by Mr Bogdani
39. Plate of an Air Pump
40. Mr Norton's Collection of Pictures NB he will'd his estate to the King & Parliamt.
41. An Account of the Stone in bladder from Leyden
42. Account of observations by a young Gentleman born blind for Mr Jn° Romley
43. De la vie de Ephemera
44. De Osteocolla
45. Agaricus Ramosus Cornu Reniferi [   ]
46. Experiments of Bulbous roots growing in Water
47. Dr Lockier in honorem Sir Isaac Newton
48. De Aquilegia Columbini
49. Christals from Buxton

VIII. *SGS Dissertations on Physical, Philosophical & Mathematical Subjects MSS in Folio*

1. The Free Enquirer
2. Exercises perform'd by the Learnd Dog
3. An Account of the Warwickshire Youth 7Ft 3 Inches
4.   "   of John Coan the Norwich Dwarf
5. The Life of the Revd Mr George Whitfield
6. Mr Falkners Letter Concerning Mr Mullers Book
7. A Specimen of Writeing Mr H. Johnson
8. Proposals for Manufacturing Cambletts at Lincoln
9. A Specimen of Writeing by the left hand
10. A Dissertation on Bridges by Mr M. Johnson
11. Oratio in Laudem honesti Viri Thome Suttoni
12. Answer to a Question in the Ladys Diary H. Burwell
13. Mr Dale Ingrams account of the Porpoise

14. A Meditation on seeing the Herse of D. of Montague
15. Revd Mr Peggs Letter about Luminous North. Phænomena
16. Description of an Orre[r]y by Mr T. Hawkes
17. Mr H. Johnson's account of an Earthquake at Gosberton
18. Of tingeing with Colours & on Marble M. Johnson
19. Of Allcoves arched Walks Grottos &c M. Johnson
20. A Discourse about Horses and Horse Races MJ
21. An Account of a Concave Mirror
22. Byenius Method of Rangeing Shells
23. Catalogus Simplicium Officinal. J. Green
24. Letter from the Revd T. Neve Junr.
25. Dissertation on Climates by M. Johnson
26. An abacus by Mr Robt. Flower
27. Observations on the Tinn Mines from Mr Bogdani
28. Ode in Exordio Orationis Cl. Christoph. Longnot
29. Dissertation on Corsica
30. Letter from M. Johnson to J. Kouwenhoven
31. Dr Stukeley on forming a Society at Ancaster
32. Epistle from the Lady Hippolyta Taurella
33. The Art of Painting upon Glass at Venice
34. Epigrams
35. Reynards Brush a poem
36. Lying In Infirmary
37. Taverners Case of Mrs Brooks sore leg
38. The Account of a Sea Monster by Mr Searson
39. [   ] Hermaphroditi
40. A Description of the comet in 1743
41. Grundy the Draining &c
42. An Alchaick Ode by H[   ]
43. Illustissimo [sic] Academiæ Cortonensis SGS
44. Construction of the Eclipse in 1739
45. History of the Condor
46. Tumba Chyndonacis
47. An Account of Thomas Kouls [   ]
48. Extract of Sir John Clarks Letter by Mr R. Gale with an Historical account
    of part of Yorkshire in three Sheets a Manuscript
49. A wonderfull Deliverance of 3 [   ]
50. A plan of the Physick Garden at Oxford
51. Dr Stewarts Dissert. on Heart with a draught and Section
52. Mr Bogdani's Draught of the Iron Oven
53. A Map of the North Level &c by Capt. Perry
54. Badeslades Scheme for the Bedford Level
55. Mr Flamsteeds Correct Tide table
56. Proposals for printing by subscription an universal History of Exp.
    Knowledge
57. Draught of Mr Rownings maching for throwing Water
58. Cambridge a poem.

APPENDIX 4

LETTERS FROM THE 1760s
relating to the SGS

The following two letters are not among the papers of the SGS; they are in the collections of the British Library. They have, however, been included here as evidence of the continued survival of the SGS as an active learned body for some years after the death of Maurice Johnson.

Letter from Walter Johnson to William Stukeley;
British Library Add MS 4440, f.260

Spalding Apr. 16.1764

Dear Dr

I have taken the Liberty to transmit to you our Observations of the Suns Eclipse on the 1st. of this Month & as I know you constantly attend the Royal Society beg you will communicate it to that learned Body. Many years since there was an Order made by that learned Society that their Works should be regularly given to the Gentlemen's literary Society in Spalding & during my Fathers Life Time they were constantly given. after his decease we did not receive them of some Time until my late Bro: John Johnson waited of you to Dr Birch[1] then we received Them again but have received none these 5 or 6 Years. I am desired by the Gents of the Society to entreat the Favour of you to enquire of Dr. Birch how this has happened as I do not conceive that the Royal Society have made any Order to the contrary. We keep up the Society with all the Spirit we can & have a great many regular Members & almost Every Thursday's Even thirteen or 14 & sometimes more regular Members attend. we greatly feel the Loss of your Amanuensis: all join in humble Wishes that you would suffer us to pay a Scribe for copying yr Minutes of the Royal Society Transactions with yr own useful & entertaining [page 2] Remarks thereon. We lately purchased out of our Savings An 18 inch Reflecting Telescope –
An Air Pump with its Apparatus –
A Compound Microscope –
& a Solar Microscope – which cost us Twenty Eight Pounds Eighteen Shillings & we entertain ourselves with Experiments at such Times as Nothing new or usefull is communicated – I believe the Account & Calculation of the Eclipse should have been signed by one of the Secretarys & directed to Dr Birch but they are both out on Journeys the Revd Mr Rowning in Suffolk and the Revd Everard

---

[1] Secretary of the RS.

Buckworth at Lincoln therefore as Treasurer I was desired to transmit it to you with the Compliments of the Society. I shall be obliged to you to write me who is the Treasurer of the Antiquarian Society for I am something in arrears there & want to pay it & take my Prints.

I am
Dear Dr
Yr. obliged & most obedient Servant
The Revd Dr Stukeley   Walt. Johnson
Queen Square
London

Letter from Revd Joseph Mills[2] *to the Spalding Gentlemen's Society,*
December 1769

[Published in Revd J. Mills, *Collection of Letters and Verses on Several Occasions* (Spalding, 1771).]

To the Gentleman's Literary Society in SPALDING.
Quid pure tranquillet –   Hor. Ep.18 l.1 – v. 102[3]
What calms the Breast, and makes the Mind serene.
Gentlemen,
You did me the Honour to accept of a Greek Epigram which I composed; I beg leave now to present you with a Copy of those Verses which I wrote upon Skaiting; and some Observations relating to Natural History, which I sent in a Letter to Mr URBAN, Author of the GENTLEMAN'S MAGAZINE.

And here I hope you will indulge me in a few Reflections upon the Benefits arising from your laudable Institution. And on this Occasion I cannot help honouring the Memory of him,* who was the Patron and Support of this Society; whose Learning and Knowledge were very extensive, and whose desire of communicating that Knowledge, was scarcely to be equalled. The Study of, [page 2] and Endeavour to promote whatever contributes to the Improvement of the Mind, is undoubtedly worthy of the Gentleman and the Scholar; and what can be a more commendable Employment, what a more suitable Exercise of our rational Faculties, than the Study and Contemplation of the Works of Nature, and the Wonders of the Creation? That Beauty and Harmony, which we behold in the Objects that surround us, serve to fill our Minds with pleasing Ideas, and excite in us a profound Veneration for the GOD of Nature. This was the Effect they had upon that excellent Philosopher Mr BOYLE, who shewed the sense he had of GOD upon his Mind, by an awful regard to his Sacred Name; and to raise in others a noble Emulation of his exalted Piety, he left an Institution for the continual Praise and Contemplation of HIM.

---

[2]   Revd Joseph Mills was the incumbent of Cowbit, following Revd Benjamin Ray, a regular SGS member. Mills became an SGS member in 1753. His book was a collection of his poems and letters; he evidently regarded the SGS as important enough for a letter to them to merit inclusion.
[3]   A quotation from a poem by the Roman poet Horace.

It is such Considerations as these, that increase in us the Affections of Admiration, Humility and Gratitude; and create in us a dutiful Complacency and Acquiescence in the Evils and Misfortunes which are incident to us, amidst the Entertainments and Delights of Nature. Which Thought is finely improved by Mr LOCKE, in his Essay on Human Understanding. 'Beyond all this, says he, we may find another Reason why GOD has scattered up and down several degrees of Pleasure and Pain in all the things that environ and affect us, and blended them together, in almost all that our Thoughts and Senses have to do with: that we finding Imperfection, Dissatisfaction and want of compleat Happiness in all the Enjoyments [page 3] which the Creatures can afford us, might be led to seek it in the Enjoyment of HIM, with whom there is fulness of Joy, and at whose Right Hand are Pleasures for evermore.'

I am, Gentlemen, your most obedient,
most humble Servant,

Cowbit, Dec.1769   J.MILLS

*Note: *The late Councellor J*****n* [Johnson, i.e. Maurice Johnson]

APPENDIX 5

FAMILY TREE OF THE JOHNSONS OF SPALDING (Simplified)

Correspondents with a letter in this volume in bold. SGS members are marked with an asterisk.

Beaupré Bell's relationship is through the Oldfields: his mother was Margaret Oldfield (1681–1720) and Mary Oldfield (d.1725), her aunt, had married Mr Ambler of Spalding (d.1727), the father of Maurice Johnson's wife Elizabeth Ambler.

Martin Johnson
of Spalding, Attorney
1589–1651

=

Jane Lynn
1592–1655

Walter Johnson,
Attorney
1620–1692

=

(2) Katherine Downes
d.1692

(1) Agnes Willesbye
d.1658

=

Martin Johnson
Barrister
1652–1705

Maurice Johnson*
Barrister
1661–1747

=

(1) Jane Johnson
of Ayscoughfee Hall
d.1703

(2) Elizabeth Oldfield
d.1724

(3) **Ann Falkner**
(née Wood), d.1742:
widow of Thomas Falkner
of Boston

Mary Lynn
of Southwick

=

Mary Johnson

=

(1) John Green
of Dunsby
1683–1709

(2) Francis Pilliod*

MAURICE JOHNSON*
Barrister, SGS Founder
1688–1755

=

Elizabeth Ambler
1690–1754

John Johnson*
Barrister, SGS Treasurer
1690–1744

Walter Johnson* = Elizabeth Cox
Clergyman
1686–1760

George Johnson*
Clergyman
1732–1786

John Green* = **Jane Johnson**
Physician   1711–1754
1708–1756

Elizabeth Johnson
(Madcap Bet) b.1713
= **Robert Butter***

Maurice Johnson*
Army Officer 1714–1793
= (1) Elizabeth Bellamy
d.1752
(2) Mary Baker

Catherine ('Kitty')
b.1715
= Revd John Lodge*

Richard Falkner*
d.1737
medical student

Henry Eustace Johnson*
East India Company
b.1733

Anne Alethea Johnson
b.1731
= Richard Wallin

Martin Johnson
Midshipman RN
1727–1744

Mary Johnson
1723–1741
= Mr Archer

John Johnson*
Clergyman
1722–1758

Walter (Wat) Johnson*
Barrister 1720–1779
= Mary Fairfax

Henrietta (Harriet)
b.1718

INDEX OF PERSONS AND PLACES

References to persons in this index relate to the content of letters in which they are mentioned. Letter-writers and recipients are listed in Appendix 1 on pp. 217–222.

Places are given locations in their present county in England, or in the country of which they currently form a part. When a page-reference is followed by '*n*' this means that there is a relevant footnote on that page of the book.

INDEX OF SUBJECTS